CHINESE YUAN
RENMINBI
DERIVATIVE PRODUCTS

CHINESE YUAN
RENMINBI
DERIVATIVE PRODUCTS

PETER G. ZHANG

Chief Financial Engineering Advisor and
Senior Director of Research & Development Center
Shanghai Futures Exchange, China

World Scientific

NEW JERSEY • LONDON • SINGAPORE • BEIJING • SHANGHAI • HONG KONG • TAIPEI • CHENNAI

Published by

World Scientific Publishing Co. Pte. Ltd.
5 Toh Tuck Link, Singapore 596224
USA office: 27 Warren Street, Suite 401–402, Hackensack, NJ 07601
UK office: 57 Shelton Street, Covent Garden, London WC2H 9HE

British Library Cataloguing-in-Publication Data
A catalogue record for this book is available from the British Library.

First published 2004
Reprinted 2005

CHINESE YUAN (Renminbi) DERIVATIVE PRODUCTS

ISBN 981-256-608-2
ISBN 981-238-927-X (pbk)

Typeset by Stallion Press
Email: enquiries@stallionpress.com

Printed in Singapore by B & JO Enterprise

Contents

Preface		vii
Acknowledgment		xi
Part I	**The Chinese Economy and Financial System**	**1**
1	Chinese Yuan Revaluation and Derivative Products	3
2	Open-Door Policy and a Quarter-Century Reform	13
3	The Chinese Economy	21
4	Banking System in China	39
5	The Chinese Capital Markets	57
6	Foreign Exchange Administration	79
Part II	**Foreign Exchange Market and Foreign Exchange Derivatives Market**	**99**
7	Foreign Exchange Market	101
8	Foreign Exchange Forwards and Swaps	107
9	Non-Deliverable Forwards and Swaps	117
10	Foreign Exchange Futures	137
11	Foreign Exchange Options	145

Part III	**The Asian Financial Crisis and Financial Derivatives**	**157**
12	The Asian Financial Crisis	159
13	FX Forwards and Futures during the Asian Crisis	175
14	NDFs during the Asian Financial Crisis	189
15	Swaps	201
16	Options, Structured Notes, and Other Products	211
Part IV	**Chinese Yuan (CNY) Derivatives**	**221**
17	CNY Forwards	223
18	CNY NDFs	235
19	Uses of CNY NDFs	267
20	Chinese Yuan Swaps	283
21	CNY Nondeliverable Options	293
22	Structured Deposits Related to CNY	317
23	CNY Structured Notes	331
24	Onshore Products and Offshore Derivatives	341
Part V	**Future Development**	**365**
25	Future Development of CNY Derivatives in China	367
Major Websites in the Chinese Financial Market		381
Further Readings		383
Index		389

Preface

Few topics have attracted as much attention worldwide as the Chinese yuan (CNY) or Renminbi (RMB) has done in the past two years. We have heard so many talks, arguments, discussions, and debates on such questions as whether the CNY should be revaluated or not, when and how much it would appreciate if it should appreciate at all. Although I have not participated in the process of financial reforms in China in the past decade or so, as I have been working in the international financial community for over a decade, since the early 1990s, I have been constantly observing the Chinese financial market, particularly the major steps of the financial reforms since the mid-1990s, when I was sent to work at Chase Manhattan Bank's Tokyo branch. I still remember clearly what happened to the Asian economies and financial markets during the Asian financial crisis.

With years of preparation from working in the international financial markets in New York, Tokyo and Hong Kong, I finally got the opportunity to work in China at the Shanghai Futures Exchange (SHFE) to prepare for the introduction of financial products in China early in September 2003. The CNY had already been pushed to revaluate for about a year when I joined SHFE, and I thought that it would be a great idea to apply my product knowledge of over-the-counter (OTC) derivative products to analyzing various derivative products on CNY trading in the offshore marketplace. Similar to the process when I wrote my first professional book, *Exotic Options — a Guide to Second Generation Options* (first edition published in 1997 and the second edition in 1998), it has been much more challenging than I initially imagined. I am very glad that I have finished the project, and now present it to you to share my experiences in relearning the Chinese economic and financial systems.

The purpose of this book is not to study the three questions mentioned at the beginning of this preface, whether the CNY should be revaluated or not, when and how much it will appreciate. These issues are research topics for economists or policy makers and are beyond the expertise of the author as a derivatives specialist.

Instead, the purpose of this book is to introduce and study existing financial derivative products based on the speculation or perception that the CNY will be revaluated in the future. As a "currency is the derivative of its underlying economy," I give a systematic review of what China has achieved in reforming her economy and financial systems in the past quarter-century so that readers can familiarize themselves with the "underlying market" of the Chinese currency.

It is well known that China has made a significant achievement in gradually transferring her economy from the previous planned economy into a market-oriented one and in reforming her financial markets in the past quarter-century. Yet it has been rather difficult to find systematic studies on related topics because there are few existing systematic and updated studies in English, and the existing studies in Chinese generally do not conform to international standards because both academic and professional practices in China are still rather different from those found internationally, and adequate quantitative and analytical methods have not been adopted widely.

As I have mentioned repeatedly in various seminars and conferences in both China and the international community in the past few years, there was neither a stock market nor a commodity futures market in China when I was sent by the State Educational Commission to study in the US in 1987. The economic reform was in the early stage of experimentation, and the decision to move toward the market-oriented economic system was made in late 1993, as I will explain in Chapter 2 of this book, so that even cash markets for commodities did not exist then. So much has changed and has been achieved in the past 17 years that I have to learn much to keep up with the fast changing environment in China, with so many unique issues in China during the economic transformation toward a more market-oriented economy further integrated into the world economy. I am glad that I can share with you my new learning curve in addition to the learning curve I experienced when I first started working in the derivatives industry in New York more than a decade ago.

The introduction and analysis in this book will be useful for international readers in hedging CNY-related risk in trade and investment and other related transactions involving CNY derivative products in the offshore market. I have tried very hard to make this book as comprehensive as possible to include almost anything about CNY derivatives.

With a greater participation of the Chinese economy in the world economy since China entered the World Trade Organization (WTO) in late 2001 (for more details please see Chapter 3, on the Chinese economy), more and more foreign direct investment (FDI), and a higher degree of financial market liberalization, China will accelerate her process of financial market innovation as required by her promises to the WTO and evidenced by the *Interim Rules on Derivatives Business of Financial Institutes* issued by the China Banking Regulatory Commission (Consultative Draft dated October 11, 2003) and the *Nine Turning Policies* issued by the State Council on February 1, 2004 (please see Chapter 18 of this book). The CNY derivative products covered in this book will have many positive implications for China's foreign exchange reform process in general and for CNY forwards and other OTC derivatives in China in particular.

Specifically, the experiences on derivative products related to the CNY accumulated in the offshore marketplace will be proved useful not only for macroeconomic and financial policies but also for product innovation in China for years to come.

Compared with my earlier book on exotic options, which was a rather technical description and analysis of most existing exotic options in which a lot of mathematic formulas had to be used because no exotic options can be explained clearly enough without mathematic formulas, this book is a rather introductory and descriptive book of CNY derivative products, and I leave deliberately the necessary technical issues for readers to refer from my earlier work on exotic options. I have tried not to use any mathematic formulas or expressions as long as I can illustrate the contents well enough.

The book was originally planned as a story-telling book, but I later realized that my story-telling ability in English is not good enough to achieve that goal. However, the book is largely illustrative rather than analytical. I hope you enjoy reading this book and thank you all for your support, and I look forward to hearing from you your comments and suggestions so that I will be able to update the various topics in coming editions of this book since we all know that it will take time for the CNY to attain full convertibility.

Peter G. Zhang
Shanghai, China
July 15, 2004

Acknowledgment

First of all, I would like to thank Mr. Jiang Yang, Chief Executive Officer of Shanghai Futures Exchange (SHFE), Mr. Hu Zheng, Mr. Peng Junheng and Mr. Lao Guangxiong, Deputy CEOs of SHFE for providing me with such a good environment at SHFE so that I can continue pursuing my career in the derivatives profession back in China and promote the development of the derivatives industry in China.

It would have been impossible to finish such a comprehensive book without the support of and help from so many of my friends in the international financial community, from whom I have learned so much since I started my professional career in New York more than a decade ago and especially in the past year or so since I started working on this project. The list would be rather long if I were to name all of them. I would like to thank Ms. Grace Lau of the Hong Kong Monetary Authority for her help in providing some of the data and information used in this book and for the useful discussions with her; I would like to thank Kevin Ho and his colleagues of UBS for useful discussions and information on some important topics of the book; I would also like to thank Steven Ng, Shenglin Ben, James Sha, and David Connor of ABN AMRO for their help in providing me with necessary data and several updates of such data.

I need to thank G-Rian Tan and Simon Flint of Bank of America for useful discussions on some of the topics; I also want to thank Mr. Lee Seungho of Bank of Korea for providing me with not only his own research paper but also other related subjects on the Korean won nondeliverable forwards. I am certainly grateful to my long-time friends Lixin Wang, Steven Zhu, Jiwen Fang and many others in the international financial community and my new friends Professor Sang Gi Min of Seoul National University, Dr. Tong Suk Kim, president of Korean Futures and Options Association, Ms. Wenli Li of the Federal Reserve Bank of Philadelphia, and Mr. Kurt Selleslagh of Capco.

I would like to thank Mr. Zhang Jianliang of BOC Hong Kong for his help. I have also received a lot of help from my colleagues at SHFE. I would like to thank Mr. Chen Han, Dr. Zeng Xin, Dr. Yang Jianming, Dr. Xi Wei, Dr. Wang Wei, Dr. Han Gaofeng, and Ms. Zhang Min of SHFE.

I wish to express my appreciation to Cheng Chen, Wang Yuhua, Li Da, Zhou Xiaozhou, Jiang Ya, and Zhou Zhen for their assistance during the course of my writing this book. Special thanks also go to Mr. Yadin Shemmer, Judy Tao, and Elisse Zhou for their help in editing and proof-reading parts of my manuscript. Of course, all remaining errors are my responsibility.

PART I

The Chinese Economy and Financial System

Dramatic changes have taken place in the Chinese economy and her financial system in the past quarter-century since China adopted the open-door policy in the late 1970s. It is highly necessary for readers to have a basic understanding of what major reform initiatives have been taken in the Chinese economy and what basic financial structure is in China currently before we start to address Chinese currency issues and the relating derivatives currently trading in various offshore business centers around the world. The purpose of this part is to provide readers with basic conditions of the Chinese economy and financial market so that they can grasp the Chinese currency revaluation issue easily.

The topic is too comprehensive to address in depth in a limited number of pages. We try to introduce the major reform initiatives in the Chinese economy in Chapter 2. Chapter 3 introduces the macroeconomy in China. Chapter 4 gives us some background information on the Chinese monetary policies and commercial banks in China. Chapter 5 introduces the stock market, bond market, fund management, commodity futures market, and other major components of the capital market in China, and Chapter 6 focuses on the foreign currency policies and foreign exchange market in China.

1

Chinese Yuan Revaluation and Derivative Products

There have been so many discussions, arguments, and debates on these questions in political spheres, professional communities, academic circles, and private meetings around the globe in the past two years or so. It would take many volumes simply to follow such discussions, arguments, and debates on the three questions mentioned above and on related questions such as the impacts of CNY revaluation on the currencies of other east Asian countries and economies.

The purpose of this chapter is neither to list all related arguments, discussions, or studies nor to classify such arguments but rather to trace the origin of the notion of CNY revaluation and how it has evolved in the past two years and then to introduce products that have been traded in the offshore market and what other products could potentially be used to take advantage of the expectations.

This chapter is organized as follows. Section 1.1 traces the origin of the CNY revaluation; Section 1.2 introduces the major arguments for revaluation of the CNY presented during the US Congress Hearing on International Economic and Exchange Rate Policy held on May 1, 2002; Section 1.3 briefly describes the pressure for CNY revaluation exerted by the US Congress on the White House; Section 1.4 introduces the pressure and efforts from other major countries besides the US for revaluation of the CNY; Section 1.5 introduces arguments put forth by academic and professional circles backing the stable policy of the CNY; Section 1.6 briefly introduces the process by which the pressure for devaluation of the CNY during and after the Asian financial crisis moved towards revaluation since late 2002; and Section 1.7 summarizes and concludes the chapter.

1.1 The Original "Legs" that Are Running

"The notion that the renminbi (RMB) is dangerously undervalued and that China is exporting deflation got legs on May 1, 2002," wrote Steve H. Hanke, a senior fellow with the Cato Institute and Professor of Applied Economics at Johns Hopkins University on March 15, 2003 in his popular article *John Snow is wrong about China exporting deflation* (Hanke, 2003). "The assembled panelists (except me) embraced the idea that China was exporting deflation. To use one of Frank Knight's favorite words, this is 'nonsense.' Deflation is always and everywhere a monetary phenomenon, and in this day and age it is a monetary area-specific problem," Professor Hanke continued.

"Unfortunately, US Treasury Secretary, John Snow, has already fallen into the trap set by those who wrongly assert that China is exporting deflation — read: China is a supercompetitive exporter of manufactured goods, one that's robbing its US counterparts of pricing power. In written responses to members of the Senate Finance Committee, prior to his confirmation, Snow indicated that he might put pressure on China to revalue its currency. This represented the first of Snow's missteps in the exchange-rate sphere. Indeed, the evidence to date suggests that he, like his predecessor, is ill equipped to handle these matters properly," he continued.

There have been many reports and arguments on potential revaluation of the CNY, yet few have referred to these original "legs" on May 1, 2002. We will retrace these legs in the following section.

1.2 The Voice of "the Congress"

During the US Department of the Treasury's Report to Congress on International Economic and Exchange Rate Policy Hearing before the Committee on Banking, Housing, and Urban Affairs of the United States Senate on May 1, 2002, many discussions and arguments were presented on the need for CNY revaluation to reduce the US–China trade deficit. We find a great number of phrases and terms being used there by political leaders and even some professionals around the world in the past two years to address the current "undervaluation" of the CNY and the need to revaluate the CNY.

"China exemplifies all that is wrong with currency markets. It has a massive trade surplus and vast inflows of foreign direct investment. In a free market, China's currency should appreciate, but it does not because of government manipulation. This is a problem that appears in different shades in many countries." (Mr. Richard L. Trumka, Secretary–Treasurer, American Federation of Labor and Congress of Industrial Organizations, see the US Department of Treasury's Report 2002, p. 39.)

"American workers are paying the price for currency manipulation. Trade cannot be fair when we allow countries to manipulate exchange rates to win illegitimate competitive advantage... Those who argue that we can do nothing about exchange rates abdicate, I believe, the national (US) interest. The historic record and the 1985 Plaza Accord intervention show that we can. Academic research shows the same. Just as we manage interest rates, so too we can manage exchange rates." (*Ibid.*)

"Now why doesn't this represent a concerted policy on the part of China to get the trade surplus, to get the foreign direct investment and sustain that position by making the purchases, huge purchases of foreign assets, in order to hold their currency in place, all to their advantage? That is not the working of the market forces. They are intervening in the workings of the market forces in order to sustain an advantage, are they not?" asked Paul S. Sarbanes, Maryland, Chairman of the Committee on Banking, Housing, and Urban Affairs (US Department of the Treasury's Report, 2002, p. 29).

"So the net result, in my judgment, is that China has a substantially undervalued exchange rate for the yuan and the direct impact, of course, is a larger trade surplus with us — export jobs they gain and export and import-competing jobs we lose." (Mr. Ernest H. Preeg, Senior Fellow in Trade and Productivity, Manufacturers Alliance/MAPI, p. 52.)

"We should request, clearly, of China that the central bank stop buying dollars at $50 billion a year and that they bring their exchange rate up by 10%, 20%, or whatever is a reasonable first step." (Mr. Preeg, p. 53, *ibid.*)

1.3 Voices Echoed "the Congress"

On July 17, 2003, four members of the US House and Senate sent a letter to Secretary John Snow, stating that "a stronger yuan would likely be helpful to certain sectors of China's economy by lowering the cost of imports, and it would help Chinese consumers suffering under artificially high prices. If China imported more goods, it could bolster the fragile economies of its neighboring countries, and it would help US exporters. (Interested readers may refer the actual letter to Secretary John Snow, 2003.)

About three months after the hearing quoted above, 16 bipartisan members of the US House and Senate signed and sent a letter to President Bush on July 31, 2003, expressing their concerns about the undervaluation of China's currency and its potential effect on jobs in the US. "China has been one of our strongest manufacturing competitors, as illustrated in our trade figures," the letter argued, "in our constituent meetings, public hearings, and independent research, however, Congress has also found that China appears to hold another advantage — a deeply undervalued currency. Economists estimate that China's currency may be undervalued by between 15% and 40%, an enormous subsidy on China's export and a nearly insurmountable advantage against US producers." (Letter to President Bush, 2003.)

Pressurized by the members of Congress, both President Bush and Secretary John Snow reiterated that they would push China to revaluate the CNY. We will analyze these in more detail in Chapter 18 of this book.

1.4 Voices from Other Continents

With the US leadership as in many other areas, other countries have followed to advocate that China should revalue the CNY. China's close neighbor Japan, the second largest economy in the world, has raised its voice, the largest following the US. The Chief of the Japanese Ministry of Finance, Masajuro Shiokawa, has long been an advocator of CNY revaluation. In his testimony to the Japanese Congress early in December 2002, he stated that the Chinese yuan is significantly undervalued and that he would propose to raise the issue at the coming G7 conference. He promised that he would like to tell China to let (the yuan) float according to market principles. He expressed the opinion that the CNY exchange rate adjustment must be considered as a key element in an effective plan to revive the world economy and that the adjustment should be accomplished in the same manner that the Japanese yen was propped up by G7 joint intervention under the Plaza Accord in the mid-1980s. It is obvious that almost all the phrases and terms used by Mr. Masajuro Shiokawa are from the US Hearing of May 1, 2002.

In an article that appeared in a British newspaper in December, Haruhiko Kuroda, then Vice Finance Minister for International Affairs, said China was exporting deflation. Finance Minister Masajuro Shiokawa also agreed, saying Beijing must allow its currency to appreciate (The Japan Times, July 31, 2003). Following their advocates, Japanese officials and the financial industry have been pushing China to revalue the CNY (Tokyo-Mitsubishi, 2003).

Europe, which also suffers from reform inertia, is also prone to using China as a kind of scapegoat. It is unfortunate that there are powerful economies following Japan's self-deceiving view because the scapegoat strategy may encourage protectionism, demonize China as a global economic threat, and eventually destroy the gains from trade that the global system has strived for (Lo, 2003).

Even in Korea, where officials rarely comment on exchange rates, its Deputy Finance Minister Kim Yong-duk expressed concerns about the effects of a weak CNY and urged the Chinese authorities to adopt a wider trading range for the yuan (Asia Weekly Financial Alert, March 2, 2003).

1.5 The Voices of Other Spheres

Nobel Laureate Robert Mundell (March 16, 2002)

Nobel Laureate Robert Mundell said on March 16, 2002 in Beijing that China's monetary policy is "excellent." Addressing an international seminar here, Mundell praised China's policy of keeping its currency's exchange rate stable. "You shouldn't change that as it is working well," he said. The Columbia University economist, known as the "father of the euro," was awarded the 1999 Nobel economics prize for his research into economic and monetary union. He said that China is lucky to have received a great deal of foreign investment, adding that China's foreign exchange reserve is growing rapidly. He said that China is now in a very strong position and should maintain that position (People's Daily, March 17, 2002). Professor Mundell expressed similar ideas in a speech delivered to the Shanghai Futures Exchange (SHFE) on September 9, 2003 during his trip to China.

Stephen S. Roach (July 7, 2003)

China's competitive prowess has little to do with the value of the renminbi (RMB) despite accusations that pegging the currency to a weaker US dollar has given China an unfair advantage, said Stephen S. Roach, chief economist of Morgan Stanley & Co., in Beijing. Roach said the theory that currency policy was to blame for China's trade surplus overlooked the country's competitiveness in labor costs, technology, infrastructure, human capital, and its passion for reform. "I can't see vigorous growth anywhere except China," Roach said, "but it is not surprising that China has strong exports, provided the considerable increase of foreign investment." The performance of both domestic companies and multinationals contributed to the booming exports (People's Daily, July 7, 2003).

International CNN (July 18, 2003)

In *United Press International*, Gregory Fossedal, a chief investment officer of the Democratic Century Fund, writes, "the author of this return to meaningful dollar diplomacy is Treasury Secretary John Snow, with a helpful hand from his undersecretary, John Taylor. The revival of a serious interest in international monetary policy at Treasury, by itself, augurs well for the US and world economy."

As the chorus of criticism grows about the perceived low value of the Chinese currency, leading economists back Beijing's assertion that the time is not yet right to float the yuan. Hong Kong-based economists for HSBC, JP Morgan, and Morgan Stanley all say that factors such as deflation, weaknesses in China's financial system, and the need for domestic stability more than offset the external pressure for revaluation (International CNN.com, July 18, 2003).

Kenneth Rogoff (July 23, 2003)

The International Monetary Fund's chief economist, Kenneth Rogoff, said the fund does not support demands that China let its currency strengthen, saying appreciation can be risky for countries. "There are some that are calling for a revaluation," Rogoff said at a Washington conference on the dollar and the world economy (IMF, July 23, 2003).

There have been many views on whether the Chinese currency is dangerously undervalued and a threat to the global economy since May 2002. We cannot go into details of so many views and arguments here, and we encounter more views in Chapter 18 when we study factors affecting the most liquid CNY derivative product trading in the offshore market — CNY nondeliverable forwards. Interested readers may also read the Special Report (August 18, 2003) for other views.

1.6 Joint Voices of G7 Industrial Nations and Beyond

The G7 industrial nations' conference on September 20, 2002 called for more exchange rate flexibility to iron out global economic imbalances, which markets said were clearly targeted at Japan, China, and other Asian countries. The call for revaluation of the CNY was specifically stated in the communiqué of the G7: "... we emphasize that more flexibility in exchange rates is desirable for major countries or economic areas to promote smooth and widespread adjustments in the international financial system, based on market mechanisms."

Besides the official statement of the G7, the private sector and officials from both industrial and emerging markets seemed also to support the G7 view but believed that the policy change would be gradual toward the CNY exchange policy. In the investor seminars held in Dubai, where the G7 conference was held, a number of comments from both industrial and emerging markets officials were unanimous that any policy change implied for the Chinese by the communiqué would be very gradual.

1.7 From Depreciation to Appreciation

Facing the impact of the Asian financial crisis and great pressure for the CNY to depreciate since 1997, the Chinese government declared that it would maintain the exchange rate of the CNY, stating that the CNY would not be devalued, and the CNY withheld the depreciation pressure, winning the appreciation of the international community. The offshore one-year CNY/US dollar (USD) nondeliverable forward implied that CNY/USD should be devaluated to above RMB 10 per USD early in 1998. We will discuss and analyze the CNY depreciation in more detail in Part III of this book.

The market sentiment over the prospect of the RMB changed dramatically from bearishness through stagnation from May 2000 to November 2001. China's accession to WTO was interpreted as strengthening Chinese competitiveness both in international trade and as an industrial location. The buying pressure of the CNY caused the exchange rate often to break through the level of 8.27 yuan in 2001. Since the summer of 2001, demands for revaluation of the RMB arose mainly in Japan, and in November the forward rate of the RMB in the NDF market recorded appreciation of the RMB against the US dollar (the dollar discount, the RMB premium) for the first time in the market history (Murase, 2002).

The pressure from the US Congress and other major countries in the world for the CNY to be revaluated from May 2002 has been reflected in the CNY derivatives products trading in the offshore market since late 2002. The CNY foreign exchange swap rates began to imply CNY discounts from late October 2002, the offshore one-year CNY nondeliverable forward changed from premiums to discount from early November 2002, and the CNY nondeliverable options indicated similar results late in 2002. We will study these major CNY derivatives and most other products trading in the offshore market in Part IV of this book after introducing the Chinese economy and financial markets and the popular foreign exchange derivatives of the developed markets in earlier parts of this book.

1.8 Summary

Led by the US Congress and government, the developed countries have formed an almost unanimous view toward CNY revaluation, as reflected in the G7 communiqué of September 2002. However, both the academic and professional fields largely disagree with the official views from the G7. Yet, the market has been led by the official views and the CNY offshore market has implied significant discounts for the CNY from many actively traded products.

Although it is not the purpose of this book to discuss whether the CNY should be revaluated or not, it is necessary to know the underlying asset of the Chinese currency — the Chinese economy and financial market — so that readers can judge such important questions as whether the CNY should be revaluated, when it should be revaluated, and how much to revaluate before they can possibly make decisions on whether to invest or speculate in all related derivative products for the CNY revaluation.

2

Open-Door Policy and a Quarter-Century Reform

In the quarter-century since the beginning of economic reforms in China from the late 1970s, economic growth in the world's most populous country has been a phenomenal 9.4% per year on average. There have been numerous studies on how China has been reforming various aspects of her economy; it is not the purpose of this chapter to give a comprehensive review of these studies as it will take numerous books to do so. The purpose of this chapter is to try to get readers familiar with major milestones in the course of reforming the previously closed and planned economy into a market oriented economy in China and to provide basic background information for readers to better understand Chinese currency — yuan or renminbi (RMB).

This chapter is organized as follows. Section 2.1 describes briefly the rural area reform, which began earlier than all other reforms in China. Section 2.2 introduces special economic zones in coastal areas that have played important roles in the whole reform process in China. Section 2.3 introduces the decade-long experiment of a market economy in China from 1993 to 2003. Section 2.4 outlines the 2008 Beijing Olympic Games and the 2010 Shanghai World

Exposition and their impacts on the Chinese economy in the years to come. Section 2.5 discusses the significance of China's entrance into the World Trade Organization (WTO) and its effects on the Chinese economy, and Section 2.6 concludes the chapter.

2.1 Household Economic Responsibility System

After nearly three decades of a planned economy, the Chinese government decided to reform her economy and adopt an open-door policy. In the late 1970s, the Chinese government shifted its policy-focus to reforming and developing the economy from ideological or class struggles. The economic reforms started with the agriculture sector rather than industry. The earliest rural reform started automatically from a small village in Anhui province (to the east of Shanghai, see Figure 2.1, map of China), where 18 families contracted land secretly from their collective farm, and then that contracting system spread soon to other parts of China in the following years. The government approved gradually this rural household economic responsibility as a legal economic identity in the following years throughout China.

The government recognized early in 1982 various economic responsibility systems as legal economic units in the rural area and secured tenures of land responsibility systems over 15 years early in 1984. The economic responsibility system adopted in these rural areas released energy from the previous collective farm system and thus increased agricultural productivity significantly in the years to follow.

2.2 Open-Door Policy and Special Economic Zones

The previous economic system was essentially a closed and planned economic system with supply, production, and consumption planned from the top (central government) down to factories and villages. This system was rigid to changes in the economic environment. After the rural household economic responsibility system was adopted successfully in the rural areas, various measures were taken

Figure 2.1 Provinces, Autonomous Regions, and Special Municipalities in China

to give more authority to local officials and plant managers in the nonrural areas, and economic reform began in the cities. A wide variety of small-scale enterprises in services and light manufacturing were also permitted.

Recognizing the importance of foreign capital, technology, and management expertise in modernizing the Chinese economy, the Chinese government started to open increasingly to foreign trade and investment. In order to attract foreign investment and accelerate the approval processes, the government decided to establish four Special Economic Zones (SEZs) along the south coast of china, offering attractive incentives for foreign firms and creating a secure economic environment. In July 1979, the State Council approved Shenzhen (formerly a border village to Hong Kong in Guangdong Province), Zhuhai (close to Macau in Guangdong Province), Shantou (in South Guangdong Province) and Xiamen (in Fujian Province on the other side of Taiwan (see Figure 2.1 for the specific locations) to start to experiment with "special zones" and then permitted these special zones to be named "Special Economic Zones" as early as in May 1980.

In these zones, China offered low tax rates, fewer bureaucratic hurdles, and permission to repatriate the profits gained, in addition to relatively cheap land and labor. At the same time, several provinces and opened coastal cities were allowed to provide similar incentives for foreign investors. Chinese firms, especially those in big cities like Shanghai, were selected for greater autonomy. Since management was no longer subject to central government control, the resident managers were now in charge of the bottom line and had a free hand in the choice of suppliers, production methods, marketing, administration, and accounting. The reforms encouraged Chinese companies to cooperate with other firms, especially foreign firms.

At the end of his visit to three SEZs (Shenzhen, Zhuhai, and Xiamen) early in 1984, the dynamic Chinese leader Deng Xiaoping talked with the concerned central government officials on further opening up additional cities as SEZs. The central government approved 14 additional cities as SEZs on May 4, 1984.

In order to attract more foreign investment, the National People's Congress passed the "Chinese–Foreign Joint Equity Ventures Law" on July 1, 1979 to secure the interest of foreign institutions and to guard the smooth management of joint-venture businesses in China. Other major laws relating to foreign investment such as "the Chinese–Foreign Joint Co-operative Ventures Law" and the "Wholly Foreign-Owned Enterprises Law" have been established and revised since then. These laws have played important roles in China's attracting direct foreign investment and other forms of cooperation in China. For a comprehensive introduction to the Chinese legal system and business environment, please refer to Chong, Kabuth, and Kukovetz.

2.3 A Decade of Experimentation with a Market Economy

The economic reforms started with the automatic household responsibility system in rural areas, and soon it spread to cities in the coastal provinces without much central planning. The early reform process could be characterized as "experimenting" or "passing the river through touching the stones in the basin of the river" in the words of Deng Xiaoping. The experimentation method proved to be valuable during the earlier stages of the reform process, yet its limitations became more and more apparent as the reforms deepened and broadened in scope. It was a painstaking effort to reform the previously closed and planned economy because a lot of ideological, political, legal, ownership, and other issues were interwoven into a network that was not ready for changes.

The early attempts to reform the economy were made either automatically from the bottom-up as the rural household responsibility system was initiated and adopted or specifically for certain economic issues such as joint ventures with foreign companies. These attempts or experiments were for specific economic issues but not for general ones such as how to transform the then existing planned economy into a market economy. The theoretical need became more and more imperative after more than a decade of practice of reforming the economy in various aspects.

In order to deepen and broaden the ongoing reform process, the Communist Party of China (CPC) made an important decision in November 1993 to establish a socialist market economy. This decision was of vital importance for further reforming the Chinese economy in the following decade as it specifies the role and usefulness of the market mechanism in the development of the Chinese economy; it emphasizes the functionality of the market in resource reallocation; and it requires that reforms at various levels should be aimed at establishing a market economy. The important decision certainly promoted and accelerated the development of the Chinese economy in the decade from 1993 to 2003, and it will continue to be useful in the years to come.

An updated new version of the decision from the CPC central committee following the 10th anniversary of the 1993 market economy decision, released on October 14, 2003, further specifies items for upgrading the market economy in China. This new version of the decision will prove to be of vital importance in guiding China on her road to further development.

2.4 The Beijing Olympic Games and the Shanghai World Exhibition

On July 13, 2001, the International Olympic Committee (IOC) officially approved Beijing's application to host the 29th Olympic Games in 2008. It is the hope of generations of Chinese to host an International Olympic Games, and the realization of this hope certainly made hundreds of millions of Chinese happy. Millions of Chinese celebrated the announcement of this news in all cities and towns throughout China in the evening of July 13th, 2001.

The 2008 Beijing Olympic Games will prove to be important for China for integrating further into the international community because not only will the direct investment and related infrastructure development for the event will boost the development of the capital city, Beijing, management, globalization, and many other "software" aspects will also be improved significantly by 2008, as evidenced by the role of the 1964 Tokyo Olympic Games and the 1988 Seoul Olympic Games in the development of Japan and South Korea, respectively. Thousands of international companies from every continent have flown to Beijing to negotiate various possible business cooperation projects with the Beijing municipal government; such cooperation will further enhance business relationships between China and the rest of the world.

With the slogan "Better city, better life, strong government backing and support of China's steadily growing economy", Shanghai beat four other cities and won 54 votes of 88 member countries in the final round and won the bid to host the 2010 World Exposition on December 3, 2002. The news provided China with the opportunity to integrate her robust economy, infrastructure, cleaner environment, and social stability with the international community. City planners hope that the Expo will accelerate infrastructure plans, renovation of old districts, and ecological improvements. The Expo will certainly accelerate Shanghai's internationalization process and re-energize the economic and financial position of the "East Pearl" in not only China but also in Asia. We will discuss Shanghai as an international financial center later in Chapter 6.

2.5 World Trade Organization (WTO) Entrance

Few events could have as important impacts on the Chinese economy and political system as China's entrance into the WTO in November 2001. After 15 years of efforts to apply for WTO membership since 1986, China was admitted officially into the WTO on November 11, 2001. China became the 143rd WTO member officially on December 11, 2001. The WTO has been changing the Chinese economy and many other aspects of life in China for over 2 years.

By signing the Sino-US agreement on China's membership in WTO in the November 1999 and its subsequent realization in December 2001, China's WTO membership has boosted her economic growth and advanced her legal and governmental reforms. The improved confidence of foreign companies in China arises from the stable returns they can get from the Chinese market. China's WTO membership has also brought about fundamental changes in the government. To meet the requirements of its WTO membership, the government has initiated a campaign to clarify and unify governmental regulations to meet the WTO rules. In the first half of 2002, more than 2300 regulations were abolished or revised by 30 departments under the State Council. These moves will certainly increase market efficiency in the Chinese economy.

China's WTO membership is bridging the gap between China and the rest of the world and thus makes it easier for China to further open up to the rest of world and participate in the development of the world economy. It is changing the legal infrastructure and accelerating government reforms necessary for perform various duties related to the WTO status. Among the major promises made to the WTO, China will cut the average import tariff from 15% to 10% and abolish 400 types of import quotas by 2005. The lower import tariff and abolishment of import quotas will smoothen international trade between China and the rest of the world.

We will discuss in more detail the promises to the WTO of the Chinese government in following chapters when we discuss the Chinese economy and financial markets.

2.6 Conclusions

We have given a bird's eye view of "the quarter-century economic reform" in China from 1978 to 2003 in this chapter. The past decade's (1993–2003) experiment with a market economy has proved to be successful, and the market economy will further release the creativity and energy of the Chinese people in the years to come. The two-and-half years experience within the WTO has shown China's capacity to adapt to the international economy and the international community. Although there will be many new issues and problems ahead, they will be resolved with the intelligence of not only China but also the international community. For a comprehensive book covering various major events in China in the past quarter-century, please refer to Wang (2003).

3

The Chinese Economy

The Chinese economy is the foundation of its currency. We need to have a brief introduction to the Chinese economy before we analyze the Chinese currency renminbi (RMB) or yuan and its related derivatives in the following chapters of this book. As there are too many aspects of the Chinese economy for us to introduce clearly, we simply try to give a brief description of the basic ingredients of the economy here in this chapter.

This chapter is organized as follows. Section 3.1 focuses on population policies and the growth of the population in the past quarter-century; Section 3.2 introduces education in China in the past 25 years; Section 3.3 discusses exports and imports of China in the same period; Section 3.4 describes the accumulation of foreign reserves in China; Section 3.5 analyzes foreign direct investment in China from 1978 to 2003; Section 3.6 describe the gross domestic product (GDP) and per capita GDP in China; Section 3.7 addresses the necessity to shift the current fiscal policy to stimulating consumption; and Section 3.8 concludes the chapter.

3.1 Population

With about a quarter of the world's population, China was already the most populous country in the world when the People's Republic of China came into being in 1949. Despite various difficulties, the large population is an invaluable asset to the country. Any economic policy would not be appropriate to China that does not consider carefully the huge population factor in China. Thus, we start our description of the Chinese economy with the population.

A large population is an invaluable asset for the country as it contains a large pool of human talents that are necessary for various types of creative activities such as research and development, a great potential for consumption, and a nearly unlimited supply of human labor, which are all necessary for sustainable development of the economy. Yet, it is also the source of serious social problems such as social welfare, education, and so on.

Recognizing the potential problems with the growing population, the Chinese government began to find appropriate measures to control population growth in the early stage of reforms. The State Council issued an order "To Better Family Planning Work" on February 9, 1982. The order proposes the popular "one family–one child" policy and the policy of encouraging later marriages. This policy has been executed in China since then and has produced significant results in controlling population growth throughout China. Table 3.1 gives the total population of China and its annual growth rate from 1977 to 2003.

The family planning policy has proved to be successful as the annual population growth rate was controlled to within 2% in the 1980s and to within 1% from 1998. Despite its great success in China, the family planning policy has been frequently criticized in the international community. The policy indeed has many limitations, and the government has recognized these limitations in allowing young couples who are both single children of their parents to have more than one child.

The National Population and Family Planning Commission (NPFPC), the government agency in charge of population, has been cooperating with various international agencies for population and family planning issues. For additional information on the Chinese

Table 3.1 Chinese Population from 1978 to 2003

Year	Population (millions)	Annual Growth Rate (%)	Year	Population (millions)	Annual Growth Rate (%)
1978	956.2	1.2	1991	1158.2	1.3
1979	968.4	1.3	1992	1171.7	1.2
1980	982.1	1.4	1993	1185.2	1.1
1981	994.4	1.2	1994	1198.5	1.1
1982	1008.5	1.4	1995	1211.2	1.1
1983	1023.2	1.5	1996	1223.9	1.0
1984	1036.3	1.3	1997	1236.3	1.0
1985	1050.9	1.4	1998	1247.6	0.9
1986	1067.1	1.5	1999	1257.9	0.8
1987	1083.6	1.5	2000	1267.4	0.8
1988	1101.7	1.7	2001	1276.3	0.7
1989	1122.3	1.9	2002	1284.5	0.6
1990	1143.3	1.9	2003	1293.5	0.7

Data source: China Statistics 2002, 1990; data for 2003 are calculated from GDP and per capita GDP for 2003 released by the China Statistics Bureau on January 20, 2004.

population, please go to the official website of the NPFPC, www.npfpc.gov.cn/.

3.2 Education

Education is the foundation for both economic development and social progress in every country. China has made significant progress in education since the beginning of the reform process. Recognizing serious problems in the education system, the Chinese government decided to restore the higher education system that was disrupted during the Great Culture Revolution between 1966 and 1976, when college students were not selected from senior high school graduates but rather from workers, peasants, and soldiers. In 1977, college students began to be selected through centralized entrance examinations from senior high school graduates and those who did not have the chance to go to colleges during the Great Culture Revolution, and at the same time hundreds of thousands of students and scholars were sent abroad to study in the developed countries around the world from the late 1970s. The author also benefited from this policy of going to college immediately after graduating from senior high school in 1980 and was sent by the government to study in the United States in 1987.

The whole education system has been rebuilt and modernized since 1977, and schools have been given a certain autonomy. Never have so many students been enrolled into various vocational schools, colleges, universities, graduate schools, and research institutes throughout China in the history of the country. The total college enrollment in 2002 reached 3.205 million (19.46% higher than in 2001), more than 10 times larger than the corresponding number in 1977; and the total number of students in formal colleges reached 9.034 million in 2002. New enrollment in adult higher education and the total number of adult students reached 2.223 million and 5.592 million in 2002, respectively, with corresponding annual growth rates of 13.47% and 22.63%. (Please see the website of the Ministry of Education of China, www.moe.edu.cn, for more details.)

Enrollment in graduate schools grew faster than formal college enrollment in 2002. The total new enrollment of all graduate schools and research institutes reached 202,600, and the total number of graduate students grew to 501,000 in 2002, up 22.65% and 27.41%, respectively.

The great majority of schools are public schools in China. A dramatic growth in the number of private schools represents another unique feature of the development of education in China. The total number of private institutions for higher education rose to 1201, with the total number of registered students 1.404 million, 273,100 more than in 2001. There is also a greater number of private elementary and high schools throughout China. (Please also see the website of the Ministry of Education of China, www.moe.edu.cn.) The progress in education provides China with sufficient talent for research and development and qualified labor for the economy to grow steadily.

Despite the great achievements in education in China in the past 27 years, there are also many serious problems in the educational system, notably the relatively low enrollment rate of basic education (elementary school enrollment rate fell from 99.1% in 1999 and 2000 to 99.05% in 2001 and to 98.58% in 2002; enrollment from elementary school to junior high school was only 97.0% in 2002; and enrollment from junior high school to senior high school was only 58.5% in 2002). Besides the lower enrollment rates of basic education, high education costs represent another critical issue. It is beyond the scope of this book to go into details of specific problems in the education system in China.

3.3 Foreign Direct Investment

Foreign direct investment (FDI) has been a necessary component of the Chinese economy since the beginning of the reforms in the late 1970s. Since the economic reform took place in 1978, China has gradually turned from a closed and planned economy to a fast-growing market-oriented open economy. The growing linkage in terms of FDI between China and rest of the world makes China play an increasingly important role in the global economy. FDI provides not only the necessary capital for many projects and new ventures but also technology, management, know-how, and more importantly, the linkage between the Chinese market and the world economy. The flows of FDI have been perfect barometers of international confidence in the Chinese economy.

Table 3.2 gives the amounts of FDI into China from 1978 to 2003. We can observe readily that the accumulated FDI from 1978 to 2003 surpassed half a trillion US dollars (US$503.3 billion). We can also observe from Table 3.2 that there have been two high-growth periods in the flow of FDI into China in the past 25 years, one from 1981 to 1984 in the early stage of the reform, with an average annual growth rate of about 100%, and the other from 1992 to 1993, when after the announcement of far-reaching reforms during Deng Xiaoping's trip to the southern Special Economic Zones and the establishment of the "socialist market economy", foreign investments were boosted considerably. FDI was affected significantly during the Asian financial crisis as it experienced negative growth for the first time in 1999.

The country's WTO entry in 2001 has made it an irreversible trend to integrate her economy into the global economic framework. Its rich, low-labor cost resource and the vast market, both of which provide much scope for profits for international companies, make foreign investors more confident in investing in China, and FDI

Table 3.2 Foreign Direct Investments and Growth in China from 1978 to 2003 (Unit: US$ billion)

Year	FDI	Annual Growth Rate (%)	Accumulated FDI	Year	FDI	Annual Growth Rate (%)	Accumulated FDI
1978–80	0.1		0.1	1992	11.0	150.00	34.0
1981	0.2	100.00	0.3	1993	27.5	150.00	61.5
1982	0.4	100.00	0.7	1994	33.8	22.91	95.3
1983	0.6	50.00	1.3	1995	37.5	10.95	132.8
1984	1.3	116.67	2.6	1996	41.7	11.20	174.5
1985	1.7	30.77	4.3	1997	45.3	8.63	219.8
1986	1.9	11.76	6.2	1998	45.6	0.66	265.4
1987	2.3	21.05	8.5	1999	40.4	−11.40	305.8
1988	3.2	39.13	11.7	2000	40.8	0.99	346.6
1989	3.4	6.25	15.1	2001	47.0	15.20	393.6
1990	3.5	2.94	18.6	2002	52.7	12.22	446.3
1991	4.4	25.71	23.0	2003	53.5	1.44	499.9

Data source: China Statistics Year Book 2001; data for 2002 and 2003 are from a news release from the Ministry of Commerce of China on January 14, 2004, http://www.mofcom.gov.cn/.

has been back on the growth path since 2001. The total foreign investment influx into China exceeded US$50 billion in 2002, making the country the largest foreign investment destination in the world. However, the FDI growth slowed significantly in 2003 largely because of the spread of the severe acute respiratory syndrome (SARS) in China in the first half of 2003 and the return of international capital flows into the United States with strong signs of economic recovery there in the same year.

According to a recent release from the Ministry of Commerce, FDI in China in the first four months of 2004 amounted to US$19.617 billion, 10.07% more compared with the same period in 2003. This FDI number seems to indicate that its growth rate has returned somewhat to the 2002 level. However, there might have been other important reasons behind the significant drop in FDI growth rate in 2003; it is beyond the scope of this book to explore such reasons.

3.4 Exports and Imports

Export and import have been playing important roles in China's economic development in the past 25 years, especially in the past decade. We will concentrate on export and import in China in the past decade briefly in this section.

3.4.1 Development in the Past Quarter-Century

As China becomes more and more international with more FDI and improvement in production and management, foreign trade is playing an increasingly important role in the Chinese economy. Table 3.3 gives the export figure and its annual growth rate, the import figure and its annual growth rate, the total trade volume and its annual growth rate, and the total trade volume as a percentage of GDP from 1978 to 2003.

3.4.2 Trade Contribution to Economy

Table 3.3 shows clearly that the Asian financial crisis hit China severely as total trade volume fell in 1998 for the first time since 1982. It also shows that total trade volume as a percentage of the GDP grew steadily from merely 9.6% in 1978 to 50.4% in 2002, and to 60.4% in 2003, indicating the higher degree of international economic participation of the Chinese economy since China's entrance in the WTO.

Table 3.3 also indicates that the total trade volume increased by 7.5% in 2001, the lowest from 1999 to 2003, and yet the figure contrasted sharply with the stagnant world economy in the year, when the world trade volume dropped by 1.5 percent compared with the previous year.

The rapid growth in China's trade volume is attributable directly to the improved trade environment following its WTO entry as total trade volume grew significantly with an annual growth rate of 21.8% and 37.1% in 2002 and 2003, respectively. China's average import tariff rate was cut from 15.6 percent early in 2002 to 12%. The former trading instability brought by bilateral negotiations has been roughly written off by a more stable multilateral trade framework. And many of the quota restrictions of other countries have been lifted on Chinese products with corresponding advantages.

Table 3.3 Foreign Trade of China from 1978 to 2003 (Unit: US$ billion)

Year	Export	Export Growth Rate (%)	Import	Import Growth Rate (%)	Ex Growth– Imp Growth (%)	Trade Volume	Trade Volume Growth Rate (%)	Trade/ GDP (%)
1978	9.8		10.9			20.6		9.6
1979	13.7	40.1	15.7	44.0	−3.9	29.3	42.1	11.3
1980	18.3	33.7	19.6	24.7	9.1	37.8	28.9	14.3
1981	22.0	20.5	22.0	12.6	7.8	44.0	16.4	15.4
1982	22.3	1.4	19.3	−12.4	13.8	41.6	−5.5	14.9
1983	22.2	−0.4	21.4	10.9	−11.3	43.6	4.8	17.0
1984	26.1	17.6	27.4	28.1	−10.6	53.6	22.8	21.8
1985	27.4	4.6	42.3	54.1	−49.5	69.6	30.0	22.7
1986	30.9	13.1	42.9	1.5	11.6	73.9	6.1	25.0
1987	39.4	27.5	43.2	0.7	26.7	82.7	11.9	25.7
1988	47.5	20.5	55.3	27.9	−7.4	102.8	24.4	25.6
1989	52.5	10.6	59.1	7.0	3.6	111.7	8.7	24.9
1990	62.1	18.2	53.4	−9.8	28.0	115.4	3.4	29.1
1991	71.9	15.8	63.8	19.6	−3.8	135.7	17.6	33.3
1992	84.9	18.1	80.6	26.3	−8.2	165.5	22.0	34.3
1993	91.7	8.0	104.0	29.0	−21.0	195.7	18.2	32.6
1994	121.0	31.9	115.6	11.2	20.7	236.6	20.9	43.7
1995	148.8	22.9	132.1	14.2	8.7	280.9	18.7	40.8
1996	151.1	1.5	138.8	5.1	−3.6	289.9	3.2	36.1
1997	182.8	21.0	142.4	2.5	18.5	325.2	12.2	36.9
1998	183.7	0.5	140.2	−1.5	2.0	324.0	−0.4	34.4
1999	194.9	6.1	165.7	18.2	−12.0	360.6	11.3	35.8
2000	249.2	27.8	225.1	35.8	−8.0	474.3	31.5	43.4
2001	266.2	6.8	243.6	8.2	−1.4	509.8	7.5	43.4
2002	325.6	22.3	295.2	21.2	1.2	620.8	21.8	50.2
2003	438.4	34.6	412.8	39.8	−5.2	851.2	37.1	60.4

Data source: Data for 1978 to 2001 are from the website of the Ministry of Foreign Trade and Economic Cooperation, www1.moftec.gov.cn/moftec_cn; and data for 2002 and 2003 are calculated using data from People's Daily, January 14, 2004 (www.people.com.cn/GB/tupian).

3.4.3 Growth of Imports

Table 3.3 indicates clearly that imports have increased significantly faster than exports in China from 1999 to 2003, with the only exception of 2002, when import growth rate was merely 1.1% lower than the corresponding export figure. The average annual growth rate of imports in the five-year period was 6.4% higher than the corresponding export figure. If we consider a longer period from 1991 to 2003, the average annual growth rate of imports in the 13-year period was about 1.0% higher than the corresponding export figure. The faster growth in Chinese imports indicates clearly that China has been contributing to the world economy recovery. According to data released by the Ministry of Finance of Japan on January 26, 2004 (Japanese Asahi News of January 28, 2004), Japanese exports to China (including Hong Kong and Taiwan) reached 13.7 trillion Japanese yen (about US$130 billion) in 2003, surpassing its exports to the USA for the first time in history. This is a good example showing that China's imports contributed to the recovery of the Japanese economy in 2003.

Studies show that the growth of China benefited not only developed countries but also developing countries as China has imported about 50% from developed countries and other half from developing countries since 1992 (Yang, 2003).

3.4.4 Contribution of Foreign Enterprises

The contribution of foreign enterprises to China's exports is of particular importance in China's exports and imports. With growing FDI in China and foreign invested enterprises (FIEs) doing business in China, the foreign enterprises' share of China's exports has been growing steadily, from merely 9.4% in the late 1980s to 50.0% in 2001 and 50.2% in 2002 (Xinhua News Agency, February 18, 2003). Exports of foreign enterprises grew faster than those of Chinese enterprises, and the total foreign enterprises' exports reached US$169.94, up 27.6% in 2002 from 2001, 5.3% higher than the total growth rate (see Table 3.3) and 10.5% higher than the exports of domestic Chinese companies.

Table 3.4 Weight of Foreign Enterprises' Export in China — From the First Quarter 2002 to the Fourth Quarter 2003 (Unit: US$ billion)

	Foreign Enterprises	Total	FE/Total (%)
2002Q1	335.5	646.6	51.89
2002Q2	398.6	773.7	51.52
2002Q3	465.0	905.6	51.35
2002Q4	500.8	930.5	53.82
2003Q1	465.0	863.3	53.86
2003Q2	560.2	1039.4	53.90
2003Q3	640.5	1174.7	54.52
2003Q4	738.9	1307.5	56.51

Data source: Official website of the Ministry of Commerce, www.mofcom.gov.cn/.

Table 3.4 gives the quarterly exports of foreign enterprises (FEs) from 2002 to 2003. We can observe that the shares of FEs in China exports have been growing steadily from over 51% early in 2002 to 56.51% in the fourth quarter of 2003. These data clearly show that foreign enterprises have been playing dominating roles in China's export and trade.

3.5 Foreign Reserve and Foreign Debt

With the steady growth of exports and imports in China in the past quarter-century, as discussed earlier in this chapter, foreign reserves have also grown significantly in the same period. As a matter of fact, foreign reserves were rather low in the early 1980s when economic reforms had just started, reaching US$10 billion for the first time in 1990. Table 3.5 gives China's foreign reserves from 1978 to 2003.

We can easily observe from Table 3.5 that, with the only exception of 1992, foreign reserves have grown from 1990 to 2003. There were two periods when foreign reserves either fell or grew with single-digit values, the first period being from 1991 to 1993, when the economy grew at over 10% annual growth rates, and the second being from 1997 to 2000, when the Chinese economy was hit severely by the Asian financial crisis. It surpassed US$100 billion and US$200 billion in 1996 and 2001, respectively. It has grown steadily from 2000 to 2003, surpassing US$400 billion in 2003,

Table 3.5 China's Foreign Reserves from 1978 to 2003 (Unit: US$ billion)

Year	Reserves	Growth Rate (%)	Year	Reserves	Growth Rate (%)
1978	0.17	−82.5	1991	21.71	95.7
1979	0.84	403.0	1992	19.44	−10.5
1980	−1.30	−254.3	1993	21.20	9.0
1981	2.71	309.0	1994	51.62	143.5
1982	6.99	158.0	1995	73.60	42.6
1983	8.90	27.4	1996	105.05	42.7
1984	8.22	−7.7	1997	139.89	33.2
1985	2.64	−67.8	1998	144.96	3.6
1986	2.07	−21.6	1999	154.68	6.7
1987	2.92	41.1	2000	165.57	7.0
1988	3.37	15.4	2001	212.17	28.1
1989	5.55	64.6	2002	286.41	35.0
1990	11.09	99.9	2003	403.25	40.8

Data source: Data for 1978 to 2002 are from the website of the State Administration of Foreign Exchange, www.safe.gov.cn; and data for 2003 are from People's Daily, January 20, 2004.

second only to that of Japan in all the world. It is worthy noting that it took China 16 years for her foreign reserve to reach US$100 billion in 1996 from merely US$11 billion in 1990; yet it took only 5 years for the number to be more than doubled from 1996 to 2001; and it took another 2 years for it to be almost re-doubled again from 2001 to 2003.

Despite the huge foreign reserves, China has also accumulated a significant amount of foreign debt. Table 3.6 provides figures of the foreign debt compared with foreign reserves from 1985 to 2002. It can be observed readily that in most of the 18 years from 1985 to 2002, the total foreign debt surpassed the total foreign reserves. The average foreign debt (FD) and foreign reserve (FR) ratio was nearly 1000% in 1980s, and it declined to about 100% as the 20th century ended.

Table 3.6 shows a new phenomenon in the Chinese economy when total foreign debt fell below total foreign reserves from 1999 to 2002. With a total foreign debt of US$168.54 in 2002, the FD/FR ratio was still as significant as 58.8%. If we take foreign debt into consideration, the net foreign reserves would be much lower than the actual foreign reserves.

Table 3.6 China's Foreign Debt and Debt/Reserve Ratio from 1978 to 2003 (Unit: US$ billion)

Year	Foreign Debt	Foreign Reserves	FD/FR (%)	Year	Foreign Debt	Foreign Reserves	FD/FR (%)
1985	15.83	2.64	598.7	1994	92.81	51.62	179.8
1986	21.48	2.07	1036.7	1995	106.59	73.60	144.8
1987	30.20	2.92	1033.2	1996	116.28	105.05	110.7
1988	40.00	3.37	1186.2	1997	130.96	139.89	93.6
1989	41.30	5.55	744.1	1998	146.04	144.96	100.7
1990	52.55	11.09	473.7	1999	151.83	154.68	98.2
1991	60.56	21.71	278.9	2000	145.73	165.57	88.0
1992	69.32	19.44	356.5	2001	170.11	212.17	80.2
1993	83.57	21.20	394.2	2002	168.54	286.41	58.8

Data source: Data for 1978 to 2002 are from the website of the State Administration of Foreign Exchange, www.safe.gov.cn; and data for 2003 are from People's Daily, January 20, 2004.

3.6 GDP and GDP per Capita

Thanks to various reform initiatives, the Chinese economy took off in the 1980s. Industry posted major gains, especially in coastal areas near Hong Kong (Guangdong Province), where foreign investment helped spur output of both domestic and export goods. Table 3.7 gives the total GDP in RMB, annual GDP growth rate, total GDP in US dollars, and GDP per capita in China from 1978 to 2003.

In the period of 1992–96, the annual growth of GDP accelerated, particularly in the coastal areas — averaging more than 10% annually according to official figures. In late 1993, China's leadership approved additional long-term reforms aimed at giving still more scope to market-oriented institutions and strengthening control over the financial system. State enterprises continue to dominate many key industries in the new "socialist market economy." The GDP surpassed US$0.5 trillion for the first time in 1993, and US$1 trillion in 2000.

The GDP in 2003 rose 9.1% from 2002 to RMB 11.67 trillion (US$1.41 trillion), according to a State Statistics Bureau release of January 20, 2004, with the remark that it was the highest annual growth rate since 1996. The average annual growth rate reached 9.40% from 1978 to 2003. The GDP growth rate of 9.1% in 2003 was even lower than the average annual growth rate from 1978 to 2003.

Table 3.7 GDP and per Capita GDP in China

Year	GDP (RMB billion)	Annual Growth Rate (%)	GDP (US$ billion)	GDP per Capita (US$)
1978	362.4	11.7	215.3	225
1979	403.8	7.6	259.7	268
1980	451.8	7.8	265.0	270
1981	486.2	5.2	285.2	287
1982	529.5	9.1	279.8	277
1983	593.5	10.9	255.0	249
1984	717.1	15.2	244.2	236
1985	896.4	13.5	305.3	290
1986	1020.2	8.8	295.5	277
1987	1196.3	11.6	321.4	297
1988	1492.8	11.3	401.1	364
1989	1690.9	4.1	449.1	400
1990	1854.8	3.8	387.8	339
1991	2161.8	9.2	406.1	351
1992	2663.8	14.2	483.0	412
1993	3463.4	13.5	601.1	507
1994	4675.9	12.6	542.5	453
1995	5847.8	10.5	700.3	578
1996	6788.5	9.6	816.5	667
1997	7446.3	8.8	898.2	727
1998	7834.5	7.8	946.3	758
1999	8206.8	7.1	991.4	788
2000	8940.4	8.0	1080.0	852
2001	9434.6	7.3	1139.9	893
2002	10,239.8	8.0	1237.1	963
2003	11,669.4	9.1	1409.9	1090

Data source: China Statistical Year Book 2001; data for 2001–2003 are from the website of National Bureau of Statistics, www.stats.gov.cn; and data in US dollars are converted using the official exchange rates of the corresponding years given in Table 6.1.

3.6.1 International Comparisons

The Chinese economy has been ranked the sixth largest economy in the world since 2001 according to official GDP figures, behind those of the USA, Japan, Germany, UK, and France. The Chinese GDP of US$1.41 trillion in 2003 is slightly lower than the French GDP of US$1.42 trillion in 2002 and the UK GDP of US$1.56 trillion the same year. With a moderate average annual growth rate of 8% from 2004 to 2006, China will likely replace France as the fifth largest economy in the world in 2004 and UK as the fourth largest economy in 2006 if

Euro and British pounds don't appreciate too much against the US dollar within the time under consideration.

3.6.2 Per Capita GDP

Despite the dramatic economic growth in China in the past quarter-century and the international GDP ranking, the per capita GDP is still extremely low. It was just over US$200 at the beginning of the reforms in 1978, reaching US$500 in about 15 years in the early 1990s. A phenomenal event is that the per capita GDP, for the first time in Chinese history, surpassed US$1000 in 2003. Compared with the previous figure of several hundred US dollars, China's per capita GDP in excess of US$1000 is a historic achievement. A per capita GDP well over US$1000 cannot change the fact that China is still a developing country with relatively low incomes. It only shows that it is an arduous, long-term and urgent task for China to accelerate development. The per capita GDP in excess of US$1000 also indicates that China's economy is approaching anther stage for more citizens to be able to consume a higher level of products and services in the years to come.

But compared with developed countries, whose GDP is well above tens of thousands of US dollars, China is lagging far behind, ranking somewhat just above the 100th in the world. The coastal areas have developed significantly, and yet the vast majority of China is still much less developed, and there remain tremendous work for China to develop to improve the general living standards for over a billion of her citizens.

3.6.3 Energy Consumption and GDP Growth

There have been doubts about the actual economic growth rates in China since the Asian financial crisis. It is too complicated for us to go into the details of such arguments as it is far beyond the scope of this book. Here we simply introduce the energy consumption in China in the past few years so that readers can familiarize themselves with more aspects of the Chinese economy.

China suffered a shortage of electricity for decades before the reform process started, and the situation was not changed until 1997, when power supply became sufficient for the first time in the history of China. Power supply and capacity were adequate for economic development for only a few years. Because of the sufficiency, the country did not expand its power capacity from the late 1990s. The shortage became more and more obvious in 2002 when supply could not meet demand and many factories had to be shut down because of the shortage. The total electricity consumption reached 1.891 trillion/kw in 2003, a 15.4% increase from the 2002 level and 6.3% higher than the corresponding GDP growth rate in 2003. About two-thirds of all provinces and special municipalities experienced an electricity shortage in 2003. It is expected that the shortage situation will not be resolved until 2005.

Another important figure is China's crude oil import. According to a recent official release on February 8, 2004, China imported 91.12 million metric tons of crude oil in 2003, 31.3% up from 69.4 million metric tons in 2002; and the total imports of oil products reached 28.24 million metric tons, 38.8% up from 2002, ranking China the second largest crude oil importer in the world, second only to the USA. The dramatic growth of crude oil indicates strong economic growth, yet it also implies that the efficiency of oil usage is extremely low in China compared with countries such as Japan as the Chinese GDP is only about 30% of the Japanese GDP and yet oil consumption is already greater than Japan.

3.7 From Stimulating Fiscal Policy to Stimulating Consumption Policy

Although China largely stayed out of the Asian crisis, her FDI and export were severely affected by the crisis, as evidenced by the drop in FDI and exports in 1998 and 1999, given in Tables 3.2 and 3.3. Besides the direct impacts on FDI and exports, the crisis has had tremendous impacts on the Chinese macroeconomic policies as the country had to struggle against over-supply and demand shortage in the domestic market and a slowdown of exports. In order to stimulate economic growth, the central government adopted a dramatic fiscal policy since 1997 through issuing government debts. This stimulative fiscal policy has been quite successful as economic growth has been sustained. The economic achievement is not without costs as government debt as a percentage of GDP has increased steadily since 1997 and the growth accelerated in 1997 and 1998. The excessive government investments have somewhat crowded out private investments and also represent "returning to the previous planed economy" because most of the major projects are again initiated and managed by government institutions, and the efficiency of such investments has been proved to be limited.

The Asian financial crisis accelerated transforming the Chinese economy from supply shortage to demand shortage. Consumer prices in 1998/99 declined for the first time since the beginning of reforms in the late 1970s. Reflecting a somewhat uncertain view of the future both domestically and internationally, the consumption growth rate fell significantly to single digits (5.9% and 6.5% in 1998 and 1999, respectively) from double digits (32.7% and 19.3% in 1994 and 1996, respectively). The stimulative fiscal policy has been successful, yet it was largely a temporary policy during a crisis environment and should not be maintained as a continuous national policy. For the stability of government policies, it is not appropriate to change this policy dramatically; however, it is highly necessary to shift the policy focus gradually from government investment to stimulate private investment and consumption. Table 3.8 gives the

Table 3.8 Consumption/GDP Ratios in Selected Countries from 1995 to 2002

Country or Region/Year	1991–95 (%)	1996–2000 (%)	2001–2002 (%)
USA	82.9	81.7	84.9
UK	84.4	83.7	85.8
Mexico	82.5	78.2	80.9
France	79.2	78.7	78.7
Euro	77.6	77.2	77.4
Canada	81.1	76.6	75.7
Italy	78.1	77.6	78.9
Spain	78.5	76.9	75.7
Germany	76.6	77.3	78.0
Japan	68.4	71.5	74.4
Korea	63.9	66.4	70.1
China	58.54	59.39	60.75

Data source: calculated using data from OECD website.

consumption/GDP ratios of the countries in the Organization for Economic Cooperation and Development (OECD) countries and China. We can observe clearly that consumption contributes more than 80% to the GDP in developed economies such as USA and UK, and it was over 70% for most OECD countries. A model of stimulating consumption in China was developed by Zhang (2003b). Interested readers may refer to that paper. It is also beyond the scope of this book to address this policy issue further. Interested readers may refer to Zhang (2003a).

3.8 Conclusions

Both exports and foreign reserves have growing steadily in China in the past quarter-century, especially in the past decade. The success has largely resulted from China's reform efforts and the open-door policy. Yet, foreign enterprises contribute significantly to China's export and have dominated China's exports since 2001. Corresponding to China's huge foreign reserves, there is large foreign debt, which amounts over 50% of the foreign reserves. Therefore, we have to pay more attention to the components of China's exports, foreign debt and other factors when we make international comparisons.

China has achieved great success in reforming her economy in the past quarter-century, with an average annual growth rate of 9.4%. The magnitude of the Chinese economy is now ranked No. 6 in the world, next to the French economy in 2003. Despite the great success, the GDP per capita is still rather low, merely US$1090 in 2003, at the level of a lower middle-income country in the world. There are a lot of challenges such as unemployment, social welfare, increasing uneven income distribution, low income of the majority of people living in the rural areas, and so on. It requires a lot of intelligence and wisdom to tackle such problems.

There are many other important issues regarding the Chinese economy such as the development of the private sector, agricultural problems, real estate development and so on. These topics are beyond the scope of this book.

4

Banking System in China

China is said to have a banking-led financial structure similar to that in Japan and Germany, where the proportion of loans to GDP is obviously higher than that in other countries. The proportion of loans to GDP is even higher in China than in both Japan and Germany. By the end of June 2003, the total assets of all banks consisted of 85% of the total assets of RMB 26.5 trillion (US$3.2 trillion) of all financial institutions in China (Tang, 2003). Because of the dominance power of banks, we start with the banking system in China in this chapter.

A better understanding of the Chinese banking system will prepare us to better understand the current situation of the Chinese financial market and prepare us to know better how foreign exchange policies are determined in China. This chapter is organized as follows. Section 4.1 introduces the People's Bank of China (PBOC), the central bank of China, its functions, and the evolvement of its functionalities; Section 4.2 introduces Chinese financial institutions in general; Section 4.3 describes Chinese banks; Section 4.4 introduces foreign banks in China; Section 4.5 introduces Chinese non-banking financial institutions; Section 4.6 introduces financial instruments in the financial market in China; Section 4.7 introduces the inter-bank market; Section 4.8 analyzes major problems existing in the Chinese financial market; Section 4.9 outlines the major promises that the Chinese government made for WTO entrance; and Section 4.10 concludes the chapter.

4.1 The PBOC

The PBOC has been the most important financial institution in China simply because every financial sector has been, to some degree, related to PBOC. Thus, the development and evolvement of the functionalities of PBOC is of particularly interest to anyone in the Chinese financial industry and to everyone who is interested in the Chinese financial industry. To a great degree, the development of the Chinese financial market is the process of stripping off specific functions from the PBOC. We will describe this in this section.

The PBOC was established on December 1, 1948, 10 months before the birth of the People's Republic of China on October 1, 1949. All existing banking institutions and assets in China were injected into the mono-bank system, PBOC. The PBOC had an administrative function within the centrally planned economy, funneling budgetary funds to the agricultural and industrial sectors. It served the functions of a retail bank, wholesale bank, and central bank concurrently. The PBOC has undergone a number of fundamental changes in the past 25 years, leading to a total restructuring of China's financial landscape.

Before 1978, the financial system was largely irrelevant to the country's macroeconomic performance. The overall paradigm of financial sector reform changed from a moderate to a more radical stance over five phases of reform, beginning in the late 1970s. Table 4.1 summarizes the major events of reforms in the financial industry.

In the first phase, from 1979 to 1988, the scope of financial reforms was limited to changes in the structure and operation of the state banking system in the earlier period. At the macrolevel, financial institutions had to be adapted to fulfilling the role of financial intermediaries. On the one hand, the decentralization of financial resources into the hands of households led to an explosion in their

Table 4.1 Major Reforming Events in the Financial Industry in China

1st Phase (1979–88)	
Sep 83	Establishment of four state-owned commercial banks
2nd Phase (1988–94)	
Oct 92	Establishment of China Securities Regulatory Commission
3rd Phase Reform (1995–2003)	
Mar 18, 1995	Enactment of "Law of People's Bank of China" by NPC
Nov 1998	Establishment of China Insurance Regulatory Commission
4th Phase (2003–present)	
Mar 10, 2003	NPC passes the State Council restructuring plan to set up China Banking Regulatory Commission
Apr 28, 2003	Establishment of China Banking Regulatory Commission
Dec 27, 2003	Enactment of new "People's Bank of China Law" by NPC

saving deposits. On the other hand, bank credit replaced the state budget as the main source of investment finance. At the microlevel, banks had to start to include profitability among the objectives of their operations. They began to learn to be more selective in granting loans to enterprises and to monitor the performance of the latter in order to contribute to some timid hardening of their budget constraints.

The real start of financial sector reforms was the abandonment of the rationing of capital, in line with the fiscal plan of specialized banks emerging from the former unified state bank to become the pillars of the new financial system and the new non-banking financial institutions (NBFIs) created. In September 1983, the State Council issued a document to redefine the function of PBOC as the central bank to oversee and administer China's financial affairs and then established the four state-owned commercial banks as institutions independent of the PBOC and the Ministry of Treasury to handle the business of loans and savings. The PBOC started to lose some of its powers, becoming the sole central bank in charge of enforcing a direct monetary policy within a system of directed capital.

The second phase, from 1988 through 1994, was characterized by the experimental nature of financial sector reforms. Within the context of a slowdown in reforms, caused by the authorities' exclusive focus on controlling inflationary pressures, most reforms were limited in scope, continuously reviewed, and sometimes reversed. The authorities faced the dilemma of re-establishing macroeconomic stability under the pressure of increasing demand for capital. This phrase also included allowing new financial intermediaries to emerge.

The third phase, from 1995 to 2003, contrasts with the previous one since an attempt at macroeconomic stabilization was this time accompanied by an acceleration in the pace of financial sector reforms. The reforms include the adoption of a new law for the central bank and for commercial banks stemming from the former specialized banks, and the transfer of policy lending from the specialized banks to new policy banks. This phase is also characterized by further stripping off of the insurance regulatory function from the PBOC through the establishment of the China Insurance Regulatory Commission (CIBC).

The fourth phase starts from the establishment of the China Banking Regulatory Commission (CBRC) and the enactment and immediate execution of the new PBOC law by the National People's Congress on December 28, 2003. This new law further strips off the function of supervising commercial banks, asset management corporations, and other loan receiving financial institutions to the newly established CBRC and designates the PBOC's major functions as being the central bank in issuing and executing monetary policies, establishing and improving the macroeconomic adjustment system, and guarding financial stability.

In 1993, PBOC was transferred into a kind of Chinese Federal Reserve System. At the National People's Congress in March 1995, a very bold attempt was made to separate the PBOC from the executive arm of the government, thus removing it from political influence through the issuance of the central bank law.

It is hardly possible to keep up a high level of stability without interventions from the state, as could be seen during the actual Asian crisis. China needs further reforms of its financial system, but as everywhere in the economy right now, the government has to face the dilemma necessary deregulation and liberalization on the one hand and increasing instability and lack of control on the other hand.

The financial system must be reformed further, improving the supervisory and regulatory functions of the PBOC and making state banks operate as independent commercial entities. The investment system has to be changed from a system controlled mainly administratively to one run on market principles. We will discuss the investment system in more detail in Chapter 5 of this book.

4.2 Financial Institutions

The financial institutions can be roughly divided into banks and non-banking institutions. In 1983, the PBOC was declared by the State Council as China's central bank, and PBOC's status was further enhanced by the enactment of the PBOC law by the National People's Congress in 1995.

Table 4.2 lists the number of financial institutions in China in November 2003.

Table 4.3 gives the assets, deposits and loan compositions of major financial institutions in China between 1993 and 2001. We can observe readily that the total assets of the four big state-owned banks of the banking industry declined from 69.07% to 60.53% from 1993 to 2001 and at the same time the share of joint stock banks increased from 5.77% to 12.27%; the total deposits share of two

Table 4.2 Financial Institutions in China

State-owned commercial banks	4
State policy banks	3
Joint stock banks	11
Asset management corporations	4
City commerce banks	112
Foreign bank branches	182
Foreign bank representative offices	209
City credit unions	731
Agriculture credit unions	35,544
Agricultural commerce banks	3
Trust and investment companies	52
Financial companies	74
Financial leasing companies	12

Data source: Tang Shuangning (2003).

Table 4.3 Asset, Deposit, and Loan Compositions of Major Financial Institutions in China

	1993	1995	1999	2000	2001
Asset Composition					
Big Four	69.07	69.08	64.32	62.56	60.53
Joint stock banks	5.77	7.55	11.86	10.19	12.27
City commerce banks	—	1.01	3.67	4.2	4.87
Foreign banks	—	2.47	2.14	2.06	2.3
Others	—	23.37	21.68	20.99	20.03
Deposit Composition					
Big Four	69.07	61.04	63.73	62.15	60.93
Joint stock banks	5.34	6.46	7.83	9.7	11.53
City commerce banks	—	0.94	4.03	4.26	4.72
Foreign banks	—	0.48	0.4	0.43	0.44
Others	—	31.08	24.01	23.46	22.38
Loan Composition					
Big Four	73.48	61.91	61.3	58.61	57.57
Joint stock banks	3.54	4.57	6.24	8.47	10.2
City commerce banks	—	0.4	2.88	3.49	4.03
Foreign banks	—	2.09	1.9	1.55	1.37
Others	—	31.03	27.68	27.88	26.83

Data source: Degree of market mechanism in Chinese financial market, China Foreign trade publisher, April 2, 2003.

groups of banks followed a similar pattern; and the loan share of the four major state-owned banks declined from 73.48% to 57.57% and that of joint stock banks increased from 3.54% to 10.2% in the same period. The similar asset and deposit compositions reflect the fact that deposits have been the major components of bank assets in most commercial banks.

The commercial banks split up as a group of specialized banks for separate sectors of the economy and a group of smaller commercial banks with either regional or nation-wide coverage, most of them established in the late 1980s. At the edge is a strong and growing competitive fringe of NBFIs that have emerged as a force in recent years. There is also an expanding presence of foreign financial institutions in the form of representative and branch offices.

As a result of the different phases of reform of the banking system, the system is now characterized by the coexistence of two components. The main one, made up of specialized state-owned commercial banks, is still under the control of the government. The second component is made up of financial intermediaries, which are either subject to less control by the authorities or manage to side-step existing regulations.

In order to ease the financing pressure on the commercial banks and allow increased transparency and accountability in lending for large state-sponsored projects, three policy banks were established in the mid-1990s: the State Development Bank (SDB), the Agricultural Development Bank (ADB), and the Ex- and Import Bank of China (EIBC). They particularly provide long-term financing of important state projects. Please see the websites of these three policy banks listed in the appendix of this book, for their specific functions and development. The SDB has been quite innovative in initiating and researching new products, and its rates of non-performing loans have been lowest, and its profitability rates have been the highest of all Chinese banks.

4.3 Chinese Banks

There are various types of commercial banks in the Chinese financial system as the financial reform deepens. These commercial banks can be grouped into the big four state-owned commercial banks, share-holding commercial banks, private commercial banks, and foreign commercial banks. We will introduce them briefly in this section.

4.3.1 Big Four State-Owned Commercial Banks

In September 1983, the State Council issued a document to redefine the function of PBOC as being the central bank to oversee and administer China's financial affairs and then established the four state-owned commercial banks, namely the Agricultural Bank of China (ABC), the Bank of China (BOC), the People's Construction Bank of China later renamed the China Construction Bank (abbreviated as CCB), and the Industrial and Commercial Bank of China (ICBC). These state-owned commercial banks were established as institutions independent from the PBOC and the Ministry of Treasury to handle the business of loans and savings. Please see the websites of these banks, listed in the appendix of this book, for more detailed introductions and their businesses. The major task for the "Big Four" is to grant policy loans to the state-owned enterprises (SOEs) of a specific economic sector. The areas of the four specialized commercial banks provide an overview of their areas of specialization.

These Big Four state-owned commercial banks still dominate the banking industry in China as they together have a combined market share of 60% in personal savings deposits, 80% in payment settlement services, and 56% in loans. Their combined asset share in the Chinese banking industry is about 60%. The Big Four banks have made loans to major SOEs for years, and their share of such loans to SOEs is still as high as 80%, and their contribution to major state projects is still as high as around 70% (Tang, 2003).

4.3.2 Nation-Wide Joint Stock Banks

A range of new banks outside the Big Four have made noticeable inroads into the Mainland's banking system in recent years. The impact of these new players is difficult to measure precisely as statistics do not segregate categories of players adequately.

The Bank of Communications (Bocom) restored business in 1987. The Bocom, which was founded in 1908, has its headquarters in Shanghai. It is also the first bank in China formed as a corporation, with a 50% state share of its registered capital. The other important joint stock commercial banks set up during this period include CITIC Industrial Bank (CITICIB), China Everbright Bank (CEB), China Merchants Bank (CMB), and Huaxia Bank (HXB).

All these joint stock banks are listed either in Hong Kong or domestically in Mainland China. Because of their share structure, they are under less government regulation and are more flexible in capital funding. Their performances have been better than the Big Four on average, despite their short operation of businesses.

4.3.3 Local Joint Stock Banks

Besides the nation-wide joint stock banks introduced above, there are a number of other joint stock banks with local business coverage. These banks include Guangdong Development Bank (GDB), Shenzhen Development Bank (SDB), Pudong Development Bank (PDB), Xingye Bank (FXB), Yantai Residence Bank (YRB), and others.

Most of these local joint stock banks have been listed in Mainland Chinese stock markets. It is easier for them than for the Big Four to raise capital so as to raise their capital adequacy ratios.

4.3.4 Private Commercial Banks

Private commercial banks have not been typical for China until recent years, but the increasing emergence of such banks is quite obviously an indication for the future. China Minsheng Banking (CMSB) Corp. was China's first privately owned bank, established in January 1996 by 59 private companies. CMSB is carving out a niche in China's growing private sector, a customer base long neglected by the larger state-owned banks. It may be China's smallest national commercial bank, a minnow compared with the state-owned giants of China's banking industry, but its aspirations are big.

Compared with the Big Four commercial banks, which are heavily burdened with non-performing loans because of historical reasons and internal management issues, the new banks are free of historical burden and find it easier to adapt to the market-oriented business environment. The increasing number of new banks have pushed the existing specialized banks to further reforms in transforming themselves into market-oriented commercial banks, which try to be more flexible and customer focused. Service at Chinese banks has improved significantly in the past decade, yet there is a long way to go to catch up with international banks.

4.4 Foreign Banks in China

The current restrictive regulatory environment has discouraged and prohibited foreign banks from playing a prominent role in China.

Foreign banks have historically not been allowed to open RMB accounts for customers, but they have been permitted to open foreign currency accounts for foreign invested enterprises (FIEs) in Special Economic Zones. Following the first foreign bank representative office (Japan Export & Import Bank) in China in 1979, hundreds of foreign banks have either established representative offices or branches in China.

The differences in banking services show some differences between Chinese and international banks in financing investment projects in China. Until the end of 1996, no foreign bank could offer many day-to-day services to foreign companies or individuals in the local currency. In January 1997, it was announced that nine foreign banks had been granted licenses to undertake business in RMB. Among this group were Citibank (USA), Hong Kong & Shanghai Banking Corporation (UK), Bank of Tokyo-Mitsubishi (Japan), Industrial Bank of Japan (Japan), Dai-Ichi Kangyo Bank (Japan), Sanwa Bank (Japan), Standard Chartered Bank (UK), and International Bank of Paris (France).

Formal approval to actually transact business in RMB would be forthcoming when the conditions of the license are fulfilled to the satisfaction of the PBOC. According to the PBOC's regulations, a foreign bank must have achieved profits in the last three years and engaged in medium- to long-term capital financing in China. Such a license is only granted to those banks located in the Pudong New Area — the new financial district of Shanghai.

These foreign banks may only operate RMB accounts for FIEs that have legal registration in Shanghai. Foreign banks are still able to lend foreign currency funds to Chinese companies with transactional approval from the regulatory authorities but under these new regulations are still not allowed to handle RMB-denominated business for local Chinese enterprises unless they have been listed on an offshore stock exchange.

The businesses of foreign banks in China are indeed restricted by existing regulations; however, this situation is changing and will change more as China moves deeper into the WTO with the promises to be executed for the WTO. According to People's Daily, September 3, 2003, the number of foreign licensed commercial banks in China's business and financial center increased to 57 in Shanghai, or 30% of the country's total of 190. Among the 57 foreign bank branches, 26 have been granted the right to engage in foreign exchange business, and the number of those conducting RMB business has reached 34. China's promises for the WTO entrance will open tremendous opportunities for foreign banks in China; we discuss this in more detail in Section 4.9 of this chapter.

4.5 Non-Banking Financial Institutions

In China, the non-state financial sector does not antedate the state banking sector; rather, it developed in response to controls over, and deficiencies in, that sector. Indeed, state banks are typically poor at solving the problems of asymmetric information and at monitoring the performance of their borrowers. In contrast, NBFIs such as credit cooperatives or less formal organizations have comparative advantages in using local information, monitoring and enforcing sanctions on borrowers. NBFIs have transformed greatly the financial sector in China. They share five main characteristics. First, they have broken the monopoly of state banks. Second, they are outside the narrow credit plan of the central government and the PBOC. Third, they are more independent than banks, have more incentives to maximize profits, and are subject to fewer regulations. Fourth, they have very substantial problems of moral hazards in NFBIs because they are mostly controlled by banks. Fifth, regulations and laws concerning NFBIs are few or are less well enforced than those concerning state-owned banks.

Shanghai is the most favored place for non-banking financial institutions, ranging from trust and investment corporations to finance companies, leasing companies, insurance companies, securities companies, and thousands of rural credit co-operatives and urban credit co-operatives, often acting *de facto* like banks.

With the bankruptcy of Guangdong CITIC during the Asian financial crisis, the government restructured the trust investment companies throughout the country and has been cautious on the development of NBFIs in China since then. The most popular NBFIs in China these days are auto-loan companies because the automobile industry has grown rapidly in China in the past few years.

4.6 Instruments of Banking Control in China

The Chinese financial system can be characterized as a system of directed capital. The direct and indirect instruments of monetary control at the disposal of the PBOC involve the regulation of interest rates and the RMB currency.

Interest rates are the main instrument of indirect monetary control in China, next to the lending by the PBOC to specialized banks and reserve requirements. The PBOC sets or regulates almost all lending and deposit rates to specialized banks and other financial institutions, as well as the guidelines for rates on the interbank market. The complex structure of interest rates set by the monetary authorities aims at minimizing the cost to state-owned banks of collecting resources selectively so as to subsidize production and investment in the state sector. This regulation of interest rates has led indirectly to great discrepancies in the efficient allocation of capital.

Recognizing the problems, the PBOC has taken a series of measures to allow the market mechanism to play more important roles in determining interest rates in the past few years. Specifically, the PBOC started the marketization of interest rates as early as 1996 when the PBOC began to deregulate interest rates in the interbank market on June 1st. Various measures have been taken in interest rate marketization since then. In its regular annual conference held in February 2004, the central bank announced that it would take more dramatic measures to accelerate the interest rate mechanism in 2004.

4.7 Inter-Bank Money Market

The inter-bank market is synonymous with the money and debt markets in the Chinese terminology. Operators on this market include banks and other financial institutions. Before 1979, the allocation of credit was vertical from the State Council to bank branches through the PBOC. The only thing a bank branch with surplus funds could do was to try to hold on to them, while a branch with a shortage of funds could in no way get in contact with another branch. The reforms in 1979 put limits on the credit banks could extend and made their lending capacity conditional on their deposit-raising abilities. In 1983, an unofficial inter-bank market was created. This horizontal interface between branches marked a change from the previous, vertical system. The experiment proved such a success that branches of other banks were included in the system. As a result of early moves to liberalize the financial sector, sporadic inter-bank trading between branches of specialized banks emerged in 1985. The reason was the increasing need for local inter-bank markets, which came from the shortage of credit through a restrictive monetary policy implemented by the PBOC in 1985. In November 1995, the PBOC announced its intention to link the banks and the most important regional money markets electronically. But still, the interest rates were tightly controlled, which makes the money market not very effective. By the end of 1987, inter-bank markets existed in nearly all regions. But the lack of proper regulatory framework and of supervision by monetary authorities allowed the creation of "finance companies" and development of unauthorized activities, such as short-term borrowing and long-term lending. As the PBOC declared that no authorities would intervene in any way, inter-bank activities of various kinds sprang up in most large cities across the country.

In 1989, these finance companies were abolished by the PBOC and in 1990; standardized operating principles of inter-bank markets came into effect. The inter-bank activities were centralized in some well-defined market places in Shanghai, Wuhan, Beijing/Tianjin, Shenyang, Xi'an, and Chongqing. In Shanghai, the market took a more structured form in August 1986, with the establishment of the "Shanghai Money Market", organized by the ICBC. The ICBC often accounts for more than three-quarters of all inter-bank activities in China, although in principle any financial institution may operate in this market after approval from the PBOC.

Starting on June 1, 1996, the PBOC lifted the restriction on the ceiling of inter-bank borrowing rate movement. When the inter-bank bond market was formed in 1997, the bond repurchase rate and price began to be decided completely by market supply and demand. Table 4.4 gives the total turnovers of transactions of major financial institutions and their market share in the inter-bank market in 2003.

Table 4.4 Turnovers of Major Financial Institutions in the Inter-Bank Market in 2003

Types of Institutions	Turnover (US$ trillion)	Market Share (%)
Big Four	1.04	30.3
Joint stock banks	0.73	21.2
City commerce banks	1.15	33.6
Credit unions	0.37	10.8
NBFIs	0.04	1.0
Insurance companies	0.08	2.5
Fund companies	0.02	0.6
Foreign banks	0.00	0.1
Total	3.44	100.0

Data source: Shanghai Securities News, January 14, 2004, p. 14.

It should be observed that the total turnover of the inter-bank market reached US$3.44 trillion, or 2.44 times the Chinese GDP of 2003. We can also note from Table 4.4 that the market share of the Big Four state-owned banks fell below that of city commerce banks, and the share of joint stock banks were ranked No.3.

There are three types of transactions in the inter-bank market, credit borrowing, government bond repurchase, and government bond. Of the US$3.44 trillion total turnover, the contributions of the three types of transaction were 47.94%, 41.21%, and 10.85%, respectively. With further measures of the PBOC to allow market forces to determine interest rates, the turnovers of the inter-bank market will grow further in the years to come.

4.8 Problems in the Chinese Banking System

Despite certain progress in the banking sector in China in the past few years, there are still many serious problems within the Chinese banking system, the most noticeable problems being high non-performing loan ratios and lower capital adequacy, the lack of modern risk management systems, and so on. It is incomplete for readers to have an understanding of the Chinese banking system without knowing these problems. We will simply discuss these major problems in this section.

4.8.1 Non-Performing Loans

The most serious problem facing the Chinese state-owned banks is their sheer scale of non-performing loans (NPLs), which resulted mainly from policy loans to SOEs and government projects and partially from inappropriate internal management. In order to raise the capital adequacy of Big Four banks during the Asian financial crisis, the Chinese government injected RMB 270 billion (US$32.6 billion) into the Big Four by issuing special government bonds in 1998, and the government stripped off RMB1.4 trillion (US$169 billion) of NPLs from the Big Four to four newly established asset management corporations (AMCs) in 1999. See Zhang (2000) for more details of these AMCs.

The combined capital injection and NPL-stripping off have not been effective enough to resolve the capital adequacy problem as NPLs accumulated to RMB 2 trillion (about US$241 billion) by the end of 2003. Despite significant declines from 1999 to 2002, the NPL ratio still remained at 21.4% (the NPL ratio at ABC, ICBC, BOC, and CBC was 30.0%, 25.7%, 18.1%, and 11.8% by September 2003, respectively), more than seven times as high as those at Citibank and HSBC (Tang, 2003). The low 21.4% NPL ratio is somewhat questionable as new loans were made at a significantly faster speed in the Big Four in 2003 than in 2002.

In order to raise the capital adequacy, the State Council injected US$45 billion of foreign reserves into the BOC and CCB, the two major state-owned banks early in January 2004. The injection of capital represents the first step in introducing a shareholding system in BOC and CCB (www.pbc.gov.cn, January 6, 2004). This injected capital will better prepare the two banks for a potential initial public offering (IPO) in the international stock market in the coming years to raise further capital. The new capital injection indicates the Chinese government's determination to accelerate reforming the state-owned commercial banks.

4.8.2 Loan-Making Procedures

Another obstacle for the state banks is their history as a part of a central planning administrative organization as well as the provincial governments' power apparatus. They have only recently been subjected to the first experiments with market conditions and therefore lack basic banking skills, most notably the ability to carry out credit risk evaluation. Not many bankers have enough credit training; most of them are rather inexperienced with market-oriented credit rating.

There are many other problems in the banking industry in China, such as the lack of risk management systems currently actively practiced in international financial institutions. It is beyond the scope of this book to study such problems in great detail.

4.9 China's WTO Promises for Commercial Banking

Senior Chinese government officials have repeatedly expressed their determination to keep the promises that China made for WTO entrance. There are many items in the application document (please see the WTO website given in the appendix of this book for the official document). We simply introduce those relating to banking in this section.

4.9.1 Geographic Coverage

For foreign currency business, there will be no geographic restriction upon accession. For local currency RMB business, the geographic restriction is given in Table 4.5.

Table 4.5 Geographic Coverage of RMB Business for Foreign Banks in China

Time	Date	Cities Permitted for RMB Business	Currency
Accession	Dec 11, 2001	Shanghai, Shenzhen, Tijian, Dalian	Foreign currency only
Year 1	Dec 11, 2002	Guangzhou, Zhuhai, Qingdao, Nanjing, Wuhan	Foreign currency only
Year 2	Dec 11, 2003	Jinan, Chengdu, Chongqing, Fuzhou	RMB for Chinese enterprises
Year 3	Dec 11, 2004	Beijing, Kunming, Xiamen	RMB for Chinese enterprises
Year 4	Dec 11, 2005	Shantou, Ningbo, Shenyang, Xi'an	RMB for Chinese enterprises
Year 5	Dec 11, 2006	No geographic restrictions	RMB for all Chinese clients

Data source: http:/www.docsonline.wto.org/DDFDocuments/t/WT/ACC/CHN49A2.doc/.

4.9.2 Clients

For foreign currency business, foreign financial institutions will be permitted to provide services in China without restriction as to clients upon accession. For local currency business, within 2 years after accession, foreign financial institutions will be permitted to provide services to Chinese enterprises. Within 5 years after accession, foreign financial institutions will be permitted to provide services to all Chinese clients.

4.9.3 License

Within 5 years after accession, any existing non-prudential measures restricting ownership, operation, and juridical form of foreign financial institutions, including on internal branching and licenses, shall be eliminated. Foreign financial institutions that meet certain conditions are permitted to establish a subsidiary of a foreign bank or a foreign finance company in China. We do not need to repeat the detailed conditions here in this book.

The above promises essentially remove all restrictions of foreign banks to conduct businesses in China within 5 years after China's accession into the WTO, that is, after December 10, 2006. So it makes sense for the foreign banks to start acquiring their own branch network by looking at well placed local banks. There will be tremendous opportunities for foreign banks in China within 3 years, when the Chinese economy grows to another stage, and the financial environment will be much improved then.

4.10 Conclusions

China will continue to be an exciting market. China's economy faces a host of problems as it changes from being a partially planned one into a market-driven net of independent entities, and the major Chinese banks will be listed in stock markets both domestically and globally.

This chapter has given a brief introduction to the structure and system of the Chinese banking system in general. The Chinese government has continued with banking and financial reforms. It has been this administration's top priority to reform the banking sector in the coming years. Besides the actions taken to inject capital into the BOC and CCB, and restructure them accordingly, additional measures will be taken to accelerate the reform process so as to meet the requirements of the challenging banking environment after December 2006. Drastic reorganization of the banking institutions and control systems have occurred to create greater transparency, such as removal of the ability of local officials to influence banking decisions. These are far reaching changes that have demonstrated the Chinese government's resolve to build a modern and efficient market economy.

5

The Chinese Capital Markets

We introduced China's banking industry in the previous chapter. The purpose of this chapter is to give a bird's eye view of China's capital markets. The capital market in China includes stock markets, bond markets, the foreign exchange market, the commodity futures market, and the insurance market. Most of these markets are somewhat underdeveloped compared with markets in the developed countries and many developing countries, but they have begun gradually to play more important roles in the Chinese economy.

This chapter is organized as follows. Section 5.1 introduces the stock market; Section 5.2 introduces the bond market; Section 5.3 introduces the fund management industry in China; Section 5.4 introduces the commodity futures market; Section 5.5 introduces the insurance market; Section 5.6 introduces the qualified foreign institutional investors (QFII) in China; Section 5.7 analyzes briefly major problems in the Chinese capital markets; Section 5.8 introduces China's WTO promises for the securities and insurance markets; Section 5.9 discusses recently announced guidelines of the State Council for further development of capital market in China; and Section 5.10 concludes the chapter.

5.1 Stock Market

5.1.1 Brief Introduction

Early forms of the stock exchange can be traced back to as early as the 1890s in Shanghai, and formal stock exchanges were established in Shanghai in the 1920s, and securities such as stocks, bonds, futures, and the like were traded actively in Shanghai in the 1930s, when Shanghai was the financial center in East Asia. Securities trading was stopped in 1949 (www.sse.com.cn).

Stock trading started with stocks being sporadically sold and bought over the counter in the early stages of the reforms in the early 1980s, and the two securities exchanges, the Shanghai Stock Exchange (SSE) and the Shenzhen Securities Exchange (SZSE), were established late in 1990. The stock market has grown steadily in China in the past 13 years. There were 1287 listed companies with a market capitalization of RMB 4.25 trillion (US$513.5 billion) by the end of 2003.

5.1.2 The Two Exchanges

Officially established on November 26, 1990 and in operation on December 19 of the same year, the SSE has become the most preeminent stock market in Mainland China in terms of number of listed companies, number of shares listed, total market value, tradeable market value, securities turnover value, and Chinese Treasury bond turnover value. December 2003 ended with over 35.6 million investors and 780 listed companies in SSE. A large number of companies from key industries, infrastructure, and high-tech sectors have not only raised capital but also improved their operation mechanism through listing on the Shanghai stock market. The SSE has about 55% of the total stocks, and the market capitalization of these stocks represents about two-thirds of the total market capitalization of all listed companies in China. Table 5.1 gives basic information on the SSE.

Located in the beautiful and dynamic border city of Shenzhen next to Hong Kong and established on December 1, 1990, the SZSE is the other stock exchange in Mainland China. SZSE has about 40%

Table 5.1 Shanghai Stock Exchange

Year	Number of Listed Companies	Market Value* (US$ billion)	Market Share of A Shares (%)	Total Turnover* (US$ billion)	Number of Members	Number of Investors (million)
1991	8	0.6		0.9	29	0.11
1992	30	10.1		5.9	171	1.11
1993	106	38.1	94.2	45.3	481	4.24
1994	171	30.2	95.5	295.7	550	5.75
1995	188	30.2	96.4	660.4	553	6.85
1996	293	65.9	97.0	332.7	523	12.08
1997	383	111.2	98.0	360.0	467	17.13
1998	438	128.3	99.1	414.7	330	19.99
1999	484	176.1	99.0	434.8	310	22.81
2000	572	325.3	98.8	602.8	305	29.58
2001	646	333.3	97.6	533.3	255	34.20
2002	715	306.4	98.3	586.3	199	35.56
2003	780	360.1	98.6	513.0	186	36.51

Data source: www.sse.com.cn
*Market value and turnover are calculated using official exchange rates in corresponding years.

of the total 1287 stocks in China, and their total market capitalization is about one-third of the total market capitalization of all listed companies in China, and its turnover of stocks represented 35.16% of total turnover of stocks in China in 2003.

Both exchanges operate on a cash-only basis without margin and short sales. Due to the lack of full convertibility of the RMB, the stocks listed in both domestic stock exchanges are divided into A and B shares. The former is only available for Chinese investors (we will discuss foreign participation in Section 5.4 of this chapter), while the latter was only tradeable by foreign investors with nomination in RMB but settlement in US$ in Shanghai or HK$ in Shenzhen until February 2001, when B shares were allowed for domestic investors. Although B shares came into being shortly after A shares in 1991, they represent only a small share of the total stock market in China, as evidenced in Table 5.1, and the liquidity of B shares has been rather low compared with A shares.

5.1.3 Share Structure, Intermediaries, and Regulation

Because the Chinese economy is still in the stage of transferring from the previous planned economy to the market-oriented economy as we discussed in Chapter 2, the major shares of most of the listed companies are held by the government or by governmental agencies. Only a small number of listed companies have no interest holdings by the government. Shares held by the government represent about two-thirds of the total shares, and these shares are not tradeable in the market place. Thus liquid shares present only about one-third of the total stocks in China.

The stock markets have been quite volatile compared with matured markets in developed countries and regions. One of the reasons for the high volatility in the domestic secondary markets is the dominance of individual investors with little experience and knowledge about securities trading. Despite the significant development, total market capitalization of all listed companies is still rather low, the stock market capitalization as a percentage of GDP being merely 36.38%, and the market capitalization of liquid stocks as a percentage of GDP was only less than 11.29% by the end of 2003, much lower than the corresponding securitization rates in all developed countries and many developing countries. With further development of the Chinese economy and especially the capital market, there is great potential for the stock market to grow in China.

There are no investment banks in China because no Chinese financial institutions can provide a full range of financial services currently provided by international investment banks. There were 133 securities companies in China by the end of 2003, with total assets of only RMB 561.8 billion (US$67.87 billion). Most securities companies are rather small, the average asset of these securities companies being just about US$0.5 billion. The total assets of all the securities companies in China were merely 20.22% of the total assets of US$335.6 billion of one single US investment bank, Goldman Sachs, in 2002. There is a long way for China's securities industry to go.

The regulatory agency of the stock market is the China Securities Regulatory Commission (CSRC), which is primarily responsible for regulating and supervising securities firms and markets. Established in 1992, 2 years after SSE was officially established, the CSRC is the major regulator in charge of all issues relating to securities listing, trading, management, and others.

5.1.4 Hong Kong Stock Exchange and International Listing

In addition, China has companies listed on the Hong Kong Stock Exchange (HKEX). A total of 247 companies from Mainland China had been listed in HKEX within the decade from 1993 to November 2003, raising total capital of US$96.56 billion, which was 50.72% of the total capital raised in HKEX in the same period and 19.2% of the accumulated FDI of US$503.3 billion in China by the end of 2003. Of these 247 companies, 189 were listed in the main board of HKEX and 89 in the growth enterprise market (GEM). The total market capitalization of these companies was US$184.59 billion by November 2003, 16% larger than the market capitalization of all liquid A shares trading in the two stock exchanges in Mainland China by the end of 2003.

Besides Hong Kong, Chinese companies have also been listed in US exchanges, Singapore stock exchange, and other international stock exchanges. With further development of the Chinese economy and a great degree of international economic and financial participation of China in the world economy, more and more Chinese companies will list their stocks in major international stock markets.

5.2 Bonds Market

The Chinese bond market began its early form when the government restarted to issue government bonds in 1981, and the bond market has developed quickly since then. There are relatively mature primary and secondary markets for government bonds. According to the issuer, there are three types of bonds in China: government bonds, issued by the Ministry of Finance (MOF), financial bonds, project-specific bonds normally issued by policy banks such as China Development Bank (CDB), and corporate bonds, normally issued by SOEs. The dominant type is the government bond, with more than 60% of the total bond market value. The second largest are the financial bonds, which are issued by financial institutions, mainly by domestic banks. Corporate bonds have the smallest share of market value since the government set very strict eligible criteria and approval procedures for state-owned enterprises (SOEs) as potential bond issuers. Table 5.2 gives the amount of debt issued, principal and interest paid, and total amount outstanding of government debt from 1981 to 2003.

We can observe that the total amount of principal and interest paid on government bonds was US$30.2 billion in 2003, and the outstanding amount reached US$232.6 billion or 16.5% of the GDP of the year.

The bonds market has been growing rapidly in size in the past seven years, and the driving forces for the boom have been the interest rate cuts since 1996 and the government stimulative fiscal policy after the Asian financial crisis as discussed in Chapter 3.

Bonds are trading in both stock exchanges and the inter-bank market. Table 5.3 gives the total bond turnover and bond repo turnover from 1994 to 2003. The total turnover of bonds in China reached 442.2 billion US$ and the bond repo turnover reached US$2.06 trillion in 2003; the corresponding total turnover was almost US$2.5 trillion in 2003, 77.2% higher than the Chinese GDP of 2003.

Corporate bonds have lagged far behind government bonds. In the year 1997, the government had the intention of improving the

Table 5.2 Domestic Government Bonds of China from 1981 to 2003

Year	Issuance (US$ billion)	Principle & Interest Paid (US$ billion)	Total Domestic Debt Outstanding (US$ billion)	Total Domestic Debt Outstanding/ GDP (%)
1981	2.9			
1982	2.3			
1983	1.8			
1984	1.4			
1985	2.1			
1986	1.8	0.2	8.4	2.86
1987	3.1	0.6	10.4	3.22
1988	3.6	0.8	13.1	3.28
1989	7.0	0.5	19.5	4.34
1990	4.1	2.4	17.1	4.41
1991	5.3	2.9	17.7	4.36
1992	8.4	6.2	19.2	3.98
1993	6.6	3.9	21.1	3.52
1994	11.9	4.2	21.8	4.02
1995	18.1	9.4	31.2	4.46
1996	22.2	15.2	38.4	4.70
1997	29.1	22.0	45.6	5.08
1998	39.0	27.1	57.5	6.08
1999	44.9	21.7	80.8	8.15
2000	50.2	18.8	112.2	10.39
2001	54.2	23.2	143.2	12.56
2002	73.5	29.8	186.8	15.10
2003	75.9	30.2	232.6	16.50

Data source: China Statistics Year Book 2003; the numbers are converted into US$ using official exchange rates given in Table 6.1.

scale and variety of the corporate bond market, yet growth in the sector has been moderate. The corporate bond market has been expanding faster since 2000, especially in 2003, with eight companies issuing corporate bonds in the year compared with the cumulative number of corporate bonds of 11 before the end of 2002. It is noticeable that corporate convertible bonds (CBs) experienced extremely high growth in 2003 as 10 companies issued CBs in 2003, compared with the total number of CBs trading in SSE by the end of 2002.

Most of the lead managers for underwriting government bonds are banks, which have the financial muscle to buy such a large

Table 5.3 Bond Market Turnovers from 1994 to 2003

Year	Bond Turnover (US$ billion)	Bond Repo Turnover (US$ billion)	Total Turnover (US$ billion)	Repo/Total Turnover (%)	Total Turnover/ GDP (%)
1994	8.3	0.6	8.9	6.5	1.6
1995	9.2	14.0	23.2	60.5	3.4
1996	49.2	149.6	198.8	75.3	24.7
1997	40.5	147.4	187.9	78.5	21.3
1998	73.5	195.8	269.3	72.7	28.6
1999	64.7	194.2	258.8	75.0	25.7
2000	52.4	349.5	401.8	87.0	36.8
2001	68.3	672.0	740.3	90.8	63.0
2002	158.5	1526.0	1684.5	90.6	130.4
2003	442.2	2056.3	2498.6	90.2	177.2

Data source: the SSE website and the PBOC website.

issuance before placing it. In the secondary market, brokers trade both, bonds and shares, from the same stock exchange seat, and trading is dominated by securities houses. Securities houses are in the process of establishing specialist departments to run their bond business, rather than just dealing with it in a general securities department.

There is huge potential in the Chinese bond market, especially the corporate bond market, because the market value of bonds as a percentage of GDP is still rather low, about 30% of GDP in China. In the United States, the market value of bonds, including corporate bonds, is equivalent to 143% of the country's GDP. In Japan, the figure is 96%, while in the 15 member nations of the European Union, the figure is 82%. On a global scale, the average market value of bonds is about 95% of the world's GDP.

5.3 Fund Management

Fund management started almost as early as the stock market in China. The first investment fund in China, "Nanshan Venture Capital Fund", was established in November 1991. Its establishment marked the beginning of the fund industry in China. At the beginning, most funds were established with the approval of the local governments or the People's Bank of China. As funds were initiated for the purpose of attracting capital, their investments covered a wide spectrum, from securities investment and equity investment in non-listed companies to real estate investment. They were named "old funds" as opposed to the relatively standardized investment funds. These old funds expanded rapidly. By the end of 1997, there were 75 old funds with more than RMB 5.8 billion in book value and RMB 10 billion in market value. However, these old funds were not standardized in many aspects, including fund initiation, fund operations, information disclosure, supervision, and regulation. Many daily operation difficulties led to a halt in offering such funds practically since 1994. This marked the early stage of fund management in China.

On November 14, 1997, the CSRC issued its "Interim Regulation on the Securities Investment Funds" to regulate the fund industry. Detailed rules were promulgated later, elaborating on fund initiation, capital raising and trading, fund trustees and managers, the rights and obligations of fund holders, fund investment operations, and supervision and management. As stipulated by the Regulation, the percentage of bond and equity investments made by a fund shall not fall below 80% of the fund's total asset value; and the percentage of investments in the national bonds shall not fall below 20% of the fund's net asset value. These rules have had a large impact on the investment behavior of the investment funds. For detailed studies comparing China's fund industry with that of the UK, read Chen *et al* (2002).

In March 1998, two new funds founded in line with the CSRC Regulation of 1997, Fund Kai Yuan and Fund Jintai (for the complete list of funds in China, please refer to the official website of CSRC), were issued nation-wide and publicly listed in April. As the new funds were only allowed to invest in publicly traded stocks and bonds in the Chinese securities markets, they were named "securities investment funds" (hereafter referred to as the closed-end funds). From the regulatory perspective, the funds are established mainly for two purposes: one is to exploit the advantages of "expert management" and provide individual investors with a good investment tool; the other is to nurture institutional investors and to promote steady and healthy development of the securities markets. The CSRC has issued a series of preferential policies (see Chen *et al* (2002) for these policies) to support the healthy development of those closed-end funds. By the end of 2003, there were 54 publicly traded closed-end funds under the management of 23 fund management companies, with a total of about US$10 billion in net asset value. Table 5.4 gives the annual turnover of securities investment funds and non-securities investment funds from 1999 to 2003. Table 5.4 shows clearly that the turnover grew significantly from 1999 to 2000, yet representing only a small percentage of the total turnover of the stock market; and it dropped significantly from 2001 to 2003. For detailed characteristics of close-end funds in China, please read Chen *et al* (2002).

By the end of 2003, there were 95 investment funds with total net assets of only US$22.1 billion, or 13.2% of the total market capitalization of tradeable stocks in China. The average fund net asset was merely US$220 million.

The release of "Rules for Experimenting Open-End funds" by the CSRC on October 8, 2002 accelerated the development of open-end funds in China, representing another stage of the fund management industry in China. A total of 38 open-end funds were issued in 2003, up 171.4% from 2002 (China Securities Daily, December 30, 2003). Because of their attractiveness and flexibility, open-end funds will flourish in China in the years to come.

Despite their relatively low turnover in the securities market, the fund management industry should have great potential to grow in China because institutional investors will certainly grow steadily as

Table 5.4 Turnover of Funds in China from 1999 to 2003 (Unit: US$ billion)

Year	Securities Investment Funds Turnover	Growth Rate (%)	Percent of Stock Turnover
1999	10.14	118.45	2.33
2000	14.00	38.03	2.32
2001	16.23	15.87	3.04
2002	6.73	−58.54	1.15
2003	4.38	−34.95	0.85

Data source: www.csrc.gov.cn.

the market becomes more and more mature. This is particularly true as more and more foreign financial institutions come over to China to form joint-fund management companies with Chinese companies.

5.4 Futures Market

5.4.1 Historical Development

Preparations and experiments for the commodity futures market started officially in 1988. The opening of the Zhengzhou grain market in 1990 moved one important step toward futures trading because the former grain trading was transferred to futures trading gradually until May 1993. The first futures exchange in China was the Shenzhen Metals Exchange, established in June 1991. The Shanghai Metals Exchange was established on May 28, 1992. Many other exchanges were established throughout China from 1992 to 1994. The CSRC approved 11 experimental exchanges in October 1994, and it approved three others before the end of April, 1995. Thus, there were 14 futures exchanges approved in China in May 1995.

The government bond futures event, with extreme speculation in March 1995, changed the whole course of futures market development since then. The government began a series of dramatic measures to control the futures market by closing down a few exchanges, de-listing contracts, restricting financial institutions from participating the futures market, increasing risk management measures, and so on. The CSRC did not approve 11 futures brokerage companies for their 1996 annual reviews in July 1997.

The "Announcement to Further Restructure and Standardize the Futures Market" of the State Council in August 1998 set the current framework of futures market in China because it ordered the then 14 exchanges to be merged into three exchanges throughout China: the Shanghai Futures Exchange (SHFE), Dalian Commodity Exchange (DCE), and Zhengzhou Commodity Exchange (CZCE). The three exchanges were established formally in December 1999. The annual turnover has increased steadily since the consolidation.

Table 5.5 gives the total market turnover of the futures market and that of SHFE from 1993 to 2003. It can be observed readily that

Table 5.5 China Futures Industry

Year	Total Turnover* (US$ billion)	Growth Rate (%)	Total Turnover in SHFE* (US$ billion)	Growth Rate (%)	Market Share of SHFE (%)	Total Turnover as Percentage of GDP
1993	95.8	981.9	82.5	831.1	86.1	16.0
1994	366.7	282.6	178.9	116.9	48.8	67.7
1995	1204.2	228.4	312.7	74.8	26.0	174.9
1996	1011.8	−16.0	167.7	−46.4	16.6	125.8
1997	737.9	−27.1	45.7	−72.7	6.2	83.6
1998	446.5	−39.5	62.5	36.6	14.0	48.0
1999	269.4	−39.7	58.9	−5.7	21.9	27.7
2000	194.3	−27.9	80.5	36.6	41.4	18.2
2001	363.7	87.2	103.2	28.2	28.4	32.0
2002	465.2	27.9	186.2	80.4	40.0	38.1
2003	1309.5	181.5	731.4	292.8	55.9	92.9

Data source: total turnover and SHFE turnover for 1999 to 2003 are from the official website of CSRC www.csrc.gov.cn; and data for 1993 to 1998 before the restructuring of the futures market are from the information department of SHFE.
*Turnovers are converted from RMB into US$ using official exchange rates in the corresponding years given in Table 6.1; and turnover as a percentage of the corresponding GDP is calculated using the GDP data from Table 3.5 of this book.

there were heavy speculative trading activities in 1995 (mainly resulting from excessive trading of government bonds futures) as total turnover as a percentage of the corresponding GDP surpassed 170%. The restructuring and consolidation had led to consecutive declines in market turnovers from 1996 to 2000, and the market has returned to the path of steady growth since the realization and settlement of the market reorganization from December 1999 to 2000.

5.4.2 Futures Contracts in China

There are only commodity futures contracts trading in three futures exchanges in China. There were over 30 futures contracts trading in various exchanges in China before 1994. The number of contracts was examined and reduced before the start of the dramatic restructuring in 1995, and the number was further reduced gradually since 1995. Currently there are only six types of active contracts trading in the three exchanges: wheat and cotton futures in CZCE, soy bean futures in DCE, copper, aluminum and natural rubber futures in SHFE. The turnovers of the three exchanges from 1993 to 2003 are given in Table 5.5.

5.4.3 The Shanghai Futures Exchange (SHFE)

Shanghai has been taking many initiatives in establishing the futures market in China. Six exchanges, Shanghai Metals Exchange (SHME), Shanghai Cereals and Oils Exchange (SHCOE), Shanghai Petroleum Exchange, Shanghai Building Materials Exchange, Shanghai Agricultural Materials Exchange, and Shanghai Chemical Exchange, were established in Shanghai between 1992 and 1995. The latter four were merged to form the Shanghai Commodity Exchange (SHCE) on April 19, 1995. Following the "announcement to further restructure and standardize the futures market" of the State Council in August 1998, the three exchanges in Shanghai, SHME, SHCOE, and SHCE, were conglomerated as SHFE, which started its formal operation in December 1999. With 219 members, the SHFE has regained its dominant position in China's futures market in 2003 with an annual market turnover of US$731.4 billion (42.5% higher than the total market turnover of stocks, US$513 billion, of the same year) and 55.9% of the total market share in China.

The SHFE organizes trading activities in strict conformity with regulations and policies, being responsible for front-end supervision and market operation, so as to provide a transparent, secure, orderly, and efficient market mechanism and an open, equitable, fair marketplace. Since its inauguration late in 1999, further improvement and progress has been seen in various aspects. Table 5.5 shows that the market turnover at SHFE has increased steadily from 2000 to 2003 with an annual growth rate of 28.2%, 80.4%, and 292.8% in 2001, 2002, and 2003, respectively.

With 219 members throughout China, among whom 82% are futures brokerages, the SHFE has released 132 distant trading terminals in 23 provinces and special municipalities in China. Based on the comparative advantages of Shanghai in finance, economy, trade, and transportation, SHFE aims to transform itself into a futures exchange with diversified products ranging from commodities to various types of financial futures and options.

The first Derivative Forum — Metals Forum of SHFE held on the same day when Shanghai Metals Exchange was established on May 28 — was a great success with over 300 international and domestic governmental officials, business executives and experts participating, showing SHFE's improved management system and confidence and great interest in China with sustainable economic growth.

5.4.4 Greater Role for China's Futures Market to Play in the World

The year 2003 marked an important change in the world commodity market as China replaced the USA as the largest copper consumption country in the world. The strong economic growth, greater demand for electricity, fast development of the automobile industry, and others have led to a higher demand for copper and other industry materials. As a result, the trading volumes of copper futures and natural rubber futures have increased significantly. As the average daily trading volume of copper futures in SHFE increases as a percentage of the world copper futures market, the role of SHFE copper futures in determining world copper futures prices has in turn increased. With the steady growth of the Chinese economy, and continuous shifting of production capacity from developed countries to China, China's role in the world commodity futures market will certainly grow in the years to come. For specific analysis of copper futures trading between SHFE and the largest copper futures exchange — London Metal Exchange (LME) — see Zhang (2003b).

5.5 Insurance Industry in China

The insurance industry was initiated in 1980. Despite steady growth in the past 23 years with an average annual growth rate of 30%, the industry is still rather small in scale compared either with the major components of the financial industry or with other countries of the world.

The enactment of the "Insurance Law" of China in 1995 marked an important milestone in the development of the insurance industry in China as it sets the legal framework for the industry. The establishment

Table 5.6 Insurance Industry in China from 1999 to 2003 (Unit: US$ billion)

	Premium Income	Bank Deposits	Investment	Government Bonds	(BD + GB)/ Investment (%)	Investment Funds	Assets
1999	16.8	11.2	10.8	6.78	166.9	0.15	31.5
2000	19.3	14.9	15.7	9.56	155.5	1.34	40.8
2001	25.5	23.3	20.7	7.96	151.2	2.09	55.5
2002	36.9	36.6	30.3	11.08	157.5	3.08	78.5
2003	40.8	48.0	45.9	14.26	135.6	4.49	110.2

Data source: Data for 1999 to 2002 are from the official website of China Insurance Regulatory Commission, www.circ.gov.cn; premium income and total assets for 2003 are from The Economic Observer, February 16, 2004, page 12, and other data for 2003 are for October 2003 from the same website.

of the China Insurance Regulatory Commission (CIRC) on November 19, 1998, represents another milestone in the development of the industry in China. The CSRC has issued over 200 rules and regulations to better supervise and monitor the industry since its inception.

Table 5.6 provides the total premium income, bank deposits, investment, holding of government bonds, sum of bank deposits (BDs) and government bond (GBs) and investment ratio, investment funds, and total assets of insurance companies in China from 1999 to 2003. Despite steady growth, the total assets of the insurance market as a percentage of GDP is still lower than 1% in 2003.

Table 5.6 reveals structural problems for the insurance industry in China. Most of the income is deposited in commercial banks, and bank deposits have been greater than the total investment from 1999 to 2003, with the only exception of 2000, when investment was slight higher than bank deposits. The sum of bank deposits and government bonds is more than 50% higher than the total investment on average. This structural problem results from regulatory restrictions for insurance income to be invested in the stock market and others and the high risk of other investments compared with bank deposits and government bonds. The CIRC has recognized the problem and is taking dramatic measures to change this situation to allow insurance companies to invest in the domestic stock market and also overseas markets.

The Chinese insurance industry has one unique characteristic in its composition: the total number of foreign and China–foreign joint insurance companies surpassed that of Chinese insurance companies in 2002, and the situation was clear in Shanghai as early as in 1997. Despite the smaller number of state-owned insurance companies, the state-owned insurance companies still dominate the market. For example, the three top state-owned insurance companies, China Life Insurance (CLI), China People's Insurance Company (PICC) and Ping An Insurance, together had 94.62% of the total revenue of the industry in 2001.

The successful initial public offering (IPO) of CLI in the United States and Hong Kong SAR on December 17 and 18 marked the beginning of another stage in the development of the insurance industry in China. The CLI IPO was the largest IPO in the world, with 25 times over-subscription world-wide and 50 times in the USA, raising capital of US$3.5 billion, reflecting world confidence in the insurance industry in China.

5.6 QFIIs and Foreign Securities Companies in China

After a year of preparation and promotion, the CSRC and PBOC jointly issued, on November 8, 2002, the draft plan for qualified foreign institutional investors (QFIIs) to invest in the securities market in China (please see the official website of CSRC for details of the relating rules).

QFIIs can be overseas fund management institutions, insurance companies, securities companies and other assets management institutions that have been approved by CSRC to invest in China's securities market and granted an investment quota by the State Administration of Foreign Exchange (hereinafter referred to as "SAFE"). Under the rules of this scheme, QFIIs can apply for investment quotas ranging from US$50 million to US$800 million. Foreign companies should also be allowed to take over or acquire stakes of domestic-listed firms through the secondary market.

By the end of June 2004, 13 overseas financial institutions had won the approval of the CSRC to be QFIIs. The names of these institutions, time of approval, and corresponding initial capital injected are given in Table 5.7. The total approved investment quota of these institutions reached US$1.825 billion. By the end of January 2004, the total injected capital of these QFIIs amounted to US$1.46 billion.

Table 5.7 Qualified Foreign Institutional Investors in China

Name of QFII	Time Approved	Capital Quota (US$m)
UBS Warburg Ltd	26-May-03	600
Nomura Securities	26-May-03	50
Citigroup Global Transaction Services	8-Jun-03	200
Morgan Stanley & Co. International Ltd	8-Jun-03	300
Goldman Sachs	4-Jul-03	50
Deautche Bank	3-Aug-03	200
HSBC	6-Aug-03	100
ING Bank N.V.	16-Sep-03	50
JP Morgan Chase	8-Oct-03	50
CS First Boston	19-Nov-03	50
Nikko Asset Management Co.	11-Feb-04	50
Standard Chartered Bank	21-May-04	75
Heng Seng Bank Limited	25-June-04	50

Data source: www.csrc.gov.cn.

Some of these institutions are applying to extend their capital base for investment.

Although the total capital quota approved for these 11 QFIIs is relatively small, just over 1% of the market value of liquid stocks in China, the QFIIs will change the landscape of China's securities market before long because they will bring with them international practices into the Chinese securities market. The international methods of securities analysis, trading strategies, risk management, internal controls, and other aspects of the QFIIs will certainly influence their Chinese competitors and also individual investors. They will also accelerate the development and improvement of institutional investors in China.

5.7 Problems Facing China's Capital Market

There are many problems in China's securities market in the course of further reforming the Chinese economy with a market mechanism to play more important roles. We will introduce a few important ones briefly in this section.

One of the major problems is high government ownership of the shares of listed companies. As introduced earlier in Section 5.1, state ownership of all the listed companies is about two-thirds on average. The government has to reduce this ownership gradually so as to use the capital proceeds to solve other urgent problems in the economy such as unemployment, social welfare, basic education, and so on. Although this general trend is well understood and accepted, the remaining problems are how to treat the liquid shares and government shares and how soon and how fast to reduce the state ownership as timing is critical for stock market performances. A research paper (Tian, 2004) shows that the stock market index would decline 0.576% for every 1% drop of government-owned shares. The concern of downward market impacts in reducing government shares is the most important factor delaying the process of reducing government shares.

The majority of investors are individual investors in the Chinese stock market; individual investors are reluctant to enter the market without knowing the schedule of government plans to reduce state-owned shares. Two recent views from two major departments of the central government, the State-Owned Assets Supervision and Administration Commission (SASAC) and the CSRC, indicated differences regarding liquidizing the government shares: the former favors equal treatment of government shares and liquid shares, and the latter favors protecting rights of liquid shares (Lu, 2004). Because of the complexity of reforming process, it takes time for the government to make such decisions.

Another major problem is the limited instruments available for risk management. There are neither financial futures nor options trading in any exchanges in China. Despite the fact that the commodity futures market is playing increasingly important roles in China, it is still largely for commodity-related institutions and investors. Matured products in the developed countries such as energy futures and options, government bond futures and options, stock index futures and options, foreign exchange futures and options are not available, so that financial institutions and individual investors cannot manage their risk profiles easily without such instruments. The exponential growth of the government bond repo market somehow indicates such a demand for risk management instruments. With further reform in the securities market, especially with more and more international financial institutions to enter China, the demand for risk management tools will be further raised. The development of financial derivatives is highly necessary and imperative at the moment. This development will surely facilitate the development of the capital market in China.

It is far beyond the scope of this book to address major problems existing in the Chinese capital market systematically, and we simply mention two major ones and leave others for future research.

5.8 China's WTO Promises in the Securities and Insurance Market

We introduced China's promises for the banking services in Chapter 4, and we will briefly introduce similar commitments on services in the securities and insurance industries in this section.

Foreign securities institutions can engage directly (without a Chinese intermediary) in the B share business. Upon accession, representative offices in China of foreign securities institutions may become special members of all Chinese stock exchanges; upon accession, foreign service suppliers would be permitted to establish joint ventures with foreign investment up to 33% to conduct domestic securities investment fund management business. Within 3 years after China's accession, foreign investment shall be increased to 49%. Within 3 years after accession, foreign securities institutions will be permitted to establish joint ventures, with foreign minority ownership not exceeding 1/3, to engage (without a Chinese intermediary) in underwriting A shares and in underwriting and trading of B and H shares as well as government and corporate debts and launching of funds.

Specific commitments can be found on the official website of WTO, given in the appendix of the book, or on the official website of CSRC.

5.9 Measures to Accelerate Capital Market Development

The State Council announced new guidelines on capital market development on February 1, 2004. These guidelines are expected to lead to a whole host of concrete reform plans for the capital market in China this year. This will include permission of higher stock investment ratios of the insurance and social security funds, wider financing channels for securities brokerages, preferential taxation to encourage capital investment, and a solid solution of the liquidity problem in exchanges.

Many aspects are included in these guidelines. The most important is that the government will accelerate market innovation to have more products available for investors. The products include not only new equity products such as exchange traded funds but also, new futures contracts on other underlying commodities. For the first time in history, the term "financial derivatives" was used in a government document, and it encourages researching and preparation of financial derivatives relating to stocks and bonds.

The State Council's declaration is undoubtedly very positive news for the securities industry as it covers almost all the crucial issues in the capital market. Many of the reforms mentioned in the document are likely to be carried out soon, such as a higher ratio of securities investment by the insurers, social security fund, and occupational pension fund, which are expected to diversify their own investment portfolio and increase the number of institutional investors in the bourses.

Securities houses, long dogged by limited financial resources, will also get more adequate funding. The State Council's declaration stated that more qualified securities houses would be allowed to go public and some would start to issue bonds. And if risk control can be enhanced, they will also get more bank loans and can even enter the inter-bank market. Implementation of such a plan still awaits parallel regulations from the securities and banking authorities.

Poor coordination between different government agencies used to affect greatly the efficiency during the reforms. But the situation is expected to change now, with the authority of the State Council document, which has asked for improved coordination. The establishment of a policy coordination system in the securities market will help stabilize market sentiment and avoid contradictions of different sectoral regulations.

5.10 Conclusions

We have introduced the major components of the capital market in China in this chapter. Despite the great growth in stock market, the securitization rate is still rather low compared with not only developed countries but also some developing countries. The ratio of shares in government hands is still somewhat too high for the market mechanism to play its roles in the market place. The bonds market has grown tremendously, particularly the government bond market. The development of the corporate bonds market will further increase the completeness of the capital market. The funds management industry is still at an early stage as the total market capitalization of all funds represents only a small percentage of the total market capitalization of all stocks in China.

The commodity futures market has grown steadily in the past two years. The commodity market will have a greater role to play as China's role in world production rises. The financial futures market is a natural extension, and further development of commodity futures as evidenced in most developed countries as commodity futures trading provides necessary experiences in margin management for financial futures trading.

The entrance of QFIIs into China's securities market will accelerate China's reform of capital market as they bring with them analyzing, operational, and risk management experiences into China.

6

Foreign Exchange Administration

China's currency is generally known as renminbi (RMB), or "People's currency", but the unit of measurement is the yuan. The terms are parallels of "sterling" and "pound" in the UK. Throughout this book, we will use Chinese yuan (CNY) or renminbi (RMB) to stand for the Chinese currency.

China's official currency, the Renminbi (RMB), is issued and managed by the People's Bank of China (PBOC). The currency is denominated in yuan, one yuan equaling 10 jiao and one jiao equaling 10 fen. The exchange rate of RMB is formulated by the PBOC and issued by the General Administration of Exchange Control (GAEC). China exercises centralized management over foreign exchange, this function being performed by the GAEC.

We have introduced the Chinese banking industry and capital market in the previous two chapters. Because of its unique features and importance to this book, we focus on the management, market, and other related issues involving foreign exchange in this chapter. To a great degree, all other chapters in Part I of this book are preparations for this chapter, so that readers will familiarize themselves with how foreign exchange is currently administered in China and it will be easier to understand how the Chinese government will structure the foreign exchange mechanism in China in the future.

This chapter is organized as follows. Section 6.1 introduces the foreign exchange regulator in China — the State Administration of Foreign Exchange — its functions and responsibilities; Section 6.2 reviews a brief history of foreign exchange administration in China; Section 6.3 introduces the present foreign exchange administration system in China; Section 6.4 discusses the current condition of capital account convertibility in China; Section 6.5 introduces China's existing foreign exchange market; Section 6.6 introduces how foreign exchange policies impact foreign invested enterprises in China; Section 6.7 briefly introduces Shanghai as the financial center in Mainland China and its determination to become an international financial center; and Section 6.8 concludes the chapter.

6.1 The State Administration of Foreign Exchange

The State Administration of Foreign Exchange (SAFE) is the major government agency to administrate various issues relating to foreign exchange and foreign currencies in China. Because of the nature of its responsibilities, it has been under the People's Bank of China administratively, and its director has been deputy governor of the PBOC.

6.1.1 Functions and Responsibilities

After the 1998 reshuffling, the major functions and responsibilities of SAFE include (see the official website of SAFE, www.safe.org.cn):

(1) creating statistical systems and balance sheets for international payments and reporting systems for statistics on international payments;
(2) analyzing foreign exchange payments and international payments, recommending policies for balancing international payments, and studying the convertibility of the RMB under the capital account;
(3) regulating and developing the foreign exchange market, forecasting supply and demand, and recommending exchange rate policies to the PBOC;

(4) regulating remittances under the current account and standardizing the administration of foreign exchange accounts;
(5) overseeing the inward/outward remittance and conversion of foreign exchange under the capital account;
(6) overseeing foreign exchange reserves;
(7) regulating foreign exchange; and
(8) participating in international financial activities.

6.1.2 Internal Set-up

SAFE has six major functional departments in charge of various major functions and responsibilities. These departments are specified as follows:

Policies and Regulations Department;
International Payments Department;
Administration and Examination Department;
Capital Account Administration Department;
Reserve Administration Department; and
General Affairs and Human Resources Department.

For specific functions and responsibility divisions among these departments, please refer to the official website of SAFE.

6.1.3 Branch Offices

SAFE has branch offices around the country. Currently, it has 294 center branch offices and 487 branch offices in all provinces, autonomous regions, and special municipalities throughout China. Please see the official website of SAFE for specific names and locations of these branch offices.

6.2 Historical Development

The administration of foreign exchange has undergone three major stages in China, in the pre-reform era, the pre-market economy era, and the market economy era. We will briefly describe these eras in this section.

6.2.1 Pre-Reform Era (1953–78)

In the early years right after the establishment of the People's Republic of China, private imports and exports still played important roles in the Chinese economy, and the RMB foreign exchange rate was adjusted in order to adjust the foreign currency income. However, China started to adopt the planned economic system in 1953, and a highly centralized and controlled foreign exchange administration system was adopted accordingly. The foreign currency business was carried on by Bank of China exclusively. China carried out the "self-reliance" closed economy policy without borrowing from foreign countries and without allowing foreign investments in China. As a planning tool with the aim of stability, the RMB exchange rate gradually moved away from import and export reality. The period lasted until 1978, when economic reforms started.

6.2.2 Pre-Market Economy Era (1979–93)

The pre-market economy era was also the period when the Chinese economy transferred itself from the previously closed and planned system toward the market oriented system. There were several stages within this era. We introduce them briefly as follows.

(1) *Adoption of the Foreign Currency Retention System*
In order to give enterprises incentives to earn foreign currency income and improve foreign currency resource reallocation, the government allowed a certain portion of the foreign currency earned or retention to be given to the earners. The retention ratios were determined by the government according to various criteria. This retention/incentive system was the first step toward foreign exchange reform. The retention system was somewhat similar to the household responsibility system introduced in the rural area at the beginning of the reform as we described in Chapter 2. The basic idea was to give participants incentives to produce more to improve productivity in the closed and planned system.

(2) *Establishing and Developing Foreign Currency Barter Market*
The adoption of the foreign currency retention system described earlier created an actual demand for a foreign currency market

between those in need and those that had retained foreign currency. The Bank of China began its foreign currency bartering business in October 1980. This business grew gradually in scope and participants from merely state-owned enterprises and collectively owned enterprises to foreign-invested companies and individuals. The swap rate was managed by the government through adding a certain range to the official exchange rate. The market force grew gradually in the late 1980s. We will introduce this market in more details in Section 6.4.

(3) *Reforming RMB Exchange Rate System*

The RMB exchange rate was not set according to market forces in the late 1970s and early 1980s. In 1981, a dual-exchange system was used in order to resolve this problem partially. An official exchange rate of RMB 1.5/US$ was used for non-trade purposes, and at the same time, another RMB exchange rate of RMB 2.8/US$ was used for import and export settlement. This dual-exchange system was effective in stimulating exports, yet it created confusion in the exchange market. This system was abolished on January 1, 1985, and the exchange rate was unified again at RMB 2.8/US$.

The official RMB/US$ exchange rate was adjusted from 1985 according to the inflation situation in China. It was adjusted to RMB 5.22/US$ on November 17, 1990. Foreign currency bartering centers were established in various parts of China from March 1988, and trading volumes increased significantly at such centers. The exchange rates trading in these centers coexisted with the official exchange rate. The official exchange rate was adjusted gradually according to market forces rather than dramatic adjustments in the early 1990s. This adjustment was essentially a managed floating system. The official exchange rate was adjusted to RMB 5.72/US$ by the end of 1993, or 9% depreciation compared with 1990. The currency bartering market was further liberalized to allow market forces to play more important roles in determining the exchange rates.

(4) *New Institutions for Foreign Currency Businesses*

The foreign exchange business was monopolized by the Bank of China before 1979. Competition was introduced into the banking system to allow other state-owned banks first and then even some non-bank financial institutions to do foreign currency business in China since the beginning of the reforming process. Currently, foreign financial institutions are also allowed to do foreign currency business in China.

(5) *Individual Participation of the Bartering Market*
Individually owned foreign currencies were allowed be deposited in banks, yet foreign currencies owned by individuals were allowed neither to be traded nor brought out of China before 1985. Foreign currencies owned by individuals were allowed to be traded in the foreign currency bartering market in November 1991. Individuals with approvals to go aboard could apply for a small amount of foreign currency at the official exchange rate.

For other detailed information of foreign exchange administration, please refer to the official website of SAFE.

6.2.3 Market Economy Era

The Communist Party of China officially announced the decision to establish a market-oriented economy on November 14, 1993 as we described in Chapter 2 of this part. The decision specifically sets the RMB exchange reforming target to float the RMB exchange rate gradually based on market supply of and demand for foreign currencies. The government has taken a series of initiatives in this era to meet the general target.

(1) *Abolishing Foreign Currency Quota Plan and Approvals*
The former foreign currency retention system and quota plans were abolished on January 1, 1994. In order to secure foreign currency supplies for various purposes, all enterprises are required to repatriate their foreign exchange receipts and sell them to designated banks at the prevailing RMB exchange rate or to open foreign exchange settlement accounts at these banks.

(2) *Adoption of the Market-Based Monitored Floating Exchange System*
The official exchange rate was unified with the market exchange rate on January 1, 1994. The unified RMB exchange was set to 8.70/US$. The RMB exchange rates have been essentially set by market supply and demand, with the PBOC announcing a daily exchange rate and market exchange being allowed to float within certain limits.

(3) *Current Account Convertibility*

The RMB was successfully made convertible conditionally in 1994, and the obligations of Article VIII of the IMF Articles of Agreement were accepted officially on December 1, 1996, and the RMB has become fully convertible for current account transactions since then. China's formal acceptance of Article VIII of the Agreement on International Currencies and Funds realized convertibility of the RMB under the current account ahead of schedule.

In 1994, reforms were carried out in the administration of foreign currencies, adopting a combination of exchange rates (from the simultaneous existence of several exchange rates to a single market exchange rate) and a unified settlement and sale of foreign exchange, and a unified inter-bank foreign exchange market was established. This had an important influence upon China's economic development and reform and opening to the outside world.

6.2.4 RMB Exchange Rates from 1978 to 2003

We have described the brief history of China's foreign exchange administration in the quarter-century since the reform process started. Table 6.1 gives the official RMB/US$ exchange rates from

Table 6.1 RMB/US$ Exchange Rate from 1978 to 2003

Year	RMB/US$	Deva/Reva (%)	Year	RMB/US$	Deva/Reva (%)
1978	168.36		1992	551.46	−3.47
1979	155.50	8.27	1993	576.20	−4.29
1980	170.50	−8.80	1994	861.87	−33.15
1981	170.50	0.00	1995	835.10	3.21
1982	189.25	−9.91	1996	831.42	0.44
1983	232.70	−18.67	1997	828.98	0.29
1984	293.66	−20.76	1998	827.91	0.13
1985	293.66	0.00	1999	827.83	0.01
1986	345.28	−14.95	2000	827.84	0.00
1987	372.21	−7.24	2001	827.70	0.02
1988	372.21	0.00	2002	827.70	0.00
1989	376.51	−1.14	2003	827.70	0.00
1991	532.33	−10.15			

Data source: China Statistical Year Book 2001; and data for 2001–03 are from the website of SAFE.

1978 to 2003 and the corresponding annual appreciation or depreciation within the same period.

6.3 Current Foreign Exchange Administration in China

As we mentioned earlier in this chapter, China began to reform her rigid foreign exchange management since the very beginning of the reform process, and it set the ultimate goal to float the RMB more than 1 decade ago, when China decided to establish the market economy system. Significant progress has been made, and yet the progress may not be as fast as what it is expected.

6.3.1 Managed Floating System

On December 28, 1993 the PBOC announced a reform program of China's foreign exchange system. The reform, based on the managed floating system we described earlier, became effective on January 1, 1994 and has remained in place to date. Some points relating to this program were discussed earlier in this chapter; the following are some of the major measures adopted at the time:

1. Introduction of a system of selling foreign exchange through banks to replace regulations requiring state approval for foreign exchange payments under the current account. Under this system, enterprises could convert the RMB into foreign exchange under the current account at designated banks upon presentation of valid documents and within given limits.
2. The PBOC published an average RMB-to-US$ exchange rate every morning based on the prices quoted on the inter-bank foreign exchange markets on the previous day and listed the exchange rates for other major currencies based on exchange rate fluctuations in international foreign exchange markets. Designated foreign exchange banks could quote prices within a narrow range fixed by PBOC.
3. Establishment of foreign debt repayment funds. In order to protect China's foreign trade credibility and strengthen the management of foreign debt repayment, China encouraged various

localities, departments, and enterprises with heavy foreign debts to establish foreign debt repayment funds by depositing an amount equivalent to a certain percentage of their outstanding debts at designated banks. Foreign exchange in these accounts could only be used for the payment of principal and interest, not other expenditures.

4. Banning free circulation of foreign currencies. Foreign currency settlements of all forms were abolished, and the issuance of foreign exchange certificates was discontinued.

6.3.2 Significant Liberalizing Measures

SAFE announced early in 2003 significant liberalization of the foreign exchange system for foreign companies operating in China. The rules came into effect from April 2003 and represent an improved investment climate. The major measures being introduced are the following.

6.3.2.1 New Account System is Introduced into the Banking System

In addition to the settlement and capital accounts, foreign investors will now be allowed to open multi-currency investment accounts for the purpose of undertaking construction and engineering contracts, exploration of natural resources, and risk investments (portfolio investors and venture capitalists). Specialized accounts are also to be permitted for acquisition of assets, expenditure related to market survey, planning, and provision of guarantees.

A new category of offshore accounts is being introduced to facilitate the transfer of investment funds from a foreign investor into an existing foreign invested enterprise. Such transfer will not require SAFE approval if a capital receipt certificate has been issued. The new bank accounts system will benefit foreign companies without a presence in China but with business dealings in the domestic market.

In the past, foreign investors' contribution of capital would only be confined to convertible currencies, imported equipment, intellectual properties, and RMB profit after tax. From April 2003 on, they will be allowed (subject to SAFE approval) to contribute new investments in the form of reserve funds from the original foreign invested enterprise, undistributed profits, unrealized investment returns, proceeds from the sale of shares or assets for reinvestment, and their own foreign exchange maintained in a domestic bank account onshore. Foreign investors can pay for the acquisition of new shares in Chinese companies by remitting capital from abroad or by utilizing RMB profits generated from China operations and other legally owned assets. This is subject to approval from SAFE.

These new measures will facilitate the contribution of capital from foreign investors, especially those classified as FDI who were unable to utilize their foreign and RMB accounts in China for mergers & aquisition (M&A)-related activities. As expected, there may be further implementation rules for the new system to be in place.

6.4 Capital Account Convertibility in China

The Asian financial crisis has important impacts not only on the economies and financial markets in the Asian countries and regions and beyond but also on the way of thinking in macroeconomic and financial policies. It led to a rethinking of the issues related to capital account liberalization. We follow in this section mostly the results from the joint seminar of the Bank for International settlement (BIS) and SAFE, *Capital Account Liberalization in China: International Perspectives* held in September 2002. The seminar was particularly timely as China prepared for the next phase of financial liberalization following its recent entry into the World Trade Organization (WTO). Interested readers may go to the website of BIS for the original paper of Andre lcard, Deputy General Manager of the BIS.

Before that crisis, it had been well understood that sound macroeconomic policies were needed to minimize the risks associated with the opening of the capital account. After that crisis, the critical role played by a well-capitalized, well-managed, and well-regulated financial system came into sharper focus. The risks of a highly leveraged corporate structure without effective shareholder discipline also became clearer. Policy-makers gained a better appreciation of the fact that successful capital account liberalization depends on a broad range of effective policies.

The current account was made convertible in China late in 1996 as we discussed earlier in this chapter. However, convertibility is still limited for the capital account. When people talk about convertibility, they normally think that China is one of the few countries still with strict capital controls. This is not exactly true, and we will explain the reasons. If we go into this issue in more detail, we will find that China's present capital account is partially convertible. Corresponding to the 43 items of the seven categories under capital account transactions set up by the IMF, some of the items have always been treated as fully or basically convertible; some of them are still strictly or totally prohibited.

Lessons and experiences of other countries in capital account liberalization indicate that economies ought to strengthen their own financial systems and supervisory infrastructure before opening up their capital accounts, and a corporate sector marked by fragile finances and poor governance may abuse systematically the opportunities provided by capital account liberalization. China's situation differs markedly from those of countries in Latin America and even some of the Asian economies. China is already largely open to international capital flows. One could even say that China has been more open to FDI than some OECD economies, especially as the country has lately encouraged outward FDI in natural resources and technology.

There are growing cross-border flows of RMB banknotes between China and its neighbors, where the RMB is sometimes treated as a hard currency. Perhaps the most striking indication of China's financial openness is the marked expansion of onshore foreign currency deposits. Such deposits by Chinese households and firms have reached 8% of local currency deposits, in part because of the government's policy of keeping onshore dollar deposit rates broadly in line with prevailing international market yields. Monthly changes in these deposits exhibit sensitivity to movements in interest rate spreads and exchange rate expectations. These aspects of financial openness favor capital account liberalization in that they point to substantial adjustments that have already occurred.

Portfolio investment liberalization has been conducted in a cautious manner in order to stay away from associated shocks. Foreign investors are allowed to invest in B shares and foreign currency-denominated bonds issued domestically and H shares and N shares issued on overseas markets except for RMB-denominated equities and bonds on the domestic markets. With the introduction and execution of the QFII mechanism in 2003, foreign institutional investors can participate in China's A shares trading. According to the WTO commitments, there is a possibility of setting up Chinese and foreign joint venture securities companies. However, their trading activities are limited to primary market underwriting and fiduciary trading on the secondary market.

6.5 The Chinese Foreign Exchange Market

The foreign exchange barter market came into being in 1980, with the Bank of China as its major initiator. Other state-owned banks began to participate in the business as they were later permitted to do foreign exchange business as described in Section 6.2. The government decided to set up an inter-bank foreign currency market in December 1993, as evidenced by the announcement by the State Council on further reforming foreign exchange administration. The inter-bank foreign exchange market — the China Foreign Exchange Trade Center (CFETCS) — was approved officially by the PBOC on February 15 and by SAFE on February 18. The CFETCS began its trial operation on March 1, 1994, and its opening ceremony was held on April 18, 1994. Its formal trading rules were approved on January 14, 1995. With only RMB and US$ cash transactions in CFETCS at the beginning, the Hong Kong dollar and Japanese yen were added to CFETCS on April 5, 1994 and March 1, 1995, respectively. The floating range for the US$, HK$ and Japanese yen has been set to 0.25%, 1.0%, and 1.0% around the official exchange rate, and prices outside the given range are considered illegal and cannot be accepted in the computer system.

CFETCS is a membership-based non-profit entity with a centralized clearing system. The number of members increased dramatically from 303 in 1994 to more than 1000 by the end of 2003. Its members include Chinese banks and their branches, foreign banks, and other non-bank financial institutions. Foreign bank members can only represent their clients' trading, and they cannot trade for proprietary purposes. There are only cash transactions in the center. Chinese enterprises left these centers on January 1, 1994, and designated banks for foreign exchange business became major players in this market. It is an entity of the PBOC outside Beijing, and the PBOC directs the center directly and intervenes according to its macroeconomic targets and RMB exchange rate stability. CFETCS connects all foreign exchange trading centers in China. The CFETCS in Shanghai now takes the function of providing a unified nation-wide spot foreign exchange rate of the RMB, through which a preparatory step is made for full convertibility of the RMB.

The turnover in CFETCS has increased steadily in the past few years. Table 6.2 provides the annual weighted average price of US$/RMB, accumulative turnover in billions of US$, and annual growth rate from 1994 to 2003.

The total turnover of CFETCS reached US$151.1 billion in 2003, 55.5% up from 2002. Only four currencies, the US dollar, the Hong Kong dollar, the Japanese yen, and the Euro are traded against the RMB in CFETCS currently. The US$ is by far the most active currency trading in CFETCS, with 97.76% of the total turnover in 2003.

There are three levels of trading activities in CFETCS, trading between clients and their banks, trading among member institutions, and trading between member institutions and the PBOC. The driving force for the market exchange rate is the supply and demand

Table 6.2 Annual Turnover of Foreign Exchange Market in China (1994–2003)

Year	Annual Weighted Average Price (US$/RMB)	Accumulative Turnover (US$ billion)	Annual Growth Rate (%)
1994	8.5829	40.8	
1995	8.3494	65.5	60.4
1996	8.3132	65.5	0.0
1997	8.2894	70.0	6.8
1998	8.279	52.0	−25.8
1999	8.2782	31.5	−39.5
2000	8.2783	42.2	34.1
2001	8.277	75.0	77.9
2002	8.2769	97.2	29.5
2003	8.2769	151.1	55.5

Data source: Data for 1994 to 2002 are from the official website of China Foreign Exchange Trade Center, www.chinamoney.com.cn, and data for 2003 are from the website of the PBOC.

relationship. The PBOC announces the base RMB exchange rate every morning based on domestic market information of the previous days and international foreign exchange market information, and designated banks set their own trading rates within a floating band of 0.25%.

The decade long operation experience of the CFETCS is very valuable for the formation of a market mechanism of the RMB exchange rate, promotion of RMB convertibility, supporting exchange rate policies, and so on. Based on such experiences, a more comprehensive convertible RMB mechanism will be designed and executed in China in the years to come.

RMB forwards were not traded in China until April 1, 1997, when it was permitted to be traded in the Bank of China, the only bank in China allowed to do such business in China at the time. We will discuss in more detail the RMB forwards market in Part IV of this book. There are no RMB futures contracts trading in China.

6.6 Foreign Invested Enterprises and Foreign Exchange Management

Foreign invested enterprises (FIEs) have been very important in the process of China's reform. FIEs are directly exposed to the RMB exchange rate risk. They are faced permanently with currency risk, which includes transfer and exchange risk. In order to attract foreign investment in China, the Chinese government has taken a series of measures to improve the environment in which the FIEs operate their businesses. As a matter of fact, FIEs in China have been granted preferential treatment in foreign exchange management. China must align the different foreign exchange management policies for FIEs and domestic enterprises. We concentrate on such measures in this section.

Under existing regulations, the foreign exchange management for FIEs covers mainly the following:

1. registration of foreign exchange;
2. the opening, utilization, and monitoring of foreign exchange accounts;

3. foreign exchange receipts and payments under the current and capital accounts;
4. balance of foreign exchange receipts and payments;
5. annual review of foreign exchange positions; and
6. foreign debts management.

The "Procedures for Bank Settlements" and "Procedures for the Management of Bank Accounts" promulgated by the PBOC in December 1988 and October 1994, respectively, provide the basis for the management of bank accounts and settlements of FIEs. There is as yet no special enactment for FIEs. In order to support FIEs in their production and operation, the PBOC issued the "Procedures for Providing Loans to Foreign Investment Enterprises by Chinese Banks" with the approval of the State Council in April 1987, providing them with a RMB financing channel.

Since 1996, the foreign currency business of foreign-invested enterprises has been directed into the banking system of settlement and sale. This was a major breakthrough in reforming the country's foreign exchange control system.

FIEs have to gain their currencies, which they need for procurement from abroad, compensation of their foreign staff, and for paying dividends to their foreign investors on a self-operating basis. The balancing of these foreign exchange positions is one of the most difficult tasks and therefore a high barrier for FIEs in China. In a transferring market like China, it is complicated to gain all the necessary currencies for daily business.

FIEs have many advantages over their Chinese counterparts because they are very familiar with most techniques existing in the international markets for hedging their currency exposures. Besides the hedging know-how, FIEs have the discretion to borrow internationally to make up the difference between their registered capital and paid-in capital. The international borrowings of foreign banks and short-term trade finance within 3 months have been included in the foreign debt statistics. The know-how to hedge currency risk, international experience, the discretion to borrow, and other advantages of the FIEs will make them more competitive in the new business environment as China enters deeper into the WTO, particularly after December 2006, when all of China's promises for the WTO will come true.

6.7 Shanghai International Financial Center

The municipal government of Shanghai has been trying to restore Shanghai's position as a leading international financial center for years. Shanghai was the financial center in East Asia in the early decades of the 20th century. The economic and financial reforms in China have reenergized Shanghai's financial status, and the city is on its way to further improving its status to reemerge as a leading international financial center in Asia in 20 years.

Shanghai has made steady progress toward its goals. Shanghai has the largest stock exchange (one of the two stock exchanges) in Mainland China, the largest futures exchange (one of the three futures exchanges) in Mainland China, the only foreign exchange market in Mainland China, the inter-bank market, and the only nation-wide gold market in Mainland China. Table 6.3 gives the total annual turnovers of the five markets in Shanghai in 2003. The total turnover of these five markets reached RMB 31.5 trillion (US$3.806 trillion) in 2003, 170% higher than China's GDP of the same year.

Shanghai has taken many initiatives to move toward its goal of being an international financial center. With the approval of SAFE, starting September 1, Shanghai will take the lead in the country to perform experiments on reform of management of foreign exchange loan of foreign-funded banks, that is to authorize foreign-funded banks operating in Shanghai to examine independently and approve

Table 6.3 Turnovers of Five Markets in Shanghai in 2003

Market	RMB (billion)	US$ (billion)	Market Share (%)
Stock market	8291.2	1001.7	26.3
Inter-bank market	17,000.0	2053.9	54.0
Foreign exchange	125.1	15.1	0.4
Futures market	6053.8	731.4	19.2
Gold market	30.0	3.6	0.1
Total	31,500.0	3805.7	100.0

Data source: Shanghai Securities News, January 15, 2004.

the interests of foreign exchange loans and the receipt and payment of fees. Over a long period of time, foreign exchange loans issued by foreign-funded banks in China were managed under the item foreign debts, and principal and interest payment had to be examined and approved by foreign exchange administrations one by one. The experiment on delegating powers to foreign-funded banks marks a significant breakthrough in administration of foreign-funded banks.

Despite the great achievements and initiatives, Shanghai is not without competition both domestically and globally. Whereas competition is normal in any market economy, it always takes time to achieve any goal with serious competition. Beijing, the capital of China, with most Chinese state-owned banks and other financial institutions headquartered there, is also planning to build itself into a financial center in China to take advantage of its political and geographic advantages over all other cities in China; Shenzhen, the border city to Hong Kong, where the other stock exchange is located, has been trying to build itself into a financial center in Mainland China; Tianjin, the other special municipality besides Shanghai and Beijing, is also trying to expand its financial businesses. Hong Kong SAR, the gateway of international capital to Mainland China, is already a financial center not only for Mainland China but also for Asia. With international experiences in almost every sector of financial businesses, a globally recognized legal system, and particularly a significant size of international financial expertise, Hong Kong's role in China's financial system will remain for years to come. Although it is true that the market mechanism is playing more important roles in more and more areas in the Chinese economy and the existing market structure has been largely the result of the previous planned economy, it will take many years for Shanghai to reach its goals without dramatic measures to refine the "software" besides building up many high-level buildings, to speed up reforming the existing systems, and particularly to accelerate to innovate in the financial system.

With the RMB authorized to be deposited in Hong Kong and the experimental floating mechanism also in Hong Kong in the future (please see Part V of this book for details), the total market capitalization of mainland companies listed in Hong Kong being greater than the total tradable A shares in Mainland China (Chapter 5, Section 5.1) and more and more good domestic enterprises to be listed in Hong Kong, the successful launching of the H share index futures in Hong Kong in December 2003 and H share index options in June 2004, Hong Kong's position as China's financial center will be further strengthened, and it will take a long time for Shanghai to catch up with Hong Kong if no dramatic measures are taken in the near future.

6.8 Conclusions

Throughout the reform era, China has experimented extensively with the structure of the foreign exchange market. Via complex rules, the authorities have allocated funds through quotas, regulated plural, dual, or unified exchange rates, and monitored retention rates and foreign exchange balancing. The overall objectives of the foreign exchange market reform have been to give incentives for export, control the exchange rate, and thereby promote macroeconomic stability. The Chinese government set the objective of floating the RMB as early as 1993 when the country began her experiment with the market-oriented economy. A lot of progress has been made in foreign exchange administration in the past quarter-century, yet the foreign exchange system is still not flexible enough to meet the dramatic development of the economy and financial market, especially after China's entry into the WTO.

Further opening of the Chinese market, especially the banking and services sectors, following China's WTO entry, will inevitably bring about new problems of foreign exchange management. China's WTO commitments have basically set the tone for its foreign exchange reform and policy adjustments. Foreign exchange management will face great pressure as the volumes of foreign exchange receipts and payments expand with fast economic growth. At the same time, the increased flow of international capital will make it imperative for China to simplify and accelerate its foreign exchange approval and verification procedures.

China entered the WTO for more than 2 years ago in December 2001, and China has been executing all her promises for the WTO entrance. We discussed the particular promises for the banking, securities, and insurance industries in the previous chapters. There is no particular WTO obligation on the foreign exchange system such as for China not to have a fixed exchange rate. As a matter of fact, the United States had a fixed exchange rate until 1971. We will discuss these issues in the following parts of this book.

PART II

Foreign Exchange Market and Foreign Exchange Derivatives Market

Our introduction to the Chinese economy and financial markets in Part I prepared us to understand better whether the Chinese yuan (CNY) or renminbi (RMB) should revalue or not, and it is necessary for us to introduce popular foreign exchange derivatives in the international marketplace before we introduce and analyze RMB derivatives in subsequent parts of this book. Foreign exchange derivatives have been trading both over-the-counter (OTC) and at exchanges around the world for over three decades, and they have become an integral part of the foreign exchange market. Yet, most of these popular foreign exchange derivatives do not exist in China.

Part II is organized as follows. Chapter 7 briefly introduces the foreign exchange market; Chapter 8 introduces foreign exchange forward market; Chapter 9 discusses non-deliverable forward market for controlled currencies; Chapter 10 introduces foreign exchange futures trading in major futures and options exchanges in the world; and Chapter 11 introduces foreign exchange options trading in both OTC marketplaces and organized exchanges.

7

Foreign Exchange Market

Before we introduce foreign exchange forward, futures, swaps, options, and other related products, it is highly necessary for us have a brief introduction to the foreign exchange (FX) market. We focus on major aspects of FX market in this chapter.

7.1 Foreign Exchange Market

After the Wars, the Bretton Woods Agreement was drawnup, in which participating countries agreed to try to maintain the value of their currencies with a narrow margin against the US dollar and a corresponding rate of gold as needed. Countries were prohibited from devaluing their currencies to their trade advantages and were only allowed to do so for devaluations of less than 10%. Into the 1950s, the ever-expanding volume of international trade led to massive movements of capital generated by post-war construction. That destabilized foreign exchange rates as setup in Bretton Woods. In the 1980s, cross-border capital movements accelerated with the advent of computers and technology, extending the market continuum through Asian, European, and American time zones. Transactions in foreign exchange rocketed from about $800 billion a day in the early 1980s to more than $1.5 trillion a day two decades later.

The FX market enables companies, fund managers and banks, to buy and sell foreign currencies, if necessary in large amounts. The motivations behind this demand for foreign currency include capital flows arising from trade in goods and services, cross-border investment, and loans and speculation on the future levels of exchange rates.

The currency market is a 24-hour market from Asia to Europe and then to America, starting every day from Asian and Australian financial centers such as Auckland (New Zealand), Sydney (Australia), Tokyo (Japan), Hong Kong, and Singapore, on to European centers such as Frankfurt (Germany), Paris (France), Zurich (Switzerland), and London (UK); then to American centers such as New York, Chicago (USA), and Toronto (Canada). It is by far the largest market, with a daily turnover exceeding US$1.5 trillion in 2002 compared with US$0.8–1.0 trillion a decade earlier in 1992. This makes the FX market the world's largest, most efficient market, dwarfing both the bond and equity markets. The largest stock exchange in the world, the New York Stock Exchange, for example, has a daily trading volume of approximately $30 billion, merely 2% of the average daily trading volume of the FX market. In turn, the FX market is by far the most liquid market in the world today. Due to the sheer size of the FX market, it is virtually impossible for individuals or companies to impact exchange rates. In fact, even central banks find it increasingly difficult to affect the exchange rates of the most liquid currencies such as the US dollar, euro, Japanese yen, Swiss franc, Canadian dollar, or Australian dollar.

7.2 Major Currencies of Foreign Exchange Market

According to a survey of the UK foreign exchange cash and derivatives market in April 2001, the US dollar remained the dominant currency in the London market, being used on one side of the transaction in 92% of all deals. The euro replaced the Deutsche mark as the second most traded currency, accounting for a larger proportion of the market than did the Deutsche mark did in 1998 but less than the sum of all euro legacy currencies. The dollar/euro was the most traded currency pair, capturing 34% of the market. The market share of the sterling/dollar increased from 14% to 20%.

The pound sterling and Japanese yen were ranked the third and fourth most actively trading currencies, with 24% and 17% of all deals, respectively. The Swiss franc and Canadian dollar were ranked No. 5 and No. 6 with 6% and 4% of all deals.

7.3 Uses of Foreign Exchange Market

Because the major purpose of transactions in the foreign exchange market is for international trade, the currencies of the major international trade participants are the most often used currencies, such as the US dollar, Euro dollar, British pound, Japanese yen and others. Besides the use for international trade, the foreign exchange market also serves the financing and investment purposes. We will return to this in the following chapter when we introduce foreign exchange derivative products.

Broadly speaking, there are three types of participants in the market: customers, banks, and brokers. Multinational corporations are in the market because they require foreign currency in the course of their cross-border trade or investment business.

7.4 Foreign Exchange Centers in the World

Unlike some financial markets, the foreign exchange market has no single location — foreign exchange is not dealt across a trading floor. Instead, trading is via telephone and computer links between dealers in different centers and, indeed, different continents. London is the world's largest foreign exchange center, with the highest average daily turnover, followed by the United States, Japan, and Singapore. Table 7.1 gives the total FX trading volume in the top eight FX centers in 1998 and 2001.

The predominant market mechanism in the major centers is still the direct inter-dealer market. In the UK, for example, the proportion

Table 7.1 Average Daily Foreign Exchange Market Turnover in Main Centers (Unit: US$ billion)

Center	April 1998	April 2001
United Kingdom	637	504
United States	351	254
Japan	149	147
Singapore	139	101
Germany	94	88
Switzerland	82	71
Hong Kong	79	67
France	72	48

Source: Bank for International Settlement, March 2002.

of total FX business transacted by brokers fell from 35% in 1995 to 27% in 1998, the remainder being conducted bilaterally between banks. Electronic brokers increased their share of total foreign exchange turnover from 5% in 1995 to 11% in 1998. Consequently, the proportion of business conducted by traditional voice brokers, who quote prices over telephone lines to dealing rooms, declined from 30% to 16%.

7.5 Singapore and Hong Kong

Among the emerging markets, Singapore and Hong Kong are the two major foreign exchange trading centers. A recent BIS survey estimates the average daily turnover in April 2001 at about US$101 billion and US$71 billion, respectively (see Table 7.1), comforting Singapore as the fourth largest foreign exchange center in the world, ahead of Switzerland, Germany, and France. Like other financial centers, most of these figures represent transactions involving the three major currencies. In Singapore, transactions in the dollar–yen currency pair represented about 22% of the total volume, while trading in the dollar–mark pair constituted 23%. In contrast, the share of transactions in the Singapore dollar was estimated at 17%. Singapore's foreign exchange market remains dominated by foreign exchange swaps and spot transactions, which made up 54% and 43%, respectively, of total foreign exchange transactions. The remaining 3% comprised outright forward transactions. Of the total turnover, 86% were transactions between financial institutions, while trading with non-bank customers accounted for 14%, reflecting the growing use of Singapore as a regional base for corporations to operate their treasury operations.

Because of the consequences of the Asian crisis, the average net daily turnover of Hong Kong's spot foreign exchange dropped by more than 20% (to US$71 billion) in April 2001, down from US$90.2 billion in April 1995. Spot deals fell by 10%, mainly because of a 32% reduction in the trading of US dollar against Deutsche mark. In contrast, the turnover of the US dollar against the Hong Kong dollar and US dollar against Japanese yen transactions experienced robust growth rates of 25% and 30%, respectively.

In Hong Kong, about 70% of all FX transactions involve the US dollar (against currencies other than the HK dollar), compared with 78% in April 1995. Transactions involving the Hong Kong dollar accounted for 24%, rising from 17% in 1995. The dollar–yen is the most heavily traded currency pair, with 26% of average net daily turnover. However, the US dollar–Hong Kong dollar pair, with 22% of average daily turnover, has replaced the US dollar–mark pair, with 20% of daily turnover, as the second commonest currency pair.

7.6 Emerging Market Currencies

Prior to the Asian crisis, the Thai baht had been perhaps the most liquid of the Asian currencies, with 1996 survey data from Singapore suggesting a total average daily trading volume on the inter-bank market of $14 billion. The volume on the spot market was $5 billion, compared with $9 billion in the swaps and forward markets. The total volumes for the Malaysian ringgit and the Indonesian rupiah were, respectively, $9.5 billion and $8.5 billion. Although the volumes on the spot market were estimated at $6 billion and $5 billion, these currencies had smaller swap and forward volumes of about $3.5 billion each. The total daily volumes for the Singapore dollar and the Hong Kong dollar were $7.5 billion and $4 billion (see Table 7.2), respectively, with $3.5 billion and $2.0 billion worth of spot transactions each. The less traded currencies of South Korea, Taiwan, India, China, and the Philippines had estimated volumes ranging between $2.4 billion for the won and $400 million for the peso. The

Table 7.2 Foreign Exchange Turnover in Asian Markets (Daily Averages in Millions of US$)

Country/Region	1998	1996	Change (%)
Hong Kong	18,711	4000	368
Singapore	17,644	7500	135
Thailand	2574	14,000	−82
South Korea	2289	2400	−5
Taiwan	1720	1100	56
India	1389	1100	26
Indonesia	972	8500	−89
Malaysia	660	9500	−93
Philippines	492	400	23
China	211	400	−47

Data source: BIS, May 1999, and Singapore Foreign Exchange Committee, 1996, Annual Report.

New Taiwan dollar and the rupee both had estimated daily volumes of $1.1 billion, while the figure for the RMB was about $400 million.

In the aftermath of the Asian financial crisis, the number of market participants had decreased, and positions were smaller than before the crisis. The size of deals shrank, with standard inter-bank and inter-broker amounts declining, for example for the baht from $10–20 million to $3 million for spot transactions and from $20 million to $10 million on forward markets. The number of inter-bank players declined on average by more than half their previous number, with, for example, the number of institutions trading on the spot market for ringgit down from 25 to 12 and on the forward market from 50 to 20. The composition of the foreign exchange market had also changed. In fact, because of the high levels of bid–ask spreads, the broker market was said to be playing an increasing role with currently about 65% of the transaction volume in Singapore, up from 5% before the crisis. In the midst of the crisis, a larger proportion of the transactions was reportedly through the broker market. On the other hand, the inter-bank market was said to be dominated by a few core international banks. Finally, hedgers, mostly equity investors, proprietary trading desks, and hedge funds, were reportedly still active on the other side of the transactions.

8

Foreign Exchange Forwards and Swaps

Forward contracts are the earliest forms of derivatives and one of the basic building units used to construct many other types of financial derivatives. Foreign exchange forwards together with foreign exchange swaps represent the major instruments in the foreign exchange market. With the development of over-the-counter (OTC) foreign exchange derivatives, the total trading volume of foreign exchange forwards and swaps as a percentage of total foreign exchange trading volume has increased steadily in the past decade and that of the corresponding spot trading volume has declined at the same time.

The purpose of this chapter is to draw a brief picture of foreign exchange instruments through introducing major derivatives instruments in the foreign exchange market. In particular, we will introduce foreign exchange forwards, foreign exchange swaps, currency swaps, and interest rate swaps involving major currencies.

This chapter is organized as follows: Section 8.1 introduces the foreign exchange forward market; Section 8.2 introduces briefly how foreign exchange forwards are priced; Section 8.3 introduces briefly FX forwards in emerging markets; Section 8.4 describes foreign exchange swaps and their applications with examples; Section 8.5 discusses currency swaps and their uses; Section 8.6 introduces interest rate swaps with major currencies; Section 8.7 outlines the future development of foreign exchange derivatives market and concludes the chapter.

8.1 Foreign Exchange Forwards

In an outright forward transaction, two currencies are exchanged at an agreed forward exchange rate for settlement more than two business days after the conclusion of the deal, locking in current exchange rates and thus eliminating the risk that exchange rates may move in the interim period. Terms are also negotiable at present in forward contracts, but the execution can be carried out at some time in the future as specified by the forward contract. Because forward contracts are not "standardized" as compared with futures contracts we will discuss in the following chapter, it is difficult to change one's position once it is specified in the agreement.

Foreign exchange forwards are used by trade companies engaging in international businesses, investment companies specializing in international investment to hedge their foreign exchange risk. Let us take an example.

Example 8.1

One importer plans to import equipment of about US$1.0 million in half a year, and the current HK$/US$ exchange rate is HK$7.79. What can he do to hedge his foreign exchange risk using Hong Kong dollar forward?

As the importer does not know what the HK$/US$ exchange rate will be in half a year and he expects that the Hong Kong dollar will appreciate against the US$, he can buy a HK$ forward contract at HK$7.765/US$ to mature in half a year. This contract actually locks the HK$/US$ exchange rate at 7.765. The amount of HK$ he needs will be $1.0 \times 7.765 =$ HK$7.765 million, that is $7.790 - 7.765 =$ HK$0.025 million = HK$25,000 less than the cash he needs at the existing exchange rate.

Table 8.1 gives the average daily trading volume of currency forwards in April of 1989, 1992, 1995, 1998 and 2001 compared with

Table 8.1 Global Foreign Exchange Turnover — Average Daily in April (Unit: US$ billion)

Year	1989	1992	1995	1998	2001
Spot	317	394	494	568	387
Weight	59.36%	50.77%	43.45%	39.72%	32.96%
Growth		24.29%	25.38%	14.98%	−31.87%
Forwards	27	58	97	128	131
Weight	5.06%	7.47%	8.53%	8.95%	11.16%
Growth		114.81%	67.24%	31.96%	2.34%
Swaps	190	324	546	734	656
Weight	35.58%	41.75%	48.02%	51.33%	55.88%
Growth		70.53%	68.52%	34.43%	−10.63%
Total	534	776	1137	1430	1174
Growth		45.32%	46.52%	25.77%	−17.90%

Data source: BIS 2002.

the corresponding volume of currency spot and swaps in the same time. Table 8.1 clearly indicates that although currency forward was smallest compared to spot and swaps trading, its accumulative growth rate was higher than the other two items; and the average daily trading volume of US$131 billion in April 2001 was about four times the average daily trading volume US$30 billion at New York Stock Exchange.

8.2 Pricing Foreign Exchange Forwards

We have introduced foreign exchange forwards in the previous section. Many may wonder how foreign exchange forwards prices are determined in general. It is our purpose to introduce how foreign exchange forwards are priced in this section.

The "arbitrage-free" or "no-free-lunch" principle is the standard textbook method for pricing all types of financial derivatives including forwards, futures, options, and so on (please see Zhang (1998) for a more detailed description of this principle and Zhang (2003) for a thorough description of how to price forwards in general). Forwards are the simplest form of derivatives, and they can also be priced using this principle.

The arbitrage-free principle can be simply understood as the no-arbitrage principle or the daily saying "there is no such thing as a free lunch". Arbitragers are traders who search for price differentials in different markets, buying at low prices in some markets and selling at high prices in others, thus making net profits without investing in any assets. Such profit opportunities are called arbitrage opportunities. Everyone would like to be an arbitrager to make money quickly out of nothing, yet it is not easy to find such opportunities without a good understanding of how different markets are working individually and interactively. Arbitrage can exist, yet it cannot last long.

As all economic and financial theories require many assumptions, we also need to make quite a few assumptions in order to price foreign exchange forwards. The comprehensive list of assumptions is rather long, and interested readers may refer to Zhang (2003c) for detailed assumptions. With these assumptions, we can obtain the forward price as follows:

$$F = Se^{(r-\mathrm{r_f})\times t}, \tag{8.1}$$

Where S, r, $\mathrm{r_f}$, and t stand for the spot price of a foreign exchange rate, domestic interest rate, foreign interest rate, and time to maturity of the forward contract in a fraction of a year or a number of years.

Example 8.2

Find the 5 month forward rate of a US dollar/Japanese yen forward contract given the US interest rate, r, is 3.0%, the Japanese interest rate is 0.5%, and the current US dollar–Japanese yen exchange rate $S = 115$ yen per US$ or $0.008696 per Japanese yen.

Substituting $S = 0.008698$, $r = 0.03$, $\mathrm{r_f} = 0.005$, and $t = 5/12$ into (8.1) yields

$$\begin{aligned} F &= 0.008696 \times \exp[(0.030 - 0.005) \times 5/12] \\ &= \$0.008787 \quad \text{or} \quad F = 113.81 \text{ yen/US\$}. \end{aligned}$$

8.3 Foreign Exchange Forwards in Emerging Markets

Foreign exchange markets in emerging markets are very different from those in developed markets. Foreign exchange markets in developing countries are predominantly spot markets. More complex financial contracts involving currency exchange are notoriously scant in emerging markets, usually with very low market turnover. Forward foreign exchange markets are undeveloped in most emerging markets. According to a recent survey by IMF (WP/04/4, Canales-Kriljenko (2004)), only 9% of survey-emerging market respondents consider their forward foreign exchange markets to be developed, liquid, and deep, while 30% of survey respondents consider them to be undeveloped, illiquid, and shallow; outright forward contracts were allowed in about 75% of the survey respondents. In countries where forward contracts are prohibited, regulations also ban contracts that yield equivalent payoffs. For example, regulations may ban swap contracts, which, combined with spot contracts, could have the same payoff as a forward contract.

The lack of forward market development may reflect many factors, including the presence of exchange rate insurance provided by the central bank. Besides limited exchange rate flexibility, the lack of forward market development may also reflect the absence of a yield curve on which to base forward prices or shallow money markets in which market-making banks can hedge the maturity risks implicit in forward positions. In turn, shallow money markets may reflect limitations on short-term capital mobility. These markets also reflect the fact that forward contracts required regulation in some countries. For example, forward contracts were allowed to cover only the exchange rate risk of legally permitted foreign exchange transactions, supported by an underlying contract of an approved international transaction in a few survey countries. In other survey countries, regulations limited contract maturity, sometimes relating it to the timing of the underlying transaction.

Most legally permitted foreign exchange activities in developing countries take place onshore, partly reflecting exchange and monetary regulations. A large number of survey respondents determine the geographical location where the domestic currency can be traded in exchange for foreign currencies. Regulations in these countries often did not authorize offshore trading of the domestic currency and restricted its export and import. In particular, about half of the survey countries actually prohibited the operation of offshore markets for their currencies.

The domestic currency can also be traded indirectly with offshore counterparties through the branches and subsidiaries of foreign banks. International voice brokers who operate in the developing countries also may connect foreign dealers willing to take positions in domestic currencies with domestic dealers willing to take positions in foreign currencies.

8.4 Foreign Exchange Swaps

Foreign exchange spot trading is for two business day delivery, and foreign exchange forwards are normally for transactions of between two business days and 1 year. Although forward contracts for more than 1 year also exist, they are rather rare. Spot transactions and forward contracts are largely for single or less-frequent transactions. For multiple or frequent transactions, foreign exchange swaps are often used.

A swap is a financial contract between two parties: one party agrees to pay a fixed rate of a pre-specified notional amount and the other party a corresponding floating rate of the same notional amount for a given period of time with pre-specified frequency. The fixed rate payer is called the buyer and the floating rate payer the seller of the swap. Payment frequencies can be monthly, quarterly, semi-annual, or annual; and notional amounts range normally from a few million to a few hundred million US dollars. The swap market is by far the largest market if we judge by notional amounts, yet only a small fraction of the notional amount, actually the difference between the fixed rate and the corresponding floating rate multiplied by the notional amount, actually matters in any swap contract.

By definition, a swap can be considered as a string of forward contracts because it includes a series of rates to be paid in the future. A foreign exchange swap is a swap with simultaneous exchanges of two currencies on specific dates specified in the contract and a reverse exchange of the same two currencies at a date further in the future at a rate agreed at the time of the contract. Short-term swaps carried out as "tomorrow/next day" transactions are included in this category. Table 8.2 lists the total amounts outstanding of foreign exchange swaps from June 1999 to December 2002. The foreign

Table 8.2 Amounts Outstanding of FX Swaps and Currency Swaps from June 1999 to December 2002 (Unit: US$ trillion)

	Jun 1999	Dec 1999	Jun 2000	Dec 2000	Jun 2003	Dec 2001	Jun 2002	Dec 2002
FX swaps*	8.3	8.3	9.0	8.6	8.9	8.6	8.6	8.7
Currency swaps	2.4	2.4	2.6	3.2	3.8	3.9	4.2	4.5
Total	10.7	10.8	11.6	11.8	12.8	12.6	12.9	13.3

*Calculated according to the ratios of FX forwards and swaps from Table 8.1 and total amounts outstanding of FX forwards and swaps.

Data source: Derivatives statistics, International financial statistics, Bank for International Settlements, 2002.

exchange swap market somewhat reached maturity as its total amounts outstanding remained between US$8.3 to US$8.9 trillion from June 1999 to December 2002 as shown in Table 8.2.

8.5 Currency Swaps

A currency swap is a contract that commits two counterparties to exchange streams of interest payments in different currencies for an agreed period of time and to exchange principal amounts in the respective currencies at an agreed exchange rate at maturity.

The first currency swap was one between the International Bank for Reconstruction (IBR) of World Bank and IBM in 1981. The IBR borrows funds internationally and loans those funds to developing countries for construction projects. It charges its borrowers an interest rate based upon the rate it has to pay for the funds. The World Bank had a definite motivation to seek the lowest cost borrowing it could find. In 1981 the relevant interest rate in the US was at 17% percent, an extreme high due to the anti-inflation tight monetary policy of the Federal Reserve Bank. In West Germany the corresponding rate was 12% and Switzerland 8%. The problem for the World Bank was that the Swiss government imposed a limit on the amount the World Bank could borrow in Switzerland. The World Bank had borrowed its allowed limit in Switzerland, and the same was true of West Germany. IBM at that time, 1981, had large amounts of Swiss franc and German Deutsche mark debt and thus had debt payments to pay in Swiss francs and deutsche marks. IBM and the World Bank worked out an arrangement in which the World Bank borrowed dollars in the US market and swapped the dollar payment obligation to IBM in exchange for taking over IBM's Swiss franc and deutsche mark obligations.

After the World Bank and IBM showed the way the market for swap grew by leaps and bounds. Now funds involved in the swap market is many trillions of dollars. Table 8.2 lists the total amounts outstanding of currency swaps from June 1999 to December 2002. The total amounts outstanding increased by more than 84.5% from US$2.4 trillion in December 1999 to US$4.5 trillion in December 2002.

8.6 Interest Rate Swaps with Major Currencies

An interest rate swap is an agreement to exchange periodic payments related to interest rates on a single currency. The swap can be fixed for floating, or floating for floating, based on different indices. Interest rate swaps appear to be the leading candidate for replacing government securities as the pre-eminent benchmark instrument. Unlike currency swaps, interest rate swaps grew significantly between June 1998 and June 2002 as shown in Table 8.3.

The notional amount of outstanding interest rate swaps increased by 32.81% from June 2001 to June 2002, to $68.274 trillion,

Table 8.3 Amounts Outstanding of Interest Rate Swaps (Unit: US$ trillion)

	Jun 1998	Dec 1998	Jun 1999	Dec 1999	Jun 2000	Dec 2000	Jun 2001	Dec 2001	Jun 2002
Interest rate swaps	29.36	36.26	38.37	43.94	47.99	48.77	51.41	58.90	68.27
Growth rate (semi-annual) (%)		23.50	5.82	14.50	9.23	1.61	5.41	14.57	15.92
Growth rate (annual) (%)			30.68		25.07		7.11		32.81

Data source: Derivatives statistics, International financial statistics, Bank for International Settlements, 2002.

about twice as large as the total world GDP in 2002. The swaps market in the euro legacy currencies was larger in notional terms than the market in dollars even before the introduction of the single currency. Since 1999, the market in euros has extended its lead over that in dollars, with swaps being used for hedging, price discovery, and other purposes for which US Treasuries tended to be used in the dollar market. The dollar market is following the lead of the euro market, increasingly using swaps for hedging and other purposes.

Table 8.4 gives the total single currency interest rate derivatives turnover net of local inter-dealer double-counting by major countries in April 2001. We can observe readily from Table 8.4 that the United Kingdom with a total market share of 35.17% had slightly more than twice the daily average turnover of the United States; the market share of other European Union member countries was 38.11%; the total market share of the rest of the world is less than 10% besides the US and EU.

Table 8.4 Single Currency Interest Rate Swaps in Major Countries — Daily Averages in Billions of US$ in April 2001

			Percent of Total
1	United Kingdom	237.76	35.17
2	United States	115.67	17.11
3	Germany	94.03	13.91
4	France	65.10	9.63
5	Netherlands	24.21	3.58
6	Italy	23.70	3.51
7	Spain	20.46	3.03
8	Japan	15.76	2.33
9	Belgium	14.09	2.08
10	Canada	9.91	1.47
11	Ireland	5.81	0.86
12	Denmark	5.79	0.86
13	Luxembourg	4.46	0.66
14	Singapore	3.19	0.47
15	Norway	2.90	0.43
16	Hong Kong SAR	2.64	0.39
Sum		645.48	95.47
Total		676.11	100.00

8.7 Conclusions

According to a BIS survey released in 2002, the turnover in traditional foreign exchange markets declined substantially between 1998 and 2001. In April 2001, the average daily turnover was $1174 billion, compared with $1430 billion in April 1998, a 17.9% decline at current exchange rates and a 14% fall when volumes are measured at constant exchange rates. The turnover did not decline uniformly across instruments. Table 8.1 indicates clearly that the spot trading volume as a percentage of total turnover has been falling steadily from 59.36% in 1989 to 32.96% in 2001; the corresponding share of foreign exchange swaps has been rising steadily from 35.58% to 55.88%; and that of foreign exchange forwards has risen from 5.06% to 11.16%. These data obviously show that foreign exchange derivatives products have been dominating the foreign exchange market since 1993 and occupying over two-thirds of the total turnover in 2001.

9

Non-Deliverable Forwards and Swaps

We introduced foreign exchange forwards, swaps, currency swaps, and single currency interest rate swaps in Chapter 8. These products are very liquid as the daily average turnover is in terms of billions of US dollars. These products are traded among financial institutions, corporations, insurance companies, and others in developed countries and regions. However, liquidity is a major issue for transactions involving foreign exchange spot, forwards, swaps, and other products in some newly developed countries and particularly in most emerging and developing countries. We focus on non-deliverable forwards and swaps of currencies with a lower level of liquidities in this chapter.

This chapter is organized as follows. Section 9.1 introduces briefly the concepts of non-deliverable forwards (NDF); Section 9.2 illustrates how NDFs work, with examples; Section 9.3 introduces the development of the NDF market; Section 9.4 introduces how to use NDFs with examples; Section 9.5 discusses the major items of a standard NDF contract; Section 9.6 introduces non-deliverable swaps (NDSs); Section 9.7 discusses major problems with the NDF and NDS markets; Section 9.8 discusses potential impacts of NDFs trading on the underlying spot market; Section 9.9 introduces major financial institutions participating in NDF and NDS markets; and Section 9.10 introduces services related to NDFs and concludes the chapter.

9.1 Non-Deliverable Forwards

Fluctuations in foreign exchange markets in the past decade, especially during the Asian financial crisis, have highlighted the need for considering currency risk on trade and investment exposures. The foreign exchange forwards market as introduced in Chapter 8 is very liquid for major currencies and can provide good hedging mechanism for hedging and speculating in the foreign exchange market. However, it cannot perform the same function for most currencies of emerging countries and even of some newly developed countries because of either lack of liquidity or other reasons such as foreign exchange regulations in these countries.

NDFs provide an offshore mechanism to hedge currencies that were previously considered "un-hedgeable" without such instruments, either due to the absence of a local forward market or limited foreign access to local currency markets. NDFs are the complement forwards for these currencies.

A good example is the new creation of an NDF market for the Indonesian rupiah. In the past, rupiah forwards were traded actively on the offshore market in Singapore and there was no need for an NDF market. But the capital regulations introduced in January 2002 eliminated offshore trading and resulted in the formation of a new NDF market the following month (the classic example of non-internationalization policies encouraging the formation of an NDF market) (Watanebe, Akama and Mifuni 2002).

An NDF is conceptually similar to an outright forward foreign exchange transaction as introduced in the previous chapter. A notional principal amount, forward exchange rate, and forward date are all agreed upon at the inception of the deal. The difference is that there will be no physical transfer of the principal amount in an NDF transaction and the settlement is normally in US dollars. The deal is agreed on the basis that net settlement will be made in US dollars, or another fully convertible currency, to reflect any differential between the agreed forward rate and the actual exchange rate on the agreed forward date. Simplistically speaking, an NDF is a cash-settled outright forward.

NDFs are synthetic foreign currency forwards contracts on non-convertible currencies or thinly traded currencies. These NDFs allow financial institutions, corporations, and investors to hedge or take exposure to local currency movements of markets such as Eastern and Central Europe currencies and the Pacific Rim currencies without actually dealing in the underlying currencies.

NDFs enable users to hedge currency exposure in foreign exchange markets where forward contracts do not exist owing to exchange controls or other regulatory restrictions. The NDF market allows offshore parties to hedge exchange rate exposures or to speculate on many Asian, African, and Eastern European currencies, without any physical transfer of these currencies and without having to deal in the local market. Therefore, local counterparty risk and the cost of holding accounts in local currencies can be avoided. Further, US dollar-settled NDFs between two offshore counterparties are not generally subject to local monetary controls. Major international financial institutions are active participants in the NDF market: they can provide guidance on hedging with NDFs for their clients.

The demand for NDFs arises principally out of liquidity issues in the underlying currency. Taiwan is a typical example of an NDF market developing out of regulatory necessity. Overseas players had been essentially barred from access to the domestic New Taiwan dollar spot and forward markets until August 6, 2003, when the Taiwan authority (Central Bank of China) authorized offshore banking units (OBUs) to transact NDFs. The local authorities actually see NDFs as a natural progression toward a free capital market. NDFs facilitate trade and investment flows by providing hedging. However, as the NDF does not involve any buying, selling, borrowing, or lending of the Taiwan dollar (TWD), it does not impact the domestic markets directly.

A fixing methodology is agreed upon when an NDF deal is contracted. It specifies how a fixing rate is to be determined on the fixing date, which is normally two working days before settlement, to reflect spot value. Generally, the fixing spot rate is based on a reference page on Reuters or Telerate with a fallback of calling four leading dealers in the relevant market for a quote. Settlement is made in the major currency: paid to, or by, the customer, and it reflects the differential between the agreed forward rate and the fixing spot rare.

9.2 How NDFs Work

Let us show how NDFs work through an example. Assume on September 9, 2003, ABC Corporation sells Korean won 1200 million NDF to XYZ Bank 3 months forward for value December 10, 2003 at the NDF rate of KW/US$1200.00.

By transacting the above, ABC has locked-in the 3-month forward KW selling rate at KW/US$1200.00, which is equivalent to ABC buying US$1 million. (KW 1200 million).

On December 9, 2003, the fixing date, at 11.00 am Seoul time, both parties will compare the NDF rate with the prevailing KW/US$ fixing rate in Telerate. There are three possible scenarios:

a. The prevailing KW/US$ rate is equal to the NDF rate, 1,200.00;
b. The prevailing KW/US$ rate is higher than the NDF rate; and
c. The prevailing KW/US$ rate is lower than the NDF rate.

Scenario (a) Assuming that the prevailing KW/US$ is exactly 1200.00 on December 9, 2003, there is no difference between the NDF and prevailing rate, and hence no payment is made by either party and the NDF expires.

Scenario (b) Assuming that the prevailing KW/US$ is 1250.00 on December 9, 2003, the KW has weakened and there is a difference of KW 50. Hence XYZ Bank will pay the difference to ABC Corporation on the settlement date (December 10, 2003).

As the settlement is in US$, XYZ Bank will have to pay ABC Corporation the difference in US$; the difference is determined as follows.

On September 9, 2003 ABC sells $\dfrac{\text{KW 1,200 million}}{\text{KW/US\$1,200.0}} = \text{US\$1,000,000.00}$

On December 10, 2003 $\dfrac{\text{KW 1,200 million}}{\text{KW/US\$1,250.0}} = \text{US\$960,000.00}$

$1{,}000{,}000.00 - 960{,}000.00 = \text{US\$40,000.00}$ (difference)

Hence on December 10, 2003, XYZ Bank pays US$40,000.00 to ABC Corporation and the NDF is settled. (Note there is no movement of the KW 1,200 million.)

Scenario (c) Assuming that the prevailing KW/US$ is 1,150.00 on December 9, 2003, the KW has strengthened and there is a difference of 50 KW. Hence ABC Corporation will pay the difference to XYZ Bank on the settlement date (December 10, 2003).

On September 9, 2003 ABC sells $\dfrac{\text{KW 1,200 million}}{\text{KW/US\$1,200.0}} = \text{US\$1,000,000.00}$

On December 10, 2003 $\dfrac{\text{KW 1,200 million}}{\text{KW/US\$ PHP 1,150.0}} = \text{US\$1,043,478.26}$

$1{,}043{,}478.26 - 1{,}000{,}000.00 = \text{US\$43,478.26}$ (difference)

Hence on December 10, 2003, ABC Corporation pays US$43,478.26 to XYZ Bank and the NDF is settled.

9.3 Development of the NDF Market

Generally, the non-internationalization of a currency leads to the development and expansion of an offshore NDF market for the currency (see Watanabe, Akama, and Mifuni (2002) for a comprehensive study). NDFs first started to be traded for Latin American currencies and Eastern European currencies in the 1990s, and they became popular for Southeast Asian currencies from the mid of 1990s.

9.3.1 NDF Distribution

According to a survey by IMF (WP/04/4, Canales-Kriljenko (2004)), 59% of the total respondents of developing and transition economies allowed NDF contracts in 2001 compared with 89% who allowed outright forward contracts; and the ratios for the pegged exchange regimes were 33% and 70% for NDF contracts and outright forward contracts. It is obvious that NDF contracts were not as popular as forward contracts.

NDF markets exist in three major regions in the world: for currencies of the Eastern European countries and Russia, those of the Latin American countries, and those of Asian countries. Most of the NDF trading takes place in New York for Latin American currencies, in London for Eastern European and Russian currencies, and in Singapore and Hong Kong for Asian currencies. NDFs are required when non-residents have hedging needs but there is no (or not enough) domestic forward trading or there is a domestic forward market but non-residents are unable to access it. In the case of Latin America and a few other countries and regions, trading taxes and the like raise the costs on the forward market. This has also led to the development of NDF markets.

9.3.2 Market Turnover

NDFs are available in several emerging market currencies. For most of these currencies, NDF prices are quoted for up to 1 year. According to recent data released by the Emerging Market Traders Association (EMTA) on May 14, 2003, the total turnover of NDFs in 14 countries reached US$187 billion in the first quarter of 2003. Table 9.1 lists the total transaction of five major NDFs, the corresponding average daily turnover, and market shares.

Table 9.1 NDF Transactions of Emerging Markets (US$ billion)

		Daily Average	**Market Share (%)**
South Korean Won	87	1.38	50.0
Brazilian real	34	0.54	19.5
Chilean peso	16	0.25	9.2
Taiwan dollar	16	0.25	9.2
PR China yuan	10	0.16	5.7
Others	11	0.17	6.3
Total	174	2.76	100.0

Source: EMTA NDF and Credit Derivatives Surveys First Quarter 2003 (based on 18 survey participants).

The biggest NDF market is the Korean won (KW/US$) and the New Taiwan Dollar (NTD/US$), with daily transactions close to US$250 millions in 1997, and the average daily transaction turnover of KW/US$ is over US$1.25 billion, more than five times as large as it was in 1997. In the first quarter of 2003, the total turnover of the Korean won reached US$87 billion, or 50.0% of the total market share. The second largest Asian NDF market is the New Taiwan Dollar (NTD/US$), with daily transactions close to US$150 million for the New Taiwan Dollar in 1997, and it reached US$250 million in the first quarter of 2003, a nearly 67% increase. The lifting of the ban on local financial institutions trading NDFs in Taiwan in August 2003 will lead to a further increase in transactions in the New Taiwan dollar.

Table 9.2 gives the total NDF turnover and those of major NDFs in the second quarter of 2003. Comparing Tables 9.1 and 9.2, we can see readily that the total NDF turnover increased nearly 84% (the significant increase was partially due to the increase in, survey participants, from 18 to 21) from the first quarter to the second quarter in 2003; Korean won, Brizilian real, and Chilean peso NDFs retained the top positions in the second quarter; and the Peruvian sol and Chilean peso NDFs had the largest surges in the second quarter.

Table 9.2 NDF Transactions of Emerging Markets (US$ billion)

		Growth Rate (%)	Daily Average	Market Share (%)
South Korean won	109	25.3	1.73	34.06
Brazilian real	65	91.2	1.03	20.31
Chilean peso	49	206.3	0.78	15.31
Purovian sol	8.5	2400.0	0.13	2.66
Colombian peso	5.9	1700.0	0.09	1.84
Others	82.6	650.9	1.31	25.81
Total	320	83.9	5.08	100.00

Source: EMTA NDF and Credit Derivatives Surveys Second Quarter 2003 (based on 21 survey participants).

Table 9.3 Asian Currencies by Average Deal Size and Turnover

	Deliverable/ Non-Deliverable Forwards		Offshore Swaps	
	Avg Deal Size ($)	**Avg Daily Turnover ($)**	**Avg Deal Size ($)**	**Avg Daily Turnover ($)**
South Korean won	5 m	1 bn–2 bn	8.5 m	150 m–200 m
Taiwanese dollar	5 m–10 m	250 m	3 m–5 m	0 m–30 m
Singaporean dollar*	20–30 m	1.5 bn–2 bn	30 m	500 m
Thai baht	2 m–5 m	50 m	3 m	10 m–20 m
Philippine peso	2 m	40 m–80 m	3 m	5 m
Indonesian rupiah*	5 m	103 m	3 m	5 m
Hong Kong dollar*	10 m–20 m	5 bn	25 m–50 m	200 m
Chinese yuan	10 m	100 m	na	na

*Statistics refer to onshore markets.
na = not available; m = million; b = billion.
Source: RISK, October 2002, p. 51.

9.3.3 Transaction Sizes

The typical inter-bank transaction size is currently US$2–5 million per trade. Table 9.3 lists the average deal size for major deliverable and non-deliverable forwards markets for major Asian currencies. The average deal size somewhat reflects the market liquidity of the corresponding currency: the higher the liquidity the larger the average deal size (with the only exception of the Chinese yuan). The Singapore and Hong Kong dollars are convertible currencies, and their average deal sizes are larger than those of other currencies.

9.4 Examples of Uses of NDFs

We will illustrate how to use NDFs to hedge foreign exchange risk in foreign investments and to speculate on foreign exchange appreciation with specific examples in this section.

Hedging Foreign Exchange Risk Using NDFs

An investor has invested US$4 million in stocks on the Korean stock market for 1 year. He expects the stock market to rise but is worried about potential KW depreciation. He wishes to hedge his foreign

Table 9.4 NDF Hedging Example

	Outcome A	Outcome B	Outcome C
US dollar/Korean won	Depreciated	—	Appreciated
Fixing spot rate	1350.00	1250.00	1150.00
Equivalent amount ($)	3,703,703.70	4,000,000.00	4,347,826.09
Settlement ($)	Bank pays customer $296,296.30	No net payment	Customer pays bank $347,826.09

exchange exposure using an NDF:

- An NDF rate of KW 1250.00 per US dollar is agreed between a bank and the customer and
- the principal amount is US$4 million.

There are three possible outcomes in 1 year's time: the KW reaches the forward rate, depreciates further, or appreciates relative to the forward rate. Examples of the three scenarios are shown below (Table 9.4).

In all outcomes, the customer has achieved the objective of hedging the KW exposure at 1250.00.

In Outcome A, the exchange loss that the customer would suffer if he sells his investment and exchanges the KW proceeds in the spot market is compensated by the proceeds of the NDF. In Outcome C, the customer's exchange gain on realization of his investment is countered by the payment he makes on the NDF.

Speculating on Foreign Exchange Appreciation Using NDFs

A speculator believes that the Chinese yuan (renminbi or RMB) will appreciate within a year but he cannot buy the RMB in the foreign exchange market because of existing RMB controls. He can simply go to his bank in Singapore, where the offshore foreign exchange market is active, for negotiating an NDF. The spot RMB/US$ rate is 8.26, and the 1-year RMB NDF rate is 2750 pips discounts, and so he buys the RMB NDF at $8.26 - 2600/10000 = 8.00$ with notional principal of US$1.0 million.

There are three possible outcomes in 1 year's time: the RMB reaches the forward rate, appreciates as the NDF rate indicated, or

Table 9.5 NDF Speculating Example

	Outcome A	Outcome B	Outcome C
US dollar/RMB	Depreciated	—	Appreciated
Fixing spot rate	8.36	8.26	8.00
Equivalent amount ($)	988,038.28	1,000,000.00	1,032,500.00
Settlement ($)	Speculator pays bank 11,961.72	No net payment	Bank pays speculator 32,500.00

depreciates relative to the forward rate. Examples of the three scenarios are shown below (Table 9.5).

In Outcome A, the customer suffers exchange loss because the RMB does not appreciate as he expects. In Outcome C, the speculator gains as he expects correctly so as to realize his speculation objective.

9.5 Master Agreement of ISDA

Agreement can be a complicated process for most financial products, especially for OTC financial products, and there is no exception with the NDF although it is simplistic in structure. Problems can arise because of contracting specifications. The good thing is that major industry organizations and committees such as the Foreign Exchange Committee (FEC) and the International Swap and Derivatives Association (ISDA) have been working on improving this situation through setting up master agreements for most products so that problems can be reduced.

As NDFs are essentially foreign exchanges in nature, the FEC has played important roles in this area. To help minimize operational risks, the FEC encourages market participants streamline and automate the confirmation process for NDF trades by adopting the following process changes for trades between inter-bank foreign exchange dealers who use the standard ISDA, International Foreign Exchange Master Agreement (IFEMA), or other master agreements. There are three major master agreements used currently in the NDF market, the FEC master agreement, ISDA Master Agreement, and the Emerging Market Traders Association (EMTA) master agreement. The three major organizations, FEC, ISDA and EMTA, have worked together in standardizing agreements for foreign exchange derivatives including NDFs.

These master agreements establish an agreement of the non-economic terms and definitions related to NDF transactions. They specify mainly the following items:

(1) *Trade terms*

The trade terms include such important terms as trade date, reference currency, reference currency notional amount, notional amount, forward rate, reference country buyer and seller, settlement currency (mostly US$), settlement date, settlement rate options, valuation date, and other terms, including business days applicable to the valuation date and to the settlement date, which are different with different reference currencies.

(2) *Disruption events and fallbacks*

Disruption events normally stand for price source disruption or other events specified in the agreement, and fallbacks may include valuation postponement, calculation agent determination, or other issues. Valuation postponement may be caused by the non-availability of settlement rate because price source disruption ceases to exist on the first business day succeeding the day.

(3) *Calculation Agent*

If the parties are unable to agree on a determination within one business day, each party agrees to be bound by the determination of an independent leading dealer in Reference Currency/Settlement Currency transactions not located in the Reference Currency jurisdiction ("independent leading dealer"), mutually selected by the parties, who shall act as the substitute Calculation Agent, with the fees and expenses of such substitute Calculation Agent (if any) to be met equally by the parties.

(4) *Account details*

The account details include account information of both buyers and sellers.

(5) *Representations*

Representations stand for such terms as non-reliance (acting for its own account, and it has made its own independent decisions to enter into such a transaction and as to whether the transaction is appropriate or proper for it, based upon its own judgment and upon advice from such advisers as it has deemed necessary), assessment, and understanding (it is capable of assessing the merits of and understanding on its own behalf or through independent professional advice and understands and accepts the terms and conditions and risks of such a transaction, and it is also capable of assuming, and assumes, the risks of the transaction).

The EMTA Template Terms for NDF transactions have been supported by the EMTA Foreign Exchange and Money Market Practices Committee (MPC), and they have been used by market participants in many countries/regions, including Hong Kong SAR, where NDFs for many Asian currencies are traded, subject to individual banks' own assessments of their acceptability. This support was expressed to the MPC member associations, including the following:

- Hong Kong Financial Markets Association
- Hong Kong Association of Banks
- Hong Kong Association of Restricted License Banks & Deposit-Taking Companies
- Hong Kong Foreign Exchange and Deposit Brokers' Association.

9.6 Non-Deliverable Swaps

NDSs are a natural progression of NDFs just as swaps are a natural progression of forwards in the foreign exchange market with convertible currencies. Because most NDFs have tenures of one business day to 1 year and also liquidity in the NDF market, especially for longer maturities, they cannot meet the need of many participants for regular multiple transactions. The development of a market for non-deliverable forwards necessarily gives scope for growth in related areas. Thus the establishment of NDF currency swaps is a natural progression. With liquidity in some NDFs up to 5 years (see table), non-deliverable cross-currency swaps provide longer-term hedging solution possibilities.

NDSs are US dollar-settled cross-currency swaps where one leg of the swap is in a non-deliverable currency and with no initial exchange of principal. However, NDSs are written out to 10 years or more, compared with NDFs, which are usually shorter than 1 year.

Most activity is in New Taiwan dollar NDSs — which see five or six trades a week, usually between US$5 million–US$10 million — with some interest in the South Korean won, Philippine peso, and Renminbi swaps.

An NDS resembles a cross-currency swap, except that there is no physical transfer of the underlying currency. The parties agree to exchange a stream of principal and interest payments in a fully convertible currency for a stream of principal and interest payments in a non-deliverable currency, over consecutive interest periods until maturity. The settlement procedures are similar to those for an NDF. The fixing rate for each period is used to convert the principal and interest payments in the restricted currency to an equivalent amount in the convertible currency. The difference is then settled in the convertible currency.

9.7 Problems with NDFs and NDSs

We have discussed several advantages of NDFs in hedging and speculating over their corresponding forward markets if they exist and over spot markets because of taxation, regulations, currency controls, and other reasons. It is these advantages that have made them so popular in the marketplace, and successes in many currencies despite government restrictions. However, there are also a lot of problems with NDF market. We simply discuss these major problems in this section.

(1) *Liquidity*

Liquidity is a natural problem with most NDFs because they came into existence because of a lack of liquidity in the onshore market and/or regulatory reasons. With the exception of major NDF markets such as those of the Korean won, New Taiwan dollar, and Brazilian real, where liquidity is not of a major problem, liquidity can be a serious problem for most other NDFs, especially when the underlying markets are volatile. If NDF buyers want to unwind contracts before maturity, there may not be the liquidity for them to do so. As long as the underlying markets are stable, liquidity should be provided for the clients, especially with institutions that have a commitment to trading the underlying foreign exchanges.

(2) *Pricing*

Pricing NDFs is probably the most difficult part of the NDF business. This again results from the non-internationalization of the underlying foreign exchange markets. Pricing structures vary according to the extent of the development of the local interest rate mechanism, the local money market, and also the degree of overseas access to that market. The "arbitrage-free" principle with which we priced foreign exchange forwards of convertible currencies in the previous chapter cannot be used to price NDFs simply because most of the conditions or assumptions are not satisfied for most local currencies on which most NDFs are written. The arbitrage-free principle represents the ideal case for pricing NDFs.

Another extreme method of pricing NDFs is the standard economic principle of "supply and demand", from which prices of any "commodities" or "products" can be determined by the equilibrium at which supply of the "commodity" equals the corresponding demand for it. For example, NDFs on the Vietnamese dong have to be priced without reference to the local money market because there does not exist such a market in Vietnam. This means that the dong NDF market is driven essentially by supply and demand. If there is no interest in dong structures at a particular price, a bank can negotiate with potential counterparties to achieve a satisfactory price. Where the domestic money market is underdeveloped, liquidity in the NDF market will also be low.

The same principle has also been used around the world to price the Chinese yuan (renminbi) since late 2002 because market fundamentals have not changed much from 2002 to 2003, yet renminbi NDF prices have changed from an over 1,000 pips premium to more than 5,000 pips discounts within about 2 years. We will discuss this further in Part IV of this book.

NDF pricing in the more developed markets (between the ideal convertible case to price forwards using the arbitrage-free method and the supply–demand case), such as the South Korean, Taiwan, Czech, and Polish markets, is more transparent.

Due to the lack of data, there have been few empirical studies as to what factors affect NDF prices in different countries, and fewer satisfactory theoretical studies on how to price NDFs. The satisfactory model of pricing NDFs should include such factors as the degree of money market development, degree of currency controls, liquidity of the underlying, difficulty in accessing the underlying market, and so on. This is beyond the scope of this book, and we leave it for special studies.

(3) *Hedging problem*

Another immediate problem remaining with NDFs is how to hedge them. Instruments are not available to offset either the foreign exchange or interest rate risk for the duration of the deals, and so institutions have to roll short-term positions over. More often, financial institutions look to do offsetting deals with investors or hedgers with different views. Yet, appropriate deals may not be easy to match.

(4) *Policy change risk*

One documentation issue that all contracts cover is what happens should a local currency cease to exist. The equivalent new currency will generally take the place. While NDFs are not subject directly to convertibility risk, convertibility changes can impact the value of NDFs. For example, the market rate of a currency will be impacted if the country moves from convertibility to a more restrictive regime, as in the case of Malaysia during the Asian financial crisis in 1997.

Another example of the policy change risk is enaction of the Argentina Exchange Law in 2002. On January 6, 2002, Argentina enacted its Public Emergency and Exchange Rate Reform Law, which announced a new foreign exchange policy, and indicated that its foreign exchange market should be open on January 9, 2002. This legal change caused Argentine peso NDFs to be unable to be priced.

(5) *Transaction costs*

Transaction Cost remains a problem for many NDFs because it can be expensive to do such transactions. Commission charges can vary from 5% to 10% for each transaction, depending upon the liquidity of the market and other factors.

(6) *Legal issues*

Despite the efforts of the Foreign Exchange Committee, ISDA, EMTA to standardize the NDF agreements, confusion could arise if the relevant fixing rate against which the NDS settles disappears, and different onshore and offshore spot markets spring up, or other issues uncovered by the agreements arise. Although the probability of this is small, after the situation in Malaysia, where currency controls were imposed in September 1997, you cannot be sure what will happen to your contracts — especially with longer-dated deals. While such low-probability events are unlikely to blow up the whole deal, the work-out process can eat quickly out of your profit margin.

9.8 Impacts of NDFs and NDSs

Derivatives could have a variety of impacts on their corresponding underlying markets: they may affect the prices/returns, volumes of the underlying markets, volatilities of the underlying assets, and others. The impacts can be particularly significant when derivatives approach maturity. There have been numerous studies on these effects since the introduction of financial derivatives. Although most of these studies conclude that derivatives have stabilizing effects on the underlying markets, there are also studies with destabilizing evidence. Interested readers can refer to Zhang (2003) for a survey of this literature.

Because of the lack of market data as for most OTC derivatives, there is little empirical evidence as to how NDFs affect their corresponding underlying foreign exchange markets. One extreme argument is that NDFs do not have any effect on the underlying local currencies because all NDFs are settled in convertible currencies such as US dollars. This argument may hold true for those NDFs with a thin turnover, and it is very difficult to access the local currencies. NDFs with moderate turnovers can have significant impacts on the local currencies.

In studying the pros and cons of measures to limit offshore use of currencies, Ishii, Otker-Robe, and Cui (2001) find good arguments supporting the idea that NDFs can affect the local currencies. Hedging, particularly speculative activities, can affect local foreign exchange markets. Foreign exchange rates formed in the NDF market affect the domestic market by the following routes.

(A) *Arbitrage between domestic and offshore markets*
When residents (domestic banks) are allowed to participate in the offshore NDF market, domestic banks will trade local currency on domestic foreign exchange markets in order to adjust positions taken in NDF trades.

(B) *Adjustment of consolidated positions within a bank*
If, for example, a customer of the Singapore branch of Bank A brings in an NDF baht sale, the branch may not cover the NDF. Instead, it may have the Bangkok branch of Bank A cover it on the Bangkok market, which will therefore influence the domestic foreign exchange market in Thailand. The scope for such trading will be limited, however, as there are position limits on the Bangkok branch of Bank A.

(C) *Market sentiment*
Trends on the NDF market will influence the sentiment of participants on the domestic foreign exchange market.

Authorities basically do not have the means of directly controlling offshore derivative products like NDFs. They can, however, insulate themselves from arbitrage between the NDF market and the domestic market by banning domestic banks from participating in the NDF market. Authorities can also issue negative messages regarding the expansion of the NDF market, which may reduce the incentives for active market making in the offshore market by foreign banks with branches in the country (this is a form of moral suasion). Still, NDFs are one potential route for speculation in emerging currencies, and so authorities must monitor trends carefully.

The Czech koruna and Polish zloty markets are two good examples of how NDFs can affect local currencies. The Czech koruna is now a convertible currency. But many users still use the NDF market. The basic reason for this is that large deals can impact local pricing. Just as in the Polish zloty market, a deal of US$75 million can be handled by an offshore player, whereas if that went through the Prague or Warsaw market, it would impact prices. A frequent and active player in offshore NDFs will take some of the risk on its own books rather than hedging the whole deal through the domestic market, which would consequently move it. See Thompson (1998, 2001) for a detailed discussion.

The Taiwan dollar NDF market also provides evidence that NDFs affect the local currencies. Taiwan's central bank had on occasion covertly intervened in the NDF market to iron out anomalies of huge differences between onshore forwards and offshore NDFs. In May 1998 the Central Bank closed the doors of NDF trading for domestic businessmen in order to ease the speculative pressure on the New Taiwan dollar. Taiwan has seen volatility in its spot market fall considerably after it allowed onshore banks to trade NDFs in August 2003.

South Korea could be labeled a success as NDFs coexist and can be traded within the country, and yet there has been no turbulence in its exchange market. We will return to this when we study what roles foreign exchange derivatives played during the Asian financial crisis, in Part III of this book.

9.9 Institutions Trading NDFs and NDSs

Most major banks offer NDFs in their emerging market departments. According to RISK magazine, JP Morgan Chase, Citibank, Standard Chartered, and Deutsche Bank are the top banks trading Korean won NDFs, Twaiwan dollar NDFs, and other NDFs; and the corresponding brokers for these major NDFs are Nittan AP and Prebon Yamane. The specific survey data are given in Table 9.6. Table 9.6 first indicates that the top banks for major Asian NDFs are stable for the three catogories with Standard Chartered Bank falling from No. 1 in all catogories in 2001 to No. 3 in 2002.

Another observation from Table 9.6 is that the market share is less concentrated with the top three banks for NDFs with a larger turnover (44% for Korean won NDF, 48% for Taiwan NDF, and 62% for other currencies) because there are more institutions participating in the markets with a higher turnover.

Table 9.6 Top Participants of Major Asian NDFs in 2002 and 2001

2002	2001	Bank	Percentage
Currency: Korean won			***Banks cited 14***
1	2	JP Morgan Chase	16
2	3	Citibank	14
3	1	Standard Chartered	12
		Total	44
		Broker	Nittan AP
Currency: Taiwan dollar			***Banks cited 12***
1	2	Deutsche Bank	20
2	3	JP Morgan Chase	16
3	1	Standard Chartered	12
		Total	48
		Broker	Prebon Yamane
Currency: Others		***Banks cited 10***	
1	2	Deutsche Bank	24
2	3	JP Morgan Chase	23
3	1	Standard Chartered	15
		Total	62
		Broker	Prebon Yamane

Data source: Asia Risk 2002.

9.10 Services to NDF/NDS Market

There are quite a few problems involving NDFs and NDSs as we discussed in Section 9.6. Some of these problems are not easy to resolve. Major futures exchanges have been approached to resolve some of these problems.

In August 1998, representatives from the NDF Russian ruble per US dollar market discussed the problems associated with a lack of a fixing for the Russian rouble per US dollar trading at the Moscow Inter-Bank Currency Exchange (MICEX). This rate was the standard "settlement rate" for NDF contracts for Russian roubles per US dollar, and the rate Chicago Mercantile Exchange (CME) used to settle its Russian rouble futures and options on futures contracts. As a result of this telephone conference call, CME was asked in collaboration with EMTA to conduct a daily survey to produce a daily reference rate. This reference rate (CME/EMTA Reference Rate) is published on a daily basis for informational purposes only via Reuters' page "EMTA," and CME also distributes the CME/EMTA Reference Rate through its normal quote distribution channels. On Friday, September 11, 1998, the International Swaps and Derivatives Association (ISDA), EMTA, and the Foreign Exchange Committee approved the addition of the CME/EMTA Reference Rate (from Reuters' page "EMTA") as another Russian rouble rate source for Annex A of the 1998 FX and Currency Option Definitions. This action enables settlement of rouble/dollar NDF transactions to the CME/EMTA Reference Rate. Please see www.cme.org.com for more detailed information.

10

Foreign Exchange Futures

"Futures markets, as their name implies, should provide a glimpse into the future. However, in truth, they often don't. The future is habitually too clouded and burdened with too many imponderables to be seen clearly."

Leo Melamed (Chairman Emeritus, CME) November 7, 1991

In 1986, Merton Miller, the 1990 Nobel Laureate in Economics, proclaimed the introduction of financial futures as "the most significant financial innovation of the last 20 years." As a consequence of this innovation, futures markets were completely transformed, experienced unparalleled growth, and became an established and indispensable tool in financial risk management. These futures markets served as the primordial soup from which today's gigantic financial derivatives markets evolved.

Foreign exchange futures contracts, firstly introduced to the International Monetary Market (IMM) of Chicago Mercantile Exchange (CME) in 1972, represents the first financial futures in the world. Financial futures on many other underlying instruments have been introduced since then. The trading volume in futures has expanded more than 20-fold during the past twenty years. According to statistics of the Bank for International Settlements, the total open interest of all financial futures around the world surpassed US$41 trillion in 2002 (see Table 10.5 of this chapter), about 30% more than the world GDP of the same year.

In this chapter we will introduce foreign exchange futures, and the differences between futures and forwards. Our purpose in this chapter is to provide a brief picture of the foreign exchange futures market.

This chapter is organized as follows: Section 10.1 introduces foreign exchange futures; Section 10.2 describes major characteristics of the futures contracts and futures markets; Section 10.3 describes briefly the major functions of foreign exchange futures; Section 10.4 outlines the differences between foreign exchange forwards and futures; Section 10.6 discusses foreign exchange futures in emerging economies; and Section 10.7 concludes the chapter.

10.1 Introduction

The early 1970s experienced two significant events in the history of the world economy. One was the abolition of the Bretton Woods agreement (which managed foreign exchange rates), and the other was the oil crisis resulting from the Organization of Petroleum Export Countries' (OPEC) oil embargo. As a result of these two historical events, financial risks increased dramatically as exchange rates fluctuated more vehemently and the inflation soared with two digits. Financial innovations aimed originally at hedging these increased risks.

The establishment of the International Monetary Market (IMM) by the CME in 1972 marked one of the most important landmarks in the history of financial derivatives. To meet the need to hedge the increased currency risks resulting from the abolition of the Bretton Woods agreement in the early 1970s, the IMM started to trade futures on foreign currencies in 1972.

The currency futures contracts somehow stimulated all other financial futures that followed. CBOT launched futures contracts on the Government National Mortgage Association-Collateralized Depository Receipt (or GNMA-CDR) in October 1975. However, the GNMA-CDR contracts were not as successful as the second futures

Table 10.1 History of Futures Trading

1972	Currency futures	IMM/CME
1975	GNMA-certificates futures	CBOT
1976	90-day T-bill futures	CME
1977	US treasury bond futures	CBOT
1981	Eurodollar futures	IMM
1982	Stock index futures	KBOT, CME, NYFE
1985	Municipal index futures	CBOT
1988	5-year US Treasury Note futures	CBOT
1989	30-day interest rate futures	CBOT
1992	3-month eurodollar futures and options	CME
2001	Equity futures	LIFFE

Source: Zhang (1995).

contract launched by the CBOT, the futures on the US Treasury Bonds, on August 22, 1977. The Treasury Bonds futures was the most actively traded futures contracts in the world.

Although the first financial futures came into existence in the United States in 1972, it took about three decades for equity futures to be traded in the United Kingdom, in 2001, and the United States, in 2002. Table 10.1 outlines the launching of major financial futures contracts in corresponding exchanges and time. Futures contracts have been launched on most financial assets, ranging from equity to stock indices, currency, bond, bond indices, precious metals, and so on.

10.2 Foreign Exchange Futures

Commodity futures contracts are standardized commodity forward contracts in which the quality of commodity, the amount of commodity, and the place and the time of deliver of the commodity are all standardized by exchanges. For example, the notional value or contract size of one US dollar/Japanese yen futures contract is 12.5 million at IMM.

Buyers and sellers of futures contracts do not even meet to make their transactions, they buy or sell through exchanges. There is no money changing hands at the time when contracts are signed as in the case of forwards. All futures exchanges, however, require participants to deposit some money as a symbol of good faith before they are allowed to trade. The required deposit is called the margin requirements. Once you deposit your money and set up your account, you have met your initial margin requirement and you may start to trade. Losses and gains of all the futures contracts are marked to the market daily, or they are settled daily at each day's close. Margin requirements actually protect exchanges from the possible bankruptcy of participants.

In cash markets, all contract terms are open to negotiation: product quality or grade, delivery location, time of delivery, mode of delivery, price, and the transactions are negotiated and fulfilled at one instant. In forward cash contracts, these terms are also negotiable, now but the execution can be carried out at some time in the future as specified by the forward contract. Because forward contracts are not "standardized", it is difficult to change one's position once it is specified in the agreement.

In futures contracts, however, the delivery unit is standardized in terms of quantity, quality, delivery time, place and mode; the transactions are executed nearly instantaneously in an organized exchange; the sale can be offset at any time between the date of original transaction and the date of delivery by buying the required number of contracts; delivery and fulfillment are guaranteed by the exchange; and the cost of transaction is minimal.

Table 10.2 lists the major currency futures contracts trading in major exchanges in the world. We can observe that CME is the largest currency futures exchange in the world, with 10 major currency futures contracts covering all major currencies of the world, and the total market share was 58.9%. The second largest exchange for currency futures was BM&F, with 36.7% of the total market share. These two exchanges have more than 90% of the total market share.

10.3 Foreign Exchange Futures Trading Volumes

With the introduction of currency options at IMM in 1972, currency futures trading volumes have increased steadily in the past three decades. Table 10.3 gives the total turnover of currency futures from 1987 to 2002. We can easily find that the total turnover reached

Table 10.2 Currency Futures Volume and Exchanges in 2003

Contract	Exchange	Volume	Percentage of Total
US dollar	BM&F	1399.86	35.2
Euro FX	CME	112.41	2.8
Japanese yen	CME	730.98	18.4
Canadian dollar	CME	393.33	9.9
Swiss franc	CME	349.89	8.8
British pounds	CME	284.47	7.1
Mexican peso	CME	238.17	6.0
Australian dollar	CME	187.25	4.7
US dollar	Kofex	98.98	2.5
Mini US dollar	BM&F	60.17	1.5
Euro/Japanese yen	Nybot	36.15	0.9
Euro FX/JY Cross rate	CME	23.73	0.6
Euro/Swiss franc	Nybot	19.67	0.5
New Zealand dollar	CME	15.41	0.4
Euro/British pound	Nybot	9.22	0.2
South African rand	CME	7.07	0.2
Large Euro/US dollar	Nybot	7.05	0.2
Euro/Canadian dollar	Nybot	6.71	0.2
Total		3980.52	100.0

Source: Futures & Options Weekly.

Table 10.3 Total Turnover (Notional Amounts) of All Exchange Currency Futures (Unit: US$ trillion)

Year	**1987**	**1988**	**1989**	**1990**	**1991**	**1992**	**1993**	**1994**
Total turnover	1.8	2.0	2.2	2.7	2.5	2.4	2.8	3.2
Annual growth rate (%)		8.1	11.5	24.2	−7.1	−5.8	17.0	14.5
Year	**1995**	**1996**	**1997**	**1998**	**1999**	**2000**	**2001**	**2002**
Total turnover	3.2	2.7	2.7	2.5	2.6	2.4	2.5	2.5
Annual growth rate (%)	−0.3	−17.3	3.2	−7.1	1.7	−6.5	3.4	0.4

Data source: Derivatives statistics, international financial statistics, Bank for International Settlement, 2003.

maturity from 1987 to 2002 because the accumulative average annual growth rate from 1987 to 2002 was merely 1.98%. The total turnover given in Table 10.3 is much smaller than the corresponding forwards turnover given in Table 8.1. For example, the corresponding annual turnover in 2001 from Table 8.1 was $32.75 trillion, and the futures turnover given in Table 10.3 is merely 7.63% of total turnover of forwards.

10.4 Differences between Forwards and Futures

We described forwards and futures briefly in the previous sections, and it is necessary for us to notice the major differences between forwards and futures. The major differences are summarized as follows:

(i) delivery unit is standardized in terms of quantity, quality, delivery time, place, and mode in all futures contracts, yet they are open for negotiations in forward contracts;
(ii) futures transactions are executed nearly instantaneously in an organized exchange, so liquidity is high for futures, yet it is difficult to change hands for forwards;
(iii) sale can be offset at any time between the date of original transaction and the date of delivery by buying the required number of contracts for futures, yet it is not feasible for forwards;
(iv) delivery and fulfillment are guaranteed by the exchange for futures but not for forwards, and thus counterparty risk is much lower for futures contracts compared with forwards;
(v) the cost of transaction is minimal for futures contracts;
(vi) an initial margin is required for futures trading, but there is no such requirements for forwards; and
(vii) a maintenance margin is required for futures trading, and the trader is subject to margin calls daily for futures, but there is no such requirement for forwards.

Although it is generally true that liquidity is higher in the futures market than in the corresponding forward market, largely because of the counterparty risk of forwards, it is not true for the foreign exchange market. The forward market has a much higher turnover than the corresponding futures market, as seen from the data of Chapter 9; this is because counterparty risk is relatively minimal in the inter-bank forward market.

10.5 Major Functions of Futures Market

10.5.1 Managing Risk

After introducing futures on major underlying assets, we can summarize the major functions of futures. The most important role of the futures markets is to provide a mechanism for managing risk, principally price risk. Producers, distributors, and users of physical commodities — as well as those exposed to fluctuations in financials such as currencies, interest rates, and stock index values — use futures contracts to hedge their exposure to risk. If the underlying market is expected to fall, the cheaper and more effective way of hedging the underlying market is sell futures contracts. Thus, disruption of a futures market can cause significant economic hardship for the users of these hedging tools.

10.5.2 Price Discovery

The other important function that futures markets perform is price discovery: they enable other markets to discover appropriate prices for commodities (and the products or services derived from commodities) by referencing quoted futures market transactions. Businesses, investors, and even government entities throughout the economy depend upon these important price discovery mechanisms. Thus, disruption of a futures market can cause widespread economic hardship for those who look to it for price discovery information.

10.5.3 Information Dissemination

Because of the leverage effects, futures markets react to various sorts of market information more quickly than their underlying markets, and thus futures markets normally lead their underlying markets in receiving information. Thus, futures markets improve market efficiency in digesting market information.

10.6 FX Futures in Developing Economies

According to an IMF (WP/04/4, Canales-Kriljenko (2004)) survey, only the currencies of a limited number of developing economies can be traded in major international exchanges and over the electronic networks created by international vendors. In particular, futures contracts on the currencies of Brazil, Mexico, Russia, and South Africa are listed on the Chicago Mercantile Exchange (CME).

South Africa also allows futures trading of the rand in the New York Board of Trade exchange. Any dealer with access to Reuters' broking systems can trade the currencies of the eight developing economies listed in them. The same applies to the currencies of Mexico and Singapore traded through EBS Spot (EBS), the electronic broking system provided by EBS Partnership, Inc., as well as to the currencies of the countries that permit offshore trading of their currencies, and have banks that make use of Reuters dealing systems.

10.7 Conclusions

The turnover of foreign exchange futures is much smaller than their corresponding forwards trading in the OTC marketplace. The turnover of futures of emerging market currencies is much smaller. Despite the smaller scale, foreign exchange futures markets are performing functions for the market participants that cannot be easily obtained from the OTC market.

11

Foreign Exchange Options

Although launched about 1 year later than the first financial futures contract, the younger brother — options have grown faster than its elder brother in terms of either trading volume or open interest. Options have been trading on essentially all financial assets, and they are basic building blocks for many other types of more sophisticated financial products. Table 11.1 shows that total turnover of all options trading in all exchanges around the world in terms of notional amounts. The total turnover of all options surpassed US$240 trillion in 2003, about 30% higher than the corresponding figure in all exchanges in 2002.

Materials on options are so extensive that it takes a few volumes to cover various aspects of their theoretical and practical properties. The purpose of this chapter is to introduce foreign exchange options trading at both exchanges and the OTC market place. We try, however, to provide a simple description of the basic foreign exchange options in this chapter.

This chapter is organized as follows: Section 11.1 introduces the basic concept of options; Section 11.2 introduces the two kinds of options — call options and put options; Section 11.3 explains option

Table 11.1 Total Turnover of All Exchange Traded Options from 1988 to 2003 (Unit: US$ trillion)

Year	1988	1989	1990	1991	1992	1993	1994	1995
Total turnover	9.3	17.0	22.4	24.6	33.1	40.4	55.9	53.4
Growth rate	−9.9%	82.9%	31.4%	9.9%	34.2%	22.3%	38.4%	−4.5%
Year	**1996**	**1997**	**1998**	**1999**	**2000**	**2001**	**2002**	**2003**
Total turnover	52.4	61.9	70.5	62.2	66.4	148.4	191.3	249.0
Growth rate	−1.9%	18.2%	13.8%	−11.8%	6.7%	123.6%	28.9%	30.2%

Data source: International financial statistics, Derivatives statistics, Bank for International Settlement, 2002, www.bis.org.

premiums; Section 11.4 compares briefly futures and options contracts; Section 11.5 introduces options on foreign exchange futures; Section 11.6 introduces non-standard or exotic options in the foreign exchange market; Section 11.7 discusses briefly foreign exchange options in emerging markets; and Section 11.8 concludes the chapter.

11.1 Introduction

Options on individual stocks were introduced in the first options exchange, the Chicago Board of Options Exchange (CBOE), in October 1973, 1 year later than the first financial futures contract at IMM of CME. Options have been introduced on most financial assets and markets since then.

Options were introduced to the foreign exchange market first in Philadelphia in 1982, 10 years later than the first futures contracts introduced at IMM. The currency options first introduced at Philadelphia exchange (PHLX) carry specified contract terms for features such as contract size, strike price intervals, expiration dates, price quoting, and premium settlement. PHLX offers standardized options on six major currencies, with either American- or European-style exercises; maturities available range from monthly to as long as 2 years, with a choice of mid-month or month-end expiration. PHLX is currently allowing users to customize all aspects of a currency option trade, including choice of exercise price, customized expiration dates of up to 2 years, and premium quotation as either units of currency or percent of underlying value.

Table 11.2 Total Turnover (Notional Amounts) of All Exchange Currency Options (Unit: US$ billion)

Year	**1987**	**1988**	**1989**	**1990**	**1991**	**1992**	**1993**	**1994**
Total turnover	996.1	1069.7	1151.4	1252.6	1429.1	1420.4	1431.2	1393.9
Annual growth rate (%)	7.4	7.6	8.8	14.1	−0.6	0.8	−2.6	
Year	**1995**	**1996**	**1997**	**1998**	**1999**	**2000**	**2001**	**2002**
Total Turnover	1326.3	1293.5	884.3	543.7	288.6	211.8	356.0	421.7
Annual growth rate (%)	4.8	−2.5	−31.6	−38.5	−46.9	−26.6	68.1	18.5

Data source: Derivatives statistics, International financial statistics, Bank for International Settlement, 2004.

Table 11.2 gives the total turnover of all exchange currency options from 1987 to 2003. The total turnover increased steadily from 1987 to 1991, declined slightly from 1992 to 1997, and then declined dramatically from 1997 to 2000. Yet it began to come back from 2000 to 2003.

11.2 Call and Put Options

There are different ways of classifing options according to their characteristics. Most often, they are classified as call options and put options. A call option is a financial contract that gives its buyer or holder the right to buy the underlying asset at a pre-specified price at or within a pre-specified time. This pre-specified price is called the exercise price or strike price of the option, and the pre-specified time is called the time-to-maturity, time-to-expiration, or tenor of the option. If the option can only be exercised at expiration, it is a European-style option; if it can be exercised either at or before expiration, it is an American option. The buyer of an option is also called the holder of the option, and the seller the writer of the option. Figure 11.1 depicts the payoff of a European call option with strike price 0.80 US dollar/Euro.

A put option, on the other hand, is a financial contract that gives its buyer or holder the right to sell the underlying asset at a pre-specified price at or within a pre-specified time. If the put option can

Figure 11.1 Payoff of a European Call Option

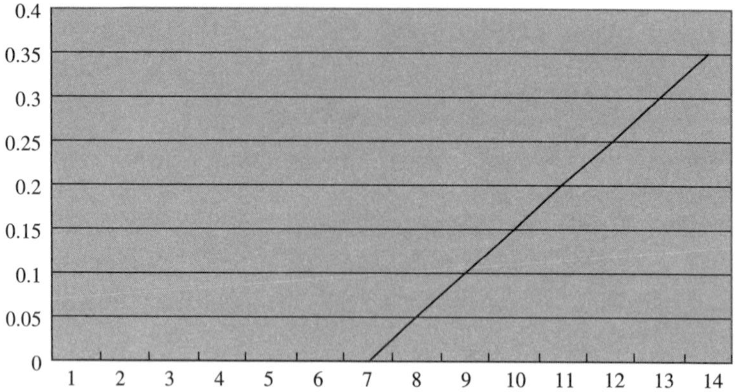

Figure 11.2 Payoff of a European Put Option

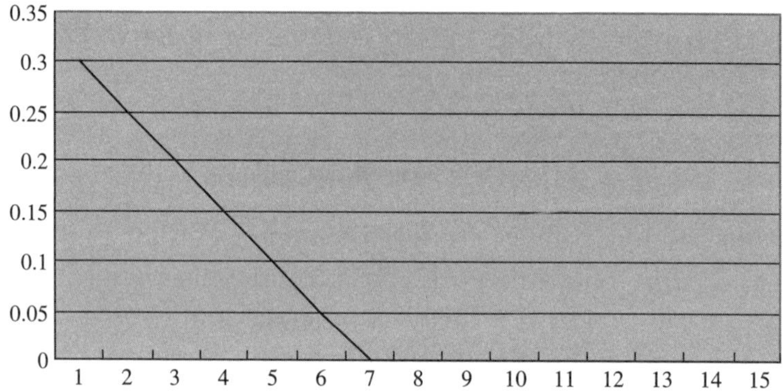

only be exercised at expiration, it is a European put option; otherwise it is an American put option. Buying a put option is similar to buying an insurance contract. Figure 11.2 depicts the payoff of a European put option with strike price 0.80 US dollar/Euro.

Compared with the payoff pattern of a European call option given in Figure 11.1, there is also one kinked point at the strike price in the put option's payoff diagram. However, the line is upward to the left rather than to the right as in the case of a European call option. The difference between the strike price and the underlying asset price at maturity is called the intrinsic value of the put option.

There is a very important difference between options and futures. Whereas a futures contract represents obligations on both sides of the contract, an option contract represents the right of the holder to buy and the obligation to the seller. Thus, if the price of the underlying asset is higher than the strike price at or before the expiration time, the call option (American) holder can simply exercise the right to take a profit by buying the underlying currency at the strike price and selling it at the higher market price. If the market price falls below the strike price, the holder can simply let the call option expire without doing anything.

11.3 Options Premiums

From the definition of a call option, we know that the buyer of the option has a positive expected payoff because the worst case is the situation when the option expires worthless, and the best case is the situation when he/she can obtain unlimited payoff if the stock price rises unlimitedly. On the other hand, the seller or writer of the call option has a negative expected payoff as he/she has to meet the obligation to sell the underlying asset at the strike price even if it is lower than the market price. There is no such thing as a free lunch for either the buyer or the writer (seller). Unlike the forwards or futures buyer, who does not pay any money, the option buyer has to pay some money to the writer to compensate the prospective loss. The amount of money the option buyer pays the writer is called the premium of the option. Thus, the worst case for the option buyer is that he/she loses the premium when the option expires worthless. That is why it is often said that call options have limited liabilities (the premiums) and unlimited payoffs or returns. In order to obtain the right to buy or sell the underlying assets, option buyers have to pay some money to compensate the writer.

All European options including currency options can be priced with the celebrated Black–Scholes pricing formula. Most textbooks on options have this formula, and we do not wish to repeat it here. Interested readers may refer to Zhang (1998) for the Black–Scholes pricing formula and its most popular extensions.

There are six parameters involved in the pricing formula: spot exchange rate, strike price, domestic and foreign interests, time to maturity, and volatility of the exchange rate. There are many studies on how to price options, yet it is beyond the scope of this book. Interested readers may refer to Zhang (1998b) on pricing various types of options.

11.4 Major Differences between Futures and Options Contracts

Options and futures share a lot of characteristics such as being written on the same underlying instruments, leverage effects, hedging functions, and so on. Yet, they are quite different in a number of aspects. It is not the purpose of this section to present a thorough comparison; we simply want to point out here the major differences between them in this section.

First, an option, when purchased, gives the buyer the right, but not the obligation, to buy or sell a specific amount of a specific asset at a specific price within a specific period of time. In comparison, a futures contract requires a buyer or seller to perform under the terms of the contract if an open position is not offset before expiration. In other words, the buyer of a futures contract is always obligated to add additional margins if the contract price moves to the opposite direction (if it goes down for a buyer or up for a seller).

Second, the option buyer has to pay a premium upfront to obtain the right, but the futures buyer needs only deposit the required initial margin and variation margin; the margin deposits are actually the buyer's own money. And the option seller (writer) needs to deposit a certain required margin in case the underlying asset price goes in the opposite direction, as for futures.

Third, the purchaser of the option can lose no more than the initial amount of money invested (premium). However, that is not the case for the buyer of a futures contract: the loss can be significant if the underlying asset price falls significantly.

Finally, an option buyer is never subject to margin calls. This enables the purchaser to maintain a market position, despite any adverse moves, without putting up additional funds. However, the corresponding option seller or writer is subject to margin calls as futures because the seller is obligated to execute his/her obligations.

11.5 Currency Futures Options

Our examples in the previous sections are actually options on exchange rates. They are foreign exchange options, currency options, or cash options. There are other popular currency options. we will introduce these options briefly in this section.

Currency options written on underlying exchange rates are actually not as actively trading as currency options written on currency futures that are actively trading in CME on CME currency futures contracts. As futures prices are generally more volatile than their corresponding spot prices because they reflect uncertainty from current time to maturity of futures contracts, options trading on futures are generally more active than options written on spot prices.

11.6 Exotic Foreign Exchange Options

11.6.1 Vanilla vs Exotic Options

We have introduced foreign exchange options and foreign exchange futures options in previous sections of this chapter. All the options are standard options or vanilla options trading at organized exchanges around the world. With the development of options, vanilla options cannot satisfy the needs of many clients, and the concept of standard options has been extended in almost every aspect of vanilla options. A lot of financial institutions are trading many such options in the over-the-counter (OTC) marketplace. These options trading at the OTC marketplace are generally called second generation options, or exotic options. It will take a lot of time to introduce all exotic options because of their variety and functionalities; interested readers may refer to Zhang (1998b) for a comprehensive introduction and analysis of most exotic foreign exchange options.

11.6.2 Development of Exotic Options

In some sense, exotic options are not new to the financial markets. Some came into existence several years before the birth of the

CBOE in 1973 (see Zhang (1998b)). The trading volume for standard options was rather thin in the pre-CBOE era, and the trading volume for non-standard options was even thinner. A few years after the establishment of CBOE, a slow and inconspicuous revolution in the options concept and trading started to take place. Toward the end of the 1970s and the beginning of the 1980s, when standard options trading at exchanges became better understood and their trading volume exploded, financial institutions began to search for alternative options forms to meet their clients' particular needs and increase their businesses. All these alternative options are called second generation options or exotic options.

Second generation options or exotic options are also called special-purpose options or customer-tailored options, implying that each type of exotic option can somehow serve a special purpose that standard options cannot. These names somehow explain why exotic options came into existence and why they have grown significantly in variety and volumes. Although there are many different kinds of exotic options, all of them are, in one way or another, either direct or indirect extension of standard options.

In the late 1980s and early 1990s, exotic options became more visible in the daily press and more popular among the financial community. Their trading has become more active in the OTC marketplace, and their users have been big corporations, financial institutions, fund managers, and recently private bankers.

11.6.3 Major FX Exotic Options

FX barrier options are the most popular FX options. A barrier FX option is essentially a conditional option in the sense that a standard call or put option is obtained if a pre-specified barrier (up barrier if it is greater than the spot rate and lower barrier if it is lower than the corresponding spot rate) is reached within the life of the barrier option, and a fixed rebate is given if the barrier is not reached.

Average rate options are also called Asian options. The only difference between an average rate option and standard option is that its payoff is determined by the average rates of the underlying FX rates within a given period of time with a given frequency of observations.

The average rate can either replace the settlement FX rate or the fixed exercise rate, depending on the nature of the options. Asian options are the second most popular FX exotic options as they serve the needs of exporters and importers for hedging their positions conveniently.

Digital options are also called binary options. Payoffs of digital options are most often a fixed amount or nothing. There are many types of FX binary options, FX barrier options, FX average rate options, and other types of FX exotic options, but it is beyond the scope of this book to introduce such options in details. Interested readers may refer to Zhang (1998a) for a comprehensive study of such options.

11.6.4 Turnovers of Major FX Exotic Options

Table 11.3 gives the major types of foreign exchange exotic options by various currency pairs in 2001. It can be clearly seen that barrier options are the most popular foreign exchange exotic options, with average rate options and binary/digital options following barrier options.

11.7 Foreign Exchange Options in Emerging Markets

Most of the FX options we have introduced so far are FX options in developed markets or with currencies in the developed economies. FX options are not so widely used in emerging economies. Table 11.4 gives the survey results of 90 emerging markets on four major types of FX derivatives. We can observe that FX options are more popular than FX futures, with 77% of the respondents permitting options and 61% permitting futures.

We can also observe from Table 11.4 that FX forwards are the most popular products in the emerging market with either pegged or intermediate exchange rate regimes, FX options and FX futures represent the second and third most popular types of products, and NDF contracts are the least favored product of all respondents.

Table 11.5 gives the notional amounts outstanding of the OTC- and exchange-traded FX derivatives in the three major regions of

Table 11.3 Exotic Foreign Exchange Options by Currency Pair and Product Category for 2001 (Unit: US$ billion)

	Barrier Options	Average Rate Options	Binary Digital Options	Other Exotic Options	Total Options
US dollar/yen	345.8	37	4.1	53.5	440.4
Market share of leading firm (%)	22.4	55.1	22.2	69.2	
US dollar/yen	327.9	23.4	7.6	41.6	400.5
Market share of leading firm (%)	23.2	35.1	—	32.3	
Euro/yen	127.7	6.4	2.2	9.3	145.6
Market share of leading firm (%)	38.9	84.1	—	34.4	
US dollar/sterling	49.1	12.9	2.3	8.1	72.4
Market share of leading firm (%)	18.9	61.3	—	39.3	
US dollar/ Australian dollar	42.2	0.8	0.3	4.8	48.1
Market share of leading firm (%)	19.9	33.6	—	28.9	
US dollar/ Canadian dollar	17.9	5.4	0.3	2.6	26.2
Market share of leading firm (%)	—	21.7	4.8	45.1	
US dollar/ Swiss franc	48.2	0.6	0.8	9.2	58.8
Market share of leading firm (%)	27.8	57.9	17.4	47.3	
Sterling/euro	33.0	3.1	2.0	4.1	42.2
Market share of leading firm (%)	33.6	39.0	25.4	52.3	
Euro/Swiss franc	14.9	0.3	0.3	4.8	20.3
Market share of leading firm (%)	16.2	65.2	—	37.3	
US dollar/all others	4.6	1.4	0.7	31.9	38.6
Market share of leading firm (%)	43.3	69.4	—	100.0	
Euro/Scandinavian currencies	8.1	0.1	0.0	1.5	9.7
Market share of leading firm	—	—	—	52.2	
US dollar/non-EU European currencies	10.8	0.6	0.1	1.5	13
Market share of leading firm	26.0	—	—	44.8	
Total	1030.2	92.0	20.6	172.9	1315.7

Source: RISK, December 2001.

Table 11.4 Forward Foreign Exchange Derivatives Allowed in Developing and Transition Economies, 2001 (in Percent of Countries Answering the Survey in Each Category)

	Market Access Emerging Markets	Exchange Rate Regime		
		Other	Pegged	Intermediate
Forward markets allowed	89	63	70	58
Forward markets not allowed	5	24	18	8
Not able to determine	7	13	12	33
Types of products allowed				
Outright forward contracts	89	63	70	58
Nondeliverable forward contracts	59	28	33	42
Futures	61	30	39	42
Options	77	30	45	42

Source: Canales-Kriljenko (2004), IMF FX survey (WP/04/4).

Table 11.5 Notional Amounts Outstanding of the Over-the-Counter and Exchange-Traded Foreign Exchange Derivatives in Emerging Markets (Unit: Billions of US Dollars; End-June 2001)

Countries and Regions	Exchange-Traded	OTC-Traded
Latin America	12.71	30.89
Brazil	12.61	25.03
Mexico	0.1	
Chile		5.86
Asia	1.36	140.64
Singapore		87.2
Hong Kong SAR	0.03	21.72
Korea	1.33	27.4
Malaysia		4.32
Europe, Middle East, and Africa	0.18	184.3
South Africa		176.66
Hungary	0.17	0.28
Poland	0.01	7.36
Total	14.24	355.82
Global Market's Total	66	20,435
Total/Global Market's Total	21.6%	1.7%

Source: IMF Global Financial Stabilities Report, Market Developments and Issues, December 2002, Chapter IV, The Role of Financial Derivatives in Emerging Markets, Table 4.1, page 55.

emerging markets by end-June 2001. Nearly 90% of the total foreign exchange derivative trading in the emerging markets in three continents took place in the organized exchange — BM&F of Brazil. In contrast, the most liquid OTC currency derivative markets are in Hong Kong SAR, Singapore, and South Africa, where the average daily turnover significantly exceeds the spot market turnover.

We can also observe from Table 11.5 that the 10 emerging markets made up 21.6% (largely because of BM&F of Brazil) of the global market's total notional outstanding of the exchanged-traded FX derivatives by end-June 2001; their share of the corresponding OTC-traded FX derivatives was merely 1.7%.

11.8 Conclusions

We have introduced the major FX derivatives products in developed and emerging markets in Part II. From our introductions, we know that various derivatives products have been actively trading in the developed economies, but they are much less developed and used in emerging markets. Of the major FX derivatives, forwards and swaps are the most popular products in emerging market with either pegged or intermediate exchange rate regimes, FX options and FX futures represent the second and third most popular types of FX products, and NDF contracts are the least favored product in most developing economies.

PART III

The Asian Financial Crisis and Financial Derivatives

The Asian financial crisis that broke out in July 1997 shocked the world financial market and the East Asian economies in particular. A lot of studies have been done by various major international organizations, academic institutions and scholars around the world. There were so many aspects of the Asian financial crisis that it would take too long simply to review the major ones. Most of these studies either aim to find out factors that caused the crisis and then what policy mistakes were made by national authorities, or to find indicators that might foresee similar crises in the future.

There are a limited number of studies that explore specifically roles financial derivatives played either before or during the crisis; many of these studies are either descriptive or simply introduce basic concepts of derivatives products involved. It is rather difficult to collect data of major derivatives traded during the crisis because of the lack-of-transparency nature of the over-the-counter (OTC) derivatives markets. The purpose of Part III is to provide a review and a brief analysis of what derivative products were involved and what roles these products played during the crisis, and then it will be logical to derive the "opposite usage" of most of these products because they were used either to hedge or to speculate on the expectation that the Asian currencies would devaluate, and most of them are currently used in the opposite direction either to hedge or to speculate on the expectation that the Chinese yuan (CNY) or Renminbi (RMB) would revalue because it is believed to be undervalued.

Part III is organized as follows.

Chapter 12 gives a brief introduction to what happened to major East Asian economies and financial markets during the Asian financial crisis, and the roles played by financial derivatives; Chapter 13 introduces the roles that currency forwards played during the crisis and central banks' intervention in the forward market; Chapter 14 studies what roles currency non-deliverable forwards (NDFs) played during the Asian financial crisis; Chapter 15 introduces various types of swaps during the Asian financial crisis, and how these swaps trading affected the Asian financial markets; Chapter 16 discusses the roles of options, structured notes and other derivatives during the crisis, and concludes Part III.

12

The Asian Financial Crisis

The Asian financial crisis, which broke out on July 2, 1997 and lasted for over a year, had affected not only all the East Asian economies and financial markets but also those in Latin America and Russia shortly afterwards, and finally led to the failure and eventual rescue of "the best, the brightest, and the most arrogant" long-term capital management (LTCM) (see Marthinsen, 2003) by New York Federal Reserve Bank later in September, 1998, astonishing the whole financial industry around the globe. We will briefly describe what happened to the Asian financial markets and what roles financial derivatives played during the Asian financial crisis in this chapter.

12.1 Thai Baht Floating and the Crisis

It has been well recognized that the Asian financial crisis started in Thailand after the Thai government failed to defend the Thai baht and allowed it to float freely on July 2, 1997. Following the July 1997 devaluation of the Thai baht, other Southeast Asian currencies over the next couple of months abandoned their close links to the US dollar and began to depreciate. The most severe pressures in foreign

Table 12.1 Currency Depreciation of Major Asian Currencies against the US Dollar between July 1, 1997 and February 3, 1998

Country	Currency	Rate of depreciation
Thailand	Baht	48% (from 26.07 to 50.00)
Malaysia	Ringgit	47% (from 2.50 to 4.75)
Philippines	Peso	27% (from 30 to 41)
Indonesia	Rupiah	85% (from 2,500 to 17,100)
South Korea	Won	49% (from 900 to 1,750)
Singapore	Sing Dollar	19% (from 1.25 to 1.55)

Data Source: Zhang (1998b: 94).

exchange markets in the third quarter of 1997 were experienced by Thailand, Malaysia, the Philippines, and Indonesia, but the currencies of Singapore and a number of other Asian countries also weakened. Table 12.1 gives the rates of depreciation of major currencies in the region from July 1, 1997 to February 3, 1998. It can be observed that the Indonesian rupiah depreciated 85 percent, and the Korean won, Thai baht, and Malaysian ringgit depreciated 49 percent, 48 percent and 47 percent, respectively, within the same period of time. Other currencies depreciated to fewer degrees.

Using an autoregressive conditional hazard (ACH) model to study speculative attacks during the Asian financial crisis, Zhiwei Zhang (2001) detects the attacking time on the Asian currencies. We present his results in Table 12.2. We can observe that the Thai baht was attacked as early as in May 1997 (we will discuss this in more detail in Chapter 13); the Indonesian rupiah, Malyasia ringgit and Philippine peso were attacked in July shortly after the Thai baht was floated. The Korean won was attacked in October 1997.

As the pressures spread to Hong Kong and Korea in late October following the depreciation of the New Taiwan dollar, the scale of the crisis worsened significantly. The extreme turbulence in emerging market currencies during the Asian crisis has been virtually without precedent. Between early October 1997 and its low in late December, the Korean won depreciated by 55 percent. Several emerging markets outside the region, notably Brazil and Russia, also began to be adversely affected by a shift in sentiment regarding emerging market vulnerabilities, as well as financial and real linkages with Asia.

Table 12.2 Identified Speculative Attacks in 1997

	Indonesia	Korea	Malaysia	Philippines	Thailand
January	0	0	0	0	0
February	0	0	0	0	0
March	0	1	0	0	0
April	0	0	0	0	0
May	0	0	0	0	1
June	0	0	0	0	0
July	1	0	1	1	1
August	1	0	1	0	1
September	0	0	1	1	0
October	1	1	0	0	0
November	0	1	0	0	1
December	1	1	1	1	1

Data source: Zhang (2001).

12.2 Singapore and Hong Kong

All countries in East Asia including the two regional banking centers in Asia, Singapore and Hong Kong, were severely affected by the crisis. We will describe how the crisis affected these two regional city financial centers in this section.

12.2.1 Singapore

The Singapore dollar was severely affected by the crisis. From a high of S$1.25 per US$ on July 1, 1997, the day before the float of the Thai baht, it went all the way down to S$1.55 per US$ on February 3, 1998, a decline of 19.35 percent over the period. However, the other regional currencies depreciated much more during the same period, as shown in Table 12.1. Although the Singapore dollar depreciated against the US dollar, it appreciated sharply against other regional currencies.

The Singapore stock market was also seriously affected by the crisis. The Straits Times Index (ST Index) was at 2055.44 in January 1997, and it dropped drastically to a 10 year low of 856.43 in September 1998, a decline of nearly 60 percent over the 20 month period. The property market saw the private property price index plunging from 270.0 in the first quarter of 1997 to 163.7 in the fourth quarter of 1998, a drop of about 40 percent over a 1 year period. The decline could have been more precipitous had the government not taken drastic measures in May 1996 to cool the private residential property market which was then showing signs of a bubble. Please see Chan and Ngiam (1998) for a more detailed study on this topic.

12.2.2 "Double Play" in Hong Kong

During the Asian financial crisis, the Hong Kong dollar suffered four major attacks. The first attack started on August 15. The currency premium increased from 178 to 826 pips on that day and further to 1157 pips on August 18; the attack on the Hong Kong dollar peaked the week of October 20, after the devaluation of the New Taiwan dollar the previous week. The currency premium hit its all-time high of 2840 pips on October 23. Reflecting some fundamental factors and the general speculative pressures in the region, by August 11 the Hang Seng Index (HSI) had slumped 36 percent in 1998, to its lowest level since January 1993.

These attacks drove up interbank interest rates to such high levels that the speculators were forced to unwind their positions and incur heavy losses. The speculators failed and the currency board was kept. But the interest rate volatility, and the consequent additional pain imposed on the community, was extreme: during the attack on October 23, 1997, the overnight interest rate shot up to nearly 300 percent (see Yam, 1999).

The Hong Kong government intervened in the stock market in order to fight speculative attacks on the Hong Kong dollar and the stock market. Between August 14 and 28, 1998, HKMA bought a total of some $15 billion in stocks and futures in the Hong Kong stock market, which constituted 7 percent of the capitalization and between 20 and 35 percent of the free float of the Hang Seng Index. The portfolio was held by the Exchange Fund Investment Limited (EFIL), according to strict guidelines, to avoid interference with the day-to-day commercial activities of the companies; see Chakravorti and Lall (2000) for more details.

The intervention was explained as being targeted at a specific group of speculators that were manipulating Hong Kong's equity and foreign exchange markets for profit in what was termed a "double play," i.e. a simultaneous attack on equity and currency markets (see Tsang, 1998). The authorities perceived certain players as selling Hong Kong dollars to drive up interest rates — taking advantage of the adjustment mechanism of Hong Kong's linked exchange rate arrangement — and depress stock prices, thus generating profits on previously established substantial short positions in the equity cash and futures markets.

12.2.3 Banking Sector Performances in the Two Banking Centers

Weston and Ford (2002) provided good results on the relative performances of the banking sector in Hong Kong and Singapore compared to those in Thailand, Malaysia, Korea, and Indonesia. Banking sector stock returns in Singapore and Hong Kong did decline during the period, but unlike the banking sectors of Thailand, Malaysia, Korea, and Indonesia, bank insolvencies did not occur. This can be explained by the higher capital cushions held by banks in Singapore and Hong Kong, more experiences of banks and the generally lower risk profile of domestic lending in the two centers.

12.3 Capital Flows and Asian Financial Crisis

According to the World Economic and Financial Surveys conducted by the International Monetary Fund (IMF) in 1998, the steady growth of foreign direct investment (FDI) flows had been a key characteristic of the surge in private capital inflows to the emerging markets during the 1990s, and one that imparted a considerable resilience to total private flows, which expanded during 1991–96 at an average annual rate of about 40 percent.

12.3.1 Capital Flows to Asian Markets

Capital flows, accounting for the largest proportion of flows since 1995, continued to grow robustly during 1997, increasing by 20 percent.

Unlike FDI flows, portfolio flows to the emerging markets had been volatile. From a peak of $104 billion in 1993, for example, they fell to less than one-fourth of this level in 1995 in the aftermath of the Mexican peso crisis, and more than doubled to $50 billion in 1996. During 1997 portfolio flows shrank by 14 percent to $43 billion. "Other" flows, which largely consisted of bank lending, were negative, that is, there were net outflows of $7.3 billion during 1997. This reflected a massive turnaround-from net bank lending inflows of over $70 billion in 1995 and in 1996.

The decline of almost $100 billion in net private capital flows to Asia in 1997 reflected a $75 billion turnaround in bank lending flows and $22 billion in portfolio flows, while FDI flows to the region remained stable. Most of the decline in total flows to the Asian region reflected declines in flows to the affected Asian countries — Thailand, Malaysia, the Philippines, Indonesia, and Korea — where net inflows of $73 billion in 1996 were replaced by net outflows of $11 billion in 1997. Most of the turnaround to these countries in turn arose from a $73 billion turnaround in net bank lending flows, with the sharpest outflows recorded from Thailand and Korea of some $18 billion each. The sharp cutbacks in private capital flows to Asia during 1997 were largely in short-term international bank credit and portfolio flows.

Table 12.3 gives the total net private capital flows, net private direct investment, net private portfolio investment, other net private capital flows, and net official flows of capital to the Eastern Asian countries severely affected by the crisis.

12.3.2 Total Amounts Owned to US Banks

Data in Table 12.3 are for the whole Asian region. Table 12.4 gives us the quarterly total amount owned by country borrowers to all US banks from September 1997 to December 1998. We can observe from Table 12.4 that Korea was the country with the largest amount owned to US banks, with over US$15 billion. We can also observe from the table that country exposures dropped significantly in all Asian countries and regions within the period under consideration.

Table 12.3 Capital Flows to Asian Crisis Countries: Recent Capital Flow Patterns (US$ billions)

	1991	1992	1993	1994	1995
Net private capital flows	24.93	20.89	20.65	33.35	38.85
Net private direct investment	5.96	6.34	6.67	6.53	8.81
Net private portfolio investment	2.53	9.49	17.09	11.3	17.65
Other net private capital flows	16.44	5.06	−3.11	15.52	12.4
Net official flows	3.41	2.68	3.27	0.86	14.94
Change in reserves	−9.68	−18.09	−20.59	−6.1	−18.99
Current account	−25.19	−16.29	−13.53	−23.21	−39.1
	1996	**1997**	**1998**	**1999**	**2000**
Net private capital flows	63.96	−8.98	−32.71	−9.06	−10.16
Net private direct investment	9.83	10.49	10.91	7.83	8.59
Net private portfolio investment	23.62	7.21	−9.28	3.62	4
Other net private capital flows	30.51	−26.68	−34.34	−20.5	−22.74
Net official flows	−3.85	14.58	17.8	−5.57	2.55
Change in reserves	−5.45	39.45	−46.95	−39.33	−22.91
Current account	−53.03	−25.46	69.9	62.95	44.8

Source: IMF, World Economic Outlook, Database tables, 2001.

Table 12.4 Country Exposure of All US Banks; Total Amount Owned by Country of Borrower (Sept 1997–Dec 1998) (Derivative Contracts Excepted, Unit: million US$)

Country/Region	Sep 97	Dec 97	Mar 98	Jun 98	Sep 98	Dec 98
China-Mainland	2595	2275	1758	1618	1351	1161
China-Taiwan	3539	3728	3211	3106	2661	2686
Indonesia	4593	4349	3031	2331	2194	2057
Korea	15,019	13,487	11,778	10,102	8,601	7,836
Malaysia	1805	1900	1262	1042	630	746
Philippines	2029	1991	1807	1730	1617	1556
Thailand	3382	2806	1546	1397	1157	887
Hong Kong	5837	5053	4054	3362	4341	3198
Singapore	3821	3131	2698	2540	2675	3502
Russia	6318	4382	5086	4842	1467	835
Brazil	16,881	17,434	19,400	18,058	14,710	14,080

Data source: Report-Statistical Releases, E16 Country Exposure Lending Survey and Country Exposure Information Report of Federal Financial Institution Examination Council (FFIEC), December 31, 1997; March 31, 30 June; 31 September and December 1998.

12.4 Derivatives Associated with Capital Flows

The volatile portfolio capital flows into and out of the affected countries and the relating derivatives products played significant roles in the Asian financial crisis. Different forms of foreign funds flowed to different recipients in developing countries before the crisis, and more importantly, derivatives emerged as an integral part of fund flows in the 1990s.

12.4.1 Derivatives and Capital Flows

Derivatives played an unprecedented role in the Asian financial crisis of 1997, as part of financial globalization in unregulated global foreign exchange, capital, and debt markets. Derivatives facilitate the growth in private fund flows by unbundling the risks associated with financial vehicles, such as bank loans, stocks, bonds, and direct physical investment, and reallocating risks more efficiently by expanding the distribution and the level of aggregate risk.

12.4.2 US Money Center Banks

It is difficult to obtain exact data on various derivatives products traded during the Asian financial crisis, yet we can obtain some aggregate data from the US Federal Financial Institution Examination Council (FFIEC). The US money-center banks are the major players of lending and relating derivatives activities around the world. Their activities involve not only lending, but also transactions hedging their foreign exchange exposure with derivatives. Kregel (1998) provides a good discussion of derivatives and global capital flows using data from the US FFIEC. We extend Table 1 of Kregel (1998) to include China-Mainland, China-Taiwan, the two banking centers Hong Kong and Singapore, and two other countries that were later affected by the Asian crisis, Russia and Brazil, and present the results in Table 12.5.

Table 12.5 gives total amounts owned by country of borrower (net of derivatives) and the cross-border exposure resulting from revaluation gains on foreign exchange and derivative products after adjustments for guarantees and external borrowings of the US money-center

Table 12.5 Country Exposure of US Money-Center Banks Loans and Derivatives (December 31, 1997) (Figures for March 31, 1998 in Parentheses) (Unit: million US$)

Country/ Region	Total Amount Owned by Country of Borrower (Derivative Excepted) (A)	Cross-Border Exposure from Foreign Exchange Revaluation and Derivatives Contracts (B)	B/A December 1997 (%)	B/A March 1998 (%)
China-Mainland	1683 (1294)	375 (380)	22.3	29.4
China-Taiwan	2580 (2068)	171 (159)	6.6	7.7
Indonesia	3000 (2284)	2266 (1612)	75.5	70.6
Korea	9791 (9155)	4633 (2890)	47.3	31.6
Malaysia	1543 (1070)	555 (266)	36.0	24.9
Philippines	1533 (1357)	40 (157)	2.6	11.6
Thailand	1771 (920)	2509 (1145)	141.7	124.5
Hong Kong	4039 (2956)	2190 (1318)	54.2	32.6
Singapore	1986 (1793)	1565 (1268)	78.8	70.7
Russia	4982 (4621)	49 (117)	1.0	2.5
Brazil	11,813 (13,157)	537 (575)	4.5	4.9

Data source: Report-Statistical Releases, E16 Country Exposure Lending Survey and Country Exposure Information Report of Federal Financial Institution Examination Council (FFIEC), December 31, 1997 and March 31, 1998.

banks. The US money center banks included six banking organizations: Bank of America, Bankers Trust, Chase Manhattan, Citicorp, First Chicago, and J.P. Morgan at the time. Table 12.5 provides us a good idea of the scale and intensity of derivatives activities of US money-center banks in countries involved in the crisis.

These figures are given for the amounts outstanding at the end of 1997 and the end of the first quarter of 1998 (in parentheses). Since derivatives exposure only results when a counterparty default places the bank under a risk of having to replace the instrument at a loss to current market conditions, the figures in the second column represent the profits for US money-center banks on their derivatives activity plus any increases in the value of their outstanding loans due to changes in exchange rates. Since US banks' exposure is primarily in dollars, the majority of these changes should be the result of changes in the valuation of derivatives contracts rather than changes in the dollar value of outstanding direct loans.

12.4.3 Derivatives/Loan Ratios

We can observe from Table 12.5 that cross-border exposure from foreign exchange revaluation and derivatives as a percentage of the corresponding total amount owned by country of borrower was the highest in Thailand at both end of 1997 and end of March 1998 (141.7 percent and 124.5 percent, respectively), reflecting dramatic Thai baht/US$ exchange fluctuations in the period and heavy speculations on the baht in the second half of 1997 since the beginning of the Asian crisis. We will discuss in more detail what happened in Thailand in this period in Chapter 13.

Closely following Thailand was Indonesia, the vast derivatives activities in Indonesia reflect the fact that the Indonesian rupiah depreciated most of all currencies, 85 percent in the time period as shown in Table 12.1. The corresponding ratio for Singapore, Hong Kong, Korea, and Malaysia was 78.8 percent, 54.2 percent, 47.3 percent and 36.0 percent, respectively by the end of 1997. We will discuss in more detail what particular derivatives products were involved in these countries and regions during the crisis, in the following chapters. The great involvement in the two banking centers, especially Singapore, reflected the fact that they provide a significant amount of financial services to the region that was heavily affected.

Table 12.6 provides similar quarterly B/A ratios defined in Table 12.5 for the same countries/regions from September 1997 in the middle of the crisis to December 1998 when the crisis was close to the end in most Asian economies. Table 12.6 provides us a good picture of derivative activities in Asia during the Asian crisis. It is worth noting that the ratio rose significantly in most major countries in East Asia with the exception of Malaysia and the Philippines (where it dropped slightly) from September 1997 to December 1997. The ratio increased dramatically in Thailand and Korea, reflecting the fact that the crisis worsened in the two countries during the time period, yet it fell significantly in the first quarter of 1998 as, then, the conditions improved there.

12.5 FX Market Volatility, Transactions Costs, and Liquidity

As market liquidity dried up, the cost of derivatives increased in Asia. Accompanying the increase in exchange market volatility,

Table 12.6 Ratios of Cross-border Foreign Exchange Revaluation and Derivatives Contracts over Total Amount Owned by Country of Borrower of All US Banks from September 1997–December 1998 (Percent)

Country/Region	Sep 97	Dec 97	Mar 98	Jun 98	Sep 98	Dec 98
China-Mainland	10.6	16.5	21.6	31.1	33.9	33.1
China-Taiwan	3.1	4.6	5.0	5.6	6.8	6.9
Indonesia	40.7	53.0	53.3	56.5	43.6	35.1
Korea	8.5	34.7	24.9	26.4	26.8	24.7
Malaysia	32.9	31.1	21.7	22.1	30.3	23.7
Philippines	3.0	2.0	8.7	6.7	12.9	9.1
Thailand	64.4	89.4	74.2	67.9	75.9	78.6
Hong Kong	38.5	45.5	33.8	32.7	24.9	26.1
Singapore	60.1	55.1	49.1	32.5	37.6	16.9
Russia	14.0	1.2	2.3	3.9	10.7	8.9
Brazil	1.5	3.3	3.0	1.4	2.6	2.5

Data source: Calculated using data from Report-Statistical Releases, E16 Country Exposure Lending Survey and Country Exposure Information Report of Federal Financial Institution Examination Council (FFIEC), December 31 1997; March 31, 30 June; 31 September and December 1998.

transactions costs in spot, forward, and other derivative markets for these currencies skyrocketed and liquidity dropped, with only modest improvements in the first half of 1998. There was also exchange market pressure in other emerging markets in the second half of 1997, notably in Latin America, Eastern Europe, and Russia. The large depreciations of the Asian currencies seriously impaired the balance sheets of already weakened and un-hedged domestic financial institutions and corporations, and led to sharp increases in non-performing loans. As a result, 1997 saw the first major reduction in private capital flows to the emerging markets in the 1990s and a general reevaluation of emerging market risk.

Higher volatility and transaction costs were associated with a drying up of liquidity. Average daily volumes fell, standard deal sizes shrank, and the number of market makers in these currencies dwindled. The number of inter-bank players declined on average by more than half their previous number with, for example, the number trading on the spot market for ringgit down from 25 to 12 and on the forward market from 50 to 20. While the crisis presumably raised the demand for hedging exchange rate risk, the higher transactions costs discouraged hedging, as evidenced by the reduced turnover on forwards, please see Singapore Foreign Exchange Market Committee (1996).

12.6 Hedge Funds

Hedge funds were actively involved in the Asian financial crisis. Although specific data of hedge funds involvement on particular products and in particular countries are difficult to obtain, yet their roles were significant. In a comprehensive study on the attacks on the Thai baht by IMF (The Asian Crisis: Capital Markets Dynamics and Spillover: 44–47), it was estimated by market participants that the Bank of Thailand forward book, at US$26 billion by the end of June 1997, and macro hedge funds accounted for some US$7 billion, more than a quarter of the total amount. In view of market participants, the baht was the only Asian currency for which the hedge funds collectively took significant short positions.

Several empirical studies have looked at the impact of hedge funds on currency market dynamics to try to determine whether such investors can "move" these markets in directions favorable to themselves, either through their own actions or through the tendency of other market participants to follow their lead. An IMF Occasional Paper from May 1998 by Barry Eichengreen and others finds some evidence that hedge funds played a leading role in precipitating the ERM crisis in 1992 by acting as market leaders that other institutional investors followed, but that they did so in response to economic fundamentals.

There is no single market strategy or approach pursued by hedge funds as a group; rather, hedge funds exhibit a wide variety of investment styles, some of which use highly quantitative techniques while others employ more subjective factors. The comprehensive Report of The US President's Working Group on Financial Markets on "Hedge Funds, Leverage, and the Lessons of Long-Term Capital Management" of April 1999 also provides good information on long term capital management's involvement in Russia. We will return to this in Chapter 16.

12.7 Institutions Involved

There were many international financial institutions and domestic institutions involved in the Asian financial crisis. It is useful for us, if we desire to have a better understanding of the crisis, to know the major players in the market during the crisis. The purpose of this section is to introduce the major players.

12.7.1 The US Money-Center Banks

The US financial institutions had been leading the world in product innovation and trading in both exchange traded products and OTC products by the time of the Asian crisis. It was the Orange County event in 1994 and its following legal procedures that made many US corporations reluctant to engage in sophisticated OTC products (see Marthinsen, 2003: 158–193), and the US trading volume of OTC derivatives products have grown somewhat less rapidly than European countries. The US money-center banks have been major "power house" for structuring and trading new products. Although the six money center banks consisted of only 39.9 percent and 39.5 percent of the total bank assets (US$3.26 trillion and US$3.39 trillion) in the US on December 31, 1997 and March 31, 1998, respectively, their total weight of cross-border exposure resulting from off-balance sheet activities of revaluation gains on foreign exchange and derivatives was 97.4 percent and 98.1 percent (calculated using data from FFIEC report — Statistical Releases) of such activities of all US banks in Asia in the same time periods, respectively.

12.7.2 European Financial Institutions

Besides the US money-center banks, European banks were also deeply involved in the Asian crisis. It was reported (Andrews, 1998) that Deutsche Bank set aside US$777 million (double its loss provisions for 1996) to cover losses of as much as US$100 million on derivatives trading in South Korea, Thailand, Indonesia, and Malaysia. Société Générale is reported to have set aside US$164 million against a total exposure of US$6.8 billion (of which US$4 billion was lent in

Korea primarily to Korean companies (Lavin, 1998). Commerz has US$3 billion in loans, Dresdner 26 percent of equity, and Deutsche 27 percent of equity in Asian loans.

12.7.3 Local Investment Banks

Not only were US and European banks involved, but much of the success of local investment banks, such as Hong Kong based Peregrine securities, was primarily in underwriting and selling debt for Asian corporations. To some degree, Peregrine played more important roles around the Asian financial crisis than most international financial institutions.

Peregrine Investments had grown dramatically to become Asia's largest investment firm outside Japan before its collapse in January 1998. The growth of Peregrine mirrors closely that of investment banking activities in Asia in the 1990s. Peregrine was a pioneer of the Asian fixed income market and the largest underwriter of Asian equity, in addition to being a major player in the Asian derivatives market.

Just as the investment bank Drexel, Burnham, Lambert is credited with pioneering the US junk bond market, Peregrine is credited with opening up the Asian local currency debt market. Peregrine's activities covered the whole gamut of investment banking activities, including equities underwriting, high-yield debt financing, asset management, and derivatives products. Peregrine intermediated a variety of derivatives instruments such as foreign exchange swaps and yield-enhancing total rate of return swaps on Asian debt and equity. Korean entities and other foreign investors reportedly took large positions on high yield Indonesian instruments through combinations of Indonesian corporate debt issuances underwritten by Peregrine as well as swaps engineered by Peregrine.

Peregrine's derivatives exposure to Indonesian corporates was reportedly 10 times larger than its exposure through direct debt instruments. With the collapse of the Indonesian rupiah, this large debt inventory went into default and led to the rapid demise of Peregrine (see Box 2.10: 45; the Asian Crisis: Capital Markets Dynamics and Spillover, IMF: 45).

12.8 Summary and Conclusions

It should also be noted that the analysis of the role of derivatives during the Asian financial crisis is seriously hampered by data availability, since the OTC derivatives transactions are not reported systematically. Thus, in many cases, anecdotal evidence and estimations of market participants on derivatives positions by major investment banks of the industrial countries are the main sources of information. The data we used so far in this chapter are aggregate data with which we cannot see trading activities clearly for particular products. We will use official data and partially anecdotal evidence to study major derivative products involved during the Asian financial crisis in the following chapters of this part.

Although it is difficult to obtain sufficient data to analyze what specific roles various types of derivatives played during the Asian financial crisis, and existing studies in this area are still limited, existing data and studies by IMF and other institutions have provided evidence that derivatives not only played important roles but also amplified the impact of the crisis (IMF). We will be able to see specific impacts of particular derivative products in the following chapters.

13

FX Forwards and Futures during the Asian Crisis

Many derivative products were involved in the Asian financial crisis. Foreign exchange forward markets are one of the primary channels for speculators to attack a fixed exchange rate regime as well as for central banks to defend the exchange rate (see Lall, 1997). Literature on speculative attacks in the foreign exchange market is comprehensive — the interested reader may refer to Lall (1997) and Frankel and Wei (2003) for classifications of the literature. It is not our purpose in this book to go into much detail of the existing academic or professional studies in this area.

In foreign exchange markets, speculators betting on a decline of the currency and taking short forward positions are bearish traders, and central banks may attempt to squeeze the bearish traders by cornering the market in the weak currency in order to maintain the fixed exchange rate regime. As foreign exchange forwards provide the most cost-effective ways to either speculate or hedge, they are the instruments most often used in the foreign exchange markets. We will concentrate on foreign exchange forwards and futures in this chapter.

Of most existing studies on foreign exchange forwards during the Asian financial crisis, the IMF working paper "The Asian

Crisis: Capital Markets Dynamics and Spillover" is the most comprehensive one on the process and roles of Asian currency forwards. We largely follow this paper in this chapter.

13.1 Central Banks' Intervention in Forward Markets

It is a well-known practice for central banks to intervene in spot foreign exchange markets as interventions are instruments for central banks to adjust macro-economy according to their macroeconomic policies and targets. Yet it is not so well-known for central banks to intervene in foreign exchange forward markets. We will briefly introduce central banks' interventions in the foreign exchange forward market in this section.

13.1.1 Interventions

The Bank of Thailand had built up a substantial forward liability, in excess of $25 billion to purchase baht and sell dollars months before July 1997. The Bank of Korea also intervened in the forward market for won, and it was reported to "test the waters" in the offshore non-deliverable forward (NDF) market for Korean won. We will study specifically the Korean won NDF market in Chapter 14 of this book. Market participants reported that the Banco do Brasil, a federally owned bank, took substantial positions on currency futures market on Brazil's futures exchange, the Bolsa de Mercadorias e Futuros (BM&F), during the period of pressures on the real in late October 1997. The Bank of England also intervened the markets for forwards for pound sterling at the time of the European Rate Mechanism (ERM) crisis in 1992, and the South African Reserve Bank conducted such interventions in the forward market for rand over extended periods.

13.1.2 Ways to Obtain Local Currency for Delivery

Foreign entities must obtain local currency in order to settle their forward contracts. There are a number of ways in which counterparties to the central bank can obtain local currency for delivery.

The straightforward benchmark case is where counterparties are foreign entities that obtain local currency directly from the central bank in exchange for foreign currency at the prevailing spot exchange rate. In this case, the purchase of local currency would result directly in an increase in the central bank's foreign exchange reserves. The subsequent delivery by the counterparties of the local currency and exchange for foreign currency, carried out at the transacted forward rate, would result in a loss of central bank reserves. Another way for foreign entities to obtain local currency is to purchase it on the spot foreign exchange market.

13.1.3 Impacts of Forward Intervention on Foreign Reserve

The central banks first gain and then lose reserves in the first straightforward way to obtain local currency. The net effect on reserves would be the difference between the prevailing spot and contracted forward exchange rates times the notional value of the forward contract settled. Specifically, reserve implications of central bank intervention in the forward market should be, as an approximation, estimated as the depreciation of the exchange rate, since the initiation of the forward contracts, times the notional value of the contracts. In the case of the Bank of Thailand (BOT) with US$26 billion forward contracts, for example, it is a $6.50 billion loss for a 25 percent devaluation.

13.2 Thai Baht Forwards and the Asian Financial Crisis

The BOT had been intervening in the forward exchange market long before the crisis broke out on July 2, 1997. Foreign exchange forward sales had effectively depleted the foreign exchange reserves in a manner that was not shown in the published spot figures of its foreign exchange position. The BOT entered into contracts with both foreign and domestic counterparties, promising to supply dollars in return for baht at the specified forward exchange rates. The counterparties were thus short baht and long dollars.

The BOT intervened in the foreign exchange market substantially by selling baht forward contracts promising to deliver dollars for baht. Including its interventions on the currency swaps market, it had by the end of June 1997 built up forward liabilities in excess of $26 billion (we will go into details later in this section). Market participants viewed the future delivery of dollars by the central bank as a claim on Thailand's foreign exchange reserves, and the realization of the buildup of the large forward book, when compared with actual holdings of reserves, contributed to the view that the defense was unsustainable. The attack on the baht and the subsequent exchange rate depreciation were exacerbated by this perception.

13.2.1 The First Episode

The first episode of notable pressure on the baht occurred as early as July 1996, following the collapse of the Bangkok Bank of Commerce and injections of liquidity by the BOT to support the financial system. This early episode of pressure was reported to have been generated largely from international commercial and investment banks.

13.2.2 The Second Episode

A second episode of serious pressure on the baht occurred in early 1997, following the release in January of poor fiscal and export data for the fourth quarter of 1996, implying both an increased monetization of the deficit and a deteriorating current account deficit. Concerns about nonperforming assets in the financial sector began to spread at about the same time, and in January market participants learned that several property developers were either unable to or had decided to stop paying interest on loans from finance companies. The February baht episode was again largely foreign investor driven. In addition to the commercial and investment banks, portfolio managers (mutual funds and proprietary trading desks) began to retrench. This time, hedge funds also reportedly took some short positions on the baht, using primarily long-dated 6 month (due in August) contracts.

13.2.3 The Most Severe Attack

The market appeared to be relatively quiet from March to the end of April in 1997, yet it gathered more energy for dramatic pressure on the baht. On the evening of Wednesday, May 7, reports circulated that the Hong Kong branch of a major Thai bank had become a large seller of baht for dollars. This led market participants to believe that Thai finance companies were scrambling to acquire dollars and other domestic entities were beginning to flee as their external financing was becoming increasingly difficult in light of growing concerns about their credit quality. During the course of the evening, it also became known that the BOT had directly contacted several foreign commercial and investment banks, offering to sell forward a large volume of dollars in exchange for baht. On Thursday and Friday, market participants estimated the BOT sold $6 billion, and the bulk of dollar buying appeared to have been local, with net reserves falling from $32 billion to $26 billion.

13.2.4 The Peak of Attack

Market participants estimated that on May 12 and May 13 the BOT lost about US$5 billion. On Wednesday, May 14, speculative attack reached its peak, with the BOT estimated to have sold over US$10 billion on that day alone. The massive intervention on the forward market by the BOT did little to reduce pressures on the baht. On Thursday, May 15, it stopped intervening, allowing interest rates to rise, and instituted capital controls segmenting the on- and offshore markets.

There were so many important events before the July 2 floating of the baht that our descriptions are also somewhat long. We tabulate these major events in Table 13.1 so as to make it easier for readers to grasp.

13.2.5 Market Participants

Market participants estimated the BOT's forward book at $26 billion by the end of June 1997, of which the macro hedge funds accounted

Table 13.1 Major Milestones before the Thai Baht Was Floated

July, 1996	Collapse of Bangkok Bank of Commerce
February 5	Somprasong Land was unable to meet a foreign debt payment
March	Thai government announced to buy US$3.9 billion in loans from finance companies to solve their liquidity problems, yet failed to execute
May 7 (Wednesday)	Hong Kong branch of a Thai Bank sold baht for US dollar; BOT contacted foreign banks
May 9 (Friday)	BOT sold US dollar for baht
May 12 (Monday)	BOT intervened in the forward market
May 13 (Tuesday)	BOT sold US$5 billion for baht
May 14 (Wednesday)	Speculative attack reached its peak and BOT sold US$10 billion for baht
May 15 (Thursday)	BOT stopped forward market intervention, raised interest rate, and instituted capital control
End of June	BOT accumulated about US$26 billion forwards
July 2, 1997	BOT floated baht exchange rate

Data source: tabulated from the IMF working paper, "The Asian Crisis: Capital Markets Dynamics and Spillover", 44–47.

for some $7 billion, "other" offshore counterparties for $8 billion, and onshore foreign banks for $9 billion, and onshore domestic banks for $2 billion. The onshore domestic banks accounted for less than 10 percent of the total amount. While some of the positions taken by banks, both domestic and foreign, were proprietary positions, many were undertaken as intermediaries on behalf of other counterparties. These also probably included hedge funds, and so their positions could have been bigger than the reported $7 billion of direct positions.

13.2.6 Market Reactions

Initial reactions to the float were, however, favorable. The stock market rose, and foreign investors were reported to be paying substantial premiums on the equity available to foreign residents. However, market sentiment quickly deteriorated due to concerns about the impact of the devaluation and high interest rates on the financial sector, and the view that the BOT's massive buildup of forward foreign exchange liabilities had depleted "net" reserves and had, therefore, limited its ability to intervene in support of the baht. The announcement of baht floating on July 2 took most by surprise. In the immediate aftermath of the baht's announced float, expectations of depreciation led the heavily indebted domestic corporate sector to rapidly purchase foreign exchange on the spot market in an attempt to hedge their foreign exchange exposures.

13.3 Korean Won Forwards

13.3.1 Foreign Reserve Deposits in Domestic Banks

As Table 12.2 indicates, the Korean won was attacked in October 1997 as the crisis spread to the north of East Asia. Official reserves of the Bank of Korea (BOK) fell from a reported \$31 billion at end-October 1997 to \$24 billion by early December. The central bank's "usable" reserves, however, were reported to be some \$6 billion. This discrepancy between measured and usable reserves arose as a result of foreign currency deposits placed by the BOK with foreign branches of domestic banks that became illiquid. That is, in light of the liquidity pressures faced by the foreign branches of Korean banks, these deposits could not be withdrawn. In January 1997, as the overseas branches of Korean banks suffered liquidity problems in the wake of the Hanbo affair, the BOK extended liquidity support to them, and by the end of March the amount of such deposits had grown to \$8 billion. Finally, as pressures grew in November, by early December such deposits had risen above \$10 billion.

In addition to measured official reserves of \$30 billion prior to the crisis, the BOK had deposits of \$30 billion with banks onshore. As the central bank sought to draw on these deposits, it discovered that these deposits too could not be accessed as they had either been on-lent to Korean corporates or invested in primarily emerging market assets that the commercial banks were either unable or unwilling to liquidate in prevailing market conditions.

Table 13.2 Foreign Exchange turnover in Korea from 1996 to 2000 (Unit: US$ billion)

	1996	1997	1998	1999	2000
Spots	1014	1398	704	1082	1372
Forwards	114	220	75	151	260
Swaps	146	216	184	412	707
Total	1273	1834	962	1645	2338
Growth Rate		44.0%	−47.5%	71.0%	42.1%

Data source: calculated using the daily average turnover data from the Bank of Korea website: www.bok.or.kr.

13.3.2 Forward Volume

According to the BOK, the Korean won forward turnover was rather low around the crisis. Table 13.2 provides the FX turnover of spots, forwards, swaps and total from 1996 to 2000. We can observe from Table 13.2 that total forwards turnover was merely US$114 billion in 1996 and it grew to US$220 billion in 1997 with an annual growth rate of nearly 100% because of extreme FX volatility in 1997. However, it dropped to only US$75 billion in 1998.

13.3.3 Derivatives Trading Value

The BOK reported (AP-DJ, 1998B) that trading in financial derivatives by South Korean banks increased by 60.1 percent in 1997 to US$556.5 billion. If we convert the Korean GDP of 453.3 trillion won in 1997 with the 1997 year-end won/US$ exchange rate of 1672, the 1997 Korean GDP was US$271.1 billion, the total derivatives trading value was 105 percent higher than its GDP in 1997. Even if we use the average won/US$ exchange rate of 1286 in 1997, the total derivatives trading value was 57.9 percent higher than its GDP in the same year.

13.3.4 Profit and Loss of Various Participants

It was reported (Park, 1998) that Korea's 26 banks booked losses of 3.92 trillion won (about US$2.35 billion converted with year-end won/US$ exchange rate of 1672 and about US$4.61 billion converted with average won/US$ exchange rate of 1286) in 1997; 39 branches of foreign banks reported net profits of 930.48 billion won (about US$560 million converted with year-end won/US$ exchange rate of 1672 and about US$720 million converted with average won/US$ exchange rate of 1286). Industrial & Commercial Bank of China (ICBC) and Credit Suisse First Boston were the only two foreign banks that reported losses.

13.4 FX Forward Market in Singapore

Singapore was directly hit by the Asian financial crisis as it provides most financial services for the region. The Singapore dollar forward turnover was significantly high during the Asian financial crisis as both local and international participants had to hedge their positions in Singapore and those Southeast Asian countries heavily affected by the crisis. Table 13.3 gives the average daily foreign exchange turnover in April 1998 compared to April 1995. Unfortunately, corresponding data for 1997 are not available. We can observe that the average turnover for the Singapore dollar forward in April 1998 was more than 50 percent more than in April 1995.

Table 13.4 provides counterparty compositions of major foreign exchange derivatives (forwards and swaps) in Singapore in April 1998 and April 1995. We can observe that financial institutions outside Singapore comprised nearly two-thirds of the total turnover in April 1998, although the growth rate of the financial institutions outside Singapore (17.8 percent) was slightly lower than the corresponding rate in Singapore (32.3 percent).

Table 13.3 Average Daily Foreign Exchange Turnover (Net Basis)

	Apr 98		Apr 95		% Change in volume
	Volume (US$b)	Share (%)	Volume (US$b)	Share (%)	
Spot	59.9	43.1	44.3	42	35.2
Forwards	4.4	3.2	2.9	2.8	51.7
Swaps	74.7	53.7	58.2	55.2	28.4
Total	139.0	100.0	105.4	100.0	31.9

Data source: Bank for International Settlements (BIS) Survey of Foreign Exchange and Derivatives Markets Activities, Date: September 29, 1998.

Table 13.4 Counterparties — Foreign Exchange in Singapore (Spot/Outright Forwards/Swaps — Daily Average)

	April 1998		April 1995		% Change in Volume
	Volume (US$b)	Share (%)	Volume (US$b)	Share (%)	
Financial Institutions	119.6	86.0	98.6	93.6	+21.3
• In Singapore	31.1	22.4	23.5	22.3	+32.3
— Banks	18.6	13.4	19.2	18.2	−3.1
— Others	12.5	9.0	4.3	4.1	+190.7
• Outside Singapore	88.5	63.6	75.1	71.3	+17.8
Non-financial Customers	19.4	14.0	6.8	6.4	+185.3
• In Singapore	11.3	8.1	3.9	3.7	+189.7
• Outside Singapore	8.1	5.9	2.9	2.7	2.7
Total	139.0	100.0	105.4	100.0	+31.9

Data source: Bank for International Settlements (BIS) Survey of Foreign Exchange and Derivatives Markets Activities, Date: September 29, 1998.

13.5 Hong Kong Dollar Forwards

Hong Kong was hit severely by the Asian financial crisis as the Hong Kong dollar was attacked four times during the crisis described in Chapter 12. As the Hong Kong dollar has been pegged to the US$ since 1984, the Hong Kong Monetary Authority (HKMA) fought against all the attacks to maintain the currency board.

13.5.1 The HKMA's Intervention Activities in the Forward Market

The HKMA also intervened in the foreign exchange forward market during the Asian financial crisis. Figure 13.1 depicts the ratio of purchases/sales of Hong Kong dollar forwards by HKMA from January 1996 to December 1998.

We can readily observe from Figure 13.1 that purchases and sales of HK$ by the HKMA were roughly the same as purchases/sales ratio stayed around 100.4 percent from January 1996 to September 1997; however, the ratio jumped to above 101.3 percent in October 1997 and January 1998, reflecting severe attacks on the HK$ and the

Figure 13.1 Ratio of HKMA Sales/Purchases of HK Dollar Forwards from January 1996 to December 1998

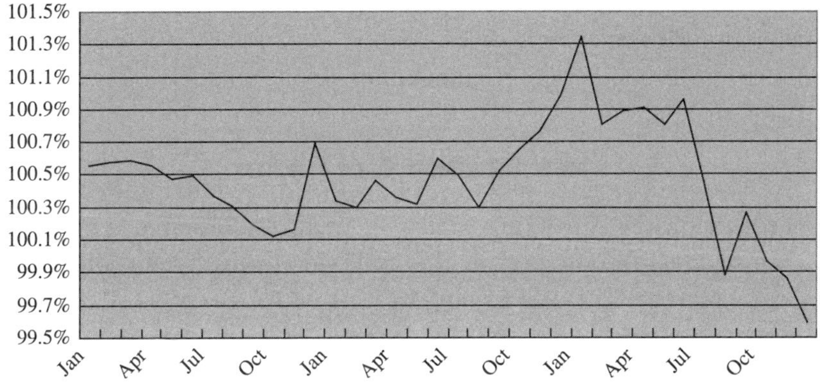

Data source: calculated using data from Hong Kong Monetary Authority, statistics, 2003.

Figure 13.2 Net Spot and Forward Positions of Hong Kong Dollar from January 1996 to December 1998 (Unit: US$ billion)

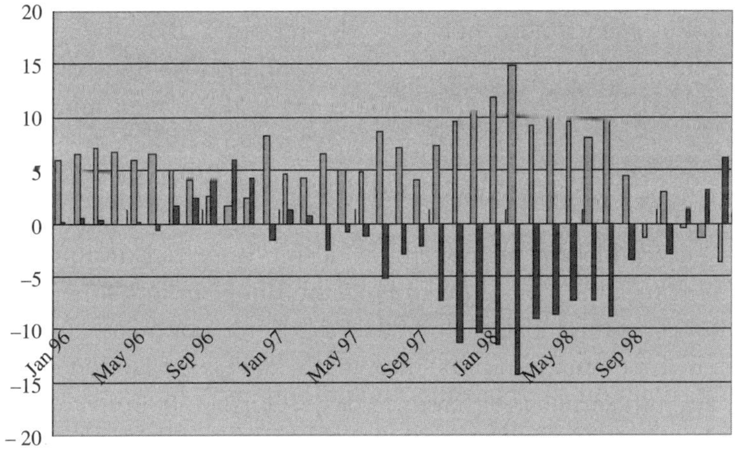

Data source: Hong Kong Monetary Authority, statistics, 2003.

HKMA had to purchase more HK$ forwards to fight against the attacks; and the ratio returned to around 100 percent from July 1998 as the crisis was about to end.

Figure 13.2 depicts the net spot positions (asset minus liabilities) and net forward positions (total purchases minus sales) from January

1996 to December 1998. It is obvious from Figure 13.2 that HKMA held more and more short positions in the spot market and more and more long positions in the forward market to fight against attacks on the currency board.

13.6 Brazilian Real Futures

Among the Latin American emerging markets, Brazil was perhaps the most severely affected in the spillover from the turbulence in financial markets in Hong Kong SAR in late October 1997. The prices of Brazilian Brady bonds fell by 18 percent in the week following October 24, the BOVESPA stock market index fell by 22 percent, and the real came under severe pressure, both on the currency futures market on the BM&F and on the spot market, with market participants reporting central bank reserve losses of $10 billion in a matter of hours at the peak of the attack. Markets were startled by the BM&F's position-taking on the futures market.

Market participants unanimously reported that the pressures on the exchange rate, which were more intense than during the Mexican crisis in early 1995, were generated predominantly by domestic entities. The BM&F increased margin requirements as the market condition worsened, resulting in further margin calls. The lack of "Chinese" and "fire walls" between the investment banks' proprietary and fund management desks caused clearing banks in New York to attribute the majority of the Brazilian investment banks' deal flows to their proprietary desks, raising concerns about their ability to meet margin calls, and resulted in a reduction of credit lines, adding further pressures for de-leveraging. In some instances, the lack of Chinese walls between the investment banks' proprietary and fund management desks also increased the size of sell orders as managers took the same positions for themselves and their clients. During this period, the revelation that Korean entities had substantial holdings of Brazilian Brady bonds, and their anticipated "dumping" in response to pressures at home, also aggravated the downward spiral in prices.

13.7 Summary and Conclusions

Foreign exchange forwards are the most popular foreign exchange derivative instruments in the foreign exchange markets. Our descriptions and analysis of foreign exchange forward trading during the Asian financial crisis convincingly indicate that forward contracts did play important roles during the Asian financial crisis.

14

NDFs during the Asian Financial Crisis

We discussed the roles played by foreign exchange forwards during the Asian financial crisis in Chapter 13. Important as foreign exchange forwards were, they either did not exist or could not be accessed for some Asian currencies during the crisis because of regulatory issues or low liquidity. In this chapter, we concentrate on roles played by foreign exchange non-deliverable forwards (NDFs) during the Asian financial crisis.

NDFs came into being during another financial crisis — the Mexican crisis. It was in 1995 that Mexico had just devalued its peso, triggering a sell-off in markets across Latin America in what became known as the "Tequila crisis" or Mexican crisis. As foreign investors watched their investments shrink, a group of US banks structured a new financial contract to insure against currency risk, structured to settle in US dollars and settled outside Latin America. The NDFs immediately found their applications in Asia and such products played their roles during the Asian financial crisis.

14.1 NDFs in Asia

Most Asian currencies were deliverable and highly liquid before the Asian crisis in 1997–98, and there was no need for NDF markets in many of the countries. Yet, NDFs started to be traded in Asia as early as in 1995, and the major currencies for NDFs were the Korean won, the New Taiwan dollar, the Philippine peso, the Indian rupee, the Chinese yun and the Vietnam dong, because these currencies are not fully convertible and there is room for NDFs to exist as we discussed in Chapter 9. Liquidity of most such NDFs was relatively low before the crisis in 1997; yet, trading activities became active after the crisis broke out early in July as capital controls were gradually imposed and exchange restrictions increased. The veracity of deliverable overseas forward markets declined, and hence, in some countries, the market simply moved to a non-deliverable context.

14.1.1 Turnovers

Average daily turnovers of Asian NDFs increased significantly in Asia in 1997 after the crisis broke out. It increased from US$600 million in the first half of 1997 to US$900 in the second half of the same year. It increased from US$250 million and US$200 million in the first half of 1997 to US$450 million and US$320 million in the second half of 1997 for the Korean won and the New Taiwan dollar, respectively.

Table 14.1 gives the average daily turnover of NDFs on four major currencies in Asia. We can see from Table 14.1 that the Korean won and the New Taiwan dollar were the two Asian currencies with the highest daily turnover, and the Indian rupee and Philippine peso NDFs were rather thinly traded.

Table 14.1 Average Daily Turnover of Major NDFs in Asia in 1998 (Unit: US$ million)

Indian Rupee	Korean Won	New Taiwan Dollar	Philippine Peso
70	450	320	75

14.1.2 Singapore and Hong Kong

Singapore and Hong Kong, the two financial centers in the region, are two major trading centers for the Asian NDFs. More Korean won and Indian rupee NDFs were traded in Singapore than in Hong Kong, yet more Chinese yuan and New Taiwan dollar NDFs were traded in Hong Kong in 1998. The major players in Singapore and Hong Kong NDF markets have been major US and European banks and investment institutions.

14.1.3 Tokyo

According to a survey conducted by the Tokyo Foreign Exchange Market Committee (TFEMC) in February–May 2003, more than half of domestic Japanese respondents (18 surveys received of 38 sent) have not conducted any NDF deals to date. However, for about 90 percent of the participants who have replied that they are dealing in NDFs, deal volumes had been increasing; foreign bank respondents (five surveys received of 14 surveys sent) traded NDFs. The survey suggests that market size has increased; 70 percent of participants in Japan and all overseas respondents have shown strong interest in NDF transactions. The same proportion of respondents noted that they are willing to consider dealing through both direct dealing and broker dealing channels. No respondent (domestic and overseas) indicated any decreases in customer NDF business, and 70 percent of all respondents seemed to have an optimistic outlook for the future prospects concerning this segment.

Of the five foreign bank respondents, the number of banks trading in the Korean won (KRW), New Taiwan dollar (NTD), Chinese yuan (CNY), Indian rupee (INR), and Philippine peso (PHP) were 5, 5, 3, 1, and 1, respectively, and the corresponding numbers were 9, 9, 2, 3, and 1 for the nine Japanese bank respondents. Therefore, major traded currencies, both domestic Japanese and foreign, were KRW and TWD, and CNY and INR followed as the third and fourth most popular NDF currencies in Asia (please see http://www.fxcomtky.com/announce/index_e.html for more details and other issues relating to Asian NDFs).

14.2 Philippine Peso NDF

The lack of a forward market in the peso, a small offshore non-deliverable forward market, and an inability to obtain credit onshore in pesos severely limited the ability of foreign investors to take positions against it. International commercial and investment banks with local operations and domestic banks, on the other hand, with access to peso credit onshore, were well placed to take short positions on the balance sheet, and appear to have been the primary source of pressure on the currency.

Despite the relatively lower turnover compared to NDFs on other Asian currencies such as the Korean won and New Taiwan dollar (see Table 14.1), Philippine peso NDFs did play some role during the crisis.

14.3 Korea Won NDF

The Korean won NDF market is the most active NDF contract in the world as evidenced in Table 9.1 with half of the world NDF turnover in the first quarter of 2003. We focus on the Korean won NDF around the Asian financial crisis in this section and will study its recent activities when we explore foreign exchange policy implications of NDF in Part V of this book.

14.3.1 Major Policy Changes

As the crisis gathered strength in Korea from October 1997 and Korean foreign reserve became tight, attacks on the Korean won became severe. On November 10, 1997, the Korean government abandoned its involvement in the currency market and, as a result, the market entered into a panic.

In December 1997, in accordance with the IMF recommendation, the Korean government eliminated the boundaries on daily movement of the won–dollar exchange rate and restrictions on foreign capital movements. On January 19, 1998 foreign creditors agreed upon a schedule for Korean debt repayments, and Korean financial markets then began to recover from the turmoil. In the meantime, in accordance with the IMF recommendation, the Korean government eliminated the daily limit on exchange rate movement and the restrictions on foreign capital inflows (see Park, 2001).

14.3.2 Development of Offshore NDF Market

In Korea, the development of the onshore currency derivatives market was constrained by a legal requirement that any forward transaction had to be certified as a hedge against future current account flows (the so-called "real demand principle"), which also spurred the development of a liquid offshore "non-deliverable" forward (NDF) market in the Korean won. In 1999, this restriction was lifted and a lot of activity moved onshore, leading to the convergence of the offshore and onshore prices.

Market participants reported during the crisis that while they believed fundamentals warranted taking a short position on the Korean won during this period, it was exceedingly difficult to do so. Foreign investors could not do this onshore as they could not obtain access to domestic credit or the forward market, which was small anyway. Offshore, the NDF market was also small, with market participants reporting considerable time and effort (half a day) to put on relatively small positions of a few million dollars. Any attempt to build up a substantial position required a continuous presence in the market and would "reveal one's hand" to the limited number of counterparties.

14.3.3 NDF Compared with the Spot Market

Turnovers of Korean won NDF are difficult to obtain around the Asian crisis as the won NDF was authorized to trade onshore in 1999. The Bank of Korea has data available from 2000, yet no specific data are available before 1999. Of the limited number of available studies on the won NDF, Park (2001) provides good evidence of the relationship between the Korean won spot and NDFs. Table 14.2 summarizes the results of Park (2001). We can observe from Table 14.2 that standard deviations, skewness (third moment) and kurtosis (fourth moment) of the won NDF were significantly greater than the

Table 14.2 Comparison between Korean Won Spot and NDFs

Variable	Mean (%)	Standard Deviation (%)	Skewness	Kurtosis
Pre-reform period ($N = 310$) (August 1996 to November 1997)				
Spot	0.06	0.279	0.660	1.283
NDS	0.083	0.537	2.300	20.050
Post-reform period ($N = 431$) (January 1997 to October 1999)				
Spot	−0.067	1.135	−0.350	9.980
NDS	−0.062	1.171	−1.150	17.000

Data source: Park (2001), Table 2, p. 369.

corresponding won spot in both pre- and post-crisis periods, implying that the NDF rate was much more volatile than the corresponding spot rate.

14.3.4 Onshore and Offshore NDF Markets

The Bank of Korea has been observing and monitoring both the onshore and offshore NDF markets closely. In a recent paper published in Korean, titled "Analysis of the Impacts of won NDF trading on Spot Market," Mr. Lee Seungho of the foreign exchange group of the International Department of BOK studies various aspects of the won NDF since 1999. The won NDF turnovers in Tables 9.1 and 9.2 in the offshore market survey by the Emerging Market Traders Association (EMTA) were many times greater (7.8 and 12.4 times in the first and second quarter of 2003, respectively) than corresponding figures in the onshore market. We will compare the offshore and onshore markets in more details in Part V of this book.

14.3.5 Comparison between Forward and NDFs

Table 13.2 clearly indicates that liquidity of the Korean won forward fell significantly in both spot and forward markets in Korea in 1998. Yet turnover in the offshore won NDF market increased dramatically, average daily turnover reached US$450 million in 1998, indicating about US$112.5 billion total turnover in 1998, 50 percent higher than the corresponding turnover of the Korean won forward market.

14.4 Taiwan

NDF contracts on the New Taiwan dollar (NTD) are probably the earliest NDF contracts in Asia. It was reported that NTD NDF contracts began to trade in Taiwan as early as 1995. We concentrate on NTW NDFs in this section.

14.4.1 Early Development of NTD NDFs

Because of support from monetary authority, NTD NDFs developed faster in Taiwan-China than in most other countries or regions. The governmental support led to one unique feature of NTD NDFs: the active participation of onshore institutions. It was reported that 13 foreign banks and six investment organizations traded NTD NDFs in Hong Kong in 1998; 10 foreign banks and two local banks traded such contracts in Singapore in 1998; and 25 foreign banks traded such contracts in Taiwan in 1998. The NTD NDF trading was banned in May 1998 because the speculative trading activities were believed to have accelerated NTD devaluation.

14.4.2 Turnover during the Asian Financial Crisis

Average daily turnover of NTD NDFs increased 60 percent to US$320 million in the second half of 1997 from US$200 million in the first half of 1997. It was reported (Sonali, 1998) that in Taiwan, the "central bank" implemented emergency measures to tighten rules on NDF trading. It said that all NDF trades would have to be reported on a daily basis, and banks would have to immediately inform the "central bank" by telephone of each NDF deal exceeding US$5 million. It was reported that the "central bank" intervened in the NTD/US$ markets on October 3 and 4, 1997, and the amount of NTD/US$ transactions for these two days were close to 2 billion US$.

14.4.3 Interventions of NTD NDF

According to Chang and Shen (2002), both Bank of Korea and "Central Bank" of China (central bank of Taiwan province of China) actively intervened in the domestic spot and forward exchange markets during the Asian financial crisis. From July 1996 to May 1997, the forward rates in both markets moved closely with the spot rate. Starting from May 1997 to December 1997, the NDF rates began to deviate from the spot, which indicates that the market was anticipating a depreciation of the New Taiwan dollar. However, the domestic forward exchange rate continued to follow the spot rates closely due to active interventions by the "Central Bank". Similar patterns for the Korean won/US$ forward rates were reported by Park and Rhee (2000).

14.4.4 Comparison between the Won NDF and NTD NDF

Maximum likelihood estimates of parameters in the regime-switching model show that the mean value of currency misalignment for NTD/US$ is much higher than that of the won/US$. It could be due to the more effective intervention by the "Central Bank" of China in the NTD/US$ spot exchange rate market than that by the Bank of Korea during the sample period. Please see Chang and Shen (2002) for a more detailed discussion on this.

14.4.5 Coexistence of Offshore and Onshore NDF Markets

The NTD NDF market has similar coexistence of both offshore and onshore markets as the Korean won NDF structure. We will study the interrelationship between the offshore and onshore markets within both markets in Part IV of this book.

14.5 Chinese Yuan NDF

14.5.1 Early Development

The CNY NDF contracts began to be first traded in Hong Kong as early as in 1996. It then spread to Singapore shortly afterwards. Hong Kong and Singapore are the two major centers for the CNY

NDFs. Participants to the CNY NDF markets are top international financial institutions, and their clients are those multinational corporations that invested in China and had incomes in CNY, those domestic Chinese companies with head offices in Hong Kong, and others. These clients had a specific need to hedge their RMB exposure because their investments and income were in RMB and there was no way for them to hedge. The development of the CNY NDF market exactly met the needs of such clients.

14.5.2 Pressure for Devaluation during the Crisis

As all other currencies in East Asia, the CNY/RMB was also under great pressure for devaluation during the Asian financial crisis. Because of the difficulty in accessing domestic RMB credit and the unavailability of the RMB forwards market, international participants could only participate in the offshore RMB NDF market which was extremely thin at the time.

Figure 14.1 depicts 12 month RMB NDFs from September 1997 to March 1998. We can readily observe from Figure 14.1 that the

Figure 14.1 Twelve Month Chinese RMB NDF from Sept 1997 to March 1998.

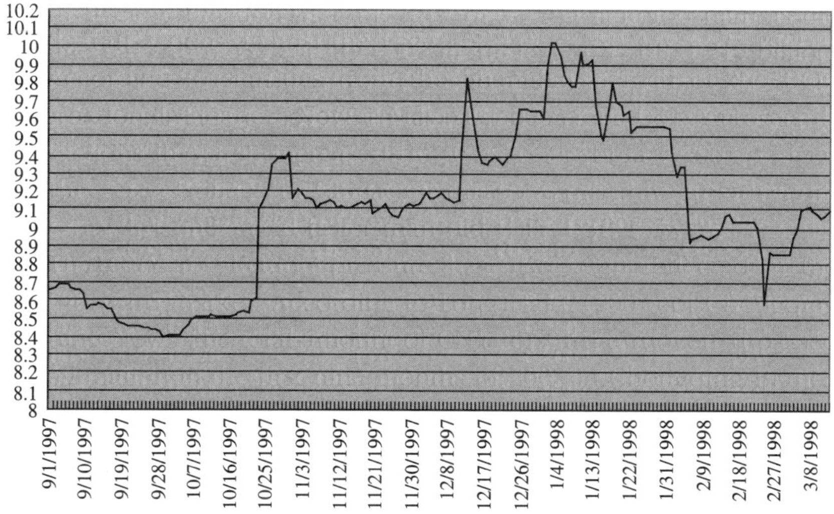

Data source: China Foreign Exchange Trading System, 1999.

12 month RMB NDF jumped late in October 1997 to around RMB 9.4/US$ from RMB 8.5/US$ when the Hong Kong dollar was severely attacked following the New Taiwan dollar devaluation; it further rose to RMB 9.8/US$ in December 1997 and to around RMB 10.0/US$ in January 1998, implying depreciation of more than 16 percent from late September 1997 (corresponding to RMB 8.4/US$).

14.5.3 Responsibility and Diminished Pressure for Devaluation

The review of history in Figure 14.1 shows that back in 1997–98, China was urged to resist devaluing the RMB to forestall a vicious currency devaluation tidal wave in Asia. China obliged and held the RMB steady to act responsibly in consideration of helping to calm the nervous Asian financial markets. The pressure for devaluation on the RMB gradually diminished from September 1999 to 2000 with the 12 month NDF slightly above RMB 8.4/US$. We will return to the CNY or RMB NDF in more detail in Part IV of this book.

14.6 Russian Ruble NDF

Although the poor state of Russia's fiscal accounts was well-known by mid-1998, the announcement of a 90-day moratorium on external debt payments on August 17, 1998 caught most market participants by surprise. At the time of the default and devaluation, the estimates of the outstanding notional of the US$ ruble NDF contracts ranged from $10 billion to $100 billion, and the total foreign exposure to the domestic bond market was around $20 billion. According to market sources, the US$–ruble foreign exchange forwards with Russian banks as counterparties were the largest source of credit losses by major swap dealers during 1997–98, exceeding the losses made on their Asian lending. The events in Russia highlighted the presence of convertibility risk even when local currency positions in emerging markets were hedged, and raised the issue of the NDF valuation when an official rate was not available. In addition, Russia's default sent shock-waves through the credit-derivatives markets, with the cost of protection increasing in all sectors, including the investment grade segment. Ambiguous and often misleading definitions of reference obligations, credit events, and settlement mechanics made it very difficult for protection buyers to enforce the contracts.

14.7 Summary

The Asian NDF market emerged in Hong Kong and Singapore for currencies such as the Korean won, New Taiwan dollar, Philippine peso, Chinese renminbi, and Indian rupee. The NDF market has attracted investors who either need to hedge currency exposure or take speculative positions but are hindered by restrictions and or illiquidity in the local forward market. Despite the growing interest in the Asian NDF market, few, so far, have studied the newly emerged offshore market and its relation with the domestic currency market.

The NDF market began trading on a full scale in Asia in 1996, and it became more active in the second half of 1997 and 1998 during the Asian crisis. However, information on trading volume is rather limited, so we cannot analyze the intensity of the market activity easily. With continuous efforts of the EMTA, which has been promoting the development of the NDF market worldwide, data on NDFs on major currencies became available in the first two quarters of 2003; yet, the survey was suspended late in 2003. We will return to this issue in Part IV of this book when we discuss CNY NDFs specifically.

15

Swaps

Structurally speaking, swaps are sets of forwards with periodic payments. Tenors of swaps are normally longer than forwards. After introducing forwards and non-deliverable forwards involved in the Asian financial crisis, we turn to the next major type of derivative products greatly involved in the crisis — swaps — in this chapter. The purpose of this chapter to introduce various types of swaps and the roles they played during the crisis.

15.1 Currency Swaps

We first introduce currency swaps in Malaysia, Indonesia, and Korea in this section.

15.1.1 Malaysian Ringgit Currency Swaps

Malaysia was greatly involved in the crisis with the ringgit devalued 47% from July 1997 to February 1998 as shown in Table 12.1. The Malaysian government adopted capital control in September 1997, a policy dramatically different from other countries. The great volume of Malaysian companies involved during the crisis clearly implies

Figure 15.1 Malaysia: Foreign Exchange Transaction (Monthly Turnover of Ringgit/US$)

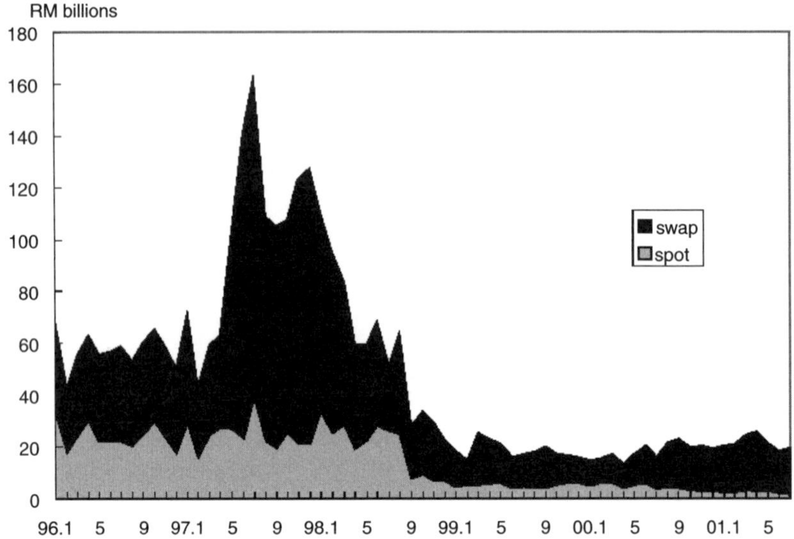

Data source: Watanabe *et al* (2002), Chart 1–2, p. 15.

the great involvement of Malaysia in derivatives during the crisis. Figure 15.1 depicts the monthly turnover of ringgit/US$ swaps and spot from January 1996 to May 2001.

Figure 15.1 clearly shows that the ringgit/US$ swap turnover was slightly higher than that of spot in the pre-crisis period from January 1996 to June 1997, and the monthly swap turnover rose from about 30–40 billion ringgit (RM) to more than RM 130 billion in July 1997 while spot turnover stayed largely the same until late in 1998 before falling dramatically. Although swap turnover fell slightly from late 1997, it remained around RM 100 billion until April 1998. Although both spot and swap turnovers dropped significantly from September 1998, when the Malaysian government adopted capital control, to May 2001, the spot turnover fell much more dramatically than the swap turnover.

15.1.2 Indonesian Rupiah Currency Swaps

Domestic banks and corporates had been bullish on the Indonesian rupiah for some time; both had entered into substantial amounts of currency swaps and sold options against the rupiah's depreciation, using the premiums as a source of income. The rupiah had tended to stay at the appreciated end of the band, and had, on previous occasions of band widening, tended to move to the appreciated end. So when Bank of Indonesia widened its intervention band from 8 percent to 12 percent on July 11, 1997 in a preemptive move designed to deter speculation, Indonesian banks bought up enough rupiah to push it up for a brief period. On the other side of these transactions were the international commercial and investment banks that had a bearish view on the rupiah, engendered by perceptions of the need for a competitive devaluation in the region, and saw the widening of the band as facilitating such a process. There were substantial foreign investor flows out of the rupiah, led by the international commercial and investment banks, and the domestic banks quickly changed sides within two days, followed soon after by the domestic corporates, as domestic entities attempted to hedge not only their external debt but also their swaps and options positions.

15.1.3 Korean Won Currency Swaps

Korean institutions were much involved in many currency swaps not only with US and European counterparties but also with Asian counterparties. Facts and data are again difficult to obtain, yet we can obtain some facts from lawsuits between Korean financial institutions and their counterparties. The lawsuits filed by a number of Korean entities shed some light on the nature of these transactions.

J.P. Morgan transacted many deals with Korean institutions. For example, in one transaction Morgan engaged in a $/won currency swap with Boram Banks. In a straight currency swap, the counterparties exchanged principal and interest payments on the currencies, so presumably Boran gave won to the US dollar, while Morgan was paying a rate linked to won interest rates (the differential in the rates when the swap was initiated in February 1997 was about 2 to 1, suggesting a substantial profit on the interest rate differential). When the swap is unwound the principal sums are usually returned at a prearranged exchange rate, so that Boram would have had to return dollars that were worth about three times as many won as at the beginning of the swap.

To transfer this risk, Boram traded a series of similar swaps with SK securities, presumably passing the dollars on to SK securities, which now carried the foreign exchange risks but was borrowing at cheap dollar interest rates against the won loans it was extending to its clients at domestic market rates. The Morgan lawsuit placed the value at $189 million. Given the changes in exchange rates, the original principal could have been less than $250 million (see Kregel, 1998). Although Boram was prepared to pay Morgan, SK filed a suit in a Korean court to block the payment, thus hoping to exonerate it from having to pay Boram the funds which would have ended up being paid to Morgan.

15.2 Credit Default Swaps

15.2.1 Credit Derivatives

Although the global credit derivatives market is still a very small part of the global derivatives markets, it remains one of its fastest-growing segments. The data collected as part of the BIS Triennial Survey showed that positions in the global credit derivatives market rose to $693 billion at the end of June 2001 from $118 billion at the end of June 1998. It had been estimated that the total volume of transaction of credit derivatives reached US$1.6 trillion in 2003 (see British Bankers Association — Credit Derivatives Survey, 2000; Wellons, 2001).

The most commonly used credit derivatives in emerging markets are credit default swaps (CDSs), total return swaps (TRSs), credit-linked notes (CLNs), and collateralized debt obligations (CDOs). The sovereign CDSs are the most liquid instruments in emerging market credit derivatives, accounting for around 85 percent of the total outstanding notional.

15.2.2 Credit Default Swaps

CDSs are the most popular credit swaps in the global market because they provide pure credit risk transfer. They were also traded during the Asian financial crisis. A credit default swap is essentially an insurance contract for one party to protect itself from unexpected credit events so that credit risk will be mitigated. The buyer of a CDS pays a certain fixed rate regularly for a given period of time within the life of the swap, say 0.25 percent, on a notional value of the swap that is often set the same as the notional amount of a loan or a bond, and the other party does not pay anything unless some specified credit events happen. The credit events may include some of the following: failure to pay, bankruptcy, repudiation, restructuring, and so on.

15.2.3 Geographical Differences and Notional Amount Outstanding

The 1998 Prebon Yamane and *Derivatives Week* survey of credit derivatives dealers provided some information about the underlying issuer. Asian issuers were almost exclusively sovereigns (93 percent). In contrast, the majority of US issuers were corporates (60 percent), with the remainder split between banks (30 percent) and sovereigns (10 percent); European issuers were more evenly split — sovereigns 45 percent, banks 29 percent, and corporates 26 percent.

As most other OTC derivatives, notional amount outstanding is not available for CDSs. We can only estimate the trading activities through indirect methods. During the financial crisis in Asia in 1997, numerous credit default swaps were triggered as the credit situation deteriorated. In some cases, protection buyers who did not own the reference asset had trouble obtaining the reference asset in the market to physically settle the swap (see Smithson and Hayt, 2000). Skinner and Diaz's (2003) empirical studies on CDSs also provide evidence that CDSs played a part during the Asian financial crisis.

15.2.4 Difficulty in Pricing Credit Default Swaps

It is rather technical to discuss how to price CDSs. When there is insufficient liquidity in the CDS market so that it is difficult to extract enough information about default probability, pricing can become rather difficult. It is beyond the scope of this book to discuss such pricing issues. Interested readers may refer to Skinner and Diaz (2003) for relating literature and pricing models.

15.3 Total Return Swaps

15.3.1 Concept of Total Return Swaps

A TRS is a contract in which at least one series of payments is based on the total rate of return (change in market price appreciation or depreciation plus interest or dividend payments) on some underlying asset, equity, bond, or a loan. The other leg of the swap is typically based on a variable interest rate such as LIBOR plus a certain spread according to the credit-worthiness of the underlying security, but may be a fixed rate or the total rate of return on some other financial instrument. Based upon what is known about the pre-crisis situation in East Asia, the total return swaps in those situations usually swapped LIBOR against the total rate of return on a government security. A total return swap replicates the position of borrowing at LIBOR in order to finance the holding of a security or security index. The returns are the same, but unlike the actual cash market transaction, it does not involve ownership.

15.3.2 Popularity in Asia

TRSs were very popular during 1995–97 in Asia because of their functionalities. These swaps seem to have played some role in the contagion of the Asian financial crisis, so we discuss them in more detail. These instruments will certainly be essential in hedging and trading credit risk.

One of the uses of TRSs in East Asia was to capture the gains from the carry trade or carry business. A profitable carry trade exists where exchange rates are fixed and interest rate differentials persist between the two economies. Then, it is possible to borrow in the low interest rate currency and lend in the high interest rate currency with no risk other than that of a failure in the fixed exchange rate. In the case of East Asia, the money center banks were willing to lend the major currencies and the East Asian banks were eager to capture carry profits from the interest rate differential of borrowing and lending.

15.3.3 Korean and Indonesian Counterparties

The use of TRSs increased the likelihood of contagion. They often involve cross-currency assets and payments and are, therefore, more likely to transfer disruptions from one market to another. Neftci (1998) claims that one reason that Korean banks engaged in so many Indonesian TRSs was that they were seeking higher rates of return in response to a rise in their funding costs. At the end of this process, Korean banks were exposed to Indonesian credit. This, however, was not visible on their balance sheets. This situation not only creates the possibility for contagion, buy may also make the contagion unpredictable and severe.

From 1995 to 1997, a significant portion of Indonesian credit was swapped out to Korean banks, which were in search of higher yields due to the high funding costs that they started to pay on their existing loans, beginning in 1996. As a result, many South Korean banks saw their profit margins shrink or even turn negative. They started to look for a way out of this situation. At the other end, Indonesian companies were in need of new funding, given the high growth of the economy.

15.3.4 J.P. Morgan and Korean Securities

Legal suits filed by J.P. Morgan and DK securities in their payments disputes, were reported to relate to TRSs. It is also the case that the issue of capital market instruments by Asian borrowers surged in 1995 and 1996. For example, Asian issuance rose from $25.2 billion in 1996. Not only were US banks involved, but much of the success of local investment banks, such as Hong Kong based Peregrine securities, was primarily in underwriting and selling debt for Asian corporations. It could only do this if it could provide reasonable guarantees for placement for these issues. The Korean Securities Supervisory Board reported that Korean institutions were operating over 100 offshore investment funds with portfolios valued at around

$3 billion, two-thirds of which represented Korean assets (see Kregel, 1998: p. 686).

15.3.5 Korean Trusts

Again, the magnitude of the change in the exchange rate witnessed after the decision to float the won would have produced capital losses on the underlying assets and thus negative won inflows, which would have been transformed into larger net dollar interest payments due to Morgan. The rush to hedge such exposure thus made the fall in the exchange. The legal cases at this stage simply involve failure of the trusts to meet periodic payments on the swaps. It is reported that more than 40 of the 100 or so such trusts had engaged in similar swaps with Morgan. Of its total of $3.4 billion of exposure to Korea, $2 billion are linked to derivative contracts. This perhaps explains why Morgan was at the forefront of the move to convert Korean banks' short-term debt into sovereign debt (see Kregel, 1998: p. 686).

15.4 Swaps in Singapore and Hong Kong

Data in the two financial centers are normally more available than in their neighboring countries or regions. We describe briefly the market activities in these two centers, in this section.

15.4.1 Singapore

The principal value of interest rate swap (IRS) transactions in 1998 averaged US$166.1 billion monthly, a significant 135.8 percent higher than in 1997. This growth was due to the increased interest rate volatility caused by the regional economic crisis. US dollar-denominated IRS remained the most widely transacted instrument. Its share of total IRS transacted rose from 59.1 percent in 1997 to 76.4 percent in 1998. Japanese yen denominated IRS accounted for 19.1 percent of the total IRS transacted, as compared to 29.7 percent for 1997. IRS transactions in other currencies decreased by 4.0 percent to account for one-twentieth of the total volume (see Singapore

Monetary Authority, 1999). Currency swap turnover is not available in 1997, the average daily turnover grew 28.4 percent to US$74.7 billion in April 1998 from April 1995 (see Table 13.3).

15.4.2 Hong Kong

Average daily net turnover of currency swaps fell from US$53.7 billion to US$43.8 billion from April 1995 to April 1998, declining by 16.9 percent; turnover of interest rate forward rate agreements fell by 75 percent and OTC interest rate options by 11 percent. Strategies based on yen interest rates diminished in the light of historically low levels of interest rates and reduced volatility. The increase of 6 percent in trading of interest rate swaps, however, partly reversed the decline in interest rate derivatives turnover. Increase in currency swaps together with a decrease in forward rate agreements was also a phenomenon seen in the other major derivatives markets. (see Turnover of Foreign Exchange and Derivatives Markets in Hong Kong, Hong Kong Monetary Authority, 1999).

15.5 Summary and Conclusions

Despite the lack of sufficient data available for systematic analysis, swaps played important roles during the Asian financial crisis, as seen from our introduction in this chapter. Similar studies on swaps and other derivatives products during the Mexican crisis have been better conducted and documented, interested readers may refer to Garber and Lall (1999).

16

Options, Structured Notes, and Other Products

Options are major components of derivative products trading in exchanges and OTC marketplaces around the world, especially in the foreign exchange market, as shown in Chapter 11. Options involved during the Asian financial crisis were currency options trading at the OTC marketplace and options embedded in traditional debt contracts. Various types of structured notes were also involved during the Asian crisis, and many such notes had embedded options. The purpose of this chapter is to introduce embedded options, currency options, structured notes, and related products during the Asian financial crisis.

16.1 "Callable" and "Put-able" Debt

16.1.1 Concepts of Embedded Options

The largest threat to financial market stability that did not directly involve foreign exchange exposure was the use of embedded derivatives, embedded options in loan and bond debt contracts. These embedded options on the debt principal enabled lenders to recall their principal in the event of economic trouble. Callable bonds are

Table 16.1 Secondary Bond Market Transactions in Debt Instruments of the Emerging Market (Unit: US$ billion)

	1993	1994	1995	1996	1997
Total turnover	1978.9	2766.2	2738.8	5296.9	5915.9
		39.8%	−1.0%	93.4%	11.7%
Debt with embedded options and warrants	57.4	142.4	593.4	1273.8	1506
Annual growth rate		148.1%	316.7%	114.7%	18.2%
Embedded turnover/total	2.9%	5.1%	21.7%	24.0%	25.5%

Data source: IMF Working Paper II: The Asian Crisis: Capital Markets, Dynamics and Spillover.

familiar financial instruments in advanced capital markets in which call options are embedded in bonds. A callable bond is a combination of a conventional bond and a call option that allows the issuer to recall the principal on the bond at a specified strike value or value after some time in the future. Callable bonds are used by borrowers to reduce their risk that they will be locked into higher than market rates of interest on their outstanding debt.

Table 16.1 provides the total turnover of debt with embedded options and warrants and the corresponding total turnover of all debt in emerging markets from 1993 to 1997. We can observe that turnover of debt with embedded options and warrants as a percentage of total turnovers increased from merely a few percent in 1993 and 1994, to over 21 percent in 1995, and to over a quarter in 1997.

16.1.2 Asian Debt with Embedded Options

The embedded options in the East Asian debt market were usually put options rather than call options; thus, it was the put rather than the call options that pose potential problems to financial market stability in emerging economies.

A put-able bond grants the lender, not the borrower, the right to reclaim its principal. Foreign lenders attached put provisions to loans and bonds in order to reduce their risk of adverse macroeconomic conditions or other circumstances which would reduce the ability of their borrowers to repay their debts. It also reduced their

Table 16.2 Put-able Bonds Issued from East Asia (US$ million due in 1999 or 2000)

Hong Kong	2642	24.8%
Indonesia	963	9.1%
Korea	3986	37.5%
Malaysia	1730	16.3%
Thailand	1313	12.3%
Total	10634	100.0%

Data source: Dodd (2000: 15).

exposure to increases in dollar or other hard currency interest rates. Table 16.2 provides the total put-able bonds in major Asian countries/region in 1999. We can observe that Korea had the highest market share of 37.5 percent with nearly US$4 billion.

16.1.3 Types of Embedded Put Options

Embedded put options were in the form of "hard" and "soft" puts. Hard puts, usually attached to a note or bond, gave the lender the right to demand principal repayment after a certain date, say, for example, a 5 year note might be put-able after 1 year. Soft puts, usually attached to loans, gave lenders the right to reschedule the terms of their credit in the event of certain adverse events. The "hard" put options are normally "Bermudian" or "Mid-Atlantic" options, implying that they are between "European" and "American" as they can be exercised at pre-specified dates within the lives of the options (for Bermudian options see Zhang, 1998). Most of the "hard" put options were closer to the European rather than the American style options. Option holders were granted the right to exercise the option only on specific days or perhaps semi-annually or annually; in only a very few cases were the options exercisable on a continuous basis like American options (for a detailed description of such options see Dodd, 2000).

16.1.4 IMF Estimation of Put-able Debts

The IMF estimated in 1999 (IMF, 1999), using available public databases, that there were $32 billion in debts put-able through the end of 2000 for all emerging countries. Of the total $32 billion, over 70 percent was from East Asian issuers. Of course a great deal had probably already been put to the borrowers since the crisis began early in 1997. Of this East Asian debt put-able through 2000, $11.5 billion were notes and bonds, and $12 billion were loans. An estimated 90 percent of the total put-able debt was issued by private, as opposed to government borrowers.

According to an IMF memo written in the summer of 1997 (IMF, July 1997), there were instances of the use of both call and put options on bond principal and coupons in East Asia. The issuer held the call option in the event that interest rates fell, and the investor held the put option in the event of a decline in the credit rating of the issuer.

16.2 Currency Options in Singapore

Transactions in currency options increased in Singapore in 1998, averaging US$61.2 billion per month, 0.9 percent higher than in 1997. The majority (85.6 percent) of the currency options transactions were transacted with counterparties outside Singapore. Table 16.3 gives the daily average turnover of FX options and other derivatives in Singapore in April 1998, April 1995 and April 2001. We can see that the average daily turnover of FX options in April 1998 was 183 percent higher than in April 1995, and 64 percent higher than in April 2001, indicating that the crisis increased turnover significantly.

Table 16.3 Average Daily Turnovers of FX Options and Other derivatives in Singapore in April 1998 and April 1995 (Unit: US$ billion)

	Apr 01	Apr 98	Apr 95
FX Options	2.80	4.60	1.20
Growth Rate		64.3%	−73.9%
FX Swaps	0.30	1.30	0.60
Growth Rate		333.3%	−53.8%

Data source: Bank for International Settlements (BIS) Survey of Foreign Exchange and Derivatives Markets Activities, Date: September 29, 1998.

16.3 Options in Hong Kong during the Asian Financial Crisis

16.3.1 Foreign Exchange and Interest Rate Options

Currency options turnover increased significantly in 1998 as volatilities in the financial market increased during the Asian crisis. Table 16.4 gives the average daily net turnover of foreign exchange options and interest rate options trading in the OTC marketplace in Hong Kong in April 1995 and April 1998, and the annualized turnovers in 1995 and 1998. We can observe easily that the annualized net turnover of foreign exchange options and interest rate options trading in Hong Kong surpassed 1998 Hong Kong GDP 10 percent and 62 percent in 1995 and 1998, respectively.

16.3.2 Stock Index Options

The "double play" in Hong Kong during the Asian financial crisis, as we discussed in Chapter 12, indicates that speculators attached the Hong Kong dollar and stock market at the same time. There are many ways to take short positions in the stock market such as selling blue chip stocks, shorting stock index futures, selling stock index call options and/or buying stock index put options. Table 16.5 provides the annual statistics of the Hang Seng Index (HSI) options from 1993 (Hang Seng Index options were launched in March 1993) to 2002.

Table 16.4 OTC Options in Hong Kong in April 95 and April 98; Average Daily Net Turnover (US$ million)

	Apr 95	Apr 98	Percent Change Over 1995	Annualized Net Turnover in 1995	Annualized Net Turnover in 1998
Foreign exchange options	625	983	57.3	154,375.0	242,801.0
Interest rate options	105	94	−10.5	25,935.0	23,218.0
Sum	730	1077	47.5	180,310.0	266,019.0
Sum/1998 HKGDP				1.10	1.62

Data source: calculated using data from Turnover of Foreign Exchange and Derivatives Markets in Hong Kong, Hong Kong Monetary Authority Quarterly Bulletin, November 1998.

Table 16.5 Annual Statistics of Hang Seng Index Options 1993–2002

Year	No. of trading days	Contract volume				Open interest		
		Average daily	Call	Put	Total	Call	Put	Total
1993	207	1426	140,520	154,697	295,217	7614	10,088	17,702
1994	248	2446	301,053	305,626	606,679	7261	8,718	15,979
1995	247	2614	310,696	334,842	645,538	9854	10,321	20,175
1996	249	4393	537,655	556,216	1,093,871	30,761	26,080	56,841
1997	245	4683	544,421	602,953	1,147,374	18,680	14,333	33,013
1998	245.5	3253	423,402	375,310	798,712	18,042	15,505	33,547
1999	244.5	2922	354,717	359,592	714,309	14,036	10,084	24,120
2000	247	2203	257,537	286,510	544,047	5750	4769	10,519
2001	241.5	2965	356,969	359,145	716,114	17,172	12,569	29,741
2002	245	4369	570,377	500,054	1,070,431	37,150	29,663	66,813

Data source: Hong Kong exchange website: www.hkex.com.hk.

We can see from Table 16.5 that the total trading volume of HSI options reached a peak in 1997; whereas the call option volume in 1997 stayed almost the same as in 1996, the put option volume increased significantly. The degrees of speculation in the HSI options can be appropriately seen from volume/open interest ratio of calls and puts. The call ratio jumped from 17.5 to 29.1, up 66.8 percent from 1996 to 1997, and that of put options jumped more significantly from 21.3 to 40.1, that is, they nearly doubled. The jumps in volume/open interest ratios of call and put options from 1996 to 1997 convincingly imply increased speculations in the stock market.

16.4 Structured Notes

16.4.1 Concepts of Structured Notes

Structured notes are investment vehicles with coupon payments and principle repayments driven by formulas that can leverage the initial capital invested. Such notes can be booked as normal investments and can avoid some regulatory issues. Structured notes became popular during the Mexican crisis when many Mexican institutions traded a large sum of such products with investment houses in

New York. Interested readers may refer to Garber (1998) for a more detailed study of such products and related literature.

Structured notes were part of the new wave of innovation in capital flows to East Asia in the 1990s. They offered issuers and investors either better yields than similarly rated securities, or better combinations or bundles of risk characteristics. In some cases, structured notes were designed to circumvent accounting rules or government regulations so as to allow lower capital charges, greater foreign exchange exposure or greater overall risk to capital.

16.4.2 Structured Notes in Asia

The structured notes used in East Asia were usually structured so that their yield was linked to the value of one or more of the currencies or stock indices in the developing economies. The issuers of these structured notes were financial institutions from advanced capital markets and the investors were often East Asian financial institutions and investors who are more willing to hold their own exchange rate risk or that of their neighboring developing countries. One reason given for this is that they are more knowledgeable of their economies and markets than investors from advanced capital markets (see Dodd, 2001).

16.4.3 Principal Exchange Rate Linked Note (PERL)

Other structured instruments were also used in the run-up to the Asian crisis. For example, one of the well-known instruments was called a PERL-principal exchange rate linked note. A PERL was a dollar-denominated instrument that generated cash flows linked to a long position in an emerging market currency. If the exchange rate remained stable, the return on the PERL was significantly higher than the return on the similarly rated dollar paper, but in the event of major depreciation, the return could become negative (for more details see Dodd, 2001).

16.4.4 South Korea

Based on the long-standing pegs of the Thai baht and Malaysian ringgit to the US dollar, a number of Korean institutions had purchased, through their offshore subsidiaries, structured notes that, in effect, borrowed in yen to finance bets on the exchange rates between the dollar and the two regional currencies. When their pegs collapsed, the investors were burdened by substantial liabilities that added to the difficulties already facing the Korean financial institutions following the depreciation of their own currency.

16.4.5 Structured Notes with Embedded Options

Many structured notes claim above-market interest rates on the notes; the above-market rate is generated by the sale of a put option on the underlying instrument, say the Thai baht as a strike price just above the current market rate that is in fact embedded in the contract. If the baht exchange rate remains constant, the written put is not exercised and the option premium received is retained by the writer and is used to meet the above-market guaranteed interest rate payable on the contract.

16.5 The Long Term Capital Management Episode

The Long Term Capital Management (LTCM) near-collapse episode in late 1988 shocked the world financial community. This episode was directly caused by the Russian default which in turn was caused by the Asian financial crisis. As LTCM traded a lot of derivative products, we briefly introduce the LTCM episode here in this section. We largely follow the Report of the (US) President's Working Group on Financial Markets (1999) in this section.

16.5.1 Background and Performances

LTCM was founded in early 1994. Although LTCM itself was a Delaware limited partnership with its main offices in Connecticut, the fund that it operates, Long-Term Capital Portfolio, L.P. ("the LTCM Fund," or "the Fund") is a Cayman Islands partnership. LTCM sought to profit from a variety of trading strategies, including convergence trades and dynamic hedging.

From its inception, the LTCM had a prominent position in the community of hedge funds, both because of the reputation of its principals, and also because of its large initial capital stake. The

LTCM Fund produced returns, net of fees, of approximately 40 percent in 1995 and 1996, and slightly less than 20 percent in 1997. At the end of 1997, LTCM returned approximately $2.7 billion in capital to its investors, reducing the capital base of the fund by about 36 percent to $4.8 billion.

16.5.2 Products Transacted

Approximately 80 percent of the LTCM Fund's balance-sheet positions were in government bonds of the G-7 countries. Nevertheless, the Fund was active in many other markets, including securities markets, exchange-traded futures, and OTC derivatives. Its activity was also geographically diverse, encompassing markets in North America, Europe, and Asia. Major products include government bonds, mortgage-backed securities, corporate bonds, emerging bonds, and equity products. The LTCM Fund took on futures positions at about a dozen major futures exchanges worldwide, including some very sizable positions.

The LTCM Fund engaged in OTC derivatives contracts with several dozen counterparties. These positions included swap, forward, and option contracts, and were predominantly focused on interest rates and equity markets; the LTCM Fund participated in the foreign exchange markets to support its activities in multiple national markets. Although the Fund sometimes held open foreign exchange positions, it was not substantially engaged in efforts to profit from foreign exchange fluctuations.

16.5.3 Portfolio Composition

Overall, the distinguishing features of the LTCM Fund were the scale of its activities, the large size of its positions in certain markets, and the extent of its leverage, both in terms of balance-sheet measures and on the basis of more meaningful measures of risk exposure in relation to capital. The Fund reportedly had over 60,000 trades on its books, including long securities positions of over $50 billion and short positions of an equivalent magnitude. At the end of August 1998, the gross notional amounts of the Fund's contracts on futures exchanges exceeded $500 billion, swaps contracts more than $750 billion, and options and other OTC derivatives over $150 billion.

16.5.4 LTCM's Near Failure

On July 31, 1998, the LTCM Fund held $4.1 billion in capital, down about 15 percent from the beginning of the year. During the single month of August (Russia's devaluation of the ruble and declaration of a debt moratorium on August 17, 1998), the LTCM Fund suffered additional losses of $1.8 billion, bringing the loss of equity for the year to over 50 percent. The Fund's capital base was now $2.3 billion, and LTCM reported to investors that it was seeking an injection of capital.

By September 21, the LTCM Fund's liquidity situation was bleak. The Federal Reserve Bank of New York provided the facilities for discussions and encouraged the firms involved to seek the least disruptive solution that they believed was in their own collective self-interest. The agreement was reached only after the firms involved became convinced that no other alternative to default was possible. Interested readers may also read pp. 218–250 of Marthinsen (2003) for a good detailed description of the LTCM episode.

16.6 Summary and Lessons

Derivatives play a useful role in hedging and risk management so as to facilitate capital flows to developing economies. They can also make fixed exchange rate systems less stable, and then later quicken the pace and deepen the impact of devaluation once it occurs. This functions to increase the systemic risk in financial markets and raises the possibility of spreading contagion amongst economies. In the wake of the crisis, they can make the process of post-crisis recovery policy making even more difficult.

We have introduced major derivatives involved during the Asian financial crisis. All derivatives products were used either to hedge or to speculate based on the expectation that the Asian currencies would devalue. Most of these products are currently used in the CNY related derivatives market based on the expectation that the CNY will revalue. We will concentrate on CNY derivatives in Part IV.

PART IV

Chinese Yuan (CNY) Derivatives

With all the preparations made in the previous three parts on the Chinese economy and financial markets, foreign exchange derivatives in developed markets, and the major foreign exchange derivative products involved in the Asian financial crisis, we are ready to start the main part of this book — CNY or RMB derivatives. Because the CNY is still tightly pegged to the USD, there are essentially no derivatives on the CNY in Mainland China besides a thin CNY forward market.

We will start with the CNY forward market — the only CNY derivative product onshore in China in Chapter 17; Chapter 18 introduces the CNY nondeliverable forwards (NDFs); Chapter 19 illustrates how CNY NDF contracts are used in practice; Chapter 20 introduces CNY nondeliverable swaps and forward swaps; Chapter 21 introduces and analyzes CNY nondeliverable options (NDOs) and options on the CNY NDFs and popular trading strategies using such options; Chapter 22 introduces various foreign currency deposits with embedded options; Chapter 23 introduces CNY structured notes; Chapter 24 analyzes channels to profit from the potential CNY revaluation using traditional products and how offshore CNY derivatives are related to traditional business transactions onshore.

17

CNY Forwards

As discussed earlier in this book, foreign exchange forwards are the basic foreign exchange instruments for hedging as well as for speculation in all developed markets and also for most countries affected during the Asian financial crisis. It is natural for us to start our introduction and analysis of CNY derivatives with CNY forwards in this chapter.

This chapter is organized as follows. Section 17.1 traces a brief history of the CNY forwards market; Section 17.2 discusses the Tentative Administrative Methods for CNY forward transactions issued by the People's Bank of China (PBOC); Section 17.3 introduces CNY forwards in the Bank of China; Section 17.4 introduces the turnover of the CNY forward transactions from 1997 to 2003; Section 17.5 explores major problems existing in the CNY forwards market; Section 17.6 discusses potentiality of the CNY forward market in China; and Section 17.7 summarizes and concludes the chapter.

17.1 Brief History of CNY Forwards

The China Foreign Exchange Trade System (CFETS) began to experiment with CNY forward transactions in April 1995, about one year after it started its operation of the cash foreign exchange business in April 1994. Because CFETS itself was in the early stage of its spot business, with many aspects to improve before its first anniversary, the first trial with CNY forwards was not successful. Recognizing the importance of CNY forwards, the PBOC studied the CNY forwards and issued *The Tentative Administrative Methods for RMB Forward Settlement* (abbreviated as *Methods*) on January 18, 1997, which provided necessary regulatory methods and cleared the way for CNY forwards to be launched later on (Ye and Li, 2000, p. 103).

Within three months after the official announcement of the tentative methods by the PBOC, the Bank of China (BOC), the only bank authorized in China then, started to transact CNY forwards business on April 1, 1997, about three years after the CFETS started foreign exchange spot trading in April 1994. Although foreign exchange forward trading is commonplace business practice in all developed markets and many developing countries, this still represented an important step in the development of the Chinese foreign exchange derivatives market. The birth of the CNY forwards made it possible for importers and other companies to hedge their foreign exchange (FX) risk.

As with other FX business, originally monopolized by the BOC and then extended to other State-owned banks, as we discussed in Chapter 7, the CNY forwards business was authorized to other state-owned banks six years after the BOC first started the first transaction. Although the China Construction Bank (CCB) and the Agriculture Bank of China obtained CNY forwards authorization from the State Administration of Foreign Exchange (SAFE) in 2002 and the Industrial and Commercial Bank (ICBC) announced that it also obtained similar authorization early in January 2003, these three state-owned banks hardly had sizable transaction until April 1, 2003, six years later than the BOC. All the four state-owned banks can now conduct CNY forwards businesses.

17.2 Tentative Methods of the PBOC

The tentative administrative methods for CNY forward trading issued by the PBOC set administrative and managerial principles for the

CNY forward business throughout China. We concentrate on the major aspects of these methods so as to have a better understanding of the CNY forwards market in China.

17.2.1 Coverage and Purpose

The methods cover foreign exchange settlement, sales, and payment for participants to hedge their FX risk in designated banks.

17.2.2 Approval for Settlement and Sales

Banks with FX business must apply for forwards authorization from the SAFE, branches of authorized banks must also apply for business approvals in the corresponding regional offices of the SAFE, and the regional offices of the SAFE will submit the applications to the SAFE head office for final approvals. Bank branches must submit certain documents such as application forms, a certificate for FX business, authorizations from the head offices of the corresponding banks, and so on.

17.2.3 Administrations

CNY forward contracts must contain information on FX sources and usage for payments. Banks must examine all required proofs, and contracts from participants who do not furnish all required information on time will not be allowed to settle when the contracts mature. Banks may require participants to pay an additional amount of security money to secure settlement of such contracts. The general margin charged is at least 3% of the notional value (Ye and Li, 2001, p. 106).

Currencies and Tenors

Essentially forwards on all full convertible currencies can be traded against the CNY. The tenor was set within 120 days when the methods were first announced, and it was extended to 180 days in 1999.

There are 14 CNY forward contracts in BOC with tenors of 7 and 20 days, 1, 1.5, 2, 2.5, 3, 3.5, 4, 4.5, 5, 5.5, 6, and 12 months, respectively. The six-month contract can be extended to another six-month period so that a tenor of a maximum of one- year can be traded.

17.3 CNY Forwards in the BOC

The BOC was first ratified to do CNY forwards transactions in China, and it has retained its monopolistic position in this business in China ever since. We will introduce BOC's forwards business in this section.

17.3.1 Current Account and Capital Account

The BOC currently provides CNY forwards exchange transactions not only for business under current account but also partly for business under capital account, such as loan repayment to the BOC, repayment of foreign debts registered by the SAFE, and other FX cash flow with the approval of the SAFE.

17.3.2 Currencies

The BOC is currently offering forwards of the CNY against eight foreign currencies including the USD, Eurodollar (EUR), Japanese yen (JPY), Australian dollar (AUD), Canadian dollar (CAD), Swiss franc (CHF), British pound (GBP), and Hong Kong dollar (HKD).

17.3.3 Procedures for CNY Forwards Transactions

There are three major steps for a CNY forwards transaction at the BOC. A general agreement for transaction of foreign exchange on the basis of maintenance of value should be agreed upon and signed between the bank and the enterprise.

After signing the agreement, the enterprise has to open a security-money account of foreign currency with the BOC and deposit in the account not less than 10% of the transaction amount as security money. Currencies for security money are confined to the USD, HKD, JPY, or EUR. In case the enterprise has loans from the BOC or is using a letter of credit from the BOC and the transactions are 100% confirmed by the BOC, the security money can be reduced or exempted accordingly after ratification according to concrete conditions.

The last step is to fill out the application form for transaction of FX on the basis of maintenance of value and bring it to the Bank for enquiries and transactions after the signature of the legal representative of the enterprise or the signature of an authorized person with the official seal. Forward transactions with loans from branches of the BOC or under letter of credit or guaranteed and confirmed can be done after enquiries by the appointed relevant branches after filling out the application form for transaction of FX on the basis of maintenance of value. In terms of the patterns of making transactions, the customer can also leave the order in advance, asking to buy whatever the currency at whatever price or submit a power of attorney to the Bank. The power of attorney will be binding lawfully, and in principle the customer should write it before the transaction; the customer can also empower in the power of attorney a person to make enquiries with the bank and conclude transactions by phone. The customer must submit a confirmation to the bank on the second working day after conclusion of business through a phone call. The transaction will be subject to a telephone recording of the bank if a divergence arises. (See the website of the BOC for more details, www.bank-of-China.com.)

17.3.4 Extension and Early Settlement

If the customer cannot make due settlement owing to some reasons and needs to postpone the time, he should submit to the bank an application for an extension three working days prior to the settlement day. And if the customer wants to settle for the concluded forwards business ahead of time, he or she should submit to the Bank an application for advance settlement three working days prior to the settlement day.

17.3.5 "Margin" Calls

A forward transaction of FX entered by a customer, like a futures contract in any exchange, could bring about floating gains or losses.

When the losses reach 80% of the security money or "margin" deposited by the customer, the Bank will at any time ask the customer to supplement the security money, and the customer should do it on time. This practice is essentially the same as the "maintenance margin" calls practiced by most futures exchanges in the world. If the customer does not supplement the "maintenance margin" on time or refuses to supplement it, the bank will impose a mandatory action according to specific conditions, and the customer will be responsible for all the expenses and losses arising thereby.

17.4 Turnover of CNY Forwards

Data on CNY forwards transactions are difficult to obtain as the product is still at the experimental stage. According to Li and Ye (2001), the total turnover of CNY forwards in the first year was just over US$767 million. Table 17.1 gives the monthly turnover of CNY forwards in 1997 at the BOC.

Table 17.2 provides annual turnover figures of the CNY forwards at the BOC and the total FX turnover in China from 1997 to 2002. We can observe that the annual turnover of CNY forwards fluctuated more significantly than did the corresponding cash turnover from 1997 to 2003. We can also observe that the forwards turnover as a percentage of the corresponding cash turnover increased from

Table 17.1 Monthly Turnover of CNY Forwards at the BOC in 1997 (Unit: US$ million)

Month	April	May	June	July	August
Payment	2.218	5.097	66.730	9.575	53.130
Sales					
Total	2.218	5.097	66.730	9.575	53.130

Month	September	October	November	December	Sum
Payment	105.610	194.906	2.999	215.301	655.566
Sales	2.812	4.191	23.488	81.180	111.671
Total	108.422	199.097	26.487	296.481	767.237

Data source: Li and Ye (2001), p. 119.

Table 17.2 Turnover of CNY Forwards at the BOC from 1997 to 2003 (Unit: US$ billion)

Year	Forward Turnover (US $b)	Growth Rate (%)	Cash Turnover (US $b)	Forward/ Cash (%)
1997	0.8		70	1.1
1998	2.1	178.0	52	4.1
1999	3.7	73.5	31.5	11.7
2000	11.4	208.1	42.2	27.0
2001	8.6	−24.7	75	11.4
2002	4.3	−49.9	97.2	4.4
2003	9.0	109.3	151.1	6.0

Data source: The BOC and Table 6.2 (Chapter 6).

merely 1.1% in 1997 to 27% in 2000 and dropped to 4.4% in 2002. Because of the experimental nature of the CNY forwards market, there is no clear pattern from the data given in Table 17.2.

Statistics released by the Industrial and Commercial Bank of China (ICBC), where CNY forwards transactions officially started from April 1, 2003, show US$55.42 million changed hands in May. Meanwhile, the figures from all banks in China authorized to handle the business — the BOC, the ICBC, the China Construction Bank, and the Agricultural Bank of China — show a rapid rise in CNY forwards transactions against the euro and a slight slow-down in forwards transactions against the USD.

According to statistics from the Shanghai Branch of the BOC (International Finance News, May 29, 2003), the CNY forwards transactions in March increased by 30% over February 2003, reflecting the FX volatilities in China. Of this 30% monthly growth, non-USD forwards increased faster than did CNY/USD forwards.

The CNY revaluation pressure has also been reflected in the CNY forward market. According to Long Haidi (2003) of Chongqing Morning News, the total amount of CNY forward turnover surpassed US$69 million in the first nine months of 2003 in Chongqing Branch of Bank of China, surpassing 160 times of that in the same period in 2002. Over 80% of the total turnover was transacted by foreign trade companies with over US$50 million and the second largest group was Motor-Cycle companies with over US$10 million. Of the 14 CNY forward contracts with 14 different tenors, the CNY forwards concentrated on the 7 tenors between half a year and one year. Turnover of CNY forwards in Shanghai Branch of BOC also increased significantly. According to People.com.cn, the total turnover of CNY forwards at BOC Shanghai Branch increased by 30% in the first quarter of 2003 (http://www.imoney.com.cn).

17.5 Examples of CNY Forward Hedging

We have introduced various aspects of the CNY forward contracts and regulations in China in previous sections in this chapter. We will illustrate how the CNY forward contracts are used in practice with two actual transactions in this section.

17.5.1 Chinese Importer with Euro Settlement

In April of 2003, H Company imported some equipment from a foreign company. The total amount of payment was Euro 100 million due on May 21, 2003. With the advice from a major Chinese bank, H Company signed a one month CNY/Euro forward contract at RMB 9.0419 per Euro with the bank on April 21, 2003. The RMB/Euro exchange rate was 9.7237 on May 21, 2003. With this CNY forward contract, H company saved $100^{*}(9.7237 - 9.0419) =$ RMB 68.2 million excluding transaction fees paid to the bank (see www.imoney.com.cn, June 5, 2003).

17.5.2 Chinese Importer Importing from Germany

In August, 2003, a company in Quanzhou, China imported some equipment from a German company with Euro 300,000 due on September 17. The importing company signed a 20-day CNY/Euro forward contract at RMB 9.0485 per Euro with the Agricultural Bank of China on August 29, 2003. The RMB/Euro exchange rate was 9.4954 on September 17, 2003. With this CNY forward contract, the importer saved $300{,}000^{*}(9.4954 - 9.0485) =$ RMB 134,100 excluding transaction fees paid to the bank (see Lin, 2003).

17.6 Existing Problems

As we saw in Chapter 7 of Part I, the spot FX market is still in an early stage of development with daily limits in China, and the CNY forwards business is still at an experimental stage despite seven years of practice in the BOC and just one year practice in other state-owned banks. As illustrated in Table 17.2, the turnovers of the CNY forwards transactions have been rather thin, and the CNY forwards transactions appear to be not as much related to activities in the FX cash market with limited data. These data imply significant problems existing in the CNY forwards experimentation. We focus on the major problems of the CNY forwards business in China in this section.

17.6.1 Significant Discrepancies between Implied and Actual Interest Rate Spreads

Theoretically, the spot and forward exchange rates must satisfy certain parity relationship as described in Section 8.1 of Chapter 8 in Part II. Yet this parity relationship appears significantly violated in the empirical study of Li and Ye (2001), using data of the first 13 months of CNY/USD forwards in the BOC. Table 17.3 gives the implied interest difference, the actual interest difference, and the difference between the implied and actual differences as a percentage of the actual interest rate difference using CNY forwards. The difference between the implied and actual interest rate differences went from −16.1% in February to 41.3% in March in 1998; and there appeared to be no specific pattern. Despite the limited sample, the empirical evidence implied a lot of problems in the market.

17.6.2 Little Volatility in Spot Market and Less Incentive for Hedging

The cash exchange rates are managed so that there is little volatility in the market, and so there is less incentive for participants either to hedge or to speculate. According to a market survey (FX Reference, No. 5, 1998; Ye and Li (2001), p. 120), only 30% of the respondents saw the actual need for hedging using forwards.

Table 17.3 Monthly Interest Rate Discrepancies from April 1997 to April 1998

Month	Apr 97	May 97	Jun 97	Jul 97	Aug 97	Sep 97	Oct 97
Implied difference	0.4630	0.4525	0.4583	0.4150	0.4308	0.3775	0.3000
Actual difference	0.3740	0.3967	0.3618	0.4179	0.3976	0.3758	0.2976
Implied–actual	0.0890	0.0558	0.0965	−0.0029	0.0332	0.0017	0.0024
(Implied–actual)/actual (%)	23.8	14.1	26.7	−0.7	8.4	0.5	0.8

Month	Nov 97	Dec 97	Jan 98	Feb 98	Mar 98	Apr 98
Implied difference	0.2517	0.3017	0.2642	0.2483	0.2375	0.0867
Actual difference	0.1819	0.2697	0.2512	0.2959	0.1681	0.0983
Implied–actual	0.0698	0.0320	0.0130	−0.0476	0.0694	−0.0116
(Implied–actual)/actual (%)	38.4	11.9	5.2	−16.1%	41.3	−11.8

Data source: Li and Ye (2001), p. 112.

17.6.3 Participation Restrictions

The PBOC restricts participants to show a specific need for using CNY forwards transactions. If evidence cannot be furnished on before the settlement date, the contract will be violated and the bank has right to terminate the contract and the participants have to bear the consequences. Such restrictions prevent participants from using the product actively.

17.6.4 Interest Rate Mechanism

As we saw in Chapter 4, an interest rate mechanism has not been established in China yet, despite significant progress in this area. Empirical evidence shows that the implied short-term interests from the interbank repurchase (repo) market and the exchange-traded repo market have significant differences (*Shanghai Securities News* reports such differences daily). Without a relatively established yield curve, it is rather difficult to price FX forward contracts.

There are many other aspects worth exploring in relation to the CNY forwards, yet they are beyond the scope of this book.

17.7 Potentiality

The FX cash market is in an early stage of development and the forwards market is still in the experimental stage in China. With growing exports and imports in China as shown in Table 3.3, the demand for both cash and forward transactions will certainly grow significantly in China in the years to come. Table 17.4 provides the ratios of FX cash and forward turnovers and the corresponding imports and trade from 1997 to 2003. We can observe that the FX cash turnover as a percentage of the total trade in China has been significantly lower than 20% since 2000 and the corresponding ratio has been merely around 2% for forwards.

As China is further integrated into the world economy more aggressively with a higher trade/GDP ratio, more domestic import and export companies are learning to follow international practices to secure their interests and guard against losses. With recent pressure on the CNY to revalue and increased FX volatility worldwide,

Table 17.4 FX Forwards and Spot Compared with Import and Total Trade

Year	Forward Turnover/ Import (%)	FX cash Turnover/ Import (%)	Forward Turnover/ Trade (%)	FX Cash Turnover/ Trade (%)
1997	0.54	49.16	0.24	21.51
1998	1.52	37.09	0.66	16.05
1999	2.23	19.01	1.03	8.74
2000	5.06	18.75	2.40	8.90
2001	3.52	30.79	1.68	14.71
2002	1.46	32.93	0.69	15.66
2003	2.18	36.60	1.06	17.75

Data source: Calculated using data from Table 3.3 (Chapter 3) and Table 17.2.

the need for hedging and trading in the FX market will certainly grow tremendously in China in the coming years.

17.8 Summary

The CNY forwards contracts transacted in the BOC are significantly different from the FX forwards contracts trading in the OTC market in most developed markets. They are actually very similar to the futures contracts trading in most futures exchanges around the world because security money is essentially the same as the margin requirement in futures exchanges, and the need for participants to supplement additional security money is the same as margin calls to satisfy the maintenance margin in futures exchanges.

The CNY forwards business is still at the early experimental stage in China, despite the fact that it has been traded on a small scale for about seven years. Because of its experimental nature, data for systematic research to explore the characteristics of the market are scarce. We leave this for future editions of this book.

18

CNY NDFs

> NDFs are now the chief tool for betting on appreciation in currency, especially in China.
>
> *Vidya Ranganathan (Reuters), August 29, 2003*

> Ironically, what began as a protection against currency devaluation has now become the chief tool for betting on currency appreciation, particularly in China — where an export boom has led to diplomatic pressure to allow the yuan to rise in value.
>
> *Feature — NDFs, the secretive side of currency trading, Forbes, August 28, 2003*

We introduced and discussed various issues on the CNY forward contracts trading onshore within China in Chapter 17. As a matter of fact, the CNY forward is the only existing CNY derivative product in China. With restrictions such as trade documents to support CNY forwards trading in China, the turnover has been extremely low, and international participants cannot access this market without meeting the same requirements.

As discussed in Chapter 8 of Part II and Chapter 14 of Part III, FX NDF contracts always find their way to offshore markets as long as the domestic currency is not fully convertible. Even if a domestic FX forwards market exists in an emerging market, a corresponding offshore

NDF market normally coexists because of liquidity problems with the domestic forwards market. The CNY is a managed currency floating within a narrow range, as we mentioned in Chapter 6, and international participants still cannot access the CNY marketplace. Thus, it is natural for offshore CNY NDFs to flourish. With strong pressure for the CNY to revalue internationally since late 2002, the CNY NDF market has become much more active than it was in its early stages from 1996 to 2000.

The CNY NDF market is the most active offshore instrument for most international participants, and it has attracted a lot of attention worldwide since late 2002. Thus, the CNY NDF naturally becomes the major content of this book. The purpose of this chapter is to study various aspects of the CNY NDF market.

This chapter is organized as follows. Section 18.1 outlines a brief history of the CNY NDF market; Section 18.2 describes the major terms of a CNY NDF contract; Section 18.3 describes the great pressure on the CNY from devaluation to revaluation in the past seven years; Section 18.4 discusses major factors affecting the CNY NDF rates; Section 18.5 introduces major CNY NDF participants; Section 18.6 estimates the CNY NDF trading volume for 2003 and the first quarter of 2004; Section 18.7 introduces the CNY realignment probability using existing CNY NDF market data; Section 18.8 explores pricing and other major problems involving the CNY NDF contracts; Section 18.9 discusses the potentiality of the CNY NDF market worldwide; and Section 18.10 summarizes and concludes the chapter.

18.1 Brief History of CNY NDF Market

The CNY NDF market came into existence in Hong Kong and Singapore as early as 1995, nearly two years before the Asian financial crisis broke out in the summer of 1997. The CNY NDF came into being because a few major multinational companies had the need to hedge their investments in China as the accumulated foreign direct investment (FDI) in China reached US$132.8 billion by the end of 1995 (see Table 5.3) and US$174.5 billion by the end of 1996. This was because there was concern that the CNY might also face devaluation following the Mexican crisis. There were also other institutions that aimed to speculate on the CNY devaluation to profit from it. The CNY NDF market gradually developed among international banks in Hong Kong and Singapore as these banks had to serve their clients for new business need. As the flow of capital into China grew larger and larger, the need for some form of risk management and risk mitigation in the exchange markets became really necessary for financial practices.

The CNY NDF market was rather less developed in the early stages, and trading was not active. In the early period, it could take a few hours or even a few days to complete a deal. Besides the low liquidity of the market, the CNY NDFs had maturities up to only six months. The 12-month CNY NDF came into the market later on. Currently the CNY NDF can be traded up to a three-year tenor, yet tenors below one year are the most liquid. CNY NDF information can be obtained from the Reuters page, PNDF Reuters Chain <CNYNDF = PREA>.

During and after the Asian financial crisis, there was tremendous pressure for the CNY to be devalued as all currencies in the region were devalued besides the CNY and the HKD, and the turnover increased moderately in the market. The 12-month CNY NDFs implied that CNY would depreciate to 10.03 per US$ in January 1998 (see Figure 14.1).

NDFs are often considered as unwelcome criticism of FX policies, a market-driven opinion about where the exchange rate should be. Because of this, most institutions prefer not to be quoted or cited for their businesses or comments because most central banks do not tolerate offshore activities such as NDFs.

The CNY NDF market has experienced dramatic changes since it came into being. We briefly described in Chapter 14 the pressure for CNY to devaluate from the the CNY NDF market during the Asian financial crisis; we will discuss the CNY revaluation reflected in the NDF market in the following sections.

18.2 CNY NDF Contract Specifications

We introduced major terms of the NDF Master Agreement in Chapter 9. These terms represent the major items that a NDF contract must contain. Here we concentrate on particular issues relating to a CNY NDF contract in this section.

18.2.1 Settlement Rates

The settlement rates are the Chinese RMB per USD, for settlement in two business days, reported by the State Administration of Exchange Control (SAEC) of the People's Republic of China, which appears on the Reuters SAEC screen page opposite the symbol "CNY =" as of 4:00 p.m., Beijing time.

18.2.2 "Drop-Dead Date" for Unscheduled Holiday

In the event the scheduled valuation date becomes subject to the Following Business Day Unscheduled Holiday Convention and if the valuation date has not occurred on or before the eighth consecutive day after the scheduled valuation day, then such eighth day, if a business day but for unscheduled holidays or the next day that would have been a business day but for unscheduled holidays shall be deemed to be the valuation date.

18.2.3 Specified Rate

This is the official fixing rate reported by the SAFE.

18.2.4 Relevant City for Business Day

Beijing, People's Republic of China.

18.3 From Devaluation to Revaluation

Few currencies have experienced as dramatic changes as the Chinese currency in the past few years. As other Asian currencies were under great pressure to be devaluated during the Asian financial crisis, the CNY was also under tremendous pressure for devaluation as shown in Table 14.1. The premium of the CNY NDF peaked at 17,509 pips (calculated using the official CNY/USD exchange rate of 8.2791 in 1998 from Table 6.1) early in January 1998, implying a one-year CNY/USD rate of RMB 10.03 or depreciation of the CNY of 17.46%.

18.3.1 From Devaluation to Revaluation

Figure 18.1 depicts the daily 12-month CNY/USD NDF rates from December 1998 to March 18, 2004. We can note from Figure 18.1 that the dramatic devaluation pressure on the CNY lost momentum in the summer of 2000, and the CNY was under slight pressure for devaluation from the summer of 2000 to November 2001. The CNY NDF was around its official exchange rate of RMB 8.277 per USD for about one year from late in 2001 to October 2002 before pressure for the CNY to be revalued began to accumulate energy.

18.3.2 Stages of the CNY Revaluation Pressure

In order to have a closer look at the recent CNY/USD NDF rates, we show daily 12-month CNY NDF rates from late in 2002 to March 2004 in Figure 18.2. Figure 18.2 clearly demonstrates significant changes in the CNY NDF rates from early November 2002, when the CNY NDF was at about the same level of the official exchange rate of RMB 8.277/USD, yet it began to change significantly since then. We can divide the CNY revaluation pressure implied by the CNY NDF market into four major stages as follows.

First stage: initial wave from mid-November to end-May 2003. The CNY NDF curve shown in Figure 18.2 indicates revaluation

Figure 18.1 From Devaluation to Revaluation of the CNY from December 1998 to March 2004

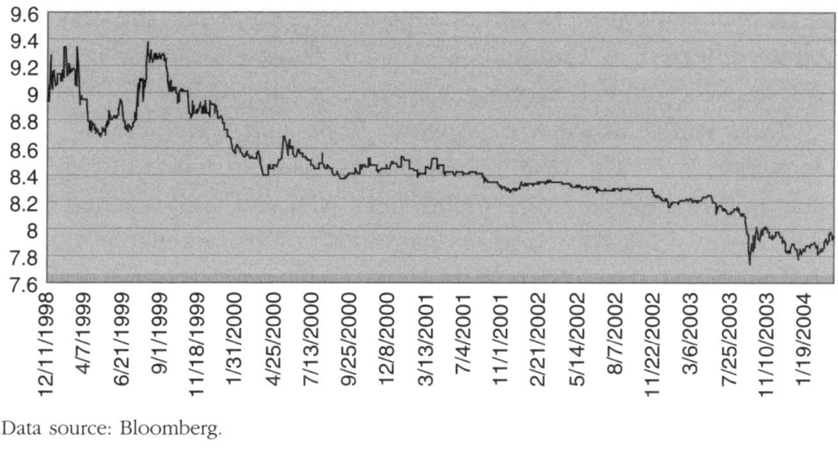

Data source: Bloomberg.

Figure 18.2 CNY Revaluation Implied from the NDF Market between April 2002 and March 2004

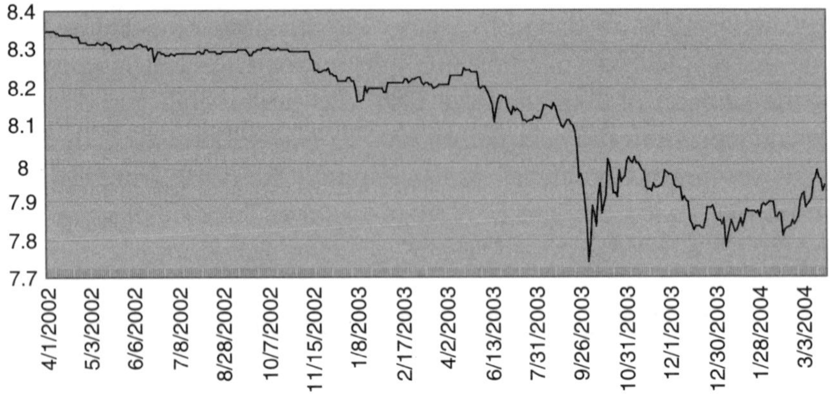

Data source: Bloomberg.

pressure from November 13, 2002, at which date the 12-month CNY NDF reflects 25 pip discounts (1 pip discount represents a 1/10,000 = 0.0001 decline in the CNY/USD rate), and the discount crossed 1000 pips to reach 1153 on January 8, 2003, reflecting 1.41% appreciation of the CNY against the USD. The revaluation pressure stayed around CNY 8.20/USD for about four months until May 30, 2003. The first stage reflected mild revaluation pressure with discounts between 300 and 1153 pips.

Second stage: significant pressure from June to September 2003. The CNY revaluation pressure continued and accelerated significantly from early June to end of September 2003, when the CNY discounts reflected in 12-month CNY NDF contracts ranged between 1000 and 2000 pips (reflecting 1.2% to 2.5% appreciation).

Third stage: dramatic pressure from mid-September to end-December 2003. The CNY revaluation pressure reached the highest point in this stage as the 12-month CNY NDF discount reached 5400 pips (about 7.1% appreciation against the official exchange rate of CNY 8.277/USD) at 4:55 p.m. in Hong Kong on October 7 versus a discount of 4325 late on October 6. The implied exchange rate was RMB 7.737 per USD, stronger than the HKD's official pegged level of 7.80 to its US counterpart for the first time in history. Although the revaluation presume weakened a little as the 12-month CNY NDF discount fell gradually to around 2700 pips on October 20 and to just above 2600 early in November, 2003, the NDF discount increased moderately to above 3000 late in November and remained between 4000 and 4500 in December 2003.

Fourth stage: stagnant pressure early January to end March 2004. The pressure on CNY revaluation remained stagnant in the first quarter of 2004, with the 12-month NDF discount fluctuating between 3000 and 5000 pips. We will study specific factors affecting the CNY/USD NDF rates in the following section

18.4 Factors and Events Affecting CNY NDF

We have introduced in Chapter 1 the calls for the CNY to be revaluated from the US Congress, the US administration, other G7 nations, officials from other emerging markets, and academic and other fields. There have been numerous important events that have affected the CNY NDF market, and the CNY NDF market has become very volatile, with daily moves being triggered by international events and news out of Mainland China and other major developed countries such as the US rather than economic and financial market fundamentals as in most other developed and developing markets. We concentrate, in the following section, on major events and news that have triggered market moves in the past year and a half since the CNY changed its stance against the USD in the offshore market place.

18.4.1 First Stage Arguments and Events (before May 2003)

We mentioned in Chapter 1 that the notion for the CNY to be revaluated started with the US hearing before the Senate Banking Committee on May 1, 2002. Although Chapter 1 introduced how the CNY revaluation process was initiated in the US, it was not the focus of Chapter 1 to outline the major steps of the whole process. The objective of this section is to review the major arguments and events that have moved the CNY NDF rates specifically.

Xie from Morgan Stanley (Hong Kong) (November 4, 2002). The earliest research paper that could be obtained publicly was that by Xie

(2002) of Morgan Stanley (Hong Kong). Xie expressed the concern that CNY revaluation would worsen China's deflation and depress its domestic demand. He also stated that China must allow the market to determine the value of its currency at some point, yet it is possible only when China's capital account is mostly open. Xie was also quoted as saying that the yuan peg to the US dollar is probably still the most appropriate currency policy in China (Hiscock, 2003).

Japanese Finance Minister Masujuro Shiokawa (December 2002). In his testimony to the Japanese Congress early in December 2002, Japanese Finance Minister Masujuro Shiokawa expressed the view that the CNY is significantly undervalued according to the purchasing power parity (PPP). He promised that he would tell China to let the yuan float according to market principles and that any coordinated and effective policy plan to revive the world economy to recover and to combat world deflation must include a major adjustment of the yuan exchange rate as a key element in the same way as the G7 joint intervention that propped up the Japanese yen under the Plaza Accord in the mid-1980s.

China's export and import data release (December 12, 2002). Chinese Customs General Administration released China's foreign trade data of the first 11 months of 2002 on December 12, and the data were reported by People's Daily on December 13, 2002. The total export and import reached US$560.2 billion, increased by 21% over the same period in 2001, and net export increased by US$27.2 billion. The one-year CNY NDF discount increased by only 50 pips from 455 pips on December 12 and 13 to 505 pips on December 16 in reaction to these important economic data.

Morgan Stanley (December 24, 2002). Asian Wall Street Journal reported that Morgan Stanley reports the five biggest hedging deals every quarter. The largest of the recently released five was related to the CNY, reflecting its business operations in China. By the end of June 2002, Morgan Stanley had hedged US$550 million worth of CNY in order to reduce the risk that the CNY might depreciate against the USD. Many institutions wanted to trade such deals as they believed that the CNY would appreciate rather than depreciate.

Zhu Rongji's speech at SAFE (January 5, 2003). Former Chinese premier Zhu Rongji visited the SAFE and made a short speech there.

"We maintained the RMB peg during the Asian financial crisis," he stated, "that was consistent with our national interests as it secured the financial stability and economic development in China." He, continued "steady growth of foreign reserve and RMB stability are important symbols of our general national economic strength and sustainable, healthy economic development."

Based on the speeches and events described above, the one-year CNY NDF in Singapore experienced significant changes on January 6, 2003. The one-year CNY NDF reached 1450 pips on that day, up from 300–650 in mid-November 2002.

The US House Commerce–Justice–State (CJS) Appropriations Subcommittee hearing (May 22, 2003). The House CJS appropriations subcommittee held a hearing on May 22 on the effect of Chinese imports on small and medium US businesses. The CJS subcommittee has funding responsibility for a number of trade-related agencies including the departments of Commerce and State, the United States Trade Representative, the International Trade Commission, and the Court of International Trade. The CJS chairman, representative Frank Wolf, expressed his concerns "about the number of jobs that are being lost in the manufacturing industry and in agriculture because of the excessive amount of goods being imported from China" and "some say that more than 1.1 million manufacturing jobs have been lost in recent years because of Chinese import, including 200,000 jobs just last year (2002)".

18.4.2 Second Stage Arguments and Events (June–September 2003)

Goldman Sachs report (June 11, 2003). In a popular paper from Goldman Sachs, Hu (2003a) argues that "the more sensible and likely alternative for China is a "regime change — replacing the currency peg with a managed float. China is likely to realize it is in its own best interest to do so, even if this means having to accept an initial appreciation of the exchange rate." Hu (2003a) believes that the CNY is undervalued about 15% on a variety of valuation metrics, and this view was further illustrated in Hu (2003b), again with the PPP. Hu expressed a similar view in a speech delivered to the American Chamber of Commerce in Hong Kong on August 29, 2003 (Hong Kong Economic Daily, August 30, 2003).

Global head of economic research of Goldman Sachs Mr. O'Neil forecast that China would allow the CNY to appreciate before the end of December 2003. He forecast specifically that the CNY would appreciate 5% to RMB 7.86/USD in the next 12 months and that the CNY would appreciate 2.5% to RMB 8.07/USD in the next six months (we have not seen any of these forecasts come true!).

Secretary Snow (June 16, 2003). In early June 2003, the US Treasury Secretary John Snow publicly commented on Washington's preference for a change in Chinese monetary policy, revealing the Bush administration's expectation that a weaker dollar would help resolve its large trade deficit. Snow suggested this week that Beijing may allow the yuan to rise, and he made it clear that he wants to see that happen. In doing so, he added his voice to those of American manufacturers, Japanese government officials, and others. Snow's comments were greeted enthusiastically by Frank Vargo, vice president for international economic affairs at the National Association of Manufacturers (Washington Post, June 18, 2003).

European countries agreed on yuan's undervaluation. At the ASEM Finance Ministers' gathering in Bali, Indonesia earlier in July, European countries agreed that the yuan's current exchange rate does not reflect the real strength of the Chinese economy. That suggests cheap Chinese goods are also flooding European countries (see Japan Times of July 31, 2003). European finance ministers pressurized Asian governments on Saturday (July 5, 2003) to allow the region's tightly managed currencies to rise against the dollar, a move that may limit any damage to Europe's economy from further euro strength (see Business News 2003).

Federal Reserve Chairman Alan Greenspan (July 17, 2003). On July 17, Federal Reserve Chairman Alan Greenspan made a remark against the Chinese foreign exchange policy and told the US Senate Banking Committee that China's pegged currency would eventually hurt China's economy (see Special Report mentioned above). The one-year CNY NDF discount jumped more than 200 pips from 1540 on July 16 to 1750 late on July 17, 2003 (Hong Kong Economic News, July 18, 2003).

Chinese Minister of Commerce Lv Fuyuan (July 29, 2003). "No country in the world makes currency adjustment decisions based on the international situation alone without analyzing its domestic situation," Chinese Minister of Commerce Lv Fuyuan told the fifth Asia–Europe Meeting of Economic Ministers in Dalian late in July (Japan Time, July 31, 2003).

Japan and the US are stepping up calls on China (July 31, 2003). Japan and the US are stepping up calls on China to revalue the yuan, charging that while growing economically, it is spreading deflation and trade deficits by exporting goods at an unfairly low exchange rate (see Japan Times of July 31, 2003). Japanese Finance Minister Masujuro Shiokawa urged China again on August 29, 2003 to let the yuan float freely before meeting the US treasury secretary (Japan Economic Newswire).

Wen meeting John Snow (September 3, 2003). Chinese premier Wen Jiaobao met US Secretary John Snow on September 3, 2003 during his visit to China. The premier repeated China's intention to maintain the CNY exchange rate and at the same time to research actively and explore a new rate mechanism that reflects market forces. The 12-month CNY NDF first rose 121 pips on September 3, 2003 and 44 pips on September 4, 2003, and then dropped 169 pips on September 5, 2003.

18.4.3 Third Stage Arguments and Events (October–December 2003)

Taylor's testimony (October 1, 2003). US Under Secretary of Treasury for International Affairs, John B. Taylor, testified before the Subcommittee on Domestic and International Monetary Policy, Trade, and Technology of the House Committee on Financial Services. Mr. Taylor mentioned the importance of recognizing that China still has significant capital controls. China's capital controls allow for more inflows than outflows, thus bolstering foreign exchange reserves. A relaxation of controls on outflows would reduce upward pressure on the yuan. The US's active engagement with China and other countries is paving the way toward freer markets. The Bush administration's effort to raise growth in the US and abroad and thereby create jobs at home is already showing signs of success. Taylor also stated that the Bush administration has also been urging the Chinese to reduce barriers to trade and capital flows (Taylor, 2003).

US legislator's pressure (October 1, 2003). The US legislators increased pressure on President Bush late in September, addressing China's alleged exchange rate market intervention to manipulate the value of the CNY, arguing that the Bush administration has not done enough. The House Financial Services Subcommittee on Domestic and International Monetary Policy, Trade, and Technology convened a hearing on October 1 to review the impact of China's exchange rate on the US economy. One day after pressing administration officials at the hearing to do more to resolve what he called "the China problem," representative Bernie Sanders introduced H.R. 3228, a bill urging the US administration to withdraw normal trade relations (NTR) status with China. The resolution has bipartisan support with 31 cosponsors. While legislators continue to pursue legislation on China's alleged currency practices, it is far from clear whether a resolution such as H.R. 3058 would impose tariffs on imports from China. (Washington Monitor, 2003, pp. 5–6.)

Rumor from Japan (October 7, 2003). Jiji Press Japan reported that the PBOC was considering revaluing the yuan by about 30% over the next five years, subject to a final decision from the State Council. The 12-month CNY NDF discount jumped 1050 pips to 5400 pips on October 7, 2003 from 4325 pips on October 6, 2003.

Snow's testimony (October 16, 2003). US Treasury Secretary John Snow testified before the US Senate Banking Committee on October 16, 2003 to discuss the US administration's exchange-rate policy, and the 12-month CNY NDF discount jumped 800 pips from 3303 to 4103 pips.

US President George Bush (mid-October 2003). Before his departure for the Asia Pacific Economic Cooperation Forum (APEC) on October 20 and 21, 2003 in Bangkok, Thailand, President Bush promised to exert pressure on China to introduce more flexibility to the yuan. He also said that the way all currencies ought to be valued is based upon the economic activity, fiscal policy, and monetary policy of their respective governments, as well as their economies' potential for growth and long-term viability (Hong Kong Economic News, October 16, 2003). The 12-month CNY NDF discount went up 800 pips late on October 16 from 3303 pips late on October 15 at 4103 pips.

Hu and Bush's joint conference (October 19, 2003). In a conference with President Bush in Bangkok on October 19, Chinese President Hu Jintao spelled out reasons why China is reluctant to let its yuan appreciate against the dollar. As China's strong economy rapidly transforms into a powerhouse, it increasingly contributes to the financial and economic stability in Asia and the world at large. Therefore, China is responsible for reviewing all economic problems carefully before taking any action. President Hu agreed to have a joint panel of experts from China and the US study the deregulation of the currency and determine the steps necessary to have the yuan's value rise and fall with international markets. President Bush stressed the importance of reducing barriers to trade, of removing restrictions on the transfer of capital, and of moving to a flexible and market-based exchange rate. The 12 month CNY NDF discount fell 900 pips from 3604 to 2704 pips on October 20, 2003.

Hearing before the US House of Representatives (October 21, 2003). Before the Committee on International Relations, House of Representatives on October 21, 2003 on US–China Ties: reassessing the Economic Relationship (108th Congress, first session), it was argued that "these formal and informal trade barriers, including the manipulation and undervaluation of China's currency, have contributed to the loss of three million manufacturing jobs in America in recent years" and "four years ago, the bilateral trade deficit that the US had with China was about $70 billion . Last year (2002), the deficit had grown to $103 billion, and this year I estimate that it will be between $120 and $130 billion" (US–China Ties, 2003, p. 5). The 12-month CNY NDF went up 125 pips on October 21, 2003.

US representatives call for tariff on Chinese imports (October 22, 2003). US representatives Sue Myrick and John Spratt introduced a bill that would impose a 27.5% tariff on Chinese imports if China refused to allow its currency to float on the open market (Bizjournals, October 22, 2003). The 12-month CNY NDF rose 351 pips on October 22, 2003.

Spokesman of the White House (October 23, 2003). The spokesman of the White House stated on October 23, 2003 that the White House would continue to negotiate with the Chinese government to allow the CNY to be revaluated in order to improve the employment situation in exports and manufacturing in the US (Hong Kong Economic News, October 24, 2003). The 12-month CNY NDF discount jumped 399 pips from 3180 late on October 22 to 3579 late on October 23, 2003.

US Commerce Secretary Donald Evans (October 28, 2003). During his trip to Beijing, the US Commerce Secretary Donald Evans said that US patience was "running thin" with China's "unfair" trade practices and that Washington "will not tolerate a stacked deck." President Bush earlier urged the Chinese to allow the yuan to move with the market, implying that China was keeping the currency artificially weak to gain a trade advantage. (See remarks by Secretary Donald Evans on www.commerce.gov/opa/speeches/Evans/2003/Oct_28_Evans_AmChamChina.htm). Asked by a reporter on China-US trade relating to Secretary Evans' speech, the spokeswoman Zhang Qiyue (of the Ministry of Foreign Affairs on the afternoon of October 28, 2003) answered that more than half of China's export to the US are completed by foreign companies in China; that the US-China trade remained surpluses from 1972 to 1993 and that the deficit began to exist only after 1993 (News conference of the Ministry of Foreign Affairs). The 12-month CNY NDF fell 699 pips on October 28, 2003.

Greenspan on China's currency and US jobs (December 11, 2003). "The story on trade and jobs, in my judgment," said Fed Chairman Greenspan, "is a bit more complex, especially with respect to China, than this strain of conventional wisdom would lead one to believe," Greenspan said in remarks prepared for the World Affairs Council of Greater Dallas. Greenspan said that if China did allow the value of its currency to float and the currency rose in value, as US manufacturers expect, it might cut Chinese exports of such goods as textiles to the United States. But he said rather than boosting production of textiles in the United States, it was "far more likely" that US imports from other low-wage countries in Asia would simply replace the Chinese textiles. Because of various complex economic forces at play, Greenspan said a rise in the value of the Chinese currency "would be unlikely to have much, if any, effect on aggregate employment in the United States" (US consulate, Hong Kong, 2003).

18.4.4 Fourth Stage Arguments and Events (January 2004–)

Governor Zhou of PBOC (January 2004). "The pressure on RMB revaluation," said Dr. Zhou, Governor of the PBOC at the BIS Conference in Hong Kong in the second week of January 2004, "has subdued significantly because of the economic recovery in the US, restructuring of state-owned banks in China, and the situation of net export from China to the US." (Beijing Morning News, January 13, 2004.)

State Council release of nine principles on capital market liberalization (February 2, 2004). The State Council of China released nine dramatic principles on further liberalizing the Chinese capital market on February 2, 2004. These principles were reported on the front pages of all major securities newspapers, implying the State Council's commitment to further liberalizing capital markets from concrete rules. It was interpreted as a necessary precursor to any FX regime change, which likely would allow the CNY to rise. The 12-month CNY NDF moved further left to 4030/3850 on Tuesday (February 3, 2004) vs 3900/3700 on Monday (February 2, 2004).

G7 reference (February 9, 2004). Like the earlier G7 Conference in September 2003, the G7 gathering in February 2004 also had significant impacts on the CNY NDF market. The G7 reference to the need for "more flexibility" looks like a veiled reference to Asia, even if no specific countries were mentioned. Interestingly, the G7 appeared to have more currencies in mind than those of just China and Japan, with European Central Bank (ECB) President Trichet suggesting that there were "quite a few" currencies where flexibility was lacking. There was again a rumor (China Business Post) that China would allow the CNY to appreciate somewhat more than currently expected either by analysts or NDF markets, and the rumor thus moved significantly, with HKD forwards following suit. Although the rumor was later denied by Chinese authorities, the pressure in this direction stayed. The 12-month CNY NDF discount jumped 401 pips from 3797 on February 9 to 4198 pips on February 10, 2004.

Greenspan — revaluing no answer (February 27, 2004). After addressing the Stanford Institute for Economic Policy Research on February 27, 2004, the US Fed Chairman, Mr. Greenspan, said "we are not quite sure what the extent, if any, of the undervaluation" of the yuan is, nor what might happen if it were to be revalued (Reuters in Palo Alto, United States, South China Morning Post, February 29, 2004). The 12-month CNY NDF fell 99 pips on February 27, 2004 and 399 pips from 4201 to 3802 on the following business day on March 1, 2004.

Chinese premier's speech to National People's Congress (March 5, 2004). Chinese premier Wen Jiabao made an important speech to the Chinese National People's Congress at its annual conference in Beijing on March 5, 2004. By revising downward the GDP growth target for 2004 to 7.0%, he gave a clear signal that the deceleration of economic growth in order to avoid overheating is a major target for China in 2004. Improving the quality of growth by rebalancing wealth between urban rural areas is key to China's administration. Mr. Wen also said that introducing more flexibility in the exchange rate is a medium-term target but that the exchange rate policy will remain unchanged in the short term. The speech reduces the scope for further widening of discounts on the CNY NDF market. The 12-month CNY NDF discount fell 145 pips from 3948 on Friday (March 5, 2004) to 3803 on the following Monday (March 8, 2004) and further to 3698 on Tuesday (March 9, 2004).

US labor data release (March 7, 2004). The US Labor Department released February unemployment data on March 7, 2004. The unemployment data was weaker than expected, 5.60%, the same as in January. The weaker labor data pushed up CNY NDF rates, and the 12-month CNY NDF went up more than 350 pips from 3950 pips on Thursday (March 4) to 4300 pips on Friday.

18.4.5 Summarizing Arguments and Events

There have been many important arguments and events, relating to what caused the CNY NDF contracts to fluctuate as we have gone through in Chapter 1 and here in this section. All these arguments and events are so numerous that it is necessary for us to summarize these events and arguments in Table 18.1 with the corresponding movements in the 12-month CNY NDF discounts.

Table 18.1 Major Arguments and Events and CNY NDF Fluctuations

	Date	Event	NDF Change
First stage	May 1, 2002	The US Senate discusses the necessity of CNY revaluation in order to reduce the US–China trade deficit	72
	May 1, 2002	Hanke says that deflation is always an everywhere phenomenon, and in this day and age it is a monctary area-specific problem	
	September 20, 2002	G7 industrial nations' conference	105
	Early in December, 2002	Japanese Finance Minister Masujuro Shiokawa's testimony to the Japanese Congress	180
	November 12, 2002	China's export and import data release	157
	November 24, 2002	Morgan Stanley reports five biggest hedging	−84
	January 5, 2003	Zhu Rongji's speech at SAFE	107
	May 22, 2003	The US House CJS Appropriations Subcommittee hearing	422
Second stage	June 11, 2003	Goldman Sachs report	300
	August 29, 2003	Hu express a similar view in a speech delivered to the American Chamber of Commerce in Hong Kong	142
	June 16, 2003	Secretary Snow commented on Washington's preference for a change in Chinese monetary policy	452
	July 5–6, 2003	ASEM Finance Ministers' gathering. European Countries agreed on yuan's undervaluation	175
	July 7, 2003	Roach says "China's competitive prowess has little to do with the value of the RMB	−193

Table 18.1 (Continued)

	Date	Event	NDF change
	July 17, 2003	Four members of the US House and Senate send a letter to Snow that a stronger yuan would likely be helpful to China	205
	July 17, 2003	Greenspan makes a remark against Chinese foreign exchange	205
	July 23, 2003	Rogoff does not support demands that China let its currency strengthen	−57
	July 29, 2003	Lü Fuyuan's speech at the fifth Asia–Europe meeting	−77
	July 31, 2003	Sixteen bipartisan members of the US House and Senate sign a letter sent to Bush Japan and the US step up calls on China	34
	September 3, 2003	Wen meets John Snow	121
Third stage	October 1, 2003	Taylor's testimony mentions the importance of recognizing that China still has significant capital control	
	October 1, 2003	US legislators address China's alleged exchange rate market intervention to manipulate the value of the CNY	1050
	October 7, 2003	Jiji Press Japan says that the PBOC is considering revaluing the yuan by about 30%	1075
	October 16, 2003	Snow testifies before the US Senate Banking Committee to discuss the US administration's exchange-rate policy	800
	Mid-October	Bush promises to exert pressure on China to introduce more flexibility in the yuan	
	October 19, 2003	In a conference with Bush, Hu Jintao spells out reasons why China is reluctant to let its yuan appreciate against the dollar	−900
	October 21, 2003	Hearing on US–China ties before the US House of Representatives	125
	October 22, 2003	US representatives call for tariff on Chinese imports	351
	October 23, 2003	White House states that it will continue to negotiate with Chinese government to allow the CNY to revaluate in order to improve the employment situation in exports and manufacturing in the US	399
	October 28, 2003	US commerce secretary Donald Evans said that the US patience was "running thin" in Beijing	699
	December 11, 2003	Greenspan: China's currency not costing US jobs	49

Table 18.1 (Continued)

	Date	Event	NDF change
Fourth stage	January 21, 2004	Bush says that China has to resolve its currency problems in order to make bilateral trade balanced and fair between the US and China	74
	February 2, 2004	State Council release of nine principles on capital market liberalization	57
	February 9, 2004	The G7 reference to the need for "more flexibility" looks like a veiled reference to Asia, even if no specific countries are mentioned	401
	February 27, 2004	Greenspan's speech at Stanford's Institute for Economic Policy Research	−99
	March 5, 2004	Premier Wen's speech to National People's Congress	−145
	March 5, 2004	US labor data release	350

18.5 CNY NDF Market Participants

It is difficult to find specific market participants for the CNY NDF as most dealers do not want to announce their transactions. We can find potential participants through two channels in this section: the RISK magazine survey and EMTA membership and surveys.

18.5.1 RISK Survey

Most international banks provide NDF businesses for their clients. According to RISK magazine, JP Morgan Chase, Citibank, Standard Chartered, and Deutsche Bank are the top banks trading the Korean won, New Taiwan dollar, and other Asian currency NDFs. The particular roles of these banks were given in Table 9.6 of Chapter 9 in Part II. Table 9.6 also lists the largest three banks providing Asian currency NDFs besides the Korean won and the New Taiwan dollar. We can observe that Standard Chartered Bank fell from No. 1 in 2001 to No. 3 in 2002 and Deutsche Bank rose from No. 2 to No. 1 from 2001 to 2002. We can also observe from Table 9.6 that JP Morgan Chase rose slightly from No. 3 in 2001 to No. 2 in 2002. We will briefly introduce these four major banks as follows.

HSBC. HSBC has been the most important bank in Hong Kong, the major CNY NDF market. Table 18.2 shows that HSBC had been

Table 18.2 Participants of CNY NDFs in 1998 and 1999

Chinese Renminbi				Banks Cited: 9
1999	**1998**	**Banks**		**% of Votes**
1 =	1	HSBC		23
1 =	3	Deutsche Bank		23
3		Chase Manhatten		19
		Broker:	1999	Prebon Yamane
			1998	Prebon Yamane

Data source: RISK magazine, 1999 and 2000.

ranked No. 1 in CNY NDF trading consecutively in 1998 and 1999. HSBC is ranked the biggest trader for the CNY by Euromoney (Kuramitsu, 2003).

Standard Chartered. Standard Chartered Bank was ranked No. 1 participant for all Asian currency NDFs including the Korean won, the New Taiwan dollar, and other currencies in 2001. Although Standard Chartered Bank's dominating position was challenged by other international banks in 2002, it was still ranked among the top three for Asian currency NDFs.

Deutsche Bank. Deutsche Bank was ranked No. 1 for CNY NDFs in 1999, up from No. 3 in 1998; it was ranked from No. 2 to No. 1 in Asian currency NDFs besides the Korean won and the New Taiwan dollar from 2001 to 2002. Thus, Deutsche Bank has been one of the major players in the CNY NDF market.

JP Morgan Chase. Chase Manhattan Bank was ranked No. 3 for CNY NDFs in 1999. After merging with JP Morgan, JP Morgan Chase's position in Asian NDFs has also strengthened.

Prebon Yamane. Prebon Yamane is a premier broker for institutions worldwide. As an intermediary in a broad range of OTC markets, Prebon Yamane is well known by its clients for enhancing liquidity and for service characterized by profound product and market knowledge. Prebon Yamane has maintained a leading market position around the world in forward FX including NDFs. Prebon Yamane was ranked No. 1 broker for New Taiwan dollar NDFs and other Asian currency NDFs besides the Korean won by RISK magazine in 2001 and 2002.

Prebon remains the number one OTC broker in Singapore, and this office once again led revenue growth in the region. It accomplished significant revenue growth in NDFs and regional currency options across a wide range of ex-Japan Asia currencies. Although their FX revenues were broadly unchanged in the prior year, the revenue in NDFs and currency options increased dramatically. The interest rate environment restricted the market volume in a number of Asian currencies, although markets denominated in Chinese RMB, the Korean won, and the Taiwanese dollar continued to expand rapidly. Prebon's Hong Kong office achieved very strong growth in revenues and profits in view of the challenging economic climate that it faced; it was recognized as the leading broker in NDFs for Greater China (i.e. Chinese RMB and New Taiwan dollar), with substantial market shares in each area (see Global Review 2003, Prebon Yamane).

18.5.2 EMTA Members

The Emerging Market Traders Association (EMTA) is one of the few major international organizations that have been taking a lot of initiatives to promote the standardization and development of NDFs around the world. Its members are also the top participants of NDF contracts around the globe. The EMTA is the only organization that has surveyed trading volumes of major NDF contracts. We provided the only surveyed NDF trading volumes in the first two quarters of 2003 in Chapter 9.

There are four types of members in the EMTA, full members, buy-side members, associate members, and affiliate members. Buy-side members are firms that invest in emerging market instruments, associate members trade emerging market instruments but are smaller and less active than full members, and affiliate members do not directly trade emerging market instruments but have a strong interest in the emerging markets trading industry. Thus, full members are major market participants of the NDF markets (see the EMTA website, www.emta.org, for more information). Table 18.3 gives the list of full members of the EMTA.

We can easily check that all the major CNY NDF participants from the RISK magazine survey are full members of the EMTA, with

Table 18.3 Full Members of the EMTA

1. ABN AMRO Bank	14. Euro Brokers Maxcor
2. AIG Trading Group	15. Fidelity Investments
3. Bank for Foreign Economic Affairs of the USSR (Vnesheconombank)	16. FleetBostonroup
	17. Goldman Sachs
	18. HSBC Bank
4. Bank of America	19. ING Financial Markets LLC
5. Barclays Capital	20. J.P. Morgan Chase
6. Bear Stearns	21. Lehman Brothers
7. BNP Paribas Securities	22. Merinvest
8. CAI/IIF	23. Merrill Lynch
9. Cargill Financial Services	24. Morgan Stanley
10. Citigroup Global Markets	25. Refco Securitiese
11. Credit Suisse First Boston	26. Santander Central Hispano
12. Deutsche Bank Securities	27. Standard Bank London
13. Dresdner Kleinwort Wasserstein	28. UBS Investment Bank

Data source: EMTA website, www.emta.org.

the only exception of Standard Chartered Bank, which falls into the group of associate members.

18.5.3 Hong Kong SAR

Because most of the foreign direct investment has flown into China through Hong Kong and due to Hong Kong's position as a regional financial center in Asia, Hong Kong has been the major offshore market for CNY NDFs since its inception.

The EMTA Template Terms for NDF transactions have been supported by the EMTA Foreign Exchange and Money Market Practices Committee (MPC). They have been used by market participants in many countries/regions including Hong Kong, where NDFs for many Asian currencies are traded. This support was expressed to the MPC member associations, including the following:

- Hong Kong Financial Markets Association (HKFMA)
- Hong Kong Association of Banks (HKAB)
- Hong Kong Association of Restricted License Banks and Deposit-Taking Companies (HKARLBDTC)
- Hong Kong Foreign Exchange and Deposit Brokers' Association.

A nonstatutory body first established in 1992 with the mandate to give advice on matters relating to the health and development of Hong Kong's foreign exchange and money markets, the MPC was restructured to play a fuller role in the development and promotion of the foreign exchange and money markets in Hong Kong and also to foster links with similar bodies elsewhere in 2000.

18.5.4 China–Taiwan

Taiwan's financial authorities announced on August 6, 2003 that they had given approval to local banks to engage in CNY-denominated NDF services, and nondelivery options (NDOs) in CNY offshore banking units (OBUs) (Wang, 2003). Because most companies in Taiwan have either invested in Mainland China or have businesses in the Mainland, they have either hedging needs or speculating demand for CNY NDF trading. Therefore, Hong Kong SAR and China–Taiwan are two major places for CNY NDF trading. Effective immediately, Taiwan is allowing local companies to use the CNY NDF market to hedge their CNY exposure.

According to China Times on October 8, 2003, authorities approved licenses to ABN Amro, Citi-bank, BNP and 6 local banks to conduct CNY NDF and non-deliverable options (NDOs) businesses. Transactions were not as active as previously expected; total turnover of both NDF and NDO surpassed US$100 million from early in August to end-September, 2003. The CNY NDF turnover was greater than 80% of the total. The major factor that prevented manufacturers to use CNY NDF was that the transaction cost was too high. We will show how participants can use CNY NDF between the Mainland and Taiwan province in the following chapter.

18.5.5 Singapore

The major participants in the Singapore NDF market are the top 20 international banks and investment organizations of the world. The clients of these banks and financial institutions are international corporations with revenues in CNY and those Chinese companies with head offices in Hong Kong. The purpose of trading the CNY NDF is either to protect currency risk involving the CNY or to speculate.

18.6 CNY NDF Volume Estimation

Because of the OTC nature of most OTC derivatives, there are no available sources for CNY NDF trading volumes. We try to estimate CNY NDF trading volumes in this section. There are two ways that we can estimate the turnover: we will use both of them separately and then reconcile the results of the two methods.

18.6.1 EMTA Survey Volume

(A) *Actual EMTA survey volume for the first two quarters of 2003.* As we mentioned earlier in this chapter, the EMTA is the only international organization that provided survey data for NDF trading volume. Table 18.4 lists the NDF turnovers of major currencies in the first two quarters of 2003. We can readily observe that the CNY NDF volumes in the first two quarters of 2003 were US$9.54 and 21.498 billion, respectively. However, these data might be very different from the

Table 18.4 NDF Turnovers in the First Two Quarters of 2003 (Unit: million US$)

	2Q 2003	1Q 2003	% change
Latin America and Caribbean total	**143,680**	**51,925**	**176.71**
Argentina	14,823	1799	724.15
Brazil	65,715	32,581	101.70
Chile	48,733	16,414	196.89
Colombia	5904	329	1696.56
Ecuador	2	0	N/A
Peru	8482	342	2378.59
Venezuela	20	461	−95.65
Eastern Europe total	**3231**	**903**	**257.60**
Russia	3231	903	257.60
Asia total	**173,397**	**121,120**	**43.16**
People's Republic of China	21,498	9,540	125.34
India	4252	2414	76.19
Indonesia	3047	4139	−26.40
Philippines	2969	2408	23.31
South Korea	109,166	86,563	26.11
Taiwan	32,465	16,055	102.21
Grand total	**320,307**	**173,948**	**84.14**

Data source: EMTA NDF and Credit Derivatives Surveys.

actual turnovers of the CNY NDF in the two periods as only a portion of the EMTA members responded to the surveys.

(B) *Difference between responding and nonresponding members.* The 1Q 2003 survey results are those of merely 18 respondents, only 64.3% of the total number of full members of the EMTA. Although the number of respondents increased from 18 to 21 in the 2Q 2003 survey, 21 only represented 75% of the total number of full members of the EMTA. According to the EMTA 2Q 2003 Emerging Markets NDF Volume Survey, released on August 13, 2003, institutions responding to the 2Q 2003 EMTA survey are given in Table 18.5 as follows.

(C) *Estimation of the actual turnovers of the first two quarters.* The turnover of 2Q 2003 given in Table 18.6 was obtained from only 50.0% of 28 full members, 17.6% of buy-side members, and 7.1% of associate members. If we neglect buy-side and associate members, the actual turnover for 2Q 2003 should be around twice the number given

Table 18.5 Respondents to 2Q 2003 EMTA Survey

Name of Institution	Type of Membership
Ashmore Investment Management	Buy-side member
Babson Mass Mutual	Not in membership list
Bank of Tokyo-Mitsubishi	Associate member
Barclays Capital	Full member
Bear Stearns	Full member
BNP Paribas	Full member
Citigroup Global Markets	Full member
Credit Suisse First Boston	Full member
Deutsche Bank	Full member
Goldman Sachs	Full member
HSBC Bank	Full member
J.P. Morgan	Full member
Lehman Brothers	Full member
Merrill Lynch	Full member
Morgan Stanley	Full member
OneWorld Investments	Not in membership list
Pharo Management	Buy-side member
Santander Central Hispano	Full member
Spinnaker Capital Limited	Buy-side member
Standard Bank	Full member
Westdeutsche Landesbank Girozentrale	Associate member

Source: Participants of EMTA Second Quarter 2003 NDF Volume Survey.

Table 18.6 Respondent Distribution of 2Q 2003 EMTA Survey

Member Type	Number	Number/Total Number (%)
Full members	14	50.0
Buy-side member	3	17.6
Associate member	2	7.1

Data source: Calculated using Table 18.5 and the EMTA website of various types of members.

Table 18.7 Quarterly Volatilities and Turnovers for CNY NDF

Quarter	Daily Standard Deviation (%)	Daily Standard Deviation/ 2Q 2003	Quarterly Turnover (US$ b)	Average Daily Turnover (US$ b)
2Q 2003	3.49	1.00	43.0	0.683
3Q 2003	5.13	1.47	63.3	1.005
4Q 2003	6.23	1.79	76.8	1.219
1Q 2004	4.38	1.25	54.0	0.856
Total 2Q 2003–1Q 2004			**237.1**	
Total 2003			**205.4**	

Data source: Calculated using data from DataStream and estimated turnovers for the first two quarters of 2003, US$22.26 and 43.00 billion, obtained in (C) of this section.

in Table 18.3, or 21.498/50.0% = US$42.996 billion. Using the same ratio of full-member respondents/total number of full-members and actual respondents in the 1Q 2003, 18, we can estimate the turnover for 1Q 2003 as 9.54/(50.0% × (18/21)) = US$22.26 billion.

(D) *Estimation of the actual turnover for the second two quarters.* Unfortunately, the EMTA stopped surveying NDF turnovers from the 3Q 2003, and we do not have any other source for CNY NDF turnovers for the third and fourth quarters of 2003 and beyond. We may use the second quarter data obtained in (C) above as a base to estimate the turnovers for the third and fourth quarters of 2003 and 1Q 2004.

Forward trading turnovers are normally proportionate to the underlying market volatilities. Fortunately, we can find CNY NDF volatilities within different quarters and then estimate quarterly turnovers using the relative CNY NDF volatilities. Table 18.7 provides the daily volatilities (standard deviations) of the daily returns of the CNY NDF from the 2Q 2003 to 1Q 2004, the magnitude of the daily volatilities compared with that in 2Q 2003, and the estimated quarterly CNY NDF turnover in the four quarters.

We can observe readily from Table 18.7 that the estimated annual turnover for CNY NDF was US$205.4 billion for 2003.

18.6.2 Hong Kong Monetary Authority Survey Volume

According to a market survey conducted by the Hong Kong Monetary Authority (HKMA) in June 2003 and February 2004, the average daily turnover of the CNY NDF worldwide was between US$100 and 200 million in 2002; it rose to around US$300 million in the first half of 2003; and it could reach US$1.00 billion in times of turbulence later in 2003. Table 18.8 gives quarterly CNY NDF turnover estimations using average daily turnovers from HKMA. The low and up-quarterly turnovers are obtained using the low and up-average daily turnovers within the daily CNY NDF turnovers provided by HKMA above.

We can observe from Table 18.8 that the total estimated annual turnover of CNY NDF for 2003 should be around US$150 billion.

18.6.3 Reconciling Results of Two Methods

Comparing the estimated results given in Tables 18.7 and 18.8, we can find that the estimation in Table 18.7 may be a little too high as the average daily turnover for 4Q 2003 in Table 17.6 is US$1.219 billion,

Table 18.8 CNY NDF Turnover Estimation Using Average Daily Turnovers from the HKMA

Quarter	Low Average Daily Turnover (US$ b)	Low Quarterly Turnover (US$ b)	Up-Average Daily Turnover (US$ b)	Up-Quarterly Turnover (US$ b)
1Q 2003	0.200	12.4	0.300	18.6
2Q 2003	0.360	22.3	0.460	28.5
3Q 2003	0.720	44.6	0.800	49.6
4Q 2003	0.900	55.8	1.000	62.0
Total 2003		**136.2**		**158.7**
Total 2003 (using average of Low and Up)			**147.5**	

Data source: Calculated using average quarterly number of working days of 62 and average daily turnovers from HKMA.

21% higher than the average daily turnover obtained by HKMA. Combining the results from Tables 18.7 and 18.8, we may conclude that the total annual CNY NDF turnover should be between US$150 billion and 200 billion.

18.7 The CNY Realignment Probability

Yu (2003) provides a thorough theoretical model using the CNY NDF data. Using an approximation technique (closed-form likelihood approximations for multivariate jump-diffusion processes widely used in finance), Yu tried to uncover the CNY realignment probability and finds the term structure of the forward realignment rate. The term structure he obtained was hump-shaped and peaked at six months from the end of 2003. The implication is that the financial market is anticipating an upward realignment in the next year, and conditioning on no realignments before then, the chance of realignment is perceived to be small in the further future. Since February 2002, the realignment intensity of the yuan has increased fivefold. The realignment probability responds quickly to news releases on domestic Chinese and foreign government interventions, the Sino–US trade surplus, and other factors as we saw in Section 18.4.

To illustrate how the term structure of the forward realignment rate responds to the news release, the term structure of the CNY realignment on August 28, August 29, and September 2 in 2003 is plotted in Figure 18.3. On August 29, 2003, before the visit of the US Treasury Secretary, the Japanese Finance Minister publicly urged China to let the yuan float freely and the state-owned enterprises in China showed improved profitability. On the same day, the level of the forward realignment rate almost doubled relative to the previous day. More interestingly, the peak of the term structure moved from ten months later to six months later, indicating the market is anticipating the yuan to appreciate sooner.

Four days later, after the diplomatic pressure receded, the peak of the term structure moved back to roughly eight months later and the level of the term structure dropped. Most of the economic theory about currency realignment is on the depreciation side, in contrast to the case of the yuan. Therefore, the results obtained by Yu

Figure 18.3 Changes of the Term Structure of CNY Realignment

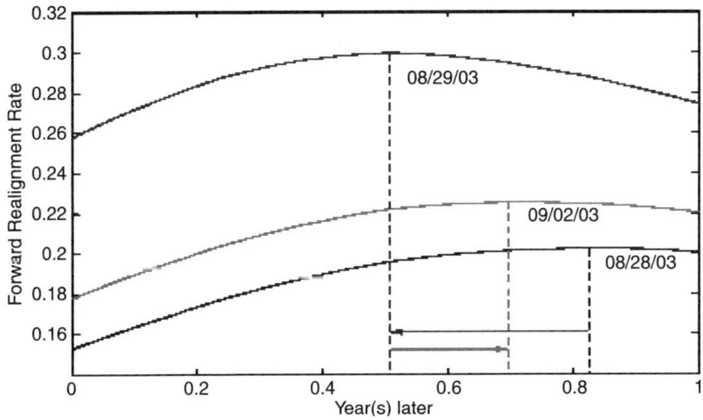

Data source: Yu (2003), Figure 9, p. 31.

lend empirical evidence to modeling currency realignment on the upward side.

18.8 Pricing and Other Problems with the CNY NDFs

Results in both Table 18.1 and Figure 18.3 show that major jumps of the CNY NDF rates coincide with major news releases on both Chinese and foreign government interventions of the FX market, Sino–US trade surpluses, Chinese foreign reserves, and so on. Because of the managed nature of the CNY exchange rate, it is not surprising that signals of the Chinese government's determination to maintain the current exchange rate play a dominant role in affecting waves of the CNY NDF changes besides calls from the US Congress, the US Department of Treasury, and other countries and international organizations.

18.8.1 Existing Theories Not Applicable

Theoretically, the spot and forward exchange rates must satisfy a certain parity relationship as we discussed in Chapter 17, yet this parity relationship cannot be used to price the CNY/USD NDF. Because you cannot go into the cash market to borrow RMB in the offshore market, the CNY NDF rates are set mainly on the perceptions of buyers and sellers or on market conditions of supply and demand.

18.8.2 No Universal Formula to Price All NDFs

We have learned from the introduction to NDFs in earlier parts of this book that they come into existence simply because there is control of either capital account or current account, so that the relating currency cannot be converted freely. Different currencies have different regulatory environments and/or administrative systems, and thus each NDF may have its own characteristics in the way its authority manages its currency. Therefore, there should not be a universal formula to price all NDFs.

18.8.3 No Reliable Formula to Price Domestic CNY Forwards

The empirical study given in Chapter 17 indicates that the CNY forward contracts cannot be priced using the parity relationship widely used to price convertible currency forwards. This is because an interest rate mechanism has not been established in China and there are a lot of controls for the CNY forward market in China. It is more difficult to price the CNY NDF contracts trading in the offshore marketplace because the CNY cannot be accessed easily.

18.8.4 Fundamental Data and NDF Fluctuations

Macroeconomic data, trade data, foreign reserves, and other data are major factors causing foreign exchange rates to fluctuate in the developed countries. Such data did affect the CNY/USD NDF rates as shown in Table 18.1, yet these data did not affect the CNY NDF as much as reports of governmental statements from both China and the US, implying that the CNY NDF is rather speculative because fundamental factors do not play important roles in determining the CNY NDF rates.

18.9 Future Development

The FX cash market is in the early stage of development and the forward market is still in an experimental stage in China. With growing exports and imports in China as shown in Table 3.3, demand for both cash and forward transactions will undoubtly grow significantly in China in coming years. Table 17.4 provides the ratios of FX cash and forward turnovers and corresponding imports and trade from 1997 to 2003. We can observe that the FX cash turnover as a percentage of total trade in China has been significantly lower than 20% since 2000 and the corresponding ratio has been around merely 2% for forwards.

As China is increasingly involved in the global market as shown in Table 3.3, more domestic import and export companies are learning to follow international practices to secure their interests and guard against losses. With recent pressure on the CNY to be revalued and increased FX volatility worldwide, the need for hedging and trading in the FX market will certainly grow tremendously in China in coming years.

18.10 Summary

The CNY NDF contracts trading in the offshore market are certainly the most popular instruments for hedgers and speculators in anticipation of the CNY revaluation. Although the CNY NDF market came into existence before the Asian financial crisis, the trading volume was rather thin until late in 2002, when the CNY was perceived to be undervalued. Thus, the instrument originally designed to hedge against currency depreciation has become a major tool for CNY revaluations.

Although the CNY NDF rates are indeed influenced by trade, economic, and capital market information, they have been largely affected by comments from government officials from China and the US, major international organizations and other countries as shown in Table 18.1. With increasing participation of Chinese enterprises in the global economy as shown in Table 3.3, further liberalization of the Chinese capital market, and greater foreign direct investment in China, the CNY NDF market will play a more important role for international investors and even domestic investors as there are no other effective instruments that can be used for investors to hedge their exposures.

19

Uses of CNY NDFs

With our study on various aspects of the CNY NDFs in Chapter 18, we can now illustrate how CNY NDFs are used in practice. Our purpose in this chapter is to illustrate how CNY NDF contracts are used in practice.

This chapter is organized as follows. Section 19.1 illustrates how CNY NDFs are traded, with specific examples; Section 19.2 shows how CNY DFNs are used in spreading; Section 19.3 illustrates with examples how bull spreaders can use CNY NDFs to trade; Section 19.4 illustrates how bear spreaders can potentially use CNY NDF contracts; Section 19.5 shows how CNY NDFs can be used in hedging; and Section 19.6 summarizes and concludes the chapter.

19.1 Trading CNY NDFs

Figure 18.2 indicates that CNY NDFs changed from premiums to discounts from November 2002 and CNY NDF rates have exhibited significant volatilities since then. In this section, we illustrate how to trade CNY NDFs, with specific examples. These examples will help us understand better specifically how offshore participants could possibly make profits or suffer losses using CNY NDFs.

Example 19.1 What is the profit or loss if one investor bought a three-month CNY NDF contract with a notional principle of US$10 million at a discount of 131 pips on June 26, 2003 and the three-month CNY NDF was at a discount of 597 pips on September 26, 2003?

Answer: The corresponding three-month CNY NDF rate on June 26 was

$$8.277 - 131/10000 = 8.277 - 0.0131 = \text{RMB } 8.2639/\text{US\$},$$

and the NDF on September 26 was

$$8.277 - 597/10000 = 8.277 - 0.0597 = \text{RMB } 8.2173/\text{US\$}.$$

Thus the net profit/loss was

$$10{,}000{,}000/(8.2173/8.2639) - 10{,}000{,}000 = \text{US\$}56{,}709.62.$$

The net profit of the transaction was US$56,709.62.

Example 19.2 What was the profit or loss if one investor bought a six-month CNY NDF contract with a notional principle of US$10 million at a discount of 3500 pips on October 7, 2003 and the six-month CNY NDF was at a discount of 2250 pips on April 7, 2004?

Answer: The corresponding six-month CNY NDF rate on October 7 was

$$8.277 - 3500/10000 = 8.277 - 0.3500 = \text{RMB } 7.927/\text{US\$},$$

and the NDF on April 7, 2004 was

$$8.277 - 2250/10000 = 8.277 - 0.2250 = \text{RMB } 8.052/\text{US\$}.$$

Thus the net profit/loss was

$$10{,}000{,}000/(8.052/7.927) - 10{,}000{,}000 = -\text{US\$}155{,}240.93.$$

The net loss of the transaction was US$155,240.93.

Example 19.3 What was the profit or loss if one investor bought a 12-month CNY NDF contract with a notional principle of US$10 million at a discount of 650 pips on March 18, 2003 and the 12-month CNY NDF was at discount of 3400 pips on March 18, 2004?

Answer: The corresponding six-month CNY NDF rate on March 18 was

$$8.277 - 650/10000 = 8.277 - 0.0650 = \text{RMB } 8.212/\text{US\$},$$

and the NDF on March 18, 2004 was

$$8.277 - 3400/10000 = 8.277 - 0.3400 = \text{RMB } 7.937/\text{US\$}.$$

Thus the net profit/loss was

$$10{,}000{,}000/(7.937/8.212) - 10{,}000{,}000 = \text{US\$}346{,}487.52.$$

The net profit of the transaction was US$346,487.52.

Example 19.4 What will the profit or loss be if one investor bought a 12-month CNY NDF contract with a notional principle of US$10 million at a discount of 5400 pips on October 7, 2003 and the 12-month CNY NDF closes at a discount of 2500 pips on October 7, 2004?

Answer: The corresponding six-month CNY NDF rate on March 18 was

$$8.277 - 5{,}400/10000 = 8.277 - 0.5400 = \text{RMB } 7.737/\text{US\$},$$

and the NDF on October 7, 2004 will be

$$8.277 - 2500/10000 = 8.277 - 0.2500 = \text{RMB } 8.027/\text{US\$}.$$

Thus the net profit/loss was

$$10{,}000{,}000/(8.027/7.737) - 10{,}000{,}000 = -\text{US\$}361{,}280.68.$$

The net loss of the transaction was US$361,280.68.

The CNY NDF rates used in the above four examples are close to the market prices, their profit and loss positions reflect the fact that trading such products is very risky as the CNY NDF rates are not based on market fundamentals but on speculations of the CNY revaluation perspectives, as analyzed by us in Chapter 18.

19.2 Spreading with CNY NDFs

According to the HKMA, calendar spreading is the most popular trading strategy with CNY NDFs. As its name implies, spreading implies buying and selling of futures contracts or NDF contracts with different tenors. In this section we concentrate on calendar spreading using CNY NDFs, with specific examples.

19.2.1 Premiums and Discounts

The basis is the most important concept involving spreading. It is defined as the price difference between the underlying instrument and the futures price. The basis also represents the price difference between various futures contracts with different expirations. The same concept can also be used for NDFs.

In general, an NDF contract is priced at a premium to its underlying spot exchange rate when the market sentiment is bearish, and at distant months may sell at increasingly higher premiums. On the other hand, NDFs are priced at a discount to the underlying spot exchange rate when the market sentiment is bullish, and at distant months may become increasingly deeper the further the contracts are from expirations.

The premiums and discounts reflected in the basis of various NDF contracts represent an important tool to NDF traders, especially to NDF spreaders. Figure 19.1 illustrates that the 12-month CNY NDF

Figure 19.1 From Premiums to Discounts of 12-month CNY NDFs between December 1998 and March 2004

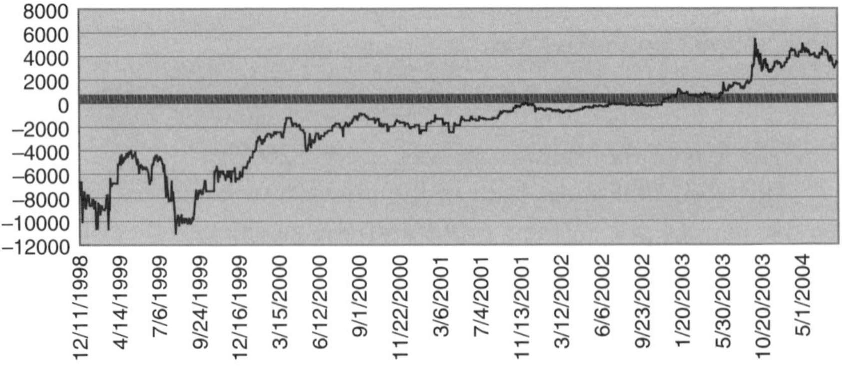

changed from premiums before November 2002 to discounts after early November 2002. The 12-month CNY NDF has changed dramatically since November 2002.

19.2.2 Spreading Strategies with CNY NDFs

A NDF spread involves establishing a long position in one NDF contract and a corresponding short position in a different NDF contract month or market. NDF contracts can be for two different settlement months, such as buying a three-month contract and selling a six-month contract on the CNY. This is known as an "intra-market" spread, "calendar spread", or "time spread".

Spreaders are not concerned with the absolute up and down price changes but with the relative price changes of the contracts. A spreader attempts to benefit from differences in the basis of two different NDF contracts that appear to be out of line in value. The spreader then purchases one contract and sells another in the hope of profiting when the price difference or spread between the two contracts widens or narrows. Figure 19.2 depicts the spreads between six-month and three-month CNY NDFs and between 6-month and 12-month CNY NDFs from January 2003 to September 2003.

We can observe readily from Figure 19.2 that the spread between six-month and three-month CNY NDFs fluctuated dramatically in the

Figure 19.2 Spread between Six-month and Three month, and 12-month and Six-month CNY NDFs from January 2003 to September 2003 (Up and Low Lines Representing 12-month/Six-month and Six-month/Three-month Spread, Respectively)

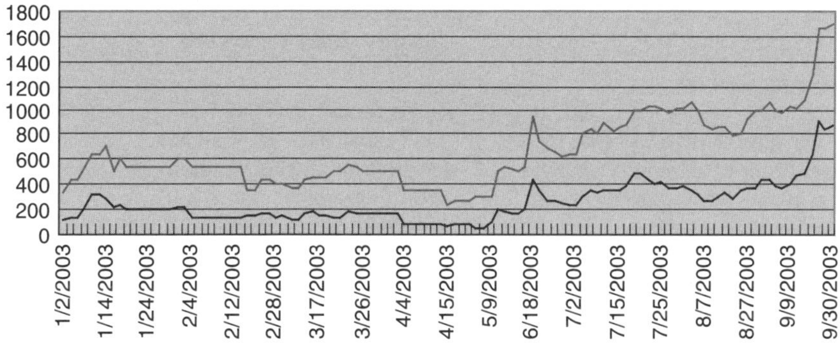

first nine months in 2003. Specifically, it remained largely between 600 pips in the first five months in 2003; between 600 and 1000 between June and August 2003, and between 1000 and 1700 in September 2003.

19.3 Bull Spread with CNY NDFs

A bull spread involves selling a nearby NDF contract and buying a distant NDF contract. Spreaders who believe that the distant month contacts will rise faster than the nearby contract or that the nearby contract will fall faster than the distant month contract would arrange a "bull spread". When the CNY is believed to be in an up-trend, prices of the more deferred contacts tend to rise faster than the nearby contracts. Let us study bull spreading with specific examples.

Example 19.5 What is the spreading result if the bull spreader sells a three-month CNY NDF contract with a notional principle of US$10 million and buys a six-month CNY NDF contract with the same principle, given the three-month and six-month NDFs at discounts of 135 and 385 pips, respectively, when the spreading position was taken on June 26, 2003, and the discounts changed to 597 and 1447 pips, respectively, on September 26, 2003?

Answer: Using the method shown in Examples 19.1–4, we can obtain the spreading result as follows.

Three-month CNY NDF	Six-month CNY NDF	Spread Basis
Spreading initiation on June 26		
Sell three-month CNY NDF at 135 pips (RMB 8.2635/US$)	Buy six-month CNY NDF at 385 pips (RMB 8.2385/US$)	250 pips
Closing position		
Buy three-month CNY NDF at 597 pips (RMB 8.2173/US$)	Sell six-month CNY NDF at 1447 pips (RMB 8.1323/US$)	850 pips
Net profit of closing position = 10.0 − 10.05622285 = − US$56,222.85	Net profit of closing position = 10.13059036 − 10.0 = US$130,590.36	
Overall spreading profit/loss = −56,222.85 + 130,590.36 = US$74,367.51		

The overall spreading profit can be approximated as the spread basis change multiplied by the notional value converted into

$$USD = \{[850 - 250]/10000\} \times 10/(8.277 - 1447/10000) = US\$73{,}780,$$

which is 99.21% of the actual profit of US$74,367.51 obtained in the above table.

There is no exact compact formula to express overall spreading profit or loss in term of the spread basis as in the case of stock index futures because the spread basis is in terms of RMB and the spread basis appears in the denominator when we convert the result into USD as shown in Examples 19.1–4.

Example 19.6 What is the spreading result if the bull spreader sells a three-month CNY NDF contract with a notional principle of US$10 million and buys a six-month CNY NDF contract with the same principle, given the three-month and six-month NDFs at discounts of 600 and 1500 pips, respectively, when the spreading position was taken on September 25, 2003, and the discounts were 400 and 1000 pips on December 25, 2003?

Answer: Using the method shown in Examples 19.1–4, we can obtain the spreading result as follows.

Three-month CNY NDF	Six-month CNY NDF	Spread Basis
Spreading initiation on September 25		
Sell three-month CNY NDF at 600 pips (RMB 8.2170/US$)	Buy six-month CNY NDF at 1,500 pips (RMB 8.1270/US$)	900 pips
Closing position		
Buy three-month CNY NDF at 400 pips (RMB 8.237/US$)	Sell six-month CNY NDF at 1,000 pips (RMB 8.177/US$)	600 pips
Net profit of closing position = 9.97571932 − 10.0 = −US$24,280.68	Net profit/loss of closing position = 9.93885288 − 10.0 = −US$61,147.12	
Overall spreading profit/loss = −61,147.12 − (−24,280.68) = −US$36,866.44		

Overall spreading profit can be approximated as spread basis change multiplied by the notional value and converted into

$$\begin{aligned} USD &= -[(900 - 600)/10000] \times 10/(8.277 - 1500/10000) \\ &= -US\$36{,}914, \end{aligned}$$

which is only 0.13% higher than the actual loss of US$36,866.44.

Example 19.7 What is the spreading result if the bull spreader sells a three-month CNY NDF contract with a notional principle of US$10 million and buys a six-month CNY NDF contract with the same principle, given the three-month and six-month NDFs at discounts of 155 and 455 pips, respectively, when the spreading position was taken on June 26, 2003, and the discounts were 600 and 1200 pips on September 26, 2003?

Answer: Using the method shown in Examples 19.1–4, we can obtain the spreading result as follows.

Three-month CNY NDF	Six-month CNY NDF	Spread Basis
Spreading initiation on June 26		
Sell three-month CNY NDF at 155 pips (RMB 8.262/US$)	Buy six-month CNY NDF at 455 pips (RMB 8.232/US$)	300 pips
Closing position		
Buy three-month CNY NDF at 600 pips (RMB 8.217/US$)	Sell six-month CNY NDF at 1200 pips (RMB 8.157/US$)	600 pips
Net profit of closing position = 10.0 − 10.05415602 = −US$54,156.02	Net profit of closing position = 10.0913326 − 10.0 = US$91,332.60	
Overall spreading profit/loss = −54,156.02 + 91,332.60 = US$37,176.58		

The overall spreading profit can be approximated as the spread basis change multiplied by the notional value converted into

$$\begin{aligned} USD &= [(600 - 300)/10000] \times 10/(8.277 - 1200/10000) \\ &= US\$36{,}788. \end{aligned}$$

Example 19.8 What is the spreading result if the bull spreader sells a three-month CNY NDF contract with a notional principle of

US$10 million and buys a six-month CNY NDF contract with the same principle, given the three-month and six-month NDFs at discounts of 1500 and 900 pips, respectively, when the spreading position was taken on September 25, 2003, and the discounts were 1000 and 600 pips on December 25, 2003?

Answer: Using the method shown in Examples 19.1–4, we can obtain the spreading result as follows.

Three-month CNY NDF	**Six-month CNY NDF**	**Spread Basis**
Spreading initiation on September 25		
Sell three-month CNY NDF at 1500 pips (RMB 8.127/US$)	Buy six-month CNY NDF at 900 pips (RMB 8.187/US$)	600 pips
Closing position		
Buy three-month CNY NDF at 1000 pips (RMB 8.177/US$)	Sell six-month CNY NDF at 600 pips (RMB 8.217/US$)	400 pips
Net profit of closing position = 9.93885288 − 10.0 = − US$61,147.12	Net profit/loss of closing position = 9.96349032 − 10.0 = −US$36,509.68	
Overall spreading profit/loss = −36,509.68 − (−61,147.23) = US$24,637.44		

The overall spreading profit can be approximated as the spread basis change multiplied by the notional value and converted into

$$\begin{aligned} \text{USD} &= [(600 - 400)/10000] \times 10/(8.277 - 1500/10000) \\ &= \text{US\$}24{,}609.33. \end{aligned}$$

We can summarize the results in the above four examples for bull spreaders as follows: a bull spreader makes money when the spread basis widens and loses money when the spread basis narrows under normal market conditions; and the bull spreader loses money when the spread basis widens and makes money when the spread basis narrows under inverted market condition. We can also observe from these examples, compared with the single trading activities in Examples 19.1–4, that losses are limited in spreading strategies compared with single transactions.

19.4 Bear Spread with CNY NDFs

A bear spread involves buying a nearby futures contract and selling a distant futures contract. Bear spreaders expect the underlying market to fall faster for the distant month as compared with the nearby month or who expect the nearby contract to rise faster than the distant month contract. In a declining market, distant contract months usually fall more rapidly than the nearby forward contracts, and bear spreaders make profits through spreading forward contracts with different expirations. Let us study, again with specific examples, bear spreading under both normal and inverted market conditions.

Example 19.9 What is the spreading result if the bear spreader buys a three-month CNY NDF contract with a notional principle of US$10 million and sells a six-month CNY NDF contract with the same principle, given the three-month and six-month NDFs at discounts of 135 and 385 pips, respectively, when the spreading position was taken on June 26, 2003, and the discounts changed to 597 and 1447 pips, respectively, on September 26, 2003?

Answer: Using the method shown in Examples 19.1–4, we can obtain the spreading result as follows.

Three-month CNY NDF	Six-month CNY NDF	Spread Basis
Spreading initiation on June 26		
Buy three-month CNY NDF at 135 pips (RMB 8.2635/US$)	Sell six-month CNY NDF at 385 pips (RMB 8.2385/US$)	250 pips
Closing position		
Sell three-month CNY NDF at 597 pips (RMB 8.2173/US$)	Buy six-month CNY NDF at 1447 pips (RMB 8.1323/US$)	850 pips
Net profit of closing position = 10.05622285 − 10.0 = US$56,222.85	Net profit of closing position = 10.0 − 10.13059036 = −US$130,590.36	
Overall spreading profit/loss = 56,222.85 − 130,590.36 = −US$74,367.51		

Example 19.10 What is the spreading result if the bear spreader buys a three-month CNY NDF contract with a notional principle of US$10 million and sells a six-month CNY NDF contract with the

same principle, given the three-month and six-month NDFs at discounts of 600 and 1500 pips, respectively, when the spreading position was taken on September 25, 2003, and the discounts were 400 and 1000 pips on December 25, 2003?

Answer: Using the method shown in Examples 19.1–4, we can obtain the spreading result as follows.

Three-month CNY NDF	Six-month CNY NDF	Spread Basis
Spreading initiation on September 25		
Buy three-month CNY NDF at 600 pips (RMB 8.2170/US$)	Sell six-month CNY NDF at 1500 pips (RMB 8.1270/US$)	900 pips
Closing position		
Sell three-month CNY NDF at 400 pips (RMB 8.237/US$)	Buy six-month CNY NDF at 1000 pips (RMB 8.177/US$)	600 pips
Net profit of closing position = 10.0 − 9.97571932 = US$24,280.68	Net profit/loss of closing position = 10.0 − 9.93885288 = US$61,147.12	
Overall spreading profit/loss = 61,147.12 − 24,280.68 = US$36,866.44		

Example 19.11 What is the spreading result if the bull spreader buys a three-month CNY NDF contract with a notional principle of US$10 million and sells a six-month CNY NDF contract with the same principle, given the three-month and six-month NDFs at discounts of 155 and 455 pips, respectively, when the spreading position was taken on June 26, 2003, and the discounts were 600 and 1200 pips on September 26, 2003?

Answer: Using the method shown in Examples 19.1–4, we can obtain the spreading result as follows.

Three-month CNY NDF	Six-month CNY NDF	Spread Basis
Spreading initiation on June 26		
Buy three-month CNY NDF at 155 pips (RMB 8.262/US$)	Sell six-month CNY NDF at 455 pips (RMB 8.232/US$)	300 pips

Closing position		
Sell three-month CNY NDF at 600 pips (RMB 8.217/US$)	Buy six-month CNY NDF at 1200 pips (RMB 8.157/US$)	600 pips
Net profit of closing position = 10.05415602 − 10.0 = US$54,156.02	Net profit of closing position = 10.0 − 10.0913326 = −US$91,332.60	
Overall spreading profit/loss = 54,156.02 − 91,332.60 = −US$37,176.58		

Example 19.12 What is the spreading result if the bull spreader buys a three-month CNY NDF contract with a notional principle of US$10 million and sells a six-month CNY NDF contract with the same principle, given the three-month and six-month NDFs at discounts of 1500 and 900 pips, respectively, when the spreading position was taken on September 25, 2003, and the discounts were 1000 and 600 pips on December 25, 2003?

Answer: Using the method shown in Examples 19.1–4, we can obtain the spreading result as follows.

Three-month CNY NDF	**Six-month CNY NDF**	**Spread Basis**
Spreading initiation on September 25		
Buy three-month CNY NDF at 1500 pips (RMB 8.127/US$)	Sell six-month CNY NDF at 900 pips (RMB 8.187/US$)	600 pips
Closing position		
Sell three-month CNY NDF at 1000 pips (RMB 8.177/US$)	Buy six-month CNY NDF at 600 pips (RMB 8.217/US$)	400 pips
Net profit of closing position = 10.0 − 9.93885288 = US$61,147.12	Net profit/loss of closing position = 10.0 − 9.96349032 = US$36,509.68	
Overall spreading profit/loss = 61,147.12 − 36,509.68 = US$24,637.44		

19.5 Hedging with CNY NDFs

Hedging is the major function of all futures and NDFs and one of the most popular purposes for futures usage. NDFs are also used to hedge FX risk by exporters, importers, and investors in countries either without a domestic currency forward market or where the domestic forward market is not easily accessible. Besides the most popular trading strategy — spreading using CNY NDFs, illustrated in Sections 19.3 and 19.4, CNY NDFs are also used to hedge investments and trade risk involving the CNY. We will illustrate how CNY NDFs are used to hedge CNY exchange risk.

Example 19.13 A major international investment bank expected to have an income of RMB 49.662 billion in about six months in October 2002 and would like to hedge its CNY risk because it believes that the CNY might depreciate. How could the bank hedge its CNY risk using the CNY NDF contracts?

Answer: The investment bank can sell a six-month CNY NDF contract with a notional amount of 49.662/8.277 = US$6 billion, and we can find the profit/loss with the CNY NDF using the methods in Examples 19.1–4 and represent the results in the following table with various possible ending results of the CNY NDF at maturity:

Six-month CNY NDF (discount/premium)	−730	−300	0	500	1000	1500
Depreciation/revaluation (%)	0.89	0.36	0.00	−0.60	−1.19	−1.78
Implied CNY/USD	8.35	8.307	8.277	8.227	8.177	8.127
Profit/loss from hedging	0.05	0.02	0.00	−0.04	−0.07	−0.11
Asset in USD without hedging	5.95	5.98	6.00	6.04	6.07	6.11

We can observe that if the CNY NDF is at a premium, the CNY NDF would yield a profit; it would result in a loss if the CNY NDF was at a discount; and the profit from the CNY NDF would make up the loss resulting from CNY depreciation. The sum of the profit or loss from the CNY NDF and the asset value without hedging would always be the same, US$6 billion, effectively hedging the asset.

Example 19.14 A major international manufacturer plans to move some of its production lines to China in order to take advantage of the lower labor costs in China. It has estimated the total amount of investment would be RMB 25 billion. The company is concerned about the potential CNY revaluation because its total investment in terms of USD would be greater if the CNY is actually revalued in about a year. How can the company hedge its risk for the potential CNY revaluation?

Answer: The company can buy a 12-month CNY NDF contract with a 2000 pips discount and a notional amount of $25/(8.277 - 2000/10000) =$ US$3.09 billion, and we can find the profit/loss with the CNY NDF using the methods in Examples 19.1–4 and represent the results in the following table with various possible ending results of the CNY NDF at maturity.

Twelve-month CNY NDF	1000	1500	2000	2500	3000	3500
CNY appreciation (%)	1.22	1.85	2.48	3.11	3.76	4.42
Implied RMB/US$	8.177	8.127	8.077	8.027	7.977	7.927
Profit from hedging (USD m)	−0.04	−0.02	0.00	0.02	0.04	0.06
Investment necessary in USD (m)	3.06	3.08	3.10	3.11	3.13	3.15

We can observe that if the CNY NDF discount turns out to be greater than 2000 pips in 12 months as expected, the profit from the long CNY NDF contract will exactly offset the additional amount for the actual investment of RMB 25 billion or US$3.09 billion, and if the CNY NDF discount turns out to be lower than 2000 pips, the loss from the long CNY NDF contract will be offset by the lower amount of investment necessary for the project. Thus, the investment risk is hedged with this CNY NDF contract.

19.6 Arbitraging between CNY Forwards and NDFs

There are many manufacturers from Taiwan province in Mainland China and they can somehow access the CNY cash market with current accounts. The newly authorized CNY NDF business in Taiwan makes it easier for Taiwan manufactures to access the CNY NDF market. As the CNY NDF rates fluctuate according to international expectation of the CNY revaluation, and the CNY forward rates exhibit lower volatility because of the exchange rate limit, there exist arbitrage opportunities between the CNY forward and CNY NDF markets and some manufacturers from Taiwan are taking such opportunities.

For example, the 12-month CNY NDF discount was at 4,201 pips on February 27, 2004, the corresponding forward CNY/USD rate is 8.277 − 4201/10000 = 7.8569 and the corresponding CNY/USD forward is not significantly different from 8.277. Thus, there exists RMB 0.42 difference for each US dollar or RMB 420,000 for each million of US dollar (see China Times, March 12, 2004, page 4).

19.7 Summary and Conclusions

With the liquidity of CNY NDFs increasing since late 2002, it has become easier for hedgers and traders to trade and hedge using CNY NDFs. We have shown with specific examples how CNY NDFs are traded with spreading and hedging strategies in this chapter. Our examples indicate that it is rather risky to trade CNY NDF contracts as the NDF prices are mainly affected by government events and official speeches rather than economic fundamental information. Although the risk of suffering a loss is somewhat reduced with spreading strategies compared with naked transactions (Examples 19.1–4), the risk is still rather significant.

The CNY NDF market has provided hedgers, spreaders, and speculators with effective tools to manage CNY related risk with higher liquidity. The market will grow further with increasing participation of China in world trade, higher foreign direct investment in China, and further liberalization of the capital market in China, as analyzed by us in Chapter 18.

20

Chinese Yuan Swaps

Foreign exchange swaps are natural extensions of FX forwards, and similarly, nondeliverable swaps (NDSs) are natural extensions of NDFs. We focus on another type of major CNY derivatives — CNY swaps — in this chapter after having introduced and discussed CNY NDFs and their uses in the previous two chapters.

This chapter is organized as follows. Section 20.1 introduces cross-currency swaps, which are the basic modules of NDSs; Section 20.2 introduces various aspects of NDSs; Section 20.3 introduces and analyzes CNY NDSs using the historical swap rates of CNY NDSs; Section 20.4 shows how to use the CNY NDSs with specific examples; Section 20.5 introduces FX forward swaps; Section 20.6 introduces CNY FX forward swaps; and Section 20.7 concludes the chapter.

20.1 Cross-Currency Swaps

A cross-currency swap (CCS) is a contract that commits two counterparties to exchange streams of interest payments in different currencies for an agreed period of time with a prespecified frequency such as quarterly, semi-annual, or annual payments and to exchange principal amounts in the respective currencies at an agreed exchange rate at maturity. A CCS is also often simply called a currency swap.

A CCS thus has two principal amounts, one for each currency. Normally, the exchange rate used to determine the two principals is the then prevailing spot rate, although for delayed start transactions, the two counterparties can either agree to use the forward FX rate or agree to set the rate two business days prior to the start of the deal. It is essential that the two counterparties agree to exchange principal amounts at maturity for CCSs.

All foreign exchange forwards can be regarded as CCSs as they are agreements to exchange two streams of cash flows (in the case of one FX forward, the stream of cash flow is one) in different currencies. Many banks manage long-term FX forwards as part of the CCS business, given their similarities. Like all FX forwards, the CCS exposes the user to foreign exchange risk. One of the major market users for CCSs is debt issuers as they can sell bonds in the "cheapest" currency and swap their exposure to their desired currency.

Currency swaps give companies extra flexibility to exploit their comparative advantage in their respective borrowing markets. They allow companies to exploit the global capital markets more efficiently. In 1995, currency swap transactions accounted for US$776.6 billion out of the US$1.5 trillion daily FX market turnovers.

20.2 Nondeliverable Swaps

20.2.1 Nondeliverable Swaps

As its name implies, an NDS resembles a CCS, with the only exception that there is no physical transfer of the nondeliverable currency involved. NDSs are natural extensions of the NDFs as swaps are natural extensions of forwards for convertible currencies. Generally speaking, NDSs are rather liquid for those controlled currencies with corresponding liquid NDFs trading in the offshore market.

An NDS is conceptually similar to a CCS. The key element in an NDS is the exchange of principal and interest on a nondeliverable basis. As its name implies, there is always one nondeliverable currency (controlled or restricted currency) and one major currency such as the USD involved in any NDS. "Nondeliverable basis" means that a payment due in the controlled currency is converted into the major currency at the prevailing spot rate. On each interest payment date and at maturity, net settlement is made in the major currency.

At the start of the transaction, the exchange rate for converting the principal amount of the controlled currency into the major currency is determined using the spot rate. In its most common form, interest payments on the controlled currency are fixed, and the major currency has fixed or floating rate payments. Exchange of interest (on a nondeliverable basis) in the two currencies occurs on each interest payment date.

For example, on an interest payment date a customer is due to pay CNY 20 million and the other counterparty, the bank, is due to pay US$2.4 million. One business day before the payments are due, the USD/CNY spot rate prevailing in the market is fixed. If the fixing rate is 8.277, the customer is due to pay US$2,416,334, resulting in a net settlement of US$16,334 made by the customer to the bank.

20.2.2 Rationale of an NDS

NDSs provide an offshore mechanism to hedge the exposures, which were previously considered "unhedgeble" either due to an absence of local funding or limited access to foreign exchange markets. Exchange of principal takes place at maturity (on a nondeliverable basis), at an exchange rate agreed upon at the start of the transaction. No fee or premium is paid using an NDS. An NDS is an off-balance sheet instrument.

20.2.3 Why Use an NDS?

An NDS may be the only viable option where one leg of the swap has a currency that is controlled or restricted, such as the Korean won, the Philippine peso, the New Taiwan dollar, the CNY, etc. The NDS market is often more liquid in the longer tenors than the forward market.

An NDS can be customized to suit individual objectives, e.g. a reducing principal during the life of the contract.

20.2.4 How Is an NDS Settled?

A fixing methodology is agreed at the beginning of the contract. It specifies how a fixing rate is to be determined, to reflect spot value, which is normally one/two working days before settlement. Generally, the fixing rate is based on a reference page on Reuters or Telerate. This rate is used to convert the interest and principal payments in the controlled currency to an equivalent amount in the major currency. The difference between the two major streams is then settled.

20.3 CNY NDSs

20.3.1 General Introduction to the CNY NDS Market

As all NDS markets are natural extensions of their corresponding NDF markets, the CNY NDS market is also a natural extension of the corresponding CNY NDF market. Most CNY NDSs are written on USD/CNY. In a typical CNY NDS contract, one party receives a fixed rate in CNY and pays floating 6m USD LIBOR. Most CNY NDSs settle in USD every six months just as in CNY NDF contracts. Tenors for most CNY NDSs are up to three years, with certain liquidity, and there is only indication of quotes for tenors beyond three years. The normal ticket size is about US$3 million.

20.3.2 Historical CNY Swap Rates

As CNY NDS contracts are similar to CNY NDF contracts, with the only exception of longer tenors, CNY NDS contracts reflect similar market sentiments of CNY depreciation and revaluation. Figure 20.1 depicts the three-year CNY swap rates, their corresponding single currency (USD) swap rates, and their spreads from January 2000 to January 2003.

We can readily observe from Figure 20.1 that the CNY CCS rate dropped steadily from the second quarter of 2000 to January 2003. This trend is largely similar to the trend shown in Figure 18.1, implying a pressure for the CNY to depreciate from 2000 to 2002 and pressure for the CNY to revalue from 2002 on.

Figure 20.1 Three-year CNY NDS and Three-year USD Swap Rates from January 2000 to January 2003

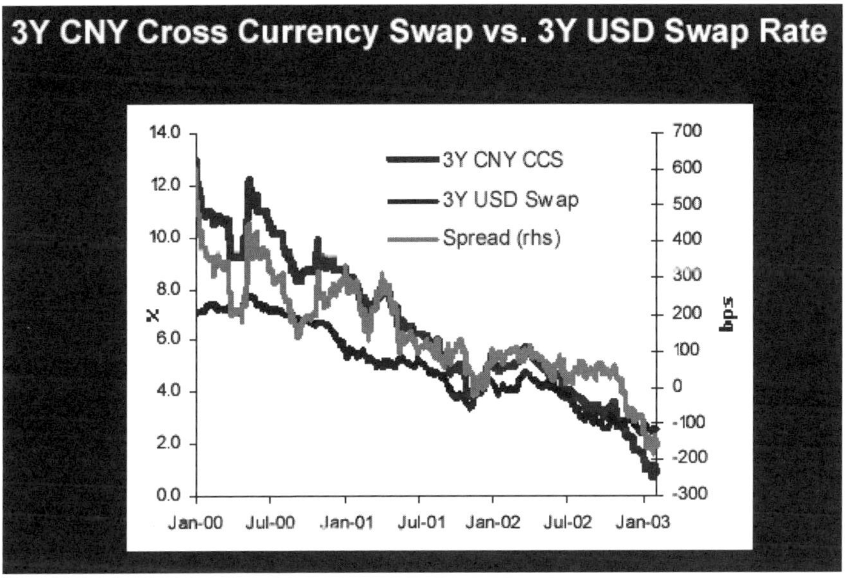

Data source: Feng (2003), p. 6.

20.3.3 Recent CNY Swap Rates

We cannot find recent changes in the CNY NDS market from Figure 20.1, which depicts the historical CNY NDS rates from 2000 to 2003. Figure 20.2 depicts the daily CNY NDS rates from April 1, 2002 to April 9, 2004.

20.4 Uses of CNY NDSs

20.4.1 Introduction to Uses of NDSs

NDSs can be used in a variety of ways for customers to achieve various targets involving nondeliverable currencies. They can be used to convert synthetically a loan in a major currency to a loan with fixed payments in a nondeliverable currency; to allow customers to manage different cash flows and timings; to fund in their most efficient currency such as the USD, euro, and Japanese yen (JY); to convert synthetically an asset with earnings in a controlled currency

Figure 20.2 Three-year CNY CCS Rates from April 1, 2000 to April 9, 2004

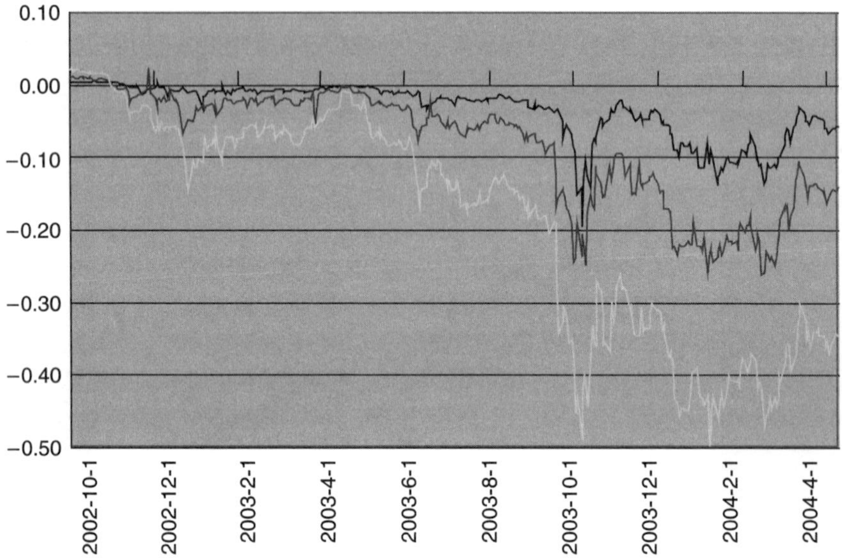

Data source: Bloomberg.

into a major currency; to allow an asset manager to invest in an overseas market where the asset has a known payout and hedge the currency risk from the investment; and so on.

We will concentrate on a few major uses here in this section and leave other issues for Chapter 24.

20.4.2 Hedging with CNY NDSs

A CNY NDS can be customized to suit individual objectives, thereby lowering the risk associated with running mismatches. Possible structures include the following: matching underlying asset/liability, the underlying exposure can be matched in terms of notional principal, rollover dates and fixed rate of the underlying asset/liability. We illustrate how to use CNY NDSs with one specific examples.

Example 20.1 Swapping a foreign currency asset

An American based investment fund buys a CNY denominated bond for RMB 2 billion. Since the liability of the fund is in USD, it wants the return from the bond in USD.

The investment, denominated in CNY, is exposed to a revaluation of the CNY as well as an increase in CNY interest rates. In order to hedge the currency risk, the fund enters into an NDS with ABC bank to exchange the fixed CNY interest stream for USD LIBOR payments.

Structure

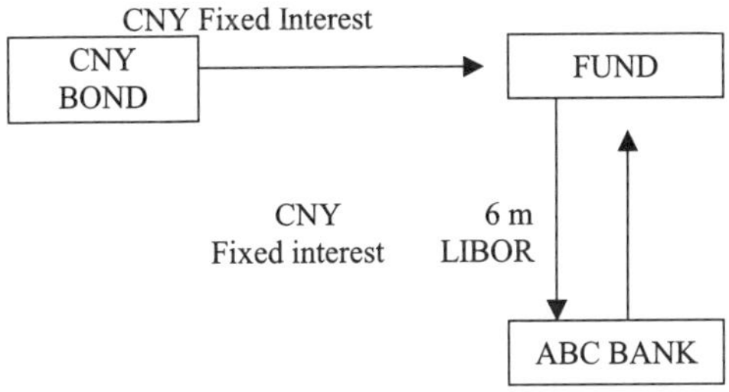

The investment in the CNY bond is 2 billion. A USD notional amount is set using the prevailing spot exchange rate at the start of the transaction. If the spot USD/CNY rate is 8.277, then the equivalent notional amount is US$241.63 million.

The fund will receive a fixed interest stream on the CNY investment that it is due to pay ABC bank. Since the swap is done on a nondeliverable basis, the interest amount is converted into USD at the prevailing USD/CNY spot rate (the fixing rate). ABC bank will pay USD LIBOR interest for six months on the notional amount of US$241.63 million.

At maturity of the CNY NDS, a notional exchange of principal takes place. The CNY 2 billion due to be paid to ABC bank by the fund is converted to USD at the fixing rate. This is netted with the USD principal of US$241.63 million, and the difference is settled.

CNY NDS information can be obtained from Reuters page PNDS and Reuters Chain <CNUSCS = PREA>.

20.5 Foreign Exchange Forward Swaps

20.5.1 Foreign Exchange Swaps

In a foreign exchange swap transaction, a trader can simultaneously sell currency for spot delivery and buy that currency for forward delivery. A foreign exchange swap involves two currencies. For example, a sale of HKD is a purchase of USD and a purchase of HKD is a sale of USD. A foreign exchange swap can be described as a simultaneous borrowing of one currency and lending of another currency.

Swaps are typically used to reduce exposure to the short-term risk of currency rate changes. For example, a US trader wants to invest in seven-day JY certificates of deposit (CDs). Then, the US trader buys JY spot, uses the funds to purchase the short-term JY CDs, and sells JY forward. The sale of JY forward protects the US trader from an appreciation of the USD against the JY, during the life of the JY CD. Traders also use foreign exchange swaps to change the maturity structure of their overall currency positions.

FX swaps are usually very short-term contracts. The majority of them have a maturity of less than one week.

20.5.2 FX Forward Swaps

In an FX forward swap transaction, a trader can simultaneously sell currency for forward delivery and buy that currency for another forward delivery with a longer tenor. Thus, a FX forward swap is essentially a FX swap with all forward transactions.

20.5.3 Nondeliverable FX Forward Swaps

A nondeliverable FX forward swap involves one controlled or restricted currency such as the Korean won, the CNY, or others and one major currency such as the USD or euro. As its name implies, a nondeliverable FX forward swap is on nondeliverable basis, or payments of the nondeliverable currency are converted into the major currency at prespecified forward rates.

20.6 CNY FX Forward Swaps

CNY FX forward swaps are another type of swap trading in the offshore market besides the CNY NDSs we introduced earlier in this chapter. We introduce CNY FX forward swaps here in this section.

There are three types of NDSs: 3-month, 6-month and 12-month swaps. Figure 20.3 depicts the 3-month, 6-month, and 12-month

Figure 20.3 CNY FX Forward Swap Rates from October 2002 to April 2004

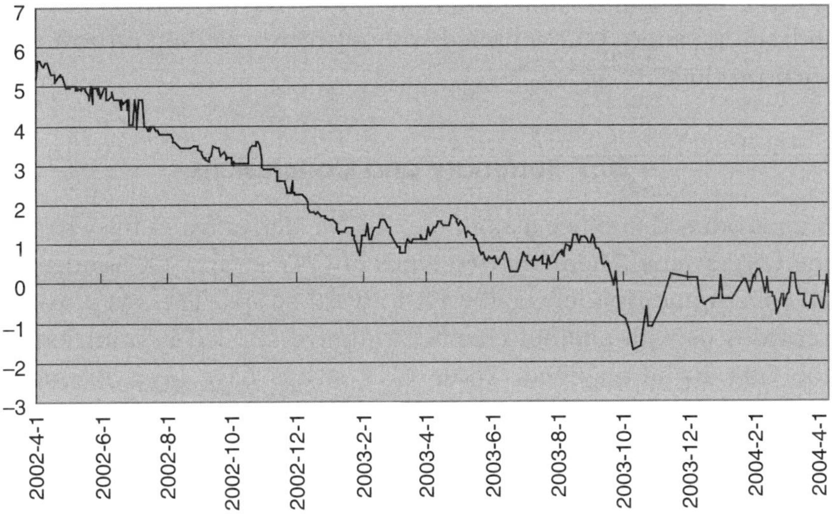

Data source: Please refer:

Lin, Wenhai, Huang Wenxian and Liu Guifeng, 2003, "CNY Forwards Helped Quanzhou Company to Hedge FX Risk," June 26, CHINA FINANCE INFORMATION NETWORK, available at http://www.imoney.com.cn, June 5, 2003.

Long, Haidi, 2003, "USD Forward Turnover Surpassed 160 Times in Chongqing BOC Branch," September 26, Chongqing Morning News, http:// www.imoney.com.cn.

CNY FX forward swap rates. We can observe that the fluctuation patterns of the CNY NDS rates resemble those of the CNY NDFs.

We can readily observe many issues from Figure 20.3. Firstly, the CNY FX forward swap rate fluctuated in a manner similar to that of the CNY NDF rates shown in Figure 18.3, reaching the lowest point of −1.725% early in October 2003 (October 9); yet there are noticeable differences between Figures 20.2 and 18.3 as the lowest CNY CCS rate was reached on October 9. Pressure for the CNY to revalue reached the highest point on October 7, 2003, with the CNY NDF reaching 5400 pips; the CNY NDF rate was largely stagnant from June 2002 to November 2002, as shown in Figure 18.3, yet the CNY FX forward swap rate dropped steadily from April 2002 to November 2002.

The noticeable differences between the CNY NDF rates in Figure 18.2 and the CNY FX forward swap rates in Figure 20.3 might provide us an indication that the CNY CCS market shows signs of CNY revaluation earlier than the CNY NDF market, yet such an indication cannot be confirmed without corresponding turnovers of such products.

20.7 Summary and Conclusions

We introduced another major type of CNY derivative in this chapter: the CNY swaps. There are two types of CNY swaps: FX nondeliverable CCSs and nondeliverable FX forward swaps. The swap market provides us with another channel to derive implied information for the CNY to be revalued. These CNY swaps have been integrated with many traditional financial transactions, and we will return to such topics in Chapter 24.

21

CNY Nondeliverable Options

We discussed in Chapter 11 that foreign currency options trading at OTC market is much more active that foreign currency options trading in exchanges around the world (Tables 11.2 and 11.3) and currency options are the second most popular currency derivative product after currency forwards in emerging markets. After introducing various aspects of CNY NDFs and NDSs and their applications in the previous three chapters, we concentrate on the second most popular offshore CNY derivative product — nondeliverable options (NDOs) — in this chapter.

This chapter is organized as follows. Section 21.1 sketches a brief history of the CNY NDOs market; Section 21.2 describes the major terms of a CNY NDO contract; Section 21.3 analyzes historical volatilities of the CNY/USD and implied volatilities from the CNY options; Section 21.4 discusses factors affecting implied volatilities of CNY NDOs; Section 21.5 discusses how to price CNY NDOs with specific examples; Section 21.6 introduces three popular option spreads using CNY options; Section 21.7 introduces the CNY and HKD put spreads; Section 21.8 introduces other popular options trading strategies; Section 21.9 introduces various aspects of options written on CNY NDFs or CNY NDFOs; and Section 21.10 concludes the chapter.

21.1 Brief Introduction to CNY NDO Market

Studies on CNY NDOs are even fewer than those on CNY NDFs. The CNY NDOs came into existence shortly after the CNY NDFs in Hong Kong, yet the volume was rather thin in the early stages. The CNY NDOs became more active late in 1997, when the Asian financial crisis spread to Northern Asia.

The participants of the CNY NDOs market are largely the same as those in the CNY NDF market. As options are more sophisticated than forwards in general, participants use various trading strategies of options to hedge their positions in the NDF market, or trade CNY options directly. An important group of CNY NDOs market participants is that of the financial institutions in Taiwan–China since late 2003, when the authorities gave the green signal for offshore banking units (OBUs) to trade CNY products in the province, as we discussed in Chapters 18 and 19.

The trading volumes of CNY NDOs have been lower than those of CNY NDFs. The average daily volume of CNY NDOs has been between one-quarter to one-half of the corresponding NDFs, although it reached two-thirds to three-quarters during volatile periods in the past 18 months.

21.2 CNY NDO Contract Specifications

We introduce the major items of a standard CNY NDO contract in this section.

21.2.1 Notional Amounts

The normal notional amount of a CNY NDO contract is between US$10 million and 30 million, with an average ticket size of around US$20 million, or about RMB 150 million.

21.2.2 Settlement Method

As their name implies, most CNY NDOs are cash settled with the USD.

21.2.3 Exercise Style

Most CNY options are European style options, or they can be exercised only at maturity.

21.2.4 Settlement Rates

Just as with the CNY NDF settlement rate determination introduced in Chapter 18, the settlement rate for CNY NDOs is RMB per USD, for settlement in two business days, as reported by the State Administration of Exchange Control (SAEC) of the People's Republic of China, appearing on the Reuters Screen SAEC Page opposite the symbol "CNY =" as of 4:00 p.m., Beijing time.

21.2.5 Tenors

Although prices are available for tenors up to three years, the liquidity is not as high for CNY options with tenors longer than one year. The CNY options are liquid for tenors up to one year, with 3 months, 6 months, and 12 months as the most popular tenors.

21.3 Historical and Implied Volatilities of CNY Options

It is well known that the secret of options trading is nothing but volatility estimation. We will discuss the major methods of volatility estimation to analyze CNY volatilities in this section.

21.3.1 Historical Estimation

The well-known practice of volatility estimation is calculation using historical data. This method is useful because it provides the general magnitudes of volatilities of the underlying instrument and indicates how the volatility fluctuates with market information. However, this method has serious limitations because the inexplicit assumption using historical estimation is that historical patterns will repeat, and we all know this is not often true. The other limitation of this method is that we cannot estimate accurately enough as

Figure 21.1 Annualized Historical Volatilities of the CNY/USD from February 2001 to March 2004 (Unit: Percent)

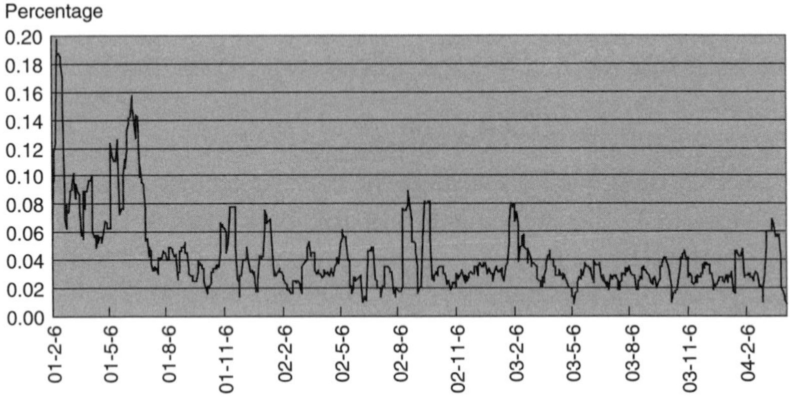

Data source: Bloomberg.

estimation results often vary with various time spans to go back history. Specifically, estimation results are most often different if we go back for one week, two weeks, one month, three months, and so on.

Figure 21.1 depicts the annualized historical volatilities (standard deviation of natural log-returns of the daily CNY/USD rates multiplied by the square root of 260) of the CNY/USD exchange rates from January 2001 to March 2004 using moving standard deviations of nine days. We can observe that the annualized volatility of the CNY/USD has been extremely low compared with volatilities of most FX rates in the world. The average annualized volatilities were 0.036% and 0.032% in 2002 and 2003, respectively. These extremely low volatilities of the CNY/USD are consistent with the PBOC's CNY/USD rate policy of floating with a maximum daily limit of 0.30%.

21.3.2 Implied Volatilities

In order to overcome the limitations of historical volatilities as discussed earlier in this section, practitioners have been using implied volatilities. Implied volatilities are those volatilities that match the observed market prices of options using certain option pricing models (the most often used pricing formula is the celebrated Black–Scholes formula or its extensions (please see Zhang (1998a) for related extensions and explanations).

Implied volatilities have quite a few advantages over historical volatilities. Of these advantages, the most obvious one is that the former contain information about the underlying instrument from the present to the time of maturity of the corresponding options. In order words, implied volatilities are "forward looking" because they contain information on the market expectation of the underlying instrument in the future, and yet historical volatilities are "backward looking".

Figure 21.2 illustrates the implied volatilities of 3-month, 6-month and 12-month CNY options from June 2002 to April 2004. It can be readily observed that the implied volatilities were largely below 2% for all options before November 2002, implying less market fluctuations; they rose moderately from November 2002 and stayed largely above 2% from November 2002 to June 2003, indicating that volatilities went up because of the pressure on the CNY revaluation; they increased almost monotonically from around 4% in July 2003 to above 10% in early October 2003, signifying tremendous pressure for the CNY to revalue within the period; and they remained around 10% until February 2004. These fluctuation patterns are very similar to the fluctuation patterns of the CNY NDFs as discussed in Chapter 18, and we will compare them more closely in the following sections of this chapter.

Figure 21.2 Implied Volatilities of the CNY Options from June 2002 to April 2004 (Unit: Percentage)

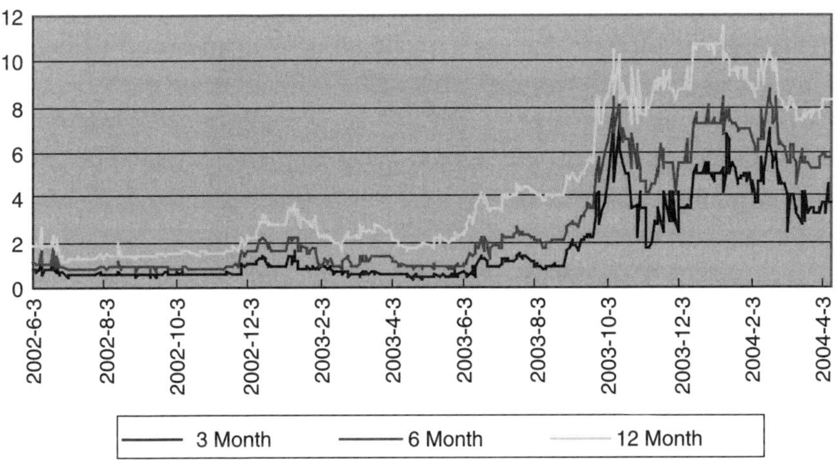

Data source: Bloomberg.

21.3.3 Volatility Smile

Implied volatilities for options with the same time to maturity and different strike prices are often different. The relationship between strike prices and their corresponding implied volatilities for the same time to maturity is called "volatility smile" in options practice. Implied volatilities have been larger for "out of the money" (OTM) options to buy RMB than for equal OTM options to sell the currency, thereby suggesting that the balance of expectations is skewed toward an appreciation of the Chinese currency against the USD. Market data indicate that the difference between implied volatilities of OTM options to buy RMB and the equal OTM options to sell the currency becomes larger when pressure for the currency to be revalued becomes stronger.

21.3.4 Term Structure of Implied Volatilities

It can be observed from Figure 21.2 that the implied volatilities of options are different with different tenors, the longer the tenor, the higher the implied volatility. The relationship between tenors of options with the same underlying instrument and corresponding implied volatilities is called the term structure of volatility. Volatilities of options with tenors other than 3 months, 6 months, or 12 months can be extrapolated using existing data so that they can be more reasonably priced.

The term structure of implied volatilities can also reflect the degree of pressure on the CNY revaluation. We can observe that the differences between implied volatilities with given tenors become narrower when the market sentiment is convergent and pressure on the CNY becomes stronger, which happened in early October 2003 and in February 2004.

21.3.5 Using Implied Volatilities and Historical Volatilities Together

In practice, traders use implied volatilities and compare them with historical volatilities so as to determine whether some options are overpriced (implied volatilities are greater than historical ones) or undervalued (implied volatilities are lower than historical ones), and then they can write or sell options if they are overpriced and buy options if they are undervalued.

21.4 Factors Affecting Implied Volatilities of CNY Options

We discussed factors affecting CNY NDFs in great details in Chapter 18 and found similar fluctuation patterns between CNY implied volatilities and CNY NDF rates in the previous section of this chapter. It is not coincident that the implied volatilities of CNY NDOs and CNY NDFs share similar fluctuation patterns because they are both affected and moved by the same information flow and events. In this section, we will compare the fluctuation patterns of the CNY NDOs and the CNY NDFs and find factors affecting the CNY NDOs' prices.

21.4.1 Implied Volatilities and NDFs

Figure 21.3 depicts the implied volatilities of 12-month CNY NDOs and corresponding 12-month CNY NDFs from June 2002 to March

Figure 21.3 Implied Volatilities of NDOs and NDFs from June 2002 to April 2004 (Unit: Percent)

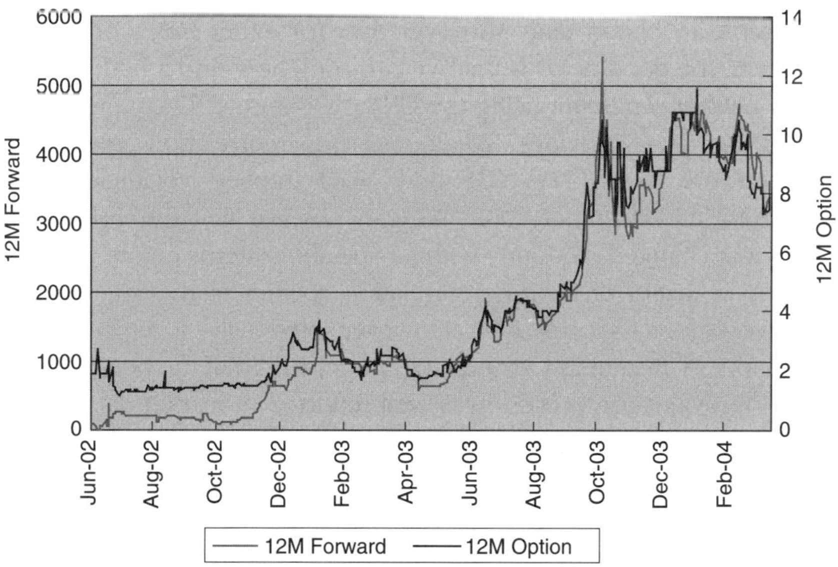

Data source: Bloomberg.

2004. We can readily observe that the fluctuation patterns of 12-month CNY NDO implied volatilities and NDFs are very similar, the correlation coefficient between these two sets of variables being as high as 98.3%.

21.4.2 Common Factors Affecting Both Markets

The high correlation coefficient between the CNY NDF and NDO markets confirms our intuition that both markets are affected by similar market information and events, as discussed systematically in Chapter 18. Higher CNY NDF rates indicate a greater possibility for the CNY to revaluate and thus push up options prices and in turn lead to higher implied volatilities.

21.4.3 Correlation Coefficient as a Measure of General Market Sentiment

Both the CNY NDF rates and CNY NDO implied volatilities shown in Figure 21.3 are extremely useful information, yet neither of them can reflect the market sentiment fully without corresponding turnovers. As we described earlier in this book, it is difficult to obtain even quarterly turnover data of the CNY NDF and NDO, and thus it is impossible to obtain daily turnover data for either NDFs or NDOs. However, the good news is that we can somehow find a better measure of market sentiment using the CNY NDF and NDO data together.

Figure 21.4 provides 20-day moving correlation coefficient between the daily CNY NDF and NDO implied volatilities from June 2002 to December 2002. We can observe that the correlation coefficient changed randomly without specific patterns before October 2002. As a matter of fact, the correlation coefficient was significantly negative before October 2002. However, obviously, it jumped from −36% to 93% from mid-October 2002, signifying that the beginning of the CNY revaluation process was well reflected in market data.

We extend our coverage in Figure 21.4 to March 2004 and present the results in Figure 21.5. We can observe readily that although the correlation coefficient has been volatile, it has been significantly greater than 50%. One obvious thing from Figure 21.5 is that the correlation coefficient dropped from above 90% to close to zero from

Figure 21.4 Moving Correlation Coefficient between NDOs and NDFs from June 2002 and December 2002

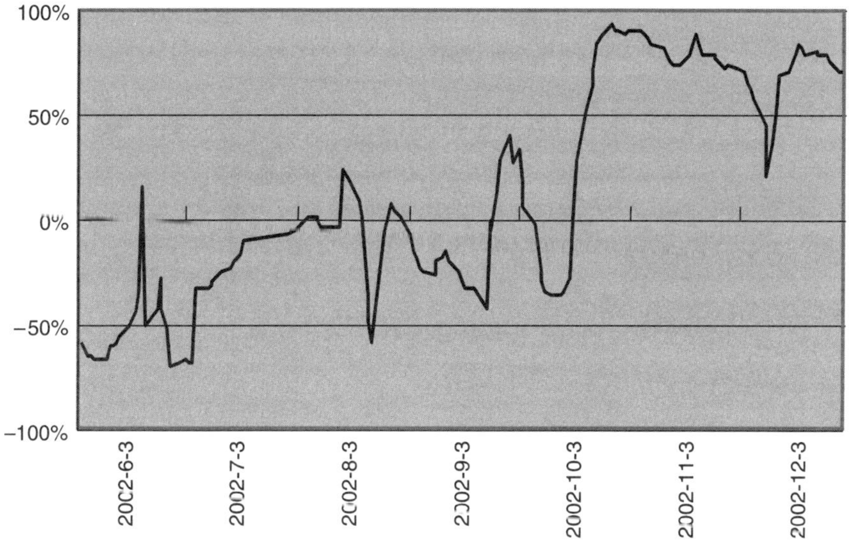

Data source: Bloomberg.

Figure 21.5 Moving Correlation Coefficient between NDOs and NDFs from June 2002 and March 2004

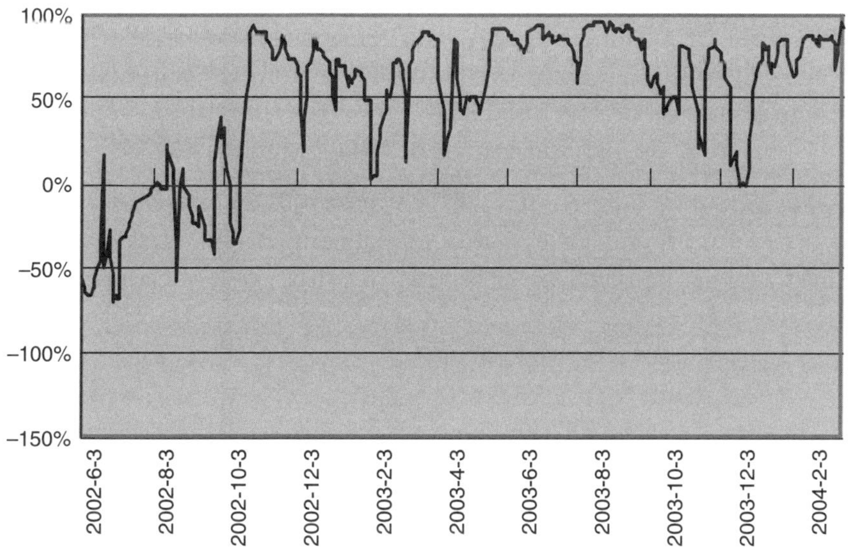

Data source: Bloomberg.

October 2002 to February 2003, implying that the market sentiment for the CNY revaluation was not as strong between October 2002 and February 2003; the correlation coefficient stayed largely above 90% between May and September 2003, implying that both the NDF and NDO markets reflect the CNY revaluation; yet the correlation coefficient began to drop from early October to around zero by the end of 2003, implying that the general sentiment for the CNY NDF was weakened; and it began to rise steadily from early 2004, signifying a new wave of speculation on the CNY.

21.5 Pricing CNY Options

In contrast to forwards or futures, prices are the most important thing for options trading as they have to be paid upfront. We will illustrate with examples in this section how the CNY options are priced. Before we start to show how to price CNY options, there is one important concept that needs to be cleared. A CNY call option written on CNY/USD is actually equivalent to the USD put option because the lower the CNY/USD exchange rate, the stronger the CNY and at the same time the weaker the USD. Thus, we use CNY call and USD put options alternatively in the rest of this book.

Example 21.1 Find the CNY call/USD put option price with spot CNY/USD = strike = 8.277 (at-the-money option (ATM)), CNY interest rate = 2.0%, US interest rate = 1.5%, time to maturity one year, volatility 10%, and notional amount USD 20 million.

Answer: Substituting $S = K = 8.277$, $r_1 = 2\% = 0.020$, $r_2 = 1.5\% = 0.015$, $\sigma = 10\% = 0.10$, and $t = 1.0$ into the extended Black–Scholes formula given on page 58 of Zhang (1998) or in any text book of options, yields

$$d_2 = [\ln(S/K) + (r_1 - r_2\sigma^2/2) \times t]/[\sigma \times \sqrt{t}] = 0.75,$$

$$d_1 = d_2 + \sigma \times \sqrt{t} = 0.75 + 0.10 = 0.85,$$

$$P = -S \times e^{-r_1 \times t} \times N(-d_1) + K \times e^{-r_2 \times t} \times N(-d_2)$$

$$= \text{RMB } 0.345 = \text{USD } 0.0417 = 4.17\%.$$

The option premium is thus $0.0417 \times 20 =$ US\$0.834 million.

Example 21.2 Find the corresponding CNY put/USD call option price with all parameters the same as in Example 21.1.

Answer: Substituting S = K = 8.277, $r_1 = 2\% = 0.020$, $r_2 = 1.5\% = 0.015$, $\sigma = 10\% = 0.10$, and t = 1.0 into the extended Black–Scholes formula yields

$$C = S \times e^{-r_1 \times t} \times N(d_1) - K \times e^{-r_2 \times t} \times N(d_2)$$
$$= \text{RMB } 0.304 = \text{USD } 0.0368 = 3.68\%.$$

The option premium is thus 0.0368 × 20 = US$0.736 million.

Example 21.3 Find the CNY call/USD put option price with strike K = 8.00 and all other parameters the same as in Example 21.1.

Answer: Substituting S = 8.277, K = 8.00, $r_1 = 2\% = 0.020$, $r_2 = 1.5\% = 0.015$, $\sigma = 10\% = 0.10$, and t = 1.0 into the extended Black–Scholes formula yields

$$P = -S \times e^{-r_1 \times t} \times N(-d_1) + K \times e^{-r_2 \times t} \times N(-d_2)$$
$$= \text{RMB } 0.216 = \text{US\$}0.0261 = 2.61\%.$$

The option premium is thus 0.0261 × 20 = US$0.522 million.

Example 21.4 Find the corresponding CNY put/USD call option price with all parameters the same as in Example 21.3.

Answer: Substituting S = 8.277, K = 8.00, $r_1 = 2\% = 0.020$, $r_2 = 1.5\% = 0.015$, $\sigma = 10\% = 0.10$, and t = 1.0 into the extended Black–Scholes formula yields

$$C = S \times e^{-r_1 \times t} \times N(d_1) - K \times e^{-r_2 \times t} \times N(d_2)$$
$$= \text{RMB } 0.448 = \text{USD } 0.0542 = 5.42\%.$$

The option premium is thus 0.0542 × 20 = US$1.084 million.

There are many other examples relating to CNY NDOs, and we leave them for following sections, when we discuss popular trading strategies using CNY NDOs.

21.6 CNY Option Spreads

There are many popular trading strategies using options. It is not our purpose to describe those popular strategies here in this section, our purpose here is to introduce the most popular trading strategies such as bullish spreads, call spreads, and put spreads.

21.6.1 CNY Bullish Spreads

A bullish spread involves buying a CNY call and selling a CNY put. Generally, call options become costly when the market becomes bullish with an underlying instrument, and the corresponding put options become cheaper, and investors and speculators often sell put options and use the premiums received from these transactions to finance the cost of the call options. Similarly, put options become costly when the market becomes bearish, and investors sell call options and use the premiums received from these transactions to finance the cost of the puts. As the pressure for the CNY to revalue gets stronger, the CNY call options becomes more costly and their corresponding put options become less costly, and thus the bullish spread has become a popular trading strategy for CNY NDOs. We illustrate such strategies with specific examples in this section.

Example 21.5 Find the price of the bullish spread to buy the CNY call option given in Example 21.1 and sell a CNY put option with volatility 5% and other parameters the same as in Example 21.2.

Answer: Following a procedure similar to that in Example 21.2, the put option premium can be readily obtained as 1.72% of the notional amount, or $1.72\% \times 20 = \text{US\$}0.344$ million. Thus, the bullish spread price is

$$\begin{aligned}(4.17\% - 1.72\%) \times 20 &= 2.45\% \times 20 \\ &= \text{US\$}0.490 \text{ million} \\ &= \text{US\$}490{,}000,\end{aligned}$$

which is only about 58.8% of the call option premium in Example 21.1.

Example 21.6 Find the price of the bullish spread to buy the CNY call option given in Example 21.1 and sell a CNY put option with strike K = 8.1, volatility 6%, and other parameters the same as in Example 21.2.

Answer: Following a procedure similar to that in Example 21.2, the put option premium can be readily obtained as 3.22% of the notional amount, or 3.50% × 20 = US$0.700 million. Thus, the spreader price is

$$\begin{aligned}(4.17\% - 3.22\%) \times 20 &= 0.95\% \times 20 \\ &= \text{US\$0.180 million} \\ &= \text{US\$180,000,}\end{aligned}$$

which is less than 23% of the call option premium in Example 21.1.

21.6.2 CNY Call Spreads

Options traders often use call spreads based on the specific bullish perspectives of the underlying instruments. We illustrate how such strategies are used with CNY NDOs in this section.

A call spread stands for buying one call option and at the same time writing (selling) another call option with a different strike price. With the generally perceived revaluation of the CNY in the offshore market, CNY option traders can simply buy an ATM call option or a slightly out-of-the money (OTM) call option and at the same time write another call option with a lower strike price. A long CNY call spread essentially captures the trader's expectation that the CNY will be revaluated within a certain range. It is more cost effective than a single call option because it actually sells off part of the profit potentiality. We will illustrate CNY call spreads with specific examples.

Example 21.7 Find the price of the CNY call spread to buy the CNY call option given in Example 21.1 and sell a CNY call option with strike price K = 8.0 and other parameters are the same as in Example 21.1.

Answer: Following the same procedure as in Example 21.1 with strike price K = 8.0, we can obtain the CNY call option with strike price K = 8.0 as C(K = 8.0) = USD 1.18%. Thus, the call spread price is

$$(4.17\% - 1.18\%) \times 20 = 2.99\% \times 20 = \text{US\$0.598 million,}$$

which is 71.7% of the call option premium in Example 21.1.

Figure 21.6 Payoff of the CNY Call Spread of Example 21.7

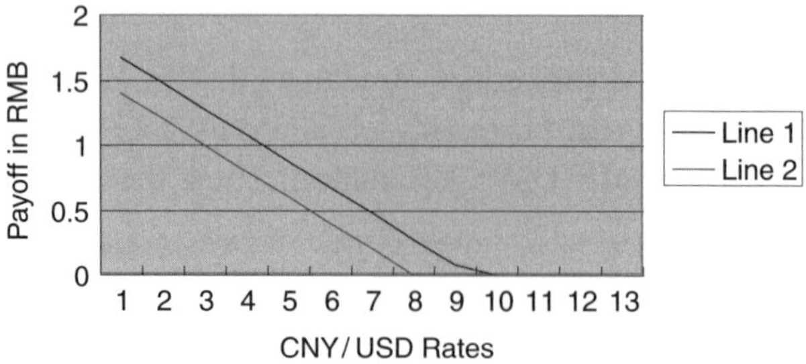

Figure 21.6 depicts the payoffs of the call spread of Example 21.7.

We can observe from Figure 21.6 that the payoff lines are actually USD put option payoff lines similar to those in Figure 11.2 because we are using the exchange rate of CNY/USD rather than USD/CNY. We can also observe that the payoff of the CNY call or USD put is given in the blue line and the other call in the red line. Thus the difference between the two lines represents the payoff of the call spread.

Example 21.8 Find the price of the CNY call spread to buy a CNY call option with strike K = 8.10, volatility 12%, and other parameters the same as in Example 21.1 and sell a CNY call option with strike price K = 7.9, volatility 8%, and other parameters the same as in Example 21.1.

Answer: Following the same procedure as in Example 21.1 with $K = 8.10$, $\sigma = 12\%$, we can obtain the CNY call option with volatility 12% as $C(\sigma = 12\% \ \& \ K = 8.10) = \text{USD } 3.89\%$; similarly we obtain $C(\sigma = 8\% \ \& \ K = 7.90) = 1.47\%$. Thus, the call spread price is

$$(3.89\% - 1.47\%) \times 20 = 2.42\% \times 20 = \text{US\$}0.484 \text{ million.}$$

21.6.3 CNY Put Spreads

Options traders also use put spreads based on the specific bearish perspectives of the underlying instruments. We illustrate in this section how such strategies are used with CNY NDOs.

A put spread stands for buying one put option and at the same time selling another put option with a different strike price. We simply illustrate the CNY put spread with one specific example.

Example 21.9 Find the price of the CNY put spread to buy the CNY put option given in Example 21.2 and sell a CNY put option with strike price K = 8.40 and other parameters the same as in Example 21.2.

Answer: Following the same procedure as in Example 21.2 with strike price K = 8.4, we can obtain the CNY put option with strike price K = 8.4 as C(K = 8.4) = USD 3.05%. Thus, the put spread price is

$$(3.68\% - 3.05\%) \times 20 = 0.63\% \times 20 = \text{US\$}0.126 \text{ million.}$$

Figure 21.7 depicts the payoffs of the put spread of Example 21.9.

We can observe from Figure 21.7 that the payoff lines are actually USD call option payoff lines similar to those of Figure 11.1 because we are using the exchange rate of CNY/USD rather than USD/CNY. We can also observe that the payoff of the CNY put or USD call is given in the blue line and the other put in the red line. Thus the difference between the two lines represents the payoff of the put spread.

Figure 21.7 Payoff of the CNY put Spread of Example 21.9

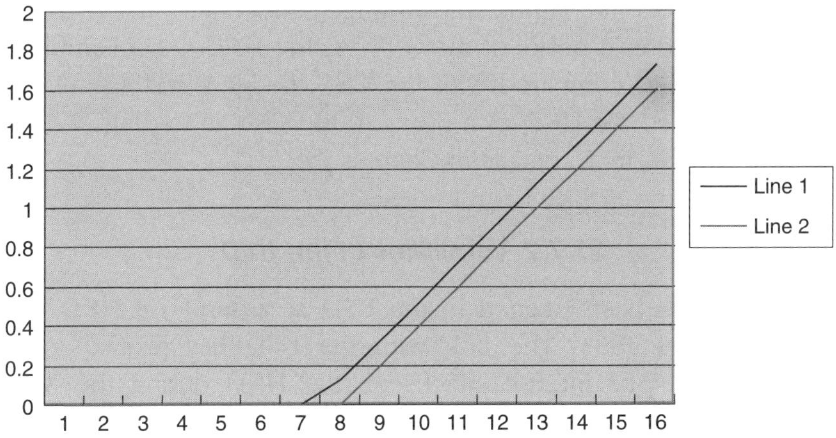

21.7 CNY and HKD Put Spread

We have introduced the CNY call spreads and put spreads in the previous section. We will introduce another popular spread widely used in the offshore market to speculate on the CNY revaluation. This spread involves selling a CNY put option and at the same time buying a put option on the HKD. This strategy is based on the expectation that the CNY will be revaluated and at the same time the HKD will be somewhat devaluated compared with the CNY. This strategy is essentially a put spread, yet it is different from the put spreads we introduced in Section 21.6 because the two put options are written on two different underlying foreign exchange rates. Before we illustrate such put spreads, it is necessary for us to introduce briefly the HKD/USD exchange rate.

21.7.1 HKD as a Proxy of the CNY

The Hong Kong economy has been more and more integrated with the Mainland Chinese economy since Hong Kong was handed over back to China as a Special Administration Region (SAR) of China on July 1, 1997. Because of the special roles that Hong Kong SAR played in China's reform process, particularly in foreign trade, foreign direct investment, equity capital raising and so on as we analyzed in Part I, and the closer economic relationship that became effective early in 2004 between the SAR and Mainland China under the Closer Economic Partnership Arrangement (CEPA), the HKD has been regarded as a proxy of the CNY. As the HKD is convertible to other currencies compared with the CNY, hedgers and speculators alike have used the HKD as a proxy to the CNY in trading. We will discuss HKD in more details in Chapter 24.

21.7.2 Volatilities of the HKD

The HKD has been pegged to the USD at around 7.8 HKD/USD since October 1983. The link with the USD has proved to be successful despite intense attacks on the HKD during the Asian

Figure 21.8 Volatilities of HKD from January 2003 to February 2004

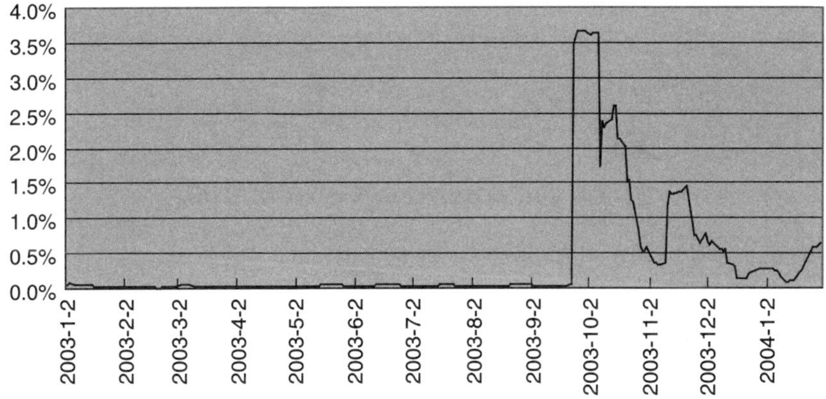

Data source: Calculated using data from the website of the HKMA.

financial crisis, when the exchange rate volatility surpassed 5% in October 1997. Figure 21.8 shows the annualized volatilities of the HKD/USD spot rates from January 2003 to January 2004. We can observe that the HKD/USD volatility has been close to zero before October 2003 and jumps to above 3.5% in October 2003, when pressure for the CNY revaluation reached the peak, and it has fallen dramatically since November 2003, although it still remains significantly higher than in the pre-October 2003 period. As a matter of fact, the HKD/USD volatility had been rather low, except during the Asian financial crisis.

21.7.3 HKD Put Options

Let us illustrate the HKD put/USD call option with an example before we illustrate the spread between the CNY put and the HKD spread.

Example 21.10 Find the price of the HKD put/USD call option given in spot HKD/USD = 7.80, with strike price K = 7.80, volatility 8%, HK dollar interest rate 1.8%, and other parameters the same as in Example 21.2.

Answer: Following the same procedure as in Example 21.2, with strike price $K = 7.8$, $\sigma = 0.08$, we can obtain the CNY put option price P = USD 3.29%. Thus, the HKD put option price is

$$3.29\% \times 20 = \text{US\$}0.658 \text{ million.}$$

21.7.4 Put Spread of CNY and HKD

Let us illustrate the spread of buying one CNY put and selling a HKD put with an example.

Example 21.11 Find the price of the spread between the CNY put in Example 21.2 and the HKD put option given in Example 21.10.

Answer: Using the results given in Examples 21.2 and 21.10, we can readily find the price of the spread to buy a HKD put and to sell a CNY put as $(3.68\% - 3.29\%) \times 20 = 0.39\% \times 20 =$ US\$0.78 million.

21.8 Other Popular Trading Strategies

We have introduced popular options trading strategies in previous sections of this chapter. There are other popular strategies trading with the CNY options. We will briefly introduce them in this section before concluding the chapter.

21.8.1 Time Spread

As the name implies, a time spread involves a long position of one option and a short position of a similar option that differs only in time to maturity with the other option. Traders use time spreads because they can take the best advantage of the price differentials of options resulting from time values. We illustrate a time spread with one specific example.

Example 21.12 Find the price of the time spread of a long CNY call/USD put option given in Example 21.1 and shortening a similar CNY call/USD put option with three months to expire and other parameters the same as in Example 21.1.

Answer: Following the same procedure as in Example 21.1 with time to maturity $t = 3/12 = 0.25$, we can obtain the CNY call option price $C(t = 0.25) = \text{USD } 2.05\%$. Thus, the price of the CNY call time spread is

$$(4.17\% - 2.05\%) \times 20 = 2.12\% \times 20 = \text{US\$}0.424 \text{ million},$$

which is only 50.8% of the CNY call option premium in Example 21.1.

21.8.2 Other Popular Options Trading Strategies

There are other popular options trading strategies widely used by options traders, such as straddles, strangles, and butterflies (please see pp. 110–116 in Zhang (1995) for specific introductions and applications of straddles and strangles). Popular as they are, all these strategies are two-sided strategies. In other words, traders can profit with these strategies when the underlying instruments move significantly away from the current spots. Yet, the ongoing CNY revaluation situation is largely one-sided, and these strategies are not so relevant.

21.9 Options on CNY NDFs or CNY NDFOs

21.9.1 Futures Options and Forward Options

Futures options or options on futures normally trade more actively than options on the corresponding underlying instruments because futures prices are generally more volatile than their corresponding underlying instruments as futures prices reflect not only information on the spot but also the uncertainty of the underlying instruments from the current time to the time of maturity of the underlying instruments.

The OTC equivalent of futures options are options written on forwards, sometimes called fractions in practice (See Zhang (1998), pp. 90–94 for examples). Although fractions are not as popular as options on the spot FX rates in general, they are popular in offshore markets because the CNY NDF market is much more active than the spot CNY, and the volatilities of the CNY NDF contracts have been much higher than both CNY/USD historical rates and implied volatilities of CNY options since 2003.

Options on CNY NDFs can be simply expressed as CNY NDFOs. It is difficult to obtain systematic data either on CNY NDFO trading volume or prices. According to Feng (2003), the daily trading volume of CNY NDFOs was about US$200 million in 2003. Although prices of CNY NDFOs are available to three years of tenor, CNY NDFOs are liquid up to one year, and the average deal size of CNY NDFOs is about USD 20 million.

21.9.2 Historical Volatilities of CNY NDFs

We will first discuss historical volatilities of the CNY NDF market using historical daily NDF rates and compare them with implied volatilities from CNY NDFOs in this section.

Although historical volatilities have certain limitations compared with implied volatilities as discussed in the previous chapter, historical volatilities give us general magnitudes of how the underlying instruments fluctuate. Using historical daily CNY NDF data from Bloomberg, we can readily find annualized nine-day moving volatilities of the CNY NDF during the Asian financial crisis and show them in Figure 21.9. We can observe that volatility of the CNY NDF was extremely low before October 1997; however, it jumped to above 30% late in October 1997 and it surpassed its peak of 34% in December 1997.

Similarly, we can obtain annualized nine-day moving volatilities of the CNY NDF from 1999 to March 2004, and we show them in

Figure 21.9 Annualized Historical Volatilities of CNY NDFs during the Asian Financial Crisis from September 1997 to February 1998

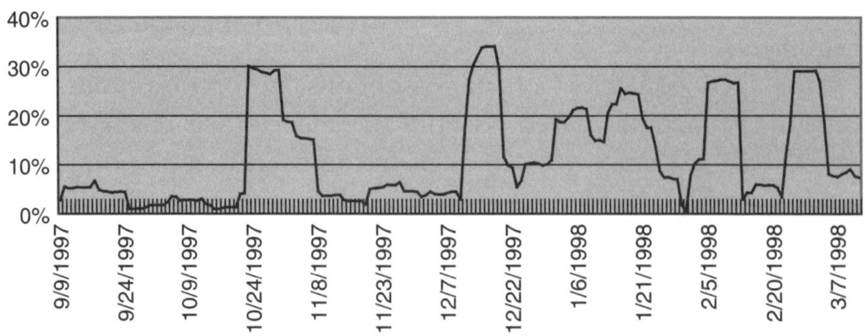

Data source: Bloomberg.

Figure 21.10 Annualized Historical Volatilities of CNY NDFs from February 1999 to March 2004

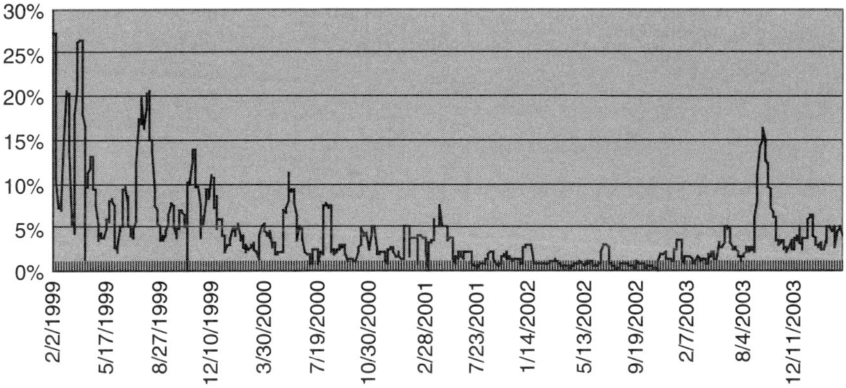

Data source: Bloomberg.

Figure 21.10. We can observe from Figure 21.10 that the volatility of the CNY NDF dropped tremendously from 27% in 1999 to close to zero early in 2002; it began to rise late in 2002 and reached its peak of 16.2% in October 2003; and it dropped significantly from its October peak and stayed at around only 5% since December 2003.

If we compare the CNY NDF volatilities in Figure 21.9 and 21.10, we can find that although the implied volatility of the CNY NDF was as high as 16.2% in October 2003, it was less than half its maximum value of 34% in October 1997 deep in the Asian financial crisis, implying that pressure on the CNY revaluation might not be as strong as the pressure for it to depreciate during the Asian financial crisis.

We can observe from Figure 21.10 that the annualized volatility of the CNY NDF fell steadily from 1999 to close to zero in 2002; yet it rose steadily from early in 2003 to above 15% in October 2003 and has stayed around 5% since December 2003, much higher than the CNY/USD spot volatilities shown in Figure 21.1.

21.9.3 Pricing CNY NDFOs

As options on futures or forwards are different from options directly on the underlying instruments, futures options or forward options are priced differently from their cash options. We will illustrate how to price CNY NDF options with specific examples in this section.

A CNY NDF call option price C is given by the following well-known formula to price futures options (see Zhang (1998a) for derivation):

$$C = e^{-r \times t} \times [\text{NDF} \times N(d_1) - K \times N(d_2)],$$
$$d_2 = [\ln(\text{NDF}/K) - t \times \sigma^2/2]/[\sigma \times \sqrt{t}], \quad \text{and}$$
$$d_1 = d_2 + \sigma \times \sqrt{t},$$

where NDF and K stand for the CNY NDF rate and strike rates, respectively, r and t for annual interest rate of CNY and time to maturity in fraction of year, and σ for the volatility of the CNY NDF option.

Similarly, A CNY NDF put option price P is given by the following formula,

$$P = e^{-r \times t} \times [K(-d_2) + \text{NDF} \times N(-d_1)],$$

where all parameters are the same as in the above call option formula.

Example 21.14 Find the CNY NDF call/USD put option price with spot CNY NDF/USD = strike = 7.90 (ATM), CNY interest rate = 2%, time to maturity one year, volatility 15%, and notional amount US$20 million.

Answer: Substituting NDF = K = 7.90, r = 2% = 0.020, σ = 15% = 0.15, and t = 1.0 into the call option pricing formula yields

$$d_2 = [\ln(S/K) - t \times \sigma^2/2]/[\sigma \times \sqrt{t}] = 0.1188,$$
$$d_1 = d_2 \times \sigma \times \sqrt{t} = 0.1188 + 0.15 = 0.2688,$$
$$C = e^{-r \times t} \times [\text{NDF} \times N(d_1) - K \times N(d_2)],$$
$$= \text{RMB } 0.463 = \text{USD } 0.0586 = 5.86\%.$$

The option premium is thus 0.0586 × 20 = US$1.172 million.

Example 21.15 Find the CNY NDF put/USD call option price with strike price K = 8.0 and all parameters the same as in Example 21.14.

Answer: Substituting NDF = 7.90, K = 8.0, r = 2% = 0.020, σ = 15% = 0.15, and t = 1.0 into the call option pricing formula yields

$$P = e^{-r\times t}\,[K\times N(-d_2) - NDF\times N(-d_1)]$$
$$= RMB\ 0.413 = USD\ 0.0522 = 5.22\%.$$

The option premium is thus $0.0522 \times 20 =$ US$1.044 million.

21.9.4 Put-Call Parity

We will introduce the well-known put–call parity and show why a bullish spread is similar to a long position of the CNY NDF in this section.

"Put–call parity" stands for the relationship between the price of a call option and the price of its corresponding put option. Specifically, we can obtain the following parity using the two pricing formulas given above:

$$C - P = e^{-r\times t}\times (NDF - K),$$

which indicates that the payoff of a NDF can be duplicated by a call and put spread with the same strike price.

Example 21.16 Find the price of the corresponding CNY NDF put/USD call option with all parameters the same as in Example 21.14 and check whether the put–call parity relationship holds.

Answer: Substituting $NDF = K = 7.90$, $r = 2\% = 0.020$, $\sigma = 15\% = 0.15$, and $t = 1.0$ into the put option pricing formula yields

$$P = e^{-r\times t}\,[K\times N(-d_2) - NDF\times N(-d_1)]$$
$$= RMB\ 0.463 = USD\ 0.0586 = 5.86\% = C \text{ in Example 21.14.}$$

The difference between the prices of the call and put options is zero and the difference the strike and spot NDF is also zero, and thus the parity holds.

21.9.5 CNY Bullish Spreads

21.9.5.1 Synthetic CNY NDFs

If we rearrange the put–call parity in Section 21.10.4, we can readily find

$$NDF = K + (C - P)\times e^{-r\times t},$$

which obviously implies that buying a call option and selling a corresponding put option essentially constructs an NDF or synthetic forward. Specifically, the put–call parity relationship largely duplicates the return of a forward contract. Thus, bullish spreads using CNY NDOs are similar to long CNY NDFs.

21.9.5.2 Risk Reversals Widening with Spot NDFs

As spot NDF rates go up, call options become more expensive, with higher implied volatilities than the implied volatilities from the corresponding puts, and thus the risk reversals widen.

21.10 Summary

We have introduced various aspects of CNY NDOs and various popular trading strategies using the CNY options in this chapter. CNY options are the second most popular CNY derivatives trading in offshore markets, and they play important roles in the offshore CNY derivatives markets. They are used to hedge positions of CNY NDFs, and various combinations of CNY NDOs make CNY NDOs an integral part of offshore CNY derivatives.

22

Structured Deposits Related to CNY

We introduced and analyzed CNY NDFs and NDOs and related trading strategies in the previous chapters. In this chapter we concentrate on another type of CNY related derivative: structured deposits including foreign currency deposits linked to CNY NDFs and CNY deposits with embedded options. Whereas most of the foreign currency deposits linked to CNY NDFs exist almost exclusively outside China, CNY deposits with embedded options exist not only in the offshore market but also in China.

Currency-linked deposits were popular in Southeast Asia before the Asian financial crisis as interests were significantly higher in countries such as Thailand. Currency NDF-linked deposits became popular for CNY NDF-linked deposits as pressure for CNY revaluation became obvious later in 2002. There are international financial institutions that offer CNY NDF-linked deposits to special investors in the US and other financial centers.

As shown in Zhang (1998), various types of exotic options are useful not only because they can be traded directly but also because they can be embedded in other products. As we will show in this chapter, many types of CNY deposits have embedded exotic options. We simply concentrate on describing these deposits and their embedded options without dwelling much on the technical issues of such options.

This chapter is organized as follows. Section 22.1 introduces NDF-linked deposits; Section 22.2 illustrates how NDF-linked deposits work using specific examples; Section 22.3 introduces currency deposits with embedded European options; Section 23.4 illustrates currency range deposits with both European and American styles; Section 23.5 introduces currency deposits with an alternative payment currency; Section 23.6 introduces currency deposits with knock-out features; Section 23.7 introduces currency deposits with principles not guaranteed; Section 23.8 deals with basket currency deposits and concludes the chapter.

22.1 Introduction to NDF-Linked Deposits

Deposits are normally made in one currency, and returns are paid as interest by commercial banks in the same currency. With market innovation, deposits can also be made in one currency with yields linked to exchange rates implied in NDFs of controlled currencies. The yield of a currency-linked deposit reflects the implied local interest rates derived from the NDF market, which may be significantly higher than the major currency interest rates. NDF currency-linked deposits are particularly suitable for asset managers who need to hold a physical asset but at the same time wish to gain access and exposure to higher-yielding markets.

There are two types of NDF currency-linked deposits in the marketplace: those only linked to principal and those linked to both principal and interest. As their names imply, the former exposes only the principal and the latter offers a higher coupon but exposes both principal and interest to exchange rate fluctuations. Neither type of deposit is principal protected. Those deposits not only have many of the same advantages as NDFs but also often allow depositors to assume a lower credit risk or to earn more interest than depositing onshore.

NDF currency-linked deposits cannot normally be withdrawn or terminated prior to the fixed maturity date. Should a currency-linked depositor wish to make an early withdrawal, the bank will endeavor to accommodate it, although the terms under which early withdrawal can be allowed will depend on market considerations.

22.2 How Does an NDF Currency-Linked Deposit Work?

Let us see in this section how an NDF currency-linked deposit works through a specific example. Assume an investor wishes to receive a CNY interest rate on US$2 million for six months and assumes the CNY currency exposure on both the principal and interest element of his deposit. He or she uses a CNY-linked deposit.

We need to make a few assumptions as follows:

(1) Assume the yuan coupon is 7.50% annually
(2) The current spot rate for yuan/USD is 8.277
(3) Interest yield at the end of the six months
= US$2 million × 7.50% × 180/360 = US$75,000.00.
(4) Principal plus interest at maturity if unlinked would be US$2,075,000.00.
(5) Linked redemption amount = US$2,075,000 × 8.277/fixing spot rate of the CNY NDF.

The four possible outcomes after six months are given in the following table.

	Situation 1	**Situation 2**	**Situation 3**	**Situation 4**
CNY NDF premium/ discount (pips)	**−3730**	**0**	**2770**	**3770**
USD/peso at fixing	8.650	8.277	8.000	7.900
Redemption amount ($)	1,985,523.12	2,075,000.00	2,146,846.88	2,174,022.15
Return ($)	−14,476.88	75,000	146,846.88	174,022.15
Annualized return (%)	−1.45	7.50	14.68	17.40

In Situation 1, the possible depreciation of the yuan has reduced the earnings on the linked deposit to a subzero return of −1.45%; in Situation 3, the appreciation of the yuan allows the investor to gain a greater return of 14.68% on the deposit than the original enhanced coupon; and in Situation 4, the appreciation of the yuan allows the investor to gain an even greater return of 17.4%.

With pressure on CNY revaluation in the offshore market, it has become increasingly possible that China will announce a change in policy regarding the RMB/USD peg. With such expectation, financial institutions are providing CNY NDF-linked deposits to special depositors or investors.

Through Everbank World Markets, a division of Florida-based First Alliance Bank is providing CNY NDF-linked deposits for sophisticated depositors with just $10,000 to open an account to bet on a yuan revaluation. The sophisticated depositors are assumed to understand the risks and rewards offered by world currencies with a convenient way to position themselves ahead of a possible change in Chinese government policy (see the specific introduction from the EverBank website given in the Further Reading section). Deposits in major currencies with the returns linked to the exchange rate of NDF currencies are also offered by other international banks.

22.3 Currency Deposits with Embedded European Options

Bullish currency deposits are the simplest type of currency deposit with embedded European digital call options (see Zhang (1998) for a comprehensive introduction of various types of digital options). They are currently used by depositors in Hong Kong, Mainland China, and other places. There are also bearish currency deposits with embedded European digital put options. We introduce such deposits in this section.

22.3.1 Deposit Currencies and Measured FX Rates

The deposit currency is usually a hard currency, and the measured FX rate is related to the deposit currency. In the case of CNY, the deposit currency can be the HKD, USD, JY or any other major currency, and the measured FX rate is CNY/USD, CNY/HKD, CNY/JY, CNY/euro, or others. The currency deposits can also be structured with CNY as the deposit currency and other FX rates as measured instruments. We will illustrate such deposits with specific examples later in this section.

22.3.2 Parameters

Besides the specified deposit currency, there are usually a few important parameters involved as follows.

(i) *Minimum amount of deposit of the specified currency.* The minimum amount can be HK$100,000, US$10,000, RMB 100,000, etc.
(ii) *Time to maturity.* The time to maturity can be six months, one year, or two years.
(iii) *Linked FX rate.* The linked FX rate can be CNY/USD, CNY/JY, CNY/euro, CNY NDF/USD, etc.
(iv) *Maximum and minimum interest rates specified.* A maximum annual interest rate R_{max}, say 4.0%, and a minimum annual interest rate R_{min}, say 1.0%, are specified in the deposit contract.
(v) *Strike FX rate.* A particular level X of the linked FX is also given as the strike price of the embedded option. If the linked FX rate surpasses X at maturity, the maximum interest rate, R_{max}, is paid in the deposit currency; and the minimum interest rate, R_{min}, is paid in the deposit currency otherwise.

22.3.3 Exercising Probabilities

The most important thing for the depositor in a currency deposit is the probability that the maximum interest rate is paid. As it is a little technical to derive the formula, we simply use results from Zhang (1998). The probability that the maximum interest rate is paid in a bullish currency deposit is actually the probability that the European digital option is exercised,

$$N\{[\ln(S_F/X) + (r_1 - r_2 - S_F)]/[\sigma \times \sqrt{t}]\},$$

where S_F stands for the spot rate of the linked FX rate; r_1 and r_2 the annual interest rates of the two currencies involved in the linked FX rate; σ the volatility of the linked FX rate; and t the time to maturity of the deposit. ln(.) is the natural logarithm function, and N(.) is the cumulative function value of the standard normal distribution. We will illustrate with specific examples how to use this formula.

Example 22.1 Given the initial CNY/USD is 8.277 and the CNY/USD volatility is 3.0%, a depositor in Hong Kong believes that the

CNY would revalue in one year and deposits HK$500,000 in a bank for one year. If the CNY/USD falls below RMB 8.00/US$, the maximum annual interest rate, 4.0% will be paid and the minimum annual interest rate, 0.80% is paid otherwise. What is the expected interest rate the depositor will receive (annual interest rate of CNY and USD are 1.5% and 2.0%)?

Answer: Substituting $r_1 = 1.5\% = 0.015$, $r_2 = 2.0\% = 0.020$, $\sigma = 3.0\% = 0.03$, and $t = 1.0$ into the probability function given above yields

$$N\{[\ln(8/8.277) + (0.015 - 0.020 - 0.03 \times 0.03/2) \times 1]/[0.03 \times \sqrt{1}]\}$$
$$= 0.094 = 9.4\%, \text{ and}$$

the expected interest yield is the weighted average of the maximum interest rate with the probability obtained above and the minimum interest rate with probability $= 1 -$ the probability obtained above:

$$4.0\% \times 9.4\% + 0.8\% \times (1 - 9.4\%) = 1.10\%.$$

Example 22.2 Given the initial CNY/USD is 8.277, one-year CNY/NDF is 2000 pips at discount, and the one-year CNY NDF volatility is 20.0%, a depositor in Hong Kong believes that the CNY would be revalued and deposits HK$500,000 in a bank for one year. If the CNY NDF rises to 4000 pips, the maximum annual interest rate of 4.0% will be paid and the minimum annual interest rate of 0.8% will be paid otherwise. What is the expected interest rate the depositor will receive?

Answer: Substituting $\sigma = 20\% = 0.20$, $t = 1.0$, $X = 8.277 - 4000/10{,}000 = 7.877$, and $S_F = 8.277 - 2000/10{,}000 = 8.077$ into the probability function given in Section 23.1.3 yields

$$N\{[\ln(7.877/8.077) + (-0.20 \times 0.20/2) \times 1.0]/[0.20 \times \sqrt{1}]\}$$
$$= 0.4108 = 41.08\%,$$

and the expected interest yield is the weighted average of the maximum interest rate with the probability obtained above and the minimum interest rate with probability $= 1 -$ the probability obtained above:

$$4.0\% \times 41.08\% + 0.8\% \times (1 - 41.08\%) = 2.11\%.$$

Currency deposits can be similarly structured with CNY as the deposit currency and the measured foreign exchange as USD/euro or JY/USD, and the average yields can be calculated as in Examples 22.1 and 22.2.

22.4 Currency Range Deposits

Currency range deposits are currency deposits with the interest rate determined depending on whether the measured FX rate will be within a given range or not. Structurally speaking, a currency range deposit has a pair of European digital call options with strike prices as the uppper and lower bounds of the given range.

22.4.1 Range and Interest Payment Specifications

For a particular currency range deposit, all parameters are the same as those of the currency deposits described in Section 22.3, with the only exception of the range specification. A particular lower level, X_{low}, and an upper level, $X_{up}(X_{low} < X_{up})$, of the linked FX are given. If the linked FX rate is within the range between X_{low} and X_{up} at maturity of the deposit, the maximum interest rate, R_{max}, will be paid in the deposit currency; and the minimum interest rate, R_{min}, will be paid in the deposit currency otherwise.

22.4.2 Exercising Probabilities

The probability that the maximum interest rate will be paid in a currency range deposit is actually the probability spread of two European digital options,

$$N\{[\ln(S_F/X_{low}) - \sigma^2/2]\}/[\sigma \times \sqrt{t}]\} - N\{[\ln(S_F/X_{up}) - \sigma^2/2]/[\sigma \times \sqrt{t}]\},$$

where all the parameters and functions are the same as in 22.3.

Let us consider a specific example before we finish this section.

Example 22.3 Given the one-year CNY NDF is 2000 pips at discount, and the one-year CNY NDF volatility is 20.0%, a depositor in Hong Kong believes that the CNY would be revalued and deposits HK$1 million in a bank for one year. If the CNY NDF ends up between 4000 and 5000 pips, the maximum annual interest rate,

10.0% will be paid, and the minimum annual interest rate, 0.8% is paid otherwise. What is the expected interest rate the depositor will receive?

Answer: Substituting $\sigma = 20.0\% = 0.20$, $t = 1.0$, $X_{low} = 8.277 - 4000/10{,}000 = 7.877$, and $X_{up} = 8.277 - 5000/10{,}000 = 7.777$ into the probability function given above yields

$$\begin{aligned} &N\{[\ln(7.877/8.077) - 0.20 \times 0.20/2] \times 1\}/[0.20 \times \sqrt{1}]\} \\ &\quad - N\{[\ln(7.777/8.077) - 0.20 \times 0.20/2] \times 1\}/[0.20 \times \sqrt{1}]\} \\ &\quad = 0.4108 - 38.62\% = 0.025 = 2.5\%, \end{aligned}$$

and the expected interest yield is the weighted average of the maximum interest rate with the probability obtained above and the minimum interest rate with probability = 1 − the probability obtained above:

$$10.0\% \times 2.5\% + 0.8\% \times (1 - 2.5\%) = 0.0103 = 1.03\%.$$

22.4.3 American Currency Range Deposits

The currency range deposits we described above are European currency range deposits because interests are paid according to whether the linked foreign exchange rate is within the range at maturity of the deposits. The interest payment is determined on whether the linked FX rate is within the range any time within the life of the deposit for an American currency range deposit. As with a European currency range deposit with a spread of two European digital call options, an American currency range deposit actually has a spread of two American digital call options with strike prices specified as X_{low} and X_{up}, respectively. It is beyond the scope of this book to describe or give numerical examples; interested readers may refer to pp. 405–409 of Zhang (1998) for American digital options to price American currency range deposits.

22.5 Dual Currency Deposits

The currency deposits we have introduced so far are deposits with interest payment in the same currency as the deposit currency.

Actually, interest can be paid in currencies other than the deposit currency. For example, the payment currency can be specified as the euro, JY, British pound, or other currency if the deposit currency is USD and the linked FX rate is specified as the CNY NDF. The analysis is similar to those we have done earlier in this chapter, and so we do not intend to go into deeper descriptions with examples in this section.

22.6 Currency Deposits with Embedded Exotic Options

We briefly introduced exotic FX options in Chapter 11 of Part II. Exotic options are useful not only because they can be traded directly in the OTC marketplace but also because they are used as building units to construct other OTC products. Currency deposits with embedded exotic options are good examples of how to build exotic features into currency deposits. We focus on introducing popular currency deposits with exotic features in this section.

22.6.1 Currency Deposits with "Knock-Out" Features

The currency deposits with "out" features are actually currency deposits with embedded knock-out options (or barrier options, see pp. 203–251, of Zhang (1998) for a comprehensive description of various types of knock-out options). The interest payment of a currency deposit with the out feature is set according to whether the linked FX rate touches some prespecified "barrier" or "trigger." If the trigger is touched any time within the life of the deposit, the knock-out feature becomes invalid, and the interest rate will be calculated with a prespecified interest rate, which can be regarded as a rebate for the knock-out option. If the trigger is never touched within the life of the deposit, interest payment can be arranged as with ordinary deposits with alternative currency payment or others. We intend not to go into the details of such products as they are beyond the scope of this book.

As there are "up-out" (triggers set higher than corresponding spot exchange rates) options and "down-out" (triggers set lower than corresponding spot exchange rates) ones, there are currency deposits with up-out features and down-out features. We intend not to give numerical examples of such products as they are rather technical and complex. Interested readers may refer to Zhang (1998) for specific examples.

22.6.2 Currency Deposits with "Knock-In" Features

The currency deposits we introduced in 22.6.1 are deposits with embedded knock-out options. Similarly, "knock-in" options can also be embedded in currency deposits. Again as there are up-in and down-in options, and there are currency deposits with up-in and down-in features. It is rather technical to discuss such products in detail, and interested readers may refer to Zhang (1998) for a comprehensive description of knock-in options, and they can be easily applied to currency deposits.

22.6.3 Currency Deposits with "Double Triggers"

The currency deposits we introduced earlier in this section are deposits with one "out" or "in" trigger. As a matter of fact, there are currency deposits with two triggers, one up and one down, the spot-linked FX rate. Interest is paid if neither the up nor the down trigger is touched during the life of the deposit; it is paid differently if the up trigger is touched and the down trigger is not touched, and it can also be paid differently if the lower trigger is touched yet the up trigger is not touched. There are different scenarios with double triggers, and again these are beyond the scope of this book. Interested readers may refer to pp. 309–318 of Zhang (1998) for a comprehensive description of double barrier options.

22.7 CNY-Linked Deposits with Principal not Guaranteed

All the currency deposits we have introduced so far are currency deposits with principal guaranteed, and so the only risk depositors face is the interest risk. There are other popular currency deposits with principal not guaranteed. We concentrate on such currency deposits in this section.

22.7.1 Currency Deposits with Principal not Guaranteed

The most important difference between a currency deposit with principal not guaranteed (CDPNG) and one with principal guaranteed is that the principal is adjusted according to the level of reference rate of the linked FX compared with the spot exchange rate in a CDPNG. Specifically, the principle is normally set as follows,

$$\text{principal} \times [n + 1 - n \times (\text{reference rate/spot rate})],$$

where n can be any integer greater than or equal to 1, and "principal" is the original principal set in the deposit.

It is obvious that the principle can go down as low as zero for a given n and possible reference rate of the linked FX. Specifically, the principal can become zero when the spot rate becomes as low as reference rate $\times$ n/(n + 1). The integer n is generally set between 2 and 10. We will illustrate the principal changes with specific examples later in this section.

22.7.2 Embedded Options

As with the principle guaranteed currency deposits that we discussed earlier in this section, most CDPNGs also have options embedded. Such options are normally European-style call options or put options, although American options and exotic options can also be embedded in. We will illustrate such deposits with specific examples.

Example 22.4 (Three-month CNY-linked CDPNG) Given a principal amount of US$1.0 million, tenor three months, fixing time as 5 p.m. Beijing Time on the expiry date, reference rate 8.277, interest rate for deposit = 10.00%, the depositor will receive the principal amount on the maturity date if the USD/CNY spot rate fixes above the reference rate, and the depositor will receive the amount given by the formula of 22.7.1, what are the principle amounts if the spot rate is 2% less and more than the reference rate with n = 10?

Answer: Substituting spot = 8.277 $\times$ (1 − 2%) = 8.1146, n = 10, reference rate = 8.277 into the principal formula in 22.7.1 yields the principal

$$\text{US\$}1.0 \times (10 + 1 - 10 \times 8.277/8.1146) = \text{US\$}0.7959 \text{ million.}$$

If the CNY is devalued 2% in two months, spot $= 8.277 \times (1 + 2\%) = 8.4425 >$ reference rate, the principal amount is the same as US\$1.0 million, and the interest payment is US\$1.0 $\times$ 10%/4 = US\$25,000.

We can observe that the depositor loses 20.41% of the principal amount if the CNY is revalued 2%.

Example 22.5 Given all other parameters are the same, what are the principal amounts if n = 2 and 5 instead of 10 in Example 22.4?

Answer: Substituting spot $= 8.277 \times (1 - 2\%) = 8.1146$, $n = 2$, reference rate = 8.277 into the principal formula in 22.7.1 yields the principal

$$\text{US\$}1.0 \times (2 + 1 - 2 \times 8.277/8.1146) = \text{US\$}0.9592 \text{ million; and}$$

substituting spot $= 8.277 \times (1 - 2\%) = 8.1146$, $n = 5$, reference rate = 8.277 into the principal formula in Section 22.7.1 yields the principal

$$\text{US\$}1.0 \times (5 + 1 - 5 \times 8.277/8.1146) = \text{US\$}0.8980 \text{ million.}$$

It is obvious that the depositor loses 4.08% and 10.20% of the principal amount if the CNY is revalued 2% and n is chosen as 2 and 5, respectively. Thus, n can be understood as an amplifier for the principal to change: the larger the value of n, the greater the leverage impacts. The probability that the principle is reduced in a CDPNG or the embedded call option is not exercised can be calculated as in Examples 22.1 and 22.2; we do not wish to repeat such calculations here.

22.7.3 Currency Deposits with Partial Principal Protection

Our examples above show that the principal amount of currency deposits can go down as low as zero if spot at maturity becomes as low as reference rate $\times$ n/(n + 1) as shown in Section 22.7.1, thus causing tremendous risk for depositors. Currency deposits with partial principal protection are structured in order to limit such risks. In general, the reference rate, the spot rate, and the amplifier must satisfy the following condition in order to guarantee $0 < k < 1$ of the principal amount:

$$\text{reference rate/spot} \leq (n + 1 - k)/n.$$

Example 22.6 Given $n = 5$, $k = 80\%$, and reference rate = 8.277, what are the principal amounts if the spot rate is 8.1115 and 7.9459, respectively?

Answer: Substituting $n = 5$, reference rate = 8.277, and spot rate = 8.1115 into the principal formula in Section 23.5.1 yields

$$\text{principal} \times (5 + 1 - 5 \times 8.277/8.1115) = 0.898 \times \text{principal},$$

and substituting $n = 5$, reference rate = 8.277, and spot rate = 7.9459 into the principal formula in Section 23.5.1 yields

$$\text{principal} \times (5 + 1 - 5 \times 8.277/7.9495) = 0.794 \times \text{principal}.$$

The principal amount falls below 80% of the principal in the case where spot rate = 7.9495 because reference rate/spot = 1.0417 > (5 + 1 − 0.80)/5 = 1.04, which violates the necessary inequality condition given before this example, and the principle amount falls, yet stays above 80% of the principal in the case where spot rate = 8.1115 because the same necessary inequality condition is satisfied.

22.8 Other Currency Deposits and Conclusions

There are many other currency deposits with various features embedded in them. All the deposits we have described are deposits with one linked FX. There are currency deposits with more than one linked FX rate. These currency deposits can also be called currency deposits with a basket of linked FX rates. There are other currency deposits with other exotic features, and they can be analyzed easily using results from Zhang (1998), yet they are beyond the scope of this book.

Standard currency deposits are straightforward products, yet they can incorporate a lot of sophisticated features to make payments more flexible and attractive. The currency deposits we have introduced so far in this chapter are popular structured currency deposits currently used in offshore markets, and some of them are actually offered by foreign banks in China.

23

CNY Structured Notes

Structured notes played important roles during not only the Asian financial crisis but also the Mexican crisis as studied in Part III of this book. Because of the flexibility of such products, they are also playing important roles in the offshore CNY derivatives market. We concentrate on various types of CNY structured notes in this chapter.

This chapter is organized as follows. Section 23.1 introduces structured notes in general; Section 23.2 introduces CNY bullish notes without limitation of upward potential; Section 23.3 illustrates CNY bullish notes with both capped and floored principals; Section 24.4 introduces CNY bullish obligations; Section 24.5 briefly discusses structured notes with embedded options; and Section 24.6 summarizes and concludes the chapter.

23.1 General Introduction

Structured notes are also known as hybrid instruments in practice. As the name implies, a structured note is actually a combination of an underlying instrument, such as a bond or a note, with one or more derivative products such as options or futures-like contracts embedded. Structured notes were part of the new wave of innovations in capital flows to East Asia in the 1990s as stated by us in Part III of this book, and they are important products involving CNY revaluation.

Structured notes offer issuers and investors either better yields than similarly rated securities or better combinations or bundles of risk characteristics. In some cases, structured notes are designed to circumvent accounting rules or government regulations so as to allow lower capital charges, greater FX exposure, or greater overall risk to capital.

Structured notes were popular during the Asian financial crisis. Financial institutions from advanced capital markets were interested in issuing these instruments in order to create long-dated futures and options positions in developing country currencies and securities. FX forward and swap markets are short-term markets; the vast majority of transactions in these markets have a maturity of one year or less.

The 1998 BIS report on FX showed that only 1.4% of FX swaps and 3.9% of forwards had maturities in excess of one year and that the majority were for seven days or less. Faced with the absence of other alternatives, these hybrid instruments were designed to create such a multiyear FX derivative. The issuer held a long-term short position in a developing country currency for the cost of the 100 or 200 basis points per year on the principal.

23.2 CNY Bullish Notes

Bullish notes can easily capture investors' expectation of CNY revaluation, and they have been invested to profit from the potential revaluation. We introduce CNY bullish notes in this section with specific examples.

A standard bullish note may have capped upside exposure and, at the same time, limited downside exposure with a certain degree of principal protection if held until maturity. We will introduce the major items of a bullish note contract first and then explain such notes with specific examples.

23.2.1 Face Amount

The face amount can normally be set as multiples of US$1.0 million, say US$2.0 million, 5.0 million, or 10.0 million.

23.2.2 Issue Price

Issue prices are often set at 100% of the face amount of the notes.

23.2.3 Redemption Value

A floor is normally set in a bullish note to limit the principal amount. Besides the floor, there is normally a multiplier set to stand for the leverage of the bullishness of the note. The multiplier is often between 1.5 and 2.5, depending on the degree of bullishness of the investors. We will illustrate this with specific examples later in this section.

23.2.4 Current Spot Rate and Strike Rate

The Current spot rate of CNY/USD is normally set at the official exchange rate of 8.2770, and the ATM option strike rate is set at 8.2770 accordingly.

23.2.5 End Rate

The end rate is normally set as the CNY per USD exchange rate one or two weeks prior to the note's final maturity. The official fixing rate is posted daily at 5 p.m. Beijing time by the PBOC on Reuters Page KFTC12 like most other CNY related products. If this source is not available, brokers normally determine the rate in a fair and commercially reasonable manner.

With the above introduction, we can illustrate how bullish CNY notes work with specific examples.

Example 23.1 What are the returns of the CNY bullish note given the spot CNY/USD rate and strike rate 8.2770, floor of the principal 95% and cap of the principal 120%, face amount US$5.0 million, cap rate 7.500, and redemption multiplier 2.0?

Table 23.1 Potential Returns of a CNY Bullish Note

Potential End Rate	Appreciation/ Depreciation (%)	Redemption at Maturity (%)	Net Return (%)
7.20	14.96	124.92	24.92
7.30	13.38	121.77	21.77
7.40	11.85	118.70	18.70
7.50	10.36	115.72	15.72
7.60	8.91	112.82	12.82
7.70	7.49	109.99	9.99
7.80	6.12	107.23	7.23
7.90	4.77	104.54	4.54
8.00	3.46	101.93	1.93
8.10	2.19	99.37	−0.63
8.20	0.94	96.88	−3.12
8.277	0.00	95.00	−5.00
8.40	−1.46	95.00	−5.00
8.60	−3.76	95.00	−5.00
8.80	−5.94	95.00	−5.00
9.00	−8.03	95.00	−5.00

Answer: Using the principal redemption formula,

$$\text{floor} \times \max[1.0,\ 2.0 \times (\text{end rate} - \text{strike rate})/\text{strike rate}]$$
$$= 95\% \times \max\ [1.0,\ 2.0 \times (\text{end rate} - 8.2770)/82.770],\ \text{and}$$

various possible end rates of the CNY/USD, we can find the potential returns of the CNY bullish note for various end rates and list them in Table 23.1.

We can observe from Table 23.1 that loss is protected to 5% as the principal is floored to 95%; yet the net returns are unlimited because there is no cap in the principal. What is noticeable is that the net return becomes larger than the degree of CNY revaluation if the CNY is revaluated below 7.8 because the multiplier is 2, yet it is lower or even negative if the CNY revaluates less than 5%.

23.3 CNY Bullish Notes with Caps and Floors

We introduced CNY bullish notes without caps in Section 23.2. We will illustrate in this section CNY bullish notes with both floored downside and capped upside exposure with a certain degree of principal protection if held until maturity. We will introduce such bullish notes with specific examples.

Example 23.2 What are the returns of the CNY bullish note in Example 24.1 if a cap of 120% is set for the principal?

Answer: Using the principal redemption formula,

$$\min\{\text{cap}, \text{floor} \times \max[1.0,\ 2.0 \times (\text{end rate} - \text{strike rate})/\text{strike rate}]\}$$
$$= \min\{120\%,\ 95\% \times \max[1.0,\ 2.0 \times (\text{end rate} - 8.2770)/82.770]\},$$

and various possible end rates of the CNY/USD, we can find the potential returns of the CNY bullish note for various end rates, and we list them in Table 23.2.

We can observe quite a few things from Table 23.2. First of all, the net return of the note is about the same as the underlying currency when the end rate is 7.90, and the net return surpasses the appreciation rate when the end rate falls between 7.50 and 7.90 because of the leverage multiplier; Secondly, the net return is negative even if the end rate slightly appreciates (between 8.10 and

Table 23.2 Potential Returns of a CNY Bullish Note

Potential End Rate	Appreciation/ Depreciation (%)	Redemption at Maturity (%)	Net Return (%)
7.20	14.96	120.00	20.00
7.30	13.38	120.00	20.00
7.40	11.85	120.00	20.00
7.50	10.36	120.00	20.00
7.60	8.91	112.82	12.82
7.70	7.49	109.99	9.99
7.80	6.12	107.23	7.23
7.90	4.77	104.54	4.54
8.00	3.46	101.93	1.93
8.10	2.19	99.37	−0.63
8.20	0.94	96.88	−3.12
8.277	0.00	95.00	−5.00
8.30	−0.28	95.00	−5.00
8.40	−1.46	95.00	−5.00
8.50	−2.62	95.00	−5.00
8.60	−3.76	95.00	−5.00

8.277) compared with the spot rate, 8.277; and the loss is locked at 5% because the principal is protected to 95%; lastly, the net return is capped at 20% for an end rate below the strike rate, 7.50 because the principal is capped at 120%.

Example 23.3 What are the returns of the CNY bullish note, given a cap of the principal of 118%, a principal floor of 90%, a redemption multiplier of 1.8, and the other parameters remaining the same as in Example 23.2?

Answer: Following a procedure similar to that used in Example 23.2, we can find the potential returns of the CNY bullish note for various end rates, and we list them in Table 23.3.

Comparing Tables 23.2 and 23.3, we can easily find that the note given in Example 23.2 should be more attractive to investors than the note given in Example 23.3 because the potential net returns are higher, yet the potential loss is also greater if the CNY is not revaluated

Table 23.3 Potential Returns of a CNY Bullish Note

Potential End Rate	Appreciation/ Depreciation (%)	Redemption at Maturity (%)	Net Return (%)
6.80	21.72	118.00	18.00
6.90	19.96	118.00	18.00
7.00	18.24	118.00	18.00
7.10	16.58	118.00	18.00
7.20	14.96	116.93	16.93
7.30	13.38	114.09	14.09
7.40	11.85	111.33	11.33
7.50	10.36	108.65	8.65
7.60	8.91	106.03	6.03
7.70	7.49	103.49	3.49
7.80	6.12	101.01	1.01
7.90	4.77	98.59	−1.41
8.00	3.46	96.23	−3.77
8.10	2.19	93.93	−6.07
8.20	0.94	91.69	−8.31
8.277	0.00	90.00	−10.00
8.30	−0.28	90.00	−10.00
8.40	−1.46	90.00	−10.00
8.50	−2.62	90.00	−10.00

or if it is revaluated for less than 5%. We will compare specifically the attractiveness of such notes later in this chapter.

23.4 Bullish Obligation on the CNY

The bullish obligation on the CNY is another investment or speculation instrument with which the investor can potentially profit from potential CNY revaluation. The payoff of a CNY bullish obligation includes two parts: the coupon and the principal. Both parts depend upon the fixing of the CNY/USD rate at maturity of the note. The coupon is set as follows.

CNY coupon rate × (spot rate/fixing rate) × number of days/360, and the principal is given as follows:

$$\left[1 + \text{multiplier} \times \left(8.277 - F_{\mathrm{m}}\right)/F_{\mathrm{m}}\right] \times \text{notional amount}$$

where F_{m} stands for the fixing rate of CNY/USD, "multiplier" for the degree of bullishness, and "notional amount" for the notional value of the note.

We will illustrate such notes here in this section with specific examples.

Example 23.4 A Hong Kong bank might buy a note with a 90-day maturity from an American investment house for US$20 million. The coupon on the note and the principal on the note are payable in US dollars. Suppose that the coupon offered in the note is 8% annually multiplied by the ratio of the current spot value of the CNY to the CNY/USD exchange rate at maturity. What are the payoffs of the note for various CNY/USD rates at maturity of the note if the multiplier is 2.8?

Using the above formula for coupon and principal payments, we can obtain payoffs of the note for various CNY/USD rate at maturity of the note, and we list the results in Table 23.4.

We can observe from Table 23.4 that the principal declines with fixing CNY/USD at maturity; particularly, it may drop to zero and negative US$8 million in the extreme cases when the CNY depreciates to 12.876 and 16.554, respectively; we can also observe that the net return or loss of the obligation note is much greater than the

Table 23.4 Payments of a CNY Bullish Obligation with Multiplier of 2.8 (Unit: US$ million)

Fixing Rate	CNY Rev/ Depr (%)	Principal Payment	Coupon Payment	Total Payment	Net Return (%)
7.50	10.4	25.802	0.441	26.243	31.2
7.60	8.9	24.988	0.436	25.424	27.1
7.70	7.5	24.196	0.430	24.626	23.1
7.80	6.1	23.425	0.424	23.849	19.2
7.90	4.8	22.672	0.419	23.091	15.5
8.00	3.5	21.939	0.414	22.353	11.8
8.10	2.2	21.224	0.409	21.632	8.2
8.20	0.9	20.526	0.404	20.930	4.6
8.277	0.0	20.000	0.400	20.400	2.0
8.30	−0.3	19.845	0.399	20.244	1.2
8.70	−4.9	17.277	0.381	17.658	−11.7
9.10	−9.0	14.935	0.364	15.299	−23.5
12.876	−35.7	(0.000)	0.257	0.257	−98.7
16.554	−50.0	(8.000)	0.200	(7.800)	−139.0

corresponding appreciation of the CNY because of the leverage effect of the note.

Example 23.5 What are the payoffs of the note for various CNY/USD rates at maturity of the note in Example 23.4 if the multiplier is 2.2?

Following the same procedure as in Example 23.4, we can obtain payoffs of the note for various CNY/USD rate at maturity of the note. We list the results in Table 23.5.

Comparing the results in Tables 23.4 and 23.5, we find that the net returns in Table 23.4 are greater than those in Table 23.5 and that the losses in Table 23.4 are also larger than in Table 23.5, resulting directly from the greater leverage effect of the larger multiplier.

23.5 Structured Notes with Embedded Options

Many structured notes have options embedded inside. A put option is actually embedded in the note introduced in Section 23.2, and a call option is embedded in the note introduced in Section 23.3, together with an embedded put option. Because of the flexible

Table 23.5 Payments of a CNY Bullish Obligation with Multiplier of 2.2 (Unit: US$ million)

Fixing Rate	CNY Rev/ Depr (%)	Principal Payment	Coupon Payment	Total Payment	Net Return (%)
7.50	10.4	24.558	0.441	25.000	25.0
7.60	8.9	23.919	0.436	24.355	21.8
7.70	7.5	23.297	0.430	23.727	18.6
7.80	6.1	22.691	0.424	23.115	15.6
7.90	4.8	22.100	0.419	22.519	12.6
8.00	3.5	21.524	0.414	21.937	9.7
8.10	2.2	20.961	0.409	21.370	6.9
8.20	0.9	20.413	0.404	20.817	4.1
8.277	0.0	20.000	0.400	20.400	2.0
8.30	−0.3	19.878	0.399	20.277	1.4
8.70	−4.9	17.861	0.381	18.241	−8.8
9.10	−9.0	16.021	0.364	16.384	−18.1
12.876	−35.7	4.285	0.257	4.542	−77.3
16.554	−50.0	(2.000)	0.200	(1.800)	−109.0

characteristics of options, structured notes become more attractive to investors because such notes can be flexible in payoff patterns and also risk profiles. We can introduce many such notes with various combinations of vanilla options and even exotic options, but these topics are beyond the scope of this book.

23.6 Summary

Structured notes exist in many forms with various combinations of options and forward-style properties. Some types of structured notes used during the Asian financial crisis and the Mexican crisis have been traded for the CNY revaluation, yet many sophisticated ones have not been used actively for CNY revaluation yet. With further development of the CNY derivatives market offshore, especially with higher liquidity of the popular CNY derivative products such as CNY NDFs, CNY NDSs, CNY NDOs, and CNY NDFOs, the CNY structured notes will become more sophisticated and trade more actively. We will discuss future development of the CNY derivatives market offshore and onshore in Part V of this book.

24

Onshore Products and Offshore Derivatives

We have introduced and analyzed major CNY derivative products in the past seven chapters of Part IV. All these products are trading in offshore marketplace besides CNY forwards trading in the interbank market between the four major Chinese state-owned commercial banks and their clients. Besides pure speculation on the CNY revaluation, most other offshore CNY derivatives trading activities should be somewhat related to the traditional financial activities onshore either directly or indirectly. The purpose of this chapter is to explore the relationship between offshore trading activities of CNY derivatives and their corresponding onshore traditional financial activities.

This chapter is organized as follows. Section 24.1 introduces hot money and estimates the amount of hot money flown into China in the past two years; Section 24.2 tries to find out ways in which hot money enters China through current and capital accounts; Section 24.3 introduces hot money flown into real estate and other related areas; Section 24.4 introduces the CNY revaluation and stock markets; Section 24.5 connects CNY revaluation and purchase of the Chinese government bonds of foreign financial institutions in China; Section 24.6 analyzes borrowings and interbank transfers of capital of foreign-invested enterprises and foreign financial institutions in China; Section 24.7 analyzes the relationship between the CNY revaluation and the HKD and provides evidence that the HKD is used as a proxy to the CNY; Section 24.8 discusses the CNY deposits in foreign financial institutions and how such deposits are linked to CNY NDF contracts offshore; Section 24.9 analyzes corporate loans of foreign banks and how such loans are related to USD swaps in the offshore market; and Section 24.10 summarizes and concludes the chapter.

24.1 CNY Revaluation and Hot Money

Hot money, also called refugee capital, is short-term capital flowing into countries mainly to speculate on asset appreciations. As shown in Chapter 12, a lot of hot money had flowed to East Asian countries not long before the Asian financial crisis broke out. A sizable amount of hot money has flowed into China since 2003. The State Administration of Foreign Exchange (SAFE), the currency regulator, first officially recognized the existence of hot money in China on October 16, 2003 (SAFE News Release). We will concentrate on hot money in the first section of this chapter.

24.1.1 Account Surpluses, Foreign Reserve, and Hot Money

There are many different sources and estimations of hot money in China, but the official source is the official data release from the SAFE. Table 24.1 gives the total foreign reserve, current account, and capital account, and the corresponding error term of Mainland China from 2001 to 2003 and 1Q2004.

We can observe from Table 24.1 that the error term changed from negative US$4.856 billion to positive US$7.800 billion from 2001 to 2002, implying that capital outflow changed from outflow to inflow from 2001 to 2002; it increased by more than 136% from 2002 to US$18.422 billion in 2003. That discrepancy, many economists suspect, was a result of inflows of hot money used to bet on an appreciation in the exchange rate of the CNY.

Despite the accumulated trade deficit of US$8.44 billion resulting from three consecutive monthly trade deficits in the first three months in 2004, the foreign reserve in China still grew by US$36.550

Table 24.1 Current Account and Capital Accounts in China from 2001 to 1Q 2004 (Unit: US$ billion)

	Foreign Reserve	Trade Surplus	Current Account	Nontrade Current Account	Capital and Financial Account	Errors
2001	212.165	22.600	17.405	(5.195)	34.775	(4.856)
2002	286.410	30.400	35.400	5.000	32.300	7.800
2003	403.250	25.600	45.900	20.300	52.700	18.422
1Q 2004	439.800	(8.440)	13.196	21.636	14.100	9.254
2004f	549.150	(33.760)	52.785	86.545	56.400	37.015

Data sources: data from 2001 to 2003 are from releases of SAFE. Foreign reserve and trade data for 1Q 2004 are from Economic Information Daily of April 29, 2004; current account data for 1Q 2004 are calculated using the same annual growth rate of current account from 2002 to 2003 divided by 4; the data for capital and financial account is the actual FDI in 1Q 2004 released by Ministry of Commerce on April 13, 2004 because the capital and financial account US$52.7 billion, was close to FDI US$53.5 billion in 2003, with a difference of merely US$0.8 billion.

billion, indicating that the hot money inflow has not slowed down but increased, if not accelerated, in 2004.

It is difficult to estimate the actual amount of hot money that has flowed into China, but the actual figure should be greater than the error term in Table 24.1. Standard & Poor estimated (Reuters, Shanghai, March 12, 2003) that US$40–50 billion in hot money flowed into China in 2003, which is more than twice as large as the error term of US$18.422 billion in Table 24.1. We will try to estimate the amount of hot money that has flowed into China in the rest of this section.

24.1.2 Capital Flows to Asia Pacific

It is helpful to know the capital flows to the Asia/Pacific region in recent years. Table 24.2 gives the total current account balance, net private flows, net direct equity investment, and net portfolio investment in the Asia/Pacific region.

Comparing the data in Tables 24.2 and 12.3 with data relating to the Asian financial crisis, we can immediately find that all major terms such as net private capital flows, net private direct investment,

Table 24.2 Capital Flows to the Asia/Pacific Region from 2001 to 2004 (Unit: US$ billion)

	2001	2002	2003e	2004f
Current account balance	48.1	70.6	80.4	58.4
Net private flows	51.3	66.3	116.7	108.0
Equity investment	64.2	59.6	87.7	94.2
Direct investment	51.8	56.8	58.3	61.5
Portfolio investment	12.4	2.8	29.4	32.7
Private creditors, net	(12.9)	6.7	29.0	13.8
Commercial banks, net	(10.4)	2.0	14.8	10.4
Nonbanks, net	(2.5)	4.7	14.2	3.4

Data source: Capital Flows to Emerging Market Economies, Institute of International Finance, Inc., April 15, 2004. e, estimate; f, forecast.

and net private portfolio investment in 2002 and 2003 all surpassed significantly their corresponding figures in 1996, one year before the crisis broke out. Specifically, the three items mentioned above in 2003 increased from their 1996 figures by 82.5%, 493.1%, and 199.1%, respectively! In other words, the net private direct investment and net private portfolio investment increased from 1996 by nearly five times and twice in 2003.

24.1.3 China' Share in the Asia/Pacific Region and Hot Money Estimation

"China continues to dominate regional cross-border transactions, with the large pipeline of commitments for new foreign investment and prospective increase in offshore share listings likely to lift total net direct equity inflows" (p. 7, IIF, 2004). China has been playing the dominant role in foreign trade and attracting international capital in the Asia/Pacific region in the past few years. We try to estimate the amount of capital that has flowed into China using the data given in Table 24 2 and our previous results in this book.

Table 24.3 gives us the current account balance ratios of China to that of the Asia/Pacific region given in Table 24.2, and the foreign direct investment ratio of China to that of the Asia/Pacific region given in Table 24.2. Average Ratio 1 is the weighted average of the current account ratio with weight 31.25% and the foreign direct

Table 24.3 Capital Flows to Mainland China from 2001 to 2003 (Unit: US$ billion)

	2001	2002	2003e
Current account balance of Mainland China	17.405	35.400	45.900
Current account ratio: China/(Asia/Pacific)(%)	36.2	50.1	57.1
FDI into China	47.0	52.7	53.5
FDI into China/direct investment in Asia/Pacific (%)	90.7	92.8	91.8
Average Ratio 1 (2002 zero)(%)	73.7	79.5	80.9
Average Ratio 2 (2002 matched)(%)	88.7	91.2	90.5
Net private flows into China (estimation 1)	37.8	52.7	94.4
Net private flows into China (estimation 2)	45.5	60.5	105.6
Estimated net private flows into China1 — FDI into China	−9.2	0.0	40.9
Estimated net private flows into China2 — FDI into China	−1.5	7.8	52.1

Data sources: current account balances of Mainland China are from Table 25.1; current account ratios are calculated using data from Table 25.2; FDI into China are from Table 3.2 of Chapter 3; FDI into China/direct Investment in Asia/Pacific are calculated using data from Table 25.2.

investment (FDI) ratio with weight 68.75%, the weights being chosen so that the FDI into China represented the estimated net private capital flow into China in 2002, or the difference between the estimated net private capital that has flowed into China and the FDI into China in 2002 was zero, and Average Ratio 2 is the weighted average of the current account ratio with weight 3.70% and the FDI ratio with weight 96.3%, the weights being chosen so that the difference between the estimated net private capital that has flowed into China and the FDI into China in 2002 matched exactly the error term or amount of hot money, US$7.80 billion, given in Table 24.1. We can estimate the total net private capital that had flowed into China using the two average ratios and the total net private capital that had flowed into the region given in Table 24.3.

Using the two weighted average ratios explained above, we estimated that net private flows into China were US$94.4 billion and

105.6 billion in 2003, respectively. Subtracting the FDI into China from the estimated net private capital flows into China yields US$40.9 billion and 52.1 billion in 2003, respectively. These should be reasonably good and conservative estimations of the hot money that flowed into China in 2003 because the corresponding values using Average Ratio 1 for 2001 and 2002 were negative US$9.2 billion and 0.0 for 2001 and 2002, respectively; and the corresponding values using Average Ratio 2 for 2001 and 2002 were negative US$1.5 billion and 7.8 billion (the matched error term, US$7.800 billion, representing the hot money that flowed into China in 2002, given in Table 24.1) for 2001 and 2002, respectively.

Our estimation of the net private capital that flowed into China other than the FDI of between US$40.9 billion and 52.1 billion in Table 24.3 are consistent with Standard & Poor's estimation of US$40–50 billion. It is beyond the scope of this book to go into great details using other methods and models to estimate the amount of hot money that flowed into China.

24.1.4 Forecast of Hot Money into China in 2004

We have estimated the hot money that flowed into China in 2003. Based on data of the foreign reserve, the trade deficit (given in Table 24.1), and the FDI of US$14.1 billion in the first quarter of 2004 (released by Ministry of Commerce on April 13, 2004, http://english.mofcom.gov.cn), we try to estimate the hot money flowing into China in 2004. Assuming that the capital account surplus in 1Q 2004 is the same as the FDI in the period (because the difference between capital and financial account and the FDI was merely US$0.8 billion in 2003) and that annual current account surplus grows at 15% from 2003 to 2004 compared with 103.4% and 29.7% in 2002 and 2003, the foreign reserve and trade deficit increase the same amount in the remaining three quarters in 2004 as in 1Q 2004, we can estimate the error term in Table 24.1 or the amount of hot money flowing into China of US$9.254 billion in 1Q 2004 to be slightly above half of the figure of US$18.422 billion for 2003, and the estimated error term, US$37.015 billion, for 2004, slightly more than double the 2003 figure.

The multipliers of the net private capital flowing into China of US$40.9 billion to US$52.1 billion over the error term, US$18.422 billion, in Table 24.1 can be easily found to be 2.22 and 2.83. Using these multipliers and the estimated error term for 2004 in Table 24.1, we can estimate the hot money flowing into China in 1Q2004 between US$20.5 billion and 26.0 billion, and the corresponding figure for 2004 would be between US$82.3 billion and 104.7 billion! If we discount such figures by 70%, the hot money to flow into China would be between US$57.6 billion and 73.3 billion! Summation of the estimated figures of between US$40.9 billion and 52.1 billion for 2003 and 2004 is between US$98.5 billion and 125.4 billion. Considering the error term as the hot money estimation of US$7.80 billion for 2002 in Table 24.1, we may find a reasonable total hot money flow into China from 2002 to 2004 between US$100 billion and 125 billion!

Our estimation is still very conservative compared with some industry reports. It was reported that the "pace of inflows (into China) has accelerated with $67 billion 'hot money' going in the last six months (by April 2004), close to $100 billion in the past year (2003)" (see Dow Jones, 2004), indicating that the total amount of capital inflows would be more than twice our estimation. It is beyond the scope of this book to go into further details of these estimations.

24.2 Current and Capital Accounts

Hot money has entered China through various channels such as capital that had flowed out of China before 2003 flowing back for investment or other purposes. It has been easier for capital to flow in than to flow out because the government has been encouraging foreign investment and various other forms of international cooperation. Hot money has entered China through three channels, current account, capital account, and transmission from overseas branches of Chinese banks into China.

24.2.1 Current Account

Of these channels, current account has been one of the major channels as it has been open. Receivables of exports can be reported so that hot money can flow into China through the trade account; actual profits of exports can also be exaggerated so that the enlarged profits can be converted into CNY. The closeness of the "nontrade current account" and the "error term" given in Table 24.1 for 2002 and 2003 convincingly confirm that current account is the major channel for hot money to enter China.

Receivables of nontrade services such as shipping, construction and others can also be manipulated so that payments can be greater than what the services are worth. Hot money can also get into China through transfer of payments between companies operating in China and their head offices overseas.

24.2.2 Capital Account

Hot money can also enter China through capital account, although it is not open yet. It has entered China through additional direct investment for existing projects or new projects and through investment in manufacturing projects, to be introduced in the following section. We will discuss such issues with specific examples later in this chapter.

24.2.3 Transfer of Deposits in Foreign Branches of Chinese Banks into China

According to the Bank for International Settlement (BIS), US$9.1 billion was withdrawn from foreign accounts and most of the deposits were transferred back to China in the second quarter of 2003; and total deposits of Chinese banks in overseas branches fell US$22.1 billion from US$92.5 billion by the end of June 2001 to US$70.4 billion. Most of this capital flew into China because of the expectation of the CNY revaluation. The transmission of capital from overseas accounts of Chinese banks into China provides us with a good information signal that Chinese banks may also participate in CNY revaluation speculation for their clients, if not for their own transactions.

It is difficult to estimate how much hot money has flowed into China through which channels specifically, and it will still remain somewhat difficult to do so as time passes. We will update any available data in this area in the following editions of this book.

24.3 CNY Revaluation and Real Estates

Like the hot money that flowed into Southeast Asian countries prior to the Asian financial crisis, a certain portion of the hot money has flowed into the real estate, production, and other sectors of the Chinese economy since 2003. The SAFE decided to probe FX acceptance and settlement operations in designated banks throughout China in August 2003, and a special examination task started to operate in September 2003. This examination largely aimed at what was believed to be massive inflows of speculative capital into the country.

The examination results show that some banks violated certain rules and regulations of foreign currency administration to allow some investment and manufacturing companies to receive foreign currencies and convert such currencies into CNY in terms of registered capital or deposit-receivables. The examination also found that most such capital was not used for manufacturing purposes but rather for real estate and securities investments or deposits in personal accounts (Shanghai Securities News, January 6, 2004). Again, it is difficult to estimate the exact amount of capital that flowed into the real estate market, and we discuss the relationship between the CNY revaluation and stock market in the following section.

Figure 24.1 shows 18-month moving correlation coefficients between monthly additional investment in real estate in China and the implied one-year USD/CNY exchange rate from one-year CNY NDFs from August 2002 to April 2004. We can observe directly from Figure 24.1 that the moving correlation coefficient declined monotonically from above 48% in August 2002 to nearly negative 2% in December 2002, yet it increased monotonically from December 2002 to August 2003, remained stagnant until January 2004, and rose dramatically from early 2004 to March 2004. The moving correlation coefficient curve in Figure 24.1 is consistent with the our analysis in Chapter 18 that the CNY NDF began to indicate revaluation with

Figure 24.1 Moving Correlation Coefficients between Monthly Additional Investment in Real Estate in China and Implied One-year USD/CNY Exchange Rate from One-year CNY NDFs from August 2002 to April 2004

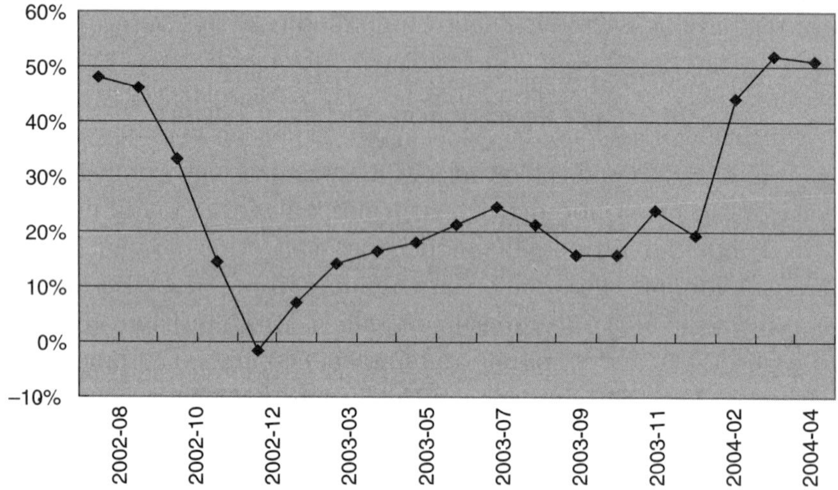

Data source: total additional monthly investments in the real estate market in China are from China Economic Information Network and CNY NDF data are the same as for Figure 18.2.

discounts from November to December 2002, and the CNY revaluation somewhat lost strength in December 2003 as shown in Figure 18.2.

The largely positive and increasing correlation coefficients indicate that the total additional investment in the real estate market in China has been increasingly positively correlated to CNY NDFs, implying that total additional investment in the real estate market in China has been somewhat responsive to offshore CNY NDF activities. Because domestic participants cannot easily participate in the offshore CNY NDF market, the increasingly positive correlation coefficients somehow provide us evidence that international capital had flowed into the Chinese real estate market since 2003. Analysis using price indexes of high-end residential apartments (data source the same as for Figure 24.1) and CNY NDF data provides similar results.

24.4 CNY Revaluation and Security Markets

Stock market investment is the most convenient and direct way of profiting from relating currency revaluations. In this section we will discuss briefly the relationship between stock market investment and the CNY revaluation.

24.4.1 H-Share Performances and the CNY Revaluation

As we introduced in Chapter 5 of this book, H-shares are Mainland Chinese stocks listed and trading in the Hong Kong Exchange. There were 92 H-shares listed in Hong Kong by the end of 2003 compared with 23 at the end of 1996. The H-share index — Hang Seng China Enterprises Index (HSCEI) — with 29 constituent H-shares outperformed all other stock indexes in Hong Kong in 2003. Figure 24.2 depicts the performances of the HSCEI compared with the Hang Seng Index (HSI) and the Hang Seng China-Affiliated Corporations Index (HSCCI) from December 2002 to December 2003.

We can readily observe from Figure 24.2 that HSCEI outperformed HSI and HSCCI tremendously from late 2002 to 2003. As a matter of fact, the HSCEI outperformed all major stock indexes in the world in 2003 (see Table 1 of SFC Quarterly Bulletin, Winter 2003). Of those factors contributing to the excellent performances of H-shares, the CNY revaluation was certainly a major factor because returns of the H-share companies would be greater in terms of the USD if the CNY is revaluated, given other things remaining unchanged. Because of the limited space of this book, we skip specific analysis of the relationship between H-share performances and CNY NDFs here.

Figure 24.2 Performances of HSCEI, HSI, and HSCCI

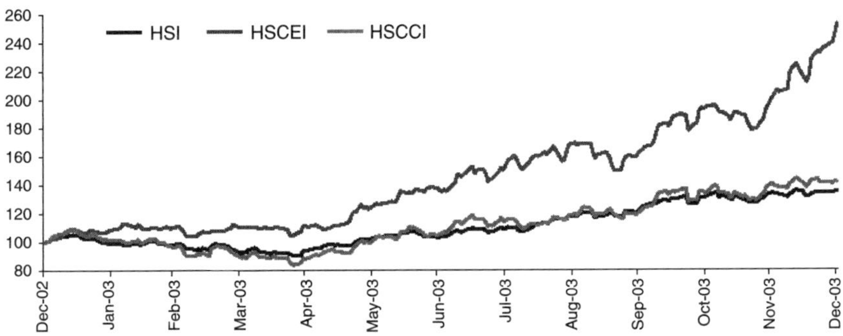

Data source: HKEx.

24.4.2 QFIIs and the CNY Revaluation

International investors can access H-shares directly in Hong Kong as the HKD is convertible, but they cannot access the domestic Mainland Chinese A-share market directly. As discussed in Chapter 5 of Part I, the SAFE approved 11 qualified foreign institutional investors QFIIs with a total capital of US$1.70 billion, and US$1.46 billion had been injected by the end of February 2004. A significant amount of this injected capital has not been invested so far. Whereas it takes time for the QFIIs to find appropriate investment targets because they do not know Chinese A-share companies well, it is reasonable to explain that some of them are reluctant to invest in A-shares simply because they are waiting for the CNY to be revaluated and then to profit from the revaluation.

24.5 CNY Revaluation and Chinese Government Bonds

Buying Chinese government bonds is another effective way to profit from CNY revaluation. According to Japan Economic News, foreign banks registered in China bought US$21.1 billion worth of Chinese government bonds in 2003, 11.6 times up from 2002. HSBC, the most aggressive among all the foreign banks in China, bought US$9.148 billion worth of Chinese government bonds in 2003, five times more than in 2002 and 43.4% of the total US$21.1 billion. The Shanghai branch of HSBC alone bought US$2.1 billion of Chinese government bonds in January 2004 (ChinaNew.com, April 25, 2004).

Although CS First Boston did not buy any Chinese government bonds before 2003, it bought US$7.31 billion in 2003, and Citigroup bought US$2.8 billion worth of Chinese government bonds in 2003. It is reported that Japanese banks bought a few billion USD worth of Chinese government bonds in 2003.

24.6 Capital Transfer from Head Offices to China Branches and International Borrowings of Foreign Companies in China

Approved by the State Council, the SAFE began to announce foreign debt data according to new international standards in 2001 to include foreign debts of foreign enterprises and financial institutions in the total debt of China.

24.6.1 Official Data and Growth of Major Components

Table 24.4 gives the total foreign debt of Mainland China, total foreign debt of foreign invested enterprises (FIEs), that of foreign financial institutions (FFIs), total short-term debt (STDs)(with maturity less than or equal to one year), and increases in STD from the previous year-end from 2001 to 2003.

Table 24.5 gives the corresponding growth rates of all the data items in Table 24.4. We can observe from Table 24.5 that the total

Table 24.4 Foreign Debt of Mainland China from 2001 to 2003 (Unit: US$ billion)

	Total Debt Outstanding	FIE Total Debt Outstanding	FFI Total Debt Outstanding	Total STD Outstanding	Increase of STD from Previous Year End
1H2001	170.410	34.070	16.12	57.530	NA
2001	170.110	35.200	17.04	50.580	(6.950)
1H2002	169.110	34.680	15.49	51.800	1.220
2002	168.538	33.158	15.046	52.976	2.396
1H2003	182.569	36.188	19.764	64.186	11.210
1–9M2003	184.085	36.398	19.395	67.395	14.419
2003	193.634	37.795	20.948	77.044	21.250

Data source: official releases of SAFE from www.safe.gov.cn.

Table 24.5 Growth of Foreign Debt of Mainland China from 2001 to 2003

	Total Debt Outstanding (%)	FIE Total Debt Outstanding (%)	FFI Total Debt Outstanding (%)	Total STD Outstanding (%)	Increase of STD from Previous Year End (%)
1H2001					
2001	−0.2	3.3	5.7	−12.1	
1H2002	−0.8	1.8	−3.9	−10.0	
2002	−0.9	−5.8	−11.7	4.7	34.5
1H2003	8.0	4.3	27.6	23.9	818.9
2003	14.9	14.0	39.2	45.4	786.9

Data source: calculated using data from Table 25.4.

foreign debt dropped slightly from 2001 semiannually to 2002, but it rose moderately from 2002 to 2003.

24.6.2 FIEs and FFIs

Tables 24.4 and 24.5 clearly show that although the foreign debt of FIEs grew at about the same rate as total foreign debt, the foreign debt of FFIs grew at a much higher rate than the total, indicating that foreign banks must have adopted dramatic different business policies since 2003 largely due to CNY revaluation. We will further illustrate this point in the composition of short-term debt as follows with specific transactions in the following sections.

24.6.3 Short-Term Debt

We can observe from Tables 25.4 and 25.5 that the short-term debt fell moderately from the first half of 2001 to the first half of 2002 and increased slightly from 2001 to 2002 but jumped significantly in the first half of 2003 over the same period in 2002 and also from 2002 to 2003. As a matter of fact, increases in STD contributed significantly to the growth of the total foreign debt in Mainland China. The STDs as a percentage of the total foreign debt increased from 29.7% in 2001 to 39.8% in 2003, a net increase of 10.1%.

24.6.4 Composition of STD Growth

Not only is the actual growth of STD of great concern but also its composition. According to a official new release from SAFE on December 16, 2003 (see SAFE official website), FFIs (mainly foreign banks) in China borrowed US$58.557 billion foreign debt in the first nine months of 2003, up from US$42.183 billion in the first half of 2003, or US$16.373 billion and 38.8% increase in 3Q 2003. This additional foreign debt by FFIs constituted 80.79% of the total new foreign debt in China in the same period, up from 77.50% in the first half of 2003, or 3.29% higher in the first nine months than in the first half of 2003.

Of this total new foreign debt of FFIs, US$55.240 billion was paid for interest and principal for existing foreign debt, up from US$38.361 billion in the first half of 2003. The interest and principal payments constituted 79.97% of the corresponding total in China in the first nine months, up from 75.82% in the first half of 2003. The net inflow of foreign debt of FFIs constituted 97.5% of the total net inflow of foreign debt in China in the same period. Such high ratios of FFIs strongly indicate that FFIs either borrowed abroad significantly or transferred capital significantly from their head offices, thus supporting our view that foreign banks have been taking dramatic measures in China.

24.7 CNY Revaluation and the HKD

Because of the close trade and economic relationship with Mainland China in the past quarter since China started the reform process, particularly because of the hand-over of Hong Kong, on July 1, 1997 to become a SAR of China, the HKD has been taken as a proxy for CNY revaluation transactions since late 2002. The Hong Kong SAR will be further integrated with the Mainland both economically and financially, with further implementation of the Closer Economic Partnership Agreement (CEPA) (signed on the sixth anniversary of the hand-over on July 1, 2003 and first implemented on January 1, 2004). Thus, the HKD and the CNY will be more closely correlated in the years to come.

24.7.1 Hong Kong Dollar Peg System

Hong Kong has been using a pegged exchange rate system since October 1983, when the value of the HKD was pegged at HK$7.8 per USD in response to currency instability and general uncertainty about Hong Kong's future in the years before its return to Mainland China. The link has served as an anchor of expectations, economic policy decisions, and confidence in Hong Kong SAR as a regional financial center. Three banks, called note-issuing banks (NIBs), have been designated to issue HKD notes in Hong Kong, the HSBC, Standard Chartered Bank, and Bank of China.

Figure 24.3 One-year CNY NDF and One-year HKD Forward from January 2000 to February 2004

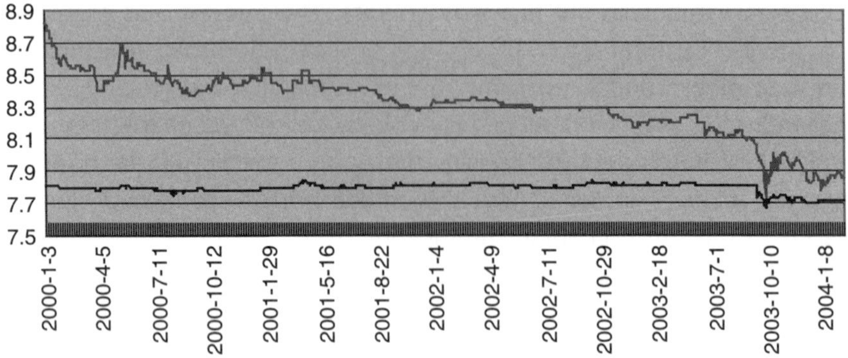

Data source: Hong Kong Monetary Authority and Bloomberg.

24.7.2 HKD Forwards and CNY Forwards

Correlation between the HKD and the CNY spot rates does not make much sense as they are both managed within narrow bands. However, from the early days of the Asian financial crisis in 1997 until recently, currency traders consistently used the forward contracts market to bet that there was at least a small chance that Hong Kong would devalue its currency in response to stagnant economic growth and deflation even more extensively than did Japan. Thus, forward rates are more informative than the managed spot rates.

Figure 24.3 shows the daily rates of the one-year CNY NDF and the one-year HKD forward from January 2000 to February 2004. We can observe readily from Figure 24.3 that the difference between the two forward rates has largely narrowed. It is worth noting that the difference between the one-year CNY nondeliverable rate and the one-year HKD forward became as small as 0.06 when the former reached its strongest point with a discount of 5400 pips early in October, as shown in Figure 18.2.

24.7.3 Correlation between HKD Forwards and CNY Forwards

Figure 24.3 shows the levels of the two forward rates, but we cannot see their correlation easily. Figure 24.4 depicts the 64-day moving correlation coefficients between the two.

Figure 24.4 Correlation Coefficients between One-year CNY NDFs and One-year HKD Forwards from January 2000 to February 2004

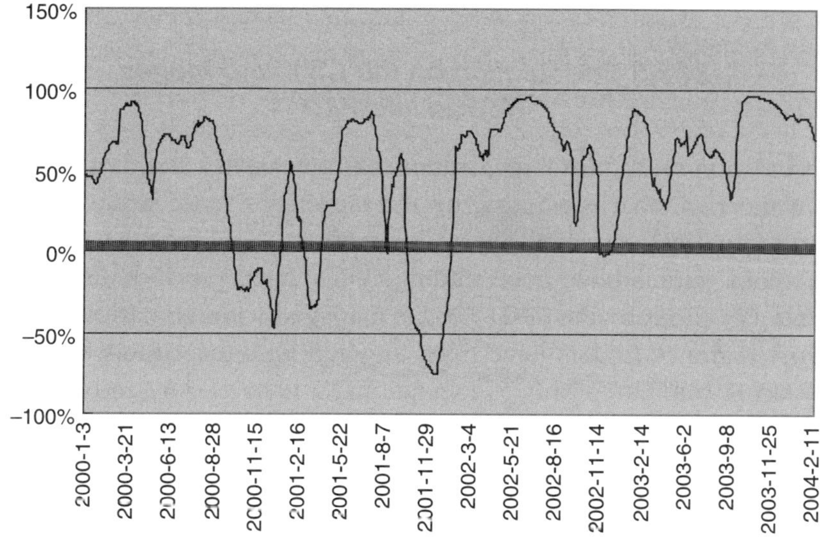

Data source: HKMA and Bloomberg.

We can observe from Figure 24.4 that the correlation coefficient between the one-year CNY NDF and the one-year HKD forward has been quite high since 2000. It fell below 75% in mid-December 2001, but it has been almost exclusively positive since early in 2002, with the only exception of late November and early December in 2002, and it has been above 50% since late in September 2003, when the CNY NDF began to reflect strong pressure for revaluation as shown in Figure 18.2.

24.7.4 Wider Band of the CNY and Its Speculative Proxy

Because of the close relationship between the CNY and the HKD and the convertibility of the latter, the HKD has been regarded as a proxy for traders to speculate on the revaluation of the former as we analyzed in Chapter 21. Based on fundamental economic linkages and closer linkages between the two as the CEPA is further implemented, a wider CNY trading band should not have adverse effects on the HKD, given the negligible amount of trade competition with the Mainland and the limited impact of exchange rate differentials on Hong Kong SAR's major export to the Mainland — financial services.

A wider trading band for the CNY might attract more speculative proxy trading of the HKD.

24.7.5 Speculation on the CNY and Money Flowed into HKD

Speculation on the CNY revaluation has produced a flood of money into the HKD that is pushing up the currency's value while driving short-term interest rates almost to zero in the Hong Kong SAR. Currency traders have been trading CNY-related products using the HKD as a proxy as the HKD/USD is managed within a narrow band. Many currency traders have been angered with the HKMA because HKMA is committed only to maintaining a floor of 7.80 and has not set a ceiling for the HKD's value.

Three days after the G7 conference as we discussed in Chapter 18, the HKD spot rate reached its highest value, of 7.702, since the Asian financial crisis in 1997, 1.22% up from the previous day. The HKMA sold HK$466 million to stabilize the currency on that day (Reference News, September 30, 2003, p. 10). This highest value happened exactly two weeks before the one-year CNY NDF reached its peak on October 7, implying that speculators participated in the HKD market much earlier than in the CNY NDF market because the former is much more liquid than the latter.

24.7.6 Convergence of the Two Highly Correlated Currencies?

The narrowed differences between the CNY and HKD forwards since October 2003 may suggest that the two currencies could be worth about the same. The possibility has reawakened discussion that continued for years in Hong Kong over whether the HKD and the CNY should converge in value. The active trading of the CNY NDFs, NDSs, NDOs, NDFOs, and other products and information implied from such products have somewhat reactivated such discussions. It is interesting to discuss this, but it is beyond the scope of this book.

24.8 Onshore CNY Deposits and Offshore CNY NDFs

Many foreign enterprises and Chinese enterprises have profits in CNY through their business operations in China. They can deposit such incomes in foreign banks to profit through using the CNY NDF contracts actively trading offshore. We illustrate in this section how such transactions can be done.

24.8.1 Onshore Transaction

An onshore foreign enterprise in China, an onshore subsidiary of a Chinese listed company in Hong Kong, or a Chinese company can deposit its income, say RMB 200 million, in a foreign bank in China for six months, one year, two years, or three years. The onshore foreign bank pays interest to its client as for a normal deposit.

24.8.2 Offshore Transaction

The head office of the foreign bank or its regional head office in Hong Kong or in Singapore will pay the head office of the Chinese-listed company in Hong Kong, or the foreign subsidiary of the Chinese company the difference according to following formula:

$$200/\text{implied CNY/USD rate} - 200/8.277,$$

where "implied CNY/USD rate" is the forward CNY/USD rate using the CNY NDF market rate as introduced and illustrated in Chapters 18 and 19. Specifically, the one-year CNY NDF discount pip is used if the deposit is made for one year, and the six-month CNY NDF discount pip is used if the deposit is made for six months; and the implied CNY/USD rate has to be calculated using information from the CNY NDS or CNY FX forward swap markets if the deposit is made beyond one year as the NDF market is not liquid. Let us illustrate how to calculate the payments with a specific example.

Example 24.1 How much does the head office of the foreign bank need to pay the offshore company — the depositor with RMB

200 million for one year — if the one-year CNY NDF is currently quoted at a discount of 4000 pips?

Answer: The implied CNY/USD exchange rate in one year can be easily found as

$$8.277 - 4000/10000 = 7.877,$$

and the amount the head office of the foreign bank pays the depositor can be readily calculated as

$$200/7.877 - 200/8.277 = 25.390 - 24.163 = \text{US\$}1.277 \text{ million.}$$

Example 24.1 gives an extreme example of using the market CNY NDF quote assuming perfect liquidity in the CNY NDF market. As a matter of fact, the CNY NDF is still not liquid enough for banks to transact as freely as they want. The bank would be exposed to significant risk for loss with the long CNY NDF contract if the CNY/USD turns out to be above 7.877 or the actual revaluation is less than RMB 0.40. Thus, the bank would negotiate with the depositor a rate above 7.877 or using a CNY NDF discount rate lower than 4000 pips in order to split the risk with the CNY NDF contract. Let us see this in the following example.

Example 24.2 How much does the head office of the foreign bank need to pay the offshore company — the depositor in Example 24.1 — if the bank and the depositor agree on payment calculated with half of the existing market CNY NDF?

Answer: The agreed implied CNY/USD exchange rate in one year can be found as $8.277 - 0.50 \times 4000/10000 = 8.077$, and the amount the head office of the foreign bank pays the depositor can be readily calculated as

$$200/8.077 - 200/8.277 = 24.762 - 24.163 = \text{US\$}0.598 \text{ million.}$$

We can easily check that the payment in Example 24.2 is about half of the payment in Example 24.1, which may be interpreted as the bank and its depositor splitting the potential profits while sharing the potential risk with the CNY NDF contract.

24.8.3 Converting CNY into USD

The foreign bank would certainly prefer to convert CNY from its clients into USD as it can easily obtain USD from its head office or regional head offices in terms of interbank capital reallocation or redistribution, and the foreign bank can make CNY loans to either Chinese companies or foreign companies in China to make additional profits as will be explained in the following sections of this chapter.

24.9 Corporate Loans of Foreign Banks

FFIs can benefit from CNY revaluation through lending either to domestic Chinese corporations or to foreign-invested companies. The loans can be either in CNY or in USD, with links with the offshore CNY NDFs. We illustrate such transactions with specific examples here in this section.

24.9.1 Onshore CNY Loans

Foreign banks were authorized in December 2003 to make CNY loans to Chinese enterprises after two years since China entered the WTO in December 2001. Corporate loans in CNY will benefit the lending foreign banks directly as both interest and principal payments will be in CNY in the years to come and such payments will be worth more in term of USD if the CNY is actually revaluated before the loans terminate.

Although it is good that there is no FX risk involved because no foreign currency is involved in such loans, there are a few problems with onshore CNY loans. First of all, foreign banks may have a limited amount of CNY to make loans; secondly, there is a CNY interest rate risk as there is no domestic interest rate swap (IRS) market, so that the CNY interest rate risk cannot be hedged easily.

24.9.2 Loans in USD

There are different types of foreign currency loans or USD loans among Chinese-designated Chinese banks, foreign banks, and other Chinese or foreign enterprises that need loans.

USD loans from Chinese banks to foreign banks in China. The examination results of the SAFE mentioned in Section 24.3 indicate that the offshore departments of some designated Chinese banks receive short-term capital from foreign institutions in the name of standard export business transactions, and these offshore departments then lend the short term capital to foreign banks in China.

USD loans from foreign banks to enterprises in China. According to Table 4.3, foreign banks were allowed to make loans in foreign currencies immediately after China entered the WTO in December 2001. Foreign banks can lend to foreign-invested companies or to China–foreign joint ventures directly. Foreign currency loans are superior to onshore CNY loans in the sense that foreign interest risk can be easily hedged for foreign banks to use offshore IRSs, and more importantly, they may arrange both interest and principal payments of such loans in the needed CNY. However, there is a mismatching of the CNY income of the companies and the foreign currency loans if the loan payments cannot be arranged in CNY.

There is one advantage of the foreign currency loans in that they can be converted into CNY by the companies receiving the loans according to foreign exchange rules. Thus, the ultimate goal of holding CNY is achieved.

24.9.3 Synthetic CNY Loans with Swaps

A synthetic CNY loan can overcome the problems of both the direct onshore CNY loans described in Section 24.9.1 and the corresponding USD loans described in Section 24.9.2. A synthetic CNY loan includes three parts: one onshore segment with the branch office of the foreign bank in Mainland China and its onshore client (foreign company, joint venture, or Chinese company), one offshore segment with the head office or regional head office of the foreign bank (either in Hong Kong or in Singapore) and the offshore office of its client, and the offshore office of the client invests the receivables in USD with its onshore company as foreign investment.

For convenience of description, we use XYZ to stand for the lending branch of the foreign bank in China and XYZ HO for its corresponding head office or regional head office. We can describe the synthetic CNY loan as follows.

Onshore segment. XYZ makes the initial loan to its client in China, and the client will make periodic interest payments to XYZ in USD until the end of the loan and pay the principal back to XYZ at the end of the loan.

Offshore segment. XYZ HO enters a cross-currency swap (CCS) with the offshore office of the client in which the former pays exactly what the client needs to pay XYZ onshore, say USD LIBOR + 1.25%; and the offshore office of the client pays XYZ HO a fixed interest rate of 3.50%.

CCS between the onshore and offshore offices of the client. Figure 24.5 depicts the cash flows of the synthetic CNY loan.

The offshore office of the client and its onshore office can enter a reverse CCS so that the offshore office can pass the USD cash flows to its onshore office for either additional investment or loan from foreign office. This transaction may somehow explain the rise in international borrowing of foreign-invested companies from abroad

Figure 24.5 Cash Flows of a Synthetic CNY Loan

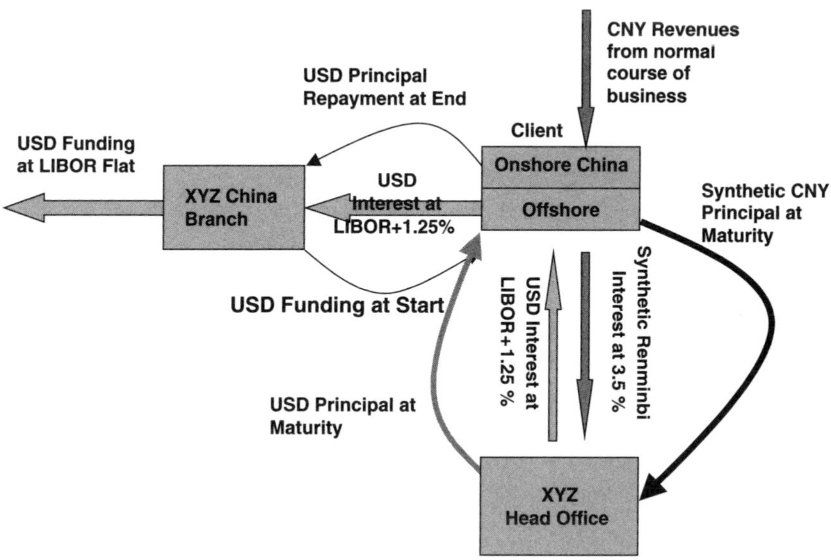

shown in Table 24.2. The onshore office of the client may simply deposit the corresponding CNY payments in a foreign bank to make some profits as explained in Section 24.6 and pay its offshore office later on. Figure 24.4 depicts the cash flows of the synthetic CNY loan.

The necessary condition for such synthetic loans is that the client must have an offshore company. As all foreign companies, most joint venture companies, and more and more Chinese companies have overseas branch companies or subsidiaries these days, this necessary condition can be easily satisfied.

24.10 Summary and Conclusions

We first introduced the traditional channels to benefit from potential CNY revaluation; these channels include deposits, international borrowing and transfer, investment in stocks, real estate, government bonds, and corporate loans, and so on. After introducing the traditional channels, we analyzed how these traditional transactions can be connected with the offshore CNY NDF, NDS, and other products. It would take another volume to further analyze the connections or relation between offshore CNY derivatives trading and traditional financial transactions onshore, but that is far beyond the scope of this book.

PART V

Future Development

We have introduced major derivative products on the Chinese yuan in Part IV based on the introduction of the underlying Chinese Economy, banking system, capital market and foreign exchange system introduced in Part I. We previously planned to write one whole chapter on the Chinese foreign exchange rate formation mechanism which has been so important and relevant to the future development of Chinese yuan derivatives markets both onshore and offshore because the rate formation mechanism will answer all the three questions we raised at the beginning of the preface. Yet, published materials on this topic are currently so limited that it is rather impossible to have one concrete chapter prior to the publication of this book because it takes time to research and design an appropriate rate formation mechanism that can reflect market forces and at the same time maintain somewhat the relative foreign exchange stability in China. We are working on this topic and plan to add that as a chapter in the subsequent edition of this book.

25

Future Development of CNY Derivatives in China

In this chapter, we focus on future development of CNY derivative products in China and also conclude this book.

This chapter is organized as follows. Section 25.1 introduces the future development of foreign trade in China; Section 25.2 introduces future development of foreign direct investment and qualified domestic institutional investors in China; Section 25.3 introduces the potentiality of the Chinese economy in coming years; Section 25.4 introduces the inter-bank derivative market in China with a brief introduction of "Interim Rules on Derivatives Business of Financial Institutes" by China Banking Regulatory Commission (CBRC); Section 25.5 introduces WTO and the CNY businesses for domestic Chinese enterprises; Section 25.6 discusses further development of the CNY forward market in China; Section 25.7 describes the likely coexistence of the onshore CNY forward and offshore CNY NDF markets; Section 25.8 relates the OTC derivatives development with exchange traded products in China; Section 25.9 discusses the potentiality of derivative markets in China; and Section 25.10 concludes the chapter and the book.

25.1 Trade Growth in China

Table 3.3 of Chapter 3 presents the annual export, import, total trade, and their corresponding annual growth rates in the Chinese economy from 1978 to 2003. It is clear from Table 3.3 that trade has grown faster than the GDP in China in the past quarter-century as the average annual growth rate of trade was 7.2 percent higher than the corresponding annual GDP growth rate of 9.4 percent. Another indicator of the faster growth of trade in China is the trade/GDP ratio, which was merely 9.6 percent in 1978 when the reform process was initiated, and went up to 50.2 percent in 2002, the first whole-year after China entered the WTO. It went up further to 60.4 in 2003.

According to statistics released by the State Statistics Bureau, export increased by 34 percent in the first quarter of 2004 and import by 41 percent, compared to the same period in 2003, and total trade increased by 38 percent in the same period. Thus, trade growth in the first quarter of 2004 was more than twice the average annual growth rate of trade in China in the past quarter-century. These 1Q2004 data imply a trade/GDP ratio of 75.9 percent using the first quarter GDP growth rate of 9.8 percent. The strong growth of trade indicates that demand for foreign exchange businesses and relating hedging businesses will grow in China in the following years.

25.2 FDI, QFIIs, and QDIIs in China

Table 3.2 gives us the total annual foreign direct investment (FDI) in China from 1978 to 2003. We can observe from Table 3.2 that China had attracted about half trillion FDI in the past quarter. According to *China Daily* (June 16, 2004), China attracted US$25.91 billion FDI in the first five months of 2004, up 11.34 percent year-on-year, according to the Chinese Ministry of Commerce, implying that the FDI growth rate is moving toward its 2002 level of 12.22 percent growth rate given in Table 3.2. The higher amount of FDI will make it more necessary for international investors to hedge their investment exposure and potential CNY incomes.

Table 5.7 gives us the total amount of approved capital US$1.8 billion of 13 authorized qualified foreign institutional investors

(QFIIs) in China by the end of June 2004. As a matter of fact, two more major international financial institutions, Merrill Lynch and Daiwa Securities, have recently received approval of their QFII statutes from the China Securities Regulatory Commission (CSRC) and these two institutions are in the process of applying for their investment quota. The increased amount of approved capital to invest in China's securities industry will also make it necessary for the QFIIs to hedge their currency exposure.

The CSRC and SAFE have been discussing specific rules on the QFII equivalent, QDII (qualified domestic institutional investor) for qualified domestic institutions to invest in the international marketplace. With the QDII's approval, more domestic investors will be allowed to invest in the international marketplace, thus creating more demand for foreign exchange businesses and relating hedging businesses in China.

25.3 Economic Growth in China

Table 3.7 gives the annual GDP in CNY and USD in China and their corresponding annual growth rates from 1978 to 2003. China achieved the average annual GDP growth rate of 9.4 percent in the past quarter. Despite the measures currently taken by the central government to curb over-heating investments in a few major industries in China, the annual GDP growth rate will not be lower than 9 percent as the GDP growth rate reached 9.8 percent in the first quarter of 2004.

The official target to quadruple the Chinese GDP from 2000 to 2020 implies an average annual growth rate of 7.18 percent. This average rate of 7.18 percent is not difficult to achieve in the coming two decades. With sustainable GDP growth, there will be more demand for foreign exchange businesses and relating hedging businesses in China.

25.4 OTC Derivatives

Similar to most countries and regions in the world in developing derivatives businesses, derivatives also developed earlier in the inter-bank market in China. In this section, we concentrate on OTC derivatives in China.

25.4.1 CBRC

We mentioned the "Interim Rules on Derivatives Business of Financial Institutes" of the CBRC in the preface of this book, but have not discussed these rules so far. Here we discuss the importance of these rules framed by the CBRC.

OTC derivative products started to trade in China some years ago, when foreign financial institutions penetrated the Chinese banking industry with their newly structured products in the early 1990s. Because of the lack of specific rules and regulations as to how derivatives should be traded in the inter-bank market, turnover of OTC derivatives was rather thin before 2002. In order to accelerate the development of inter-bank derivatives trading, the newly established CBRC drafted the "Interim Rules on Derivatives Business of Financial Institutes" and released the draft on October 11, 2003. These rules were officially released on February 4, 2004. The release of these rules will prove to be of tremendous significance in the inter-bank derivatives market as it signifies that the government has recognized the usefulness of financial derivatives and promotes their development throughout China. The CBRC has given licenses for derivatives trading to the four state-owned banks and Min Sheng Bank. For details of these interim rules, please visit the CBRC website given in the list of useful websites at the end of this book.

According to International Financial News (June 18, 2004, p. 13), all the four major state owned commercial banks, Minsheng Bank and Everbright Bank had received licenses for inter-bank derivatives businesses; and three foreign banks including Citibank, Standard Chartered Bank and Nanyang Commercial Bank also received similar approvals. The CBRC rules that no financial institutions should operate derivatives businesses without the CBRC approval from September 1, 2004.

25.4.2 OTC Derivatives Onshore

Encouraged by the CBRC interim rules, Chinese banks have accelerated the trading of derivative products in 2004. According to a report by the Asian Development Bank (ADB) (Murray, 2004), China has entered into 16 bilateral currency swap arrangements worth US$36.5

billion among 13 (ASEAN+ China, Japan, and South Korea) members. Specifically, China has signed currency swap arrangements with Thailand to the tune of US$2 billion, with Japan worth US$3 billion, with Korea worth US$2 billion, with Malaysia worth US$1.5 billion, and with Philippines to the tune of US$1 billion.

The four state-owned banks currently trade various types of OTC derivative products such as FX swaps, FX options, interest rate swaps, interest rate options, and so on with their clients and then offset their positions with major international financial institutions.

25.4.3 OTC Derivatives with US Banks

It is difficult to obtain data for OTC derivatives any where, and it is more difficult to do so for OTC derivatives in China as it is still in the early experimental stage. Besides the derivatives volume from the ABD given above, the data from the Report of Federal Financial Institution Examination Council (FFIEC) that we used in Chapter 12 also shed some light of inter-bank derivatives trading offshore between Chinese and US banks. Table 25.1 summarizes the ratio of cross-border foreign exchange revaluation and derivatives contracts

Table 25.1 Ratios of Cross-border Foreign Exchange Revaluation and Derivatives Contracts Over Total Amount Owned by Country of Borrower from December 1997 to December 2003 (all values are in percentage)

Country/ Region	Dec 1997	Dec 1998	Dec 1999	Dec 2000	Dec 2001	Dec 2002	Dec 2003
China — Mainland	16.5	33.1	31.9	40.6	44.0	57.5	21.9
China — Taiwan	4.6	6.9	3.7	4.0	4.5	5.6	4.8
Indonesia	53.0	35.1	4.1	6.0	8.5	12.3	12.5
Korea	34.7	24.7	7.7	9.2	9.8	7.8	7.4
Malaysia	31.1	23.7	7.3	5.6	19.7	19.3	15.1
Philippines	2.0	9.1	4.4	8.0	4.0	2.1	2.7
Thailand	89.4	78.6	37.1	50.4	33.8	20.0	22.2
Hong Kong	45.5	26.1	14.2	11.2	9.4	9.7	10.6
Singapore	55.1	16.9	10.7	13.2	6.9	16.7	23.2

Data source: same as Table 12.6 with updated data.

over total amount owned by nine major countries and regions in Asia from December 1997 to December 2003.

We can observe from Table 25.1 that whereas the ratios have largely declined in major countries that were heavily affected by the Asian financial crisis, they largely increased steadily from a mere 16.5 percent in December 1997 to 57.5 percent in December 2002 with Mainland Chinese banks, a value almost three times as large as the second largest ratio (20 percent in Thailand at the same time). Although the ratio fell dramatically to 21.9 percent in December 2003, it was still almost as high as those in Thailand and Singapore. Although further studies are needed to find the cause for such a fall in the ratio from December 2002 to December 2003 for Mainland Chinese banks, these systematic results give us some indication of how fast the Chinese banks have been adopting derivatives concepts and practising trading in such products with American banks in the past 7 years compared to other countries and regions in the Asia Pacific region.

25.5 WTO and CNY Derivative Business

According to the WTO time table for foreign financial operations in China given in Table 4.5, foreign banks will receive national treatment after December 11, 2006. There are foreign banks that have already obtained licenses for RMB businesses. As a matter of fact, foreign banks have already started to provide value-added services for both Chinese enterprises and depositors, and most of such value-added services are related to derivatives as we analyzed in Part IV of this book. In order to compete with foreign banks in China in the coming years, Chinese banks are making preparations in product innovation as they do not want to lose their own existing businesses in RMB in China. Therefore, product innovation and particularly, RMB related derivatives will accelerate in the years to come in China.

25.6 Further Development of the CNY Forward Market

The onshore CNY forward market is still at the experimental stage as we analyzed in Chapter 17. Seven years of experimentation has not yielded satisfactory results because of regulatory and other issues. The existing legal requirement on CNY forward is very similar to the previous Korean one that any forward transaction has to be certified as a hedge against future current account flows or the so called "real demand principle". The "real demand principle" restriction was lifted in Korea in 1999, because of which the Korean forward market has developed smoothly since then.

The Chinese government has recognized the existing problems and has been working on ways to improve the CNY forward market. There is plenty of room for the CNY forward market to grow, yet it will have to develop in line with the CNY exchange rate formation mechanism that is currently being researched and to be adopted in the future.

25.7 Coexistence of Onshore and Offshore Markets

Our introductions to the NDF contracts in Chapter 9 of Part II, Chapter 14 of Part III and Chapters 18 and 19 of Part IV indicate that the NDFs are offshore instruments that most central banks normally do not like because transactions of such products provide information that is somewhat critical of central banks policies. Yet, central banks cannot control such offshore marketplaces and most often they have managed to use information from such offshore products to better manage their onshore markets. In this section we concentrate on the coexistence of onshore and offshore markets for Korean won (KW) and New Taiwan dollar and infer what would happen to the CNY products.

25.7.1 Onshore and Offshore NDFs for the Korean Won

The Asian financial crisis accelerated the foreign exchange reform in South Korea. South Korea carried on the similar "real demand principle" as it is currently practised in China for its forward market until the first stage foreign exchange deregulation policy was adopted in April 1999 (see Lee, 2003). Both residents and non-residents could trade in onshore KW forwards and non-deliverable forwards (NDFs) freely with authorized foreign exchange banks in Korea since April 1999. The

Table 25.2 Average Daily Korean won NDF Turnover from 2000 to 2003 (Unit: US$ billion)

Quarter/Year	Turnover	Growth Rate (%)
2000	0.40	
2001	0.51	27.5
1Q2002	0.55	
2Q2002	0.63	14.5
3Q2002	0.69	9.5
4Q2002	0.79	14.5
2002	0.67	31.4
1Q2003	1.11	
2Q2003	0.88	−20.7
3Q2003	1.13	28.4
4Q2003	2.20	94.7
2003	1.33	98.5

Data source: data from 2000 to 1Q2003 are from Table 1 of Lee (2003) and data from 2Q to 4Q2003 were obtained through telephone from Mr Lee.

KW NDF contracts provide currently non-residents with effective tools for both hedging and speculating before KW becomes international.

Somewhat similar to the Korean stock index (KOSPI 200) futures and options that have been trading most actively in the world in the past few years since 2001, the KW NDF market has grown tremendously and has become the most actively trading NDF contract in the world as shown in Tables 9.1–9.3. Table 25.2 gives the average daily turnover of KW NDF from 2000 to 2003 and average daily turnover in four quarters in 2002 and 2003. We can observe from Table 25.2 that the average daily turnover of KW NDF increased from a mere US$0.40 billion in 2000 to US$1.33 billion in 2003.

Table 25.3 provides us with the weights of KW NDF market participation of domestic and foreign banks from 2000 to 2003. We can readily observe from Table 25.3 that the KW NDF was largely a market for foreign banks in the early stage shortly after the first stage deregulation because domestic banks only had 14.2 percent of the total market share compared to 85.8 percent of foreign banks, yet domestic banks have become more and more active in the KW NDF market with their weights increasing steadily to 41.5 percent in March 2003, whereas that of the foreign banks declined steadily

Table 25.3 Weights of KW NDF between Domestic and Foreign Banks

	2000	2001	2002				Mar 2003
			March	June	Sept	Dec	
Domestic banks	14.2	26.6	25.6	28.7	39.1	36.5	41.5
Foreign banks	85.8	73.4	74.4	71.3	60.9	63.5	58.5

Data source: Table 2 of Lee (2003).

from 85.8 percent in 2000 to 58.5 percent in March 2003. It is reasonable to estimate that weights of domestic and foreign banks are about the same in 2004 from the data given in Table 25.3.

The empirical study of Lee (2003) provides evidence that, besides the basic function for non-residents to hedge their KW exchange risk, the KW NDF contracts are also used to speculate according to the Japanese yen/US dollar exchange rate fluctuations; that trading of KW NDF not only affects the spot KW exchange rate, but also the KW exchange turnover, particularly KW currency swap turnover. Park (2001) also provides evidence of the effects of KW NDF on the cash market. With increasing foreign capital flow into South Korea despite the less than full convertibility of the won, trading in KW NDF will continue to grow, concluded Mr Lee of the Bank of Korea. Therefore, it is highly necessary for the Bank of Korea to monitor closely the movement of the KW NDF trading activities. It is beyond the scope of this section to go into more details of the KW NDF experiences.

25.7.2 Onshore and Offshore NDFs for the New Taiwan Dollar and other Currencies

Although the New Taiwan dollar (NTD) NDF has almost the same long history as the KW NDF, the NTD NDFs were not allowed for domestic financial institutions to trade until August 6, 2003. Thus, the coexistence of onshore and offshore NTD NDF has a much shorter history than the KW NDFs. According to Chang and Shen (2003), the NTD NDF rates began to deviate from the spot rate from May 1997 to December 1997, which indicates that the market was anticipating a depreciation of the NTD. However, the domestic forward exchange rate continued to follow closely with the spot rates due to active interventions by the monetary authority in Taiwan. Chang and Shen (2003) show that the mean value of currency misalignment for NTD/USD was much higher than that of the KW/USD. It could be due to the more effective intervention by the monetary authority in the NTD/USD spot exchange rate market than that by the Bank of Korea.

There are a few other currencies such as the Czech koruna and Polish zloty with both onshore forwards and offshore NDF as we mentioned in the introduction in Chapter 9 earlier. Evidence from Lee (2003) and arguments from Ishii (2001) indicate that trading of offshore NDF does impact both the relating foreign exchange rate and foreign exchange turnover, yet it is beyond the scope of this book to go into more details in this area.

25.7.3 Onshore Forwards and Offshore NDF for the CNY

Experiences of South Korea and Taiwan–China indicate that the monetary authorities will recognize the existence of such products in due course. With growing foreign direct investment and QFIIs, trade and other factors, demand for hedging CNY related risk will also grow. Yet it takes time for onshore CNY derivative market to develop; thus, the offshore CNY derivatives market has its reason to exist. Additionally, the Chinese government will recognize the offshore CNY derivative market in due course because it provides useful information for the future CNY rate formation mechanism.

25.8 OTC and Exchange Traded Derivatives

Encouraged by the CBRC Interim Rules for inter-bank derivatives, the OTC derivatives market has developed rather rapidly since 2002 as we analyzed earlier. Experiences from all developed markets and most developing markets clearly show that exchange traded products are highly necessary for the OTC products to develop further because the former provide necessary pricing, hedging, and risk management parameters for managing the OTC derivatives portfolios. The OTC derivatives books in all Chinese banks will have to be managed with parameters from established international futures and options exchanges if the domestic exchange traded derivatives products are not launched on time. Therefore, it is highly necessary and imperative for exchanges to launch derivatives products to meet the hedging and risk management need of the fast growing OTC market. Please refer to Zhang (2004) for a detailed description of the relationship between OTC and exchange traded products in China.

Fortunately, the State Council has recognized the necessity of exchange traded derivatives as is evident from the nine guidelines for further reforming the capital market discussed in Section 5.9. With these guidelines from the State Council and the Interim Rules for inter-bank derivatives by the CBRC, both OTC and exchange traded derivatives markets will develop parallely in coming years, and the spring of the Chinese derivatives market will eventually come after a few more years of preparation.

25.9 Potentiality of Derivatives Trading in China

The commodity futures business has been growing rapidly in the past 2 years in China as we mentioned in Chapter 5, yet financial futures contracts, or financial derivatives have not started in exchanges in China. As China enters further into the WTO, especially with the guidelines from the State Council issued early in February 2004 and the Interim Rules for inter-bank derivatives trading issued by the CBRC, financial derivatives will boom in both the OTC marketplace and exchanges in China in the coming years. The purpose of this section is to estimate the potential market sizes of derivative markets in China from 2006 to 2010.

25.9.1 Foreign Exchange Derivatives

Table 8.1 gives us the composition of global foreign exchange turnover from 1989 to 2001. We can observe that the weight of spot turnover declined steadily from 59.36 percent in 1989 to 32.96 percent in 2001; that of forwards grew steadily from merely 5.06 percent in 1989 to 11.16 percent in 2001; and that of swaps up steadily from 35.58 percent to 55.88 percent. Using the average daily total turnover of USD 1.5 trillion foreign exchange turnover and world GDP of USD 36 trillion in 2003, we can find the total world annual

Table 25.4 Estimated Turnovers of Foreign Exchange In China between 2006 and 2010

Year	2006	2007	2008	2009	2010
Chinese GDP (US$ trillion)	1.78	1.92	2.07	2.24	2.42
Chinese Ratio/ world ratio	10.00%	15.00%	25.00%	40.00%	55.00%
FX spot turnover in China (US$ trillion)	0.5	0.9	1.6	2.7	4.1
FX forward turnover in China (US$ trillion)	0.2	0.4	0.6	1.1	1.6
Swap turnover in China (US$ trillion)	1.1	1.7	3.1	5.3	7.9
Total turnover in China (US$ trillion)	1.8	2.9	5.3	9.1	13.6

spot, forward, and swap turnover as USD 110, 44, and 213 trillion, respectively, assuming 245 working days and their weights in the total volume as 30, 12, and 58 percent, respectively. Assuming further that the Chinese GDP will grow at a constant annual rate of 8 percent from 2003 to 2010, we can find the corresponding Chinese GDP from Year 2006 to Year 2010, and we can estimate the corresponding turnover of spot, forward, and swap turnovers in China between 2006 and 2010 assuming that the derivative turnover/GDP ratio is merely a fraction (10–55 percent) of the corresponding world ratio. Table 25.4 gives the estimated results.

25.9.2 Exchange Traded Derivatives

According to BIS data, the total turnover of exchange traded derivatives (ETD) in the world grew at an average growth rate of over 17 percent from 1998 to 2003. The total turnover of ETD reached US$873.7 trillion in 2003; the ETD turnover/GDP ratio was 24.3 with total world GDP US$36 trillion in 2003. Assuming that the total ETD turnover/GDP will grow at an average rate of 10 percent, we can obtain the world ETD turnover/GDP ratios from 2006 to 2010; and assuming further that the ETD turnover/GDP ratio in China is merely 8–50 percent of the corresponding world ratio, we can estimate the ETD turnover of ETD in China from 2006 to 2010 using the GDP

Table 25.5 Turnover of Exchange Traded Derivatives in China Estimated for 2006 and 2010

Year	2006	2007	2008	2009	2010
Chinese GDP (US$ trillion)	1.78	1.92	2.07	2.24	2.42
Total turnover of world ETD/world GDP	35.5	39.1	43.0	47.3	52.0
Chinese ratio/ world ratio	8.00%	15.00%	25.00%	40.00%	50.00%
Total turnover of ETD in China (US$ trillion)	5.1	11.3	22.2	42.4	62.9

Table 25.6 Total Year-end Notional Amount of OTC Derivatives in China

Year	2006	2007	2008	2009	2010
Chinese GDP (US$ trillion)	1.78	1.92	2.07	2.24	2.42
Total notional amount outstanding of all OTC derivatives in the world/ world GDP	8.6	9.7	10.8	12.1	13.6
Chinese ratio/world ratio	25.00%	35.00%	45.00%	55.00%	65.00%
Total notional amount outstanding of all OTC derivatives in China	3.8	6.5	10.1	14.9	21.3

annual growth rate of 8 percent. We list the estimated results in Table 25.5. We can observe that the ETD turnover will be around US$5 trillion in 2006 to over US$60 trillion in 2010.

25.9.3 OTC Derivatives

Total notional amount of all OTC derivatives reached US$197.2 trillion in December 2003 from US$80.3 trillion in 1998 with an average annual growth rate of 19.7 percent. The total notional amount of all OTC derivatives in the world/GDP was 5.5 in 2003. Using the average annual growth rate of notional amount of all OTC derivatives in the world/GDP 12 percent and following similar procedure as above for ETDs given in Table 25.5, we can readily find the total year-end notional amount of all OTC derivatives in China from 2006 to 2010. The results are given in Table 25.6. We use a higher Chinese ratio/world ratio in Table 25.6 for OTC products than that for ETD in Table 25.5 for 2006 because the OTC derivatives market is growing rapidly as we discussed in Section 25.4. Notional amount outstanding for OTC derivatives would be more than twice the corresponding Chinese GDP in 2006.

25.10 Summary and Conclusions

With sustainable economic growth, foreign direct investment, qualified foreign institutional investors, and qualified domestic institutional investors, the demand for hedging currency risk will certainly be higher from both international and domestic enterprises and individual investors in China in the coming years. As measures to accelerate the reform of the capital market, as outlined in the nine guidelines from the State Council and the interim rules for inter-bank derivatives by the China Banking Regulatory Commission are gradually taken, derivatives will grow gradually in both the OTC marketplace and exchanges in China. As the first- 5-year time limit of China's WTO status gets closer, additional and more dramatic measures will be taken to accelerate the development of derivatives industry in China.

Let us work together to explore the potential of such huge market in China in the coming years.

Major Websites in the Chinese Financial Market

State Development and Reforming Commission (SDRC)	http:/www.sdrc.gov.cn/
State-owned Assets Supervision and Administration Commission (SASAC)	http:/www.sasac.gov.cn/
National Bureau of Statistics of China (NBSC)	http://www.stats.gov.cn/
Ministry of Finance (MOF)	http://www.mof.gov.cn
People's Bank of China (PBOC)	http://www.pbc.gov.cn/
Ministry of Education (MOE)	http://www.moe.edu.cn/
Ministry of Commerce (MOC)	http://www.mofcom.gov.cn/
National Population and Family Planning Commission (NPFPC)	http://www.npfpc.gov.cn/
China Insurance Regulatory Commission (CIRC)	http://www.circ.gov.cn
China Banking Regulatory Commission (CBRC)	http://www.cbrc.gov.cn
China Securities Regulatory Commission (CSRC)	http://www.csrc.gov.cn/cn/
State Administration of Foreign Exchange (SAFE)	http://www.safe.gov.cn
Customs General Administration (CGAPRC)	http://www.customs.gov.cn/
China Foreign Exchange Trade Center (CFETCS)	http://www.chinamoney.com.cn/
Industry and Commercial Bank of China (ICBC)	http://www.icbc.com.cn
Bank of China (BOC)	http://www.boc.com.cn
China Construction Bank (CCB)	http://www.ccb.com.cn
Agriculture Bank of China (ABC)	http://www.abchina.com
The China Development Bank (SDB)	http://www.cdb.com.cn
Export and Import Bank of China (EIBC)	http://www.eximbank.gov.cn
Shanghai Stock Exchange (SSE)	http://www.sse.com.cn/
Shenzhen Stock Exchange (SZSE)	http://www.szse.com.cn/

Shanghai Futures Exchange (SFFE)	http://shfe.com.cn/
Dalian Commodity Exchange (DCE)	http://www.dce.com.cn/
Zhengzhou Commodity Exchange (CZCE)	http://www.czce.com.cn/
People's Daily	http://english.peopledaily.com.cn/
China Daily	http://www.chinadaily.com.cn/
The Hong Kong Monetary Authority (HKMA)	http://www.info.gov.hk/hkma/
International Monetary Fund (IMF)	http://www.imf.org/
Bank for International Settlements (BIS)	http://www.bis.org/
World Trade Organization (WTO)	http:/www.docsonline.wto.org/DDFDocuments/t/WT/ACC/CHN49A2.doc/
Hong Kong Monetary Authority (HKMA)	http://www.info.gov.hk/hkma/eng/statistics/msb/index.htm
Hong Kong Securities and Futures Commission (HKSFC)	http://www.hksfc.org
Hong Kong Institute for Monetary Research (HKIMR)	https://www.hkimr.org/general_papers.asp
Tokyo Foreign Exchange Market Committee	http://www.fxcomtky.com/announce/index_e.html
Caijing	http://www.caijing.com.cn/

Further Readings

Andrews, E. L. 1998, "Huge German bank covering risks in Asia." *New York Times*, January 29.

Asia Weekly Financial Alert, March 2, 2003, CN7 band widening called for, 14755203, Vol. 6(20).

Bizjournals, October 22, 2003, available via the World Wide Web at http://www.bizjournals.com/charlotte/stories/2003/10/20/daily32.html.

British Bankers Association — Credit Derivatives Survey, 2000.

Brown, Stephen J., William N. Goetzmann and James M. Park, 1998, *Hedge Funds and the Asian Currency Crisis of 1997*, NBER Working Paper No. 6427 (February).

Business News, 2003, available via the World Wide Web at http://www.jang.com.pk/thenews/jul2003-daily/07-07-2003/business/b14.htm.

Canales-Kriljenko, Jorge Iván, 2004, "Foreign Exchange Market Organization in Selected Developing and Transition Economies: Evidence from a Survey," IMF Working Paper, Monetary and Financial Systems Department, Authorized for distribution by Shogo Ishii, WP/04/4.

Chakravorti, Sujit and Subir Lall, 2000, "The Double Play: Simultaneous Speculative Attacks on Currency and Equity Markets," Federal Reserve Bank of Chicago and International Monetary Fund, December.

Chan, K.S. and K.J. Ngiam (1998) "Currency crisis and the modified currency board system in Singapore." *Pacific Economic Review*, 3, 243–263.

Chang, Yuanchen and Chung-hua Shen, 2002, Modeling the degree of currency misalignment around the Asian financial crisis: evidence from Taiwan and Korea's non-delivery forward exchange markets. *Taiwan Academy of Management Journal*, 2, 2, 39–51.

Chapman, Robert, 1998, The derivatives mess. *The International Forecaster*, November 9: http://www.usagold.com/DerivativesChapman.html

Chen, Gongmeng, Oliver Rui, and Yexiao Xu, 2002, "A First Look at Closed-End Funds in China," http://www.pbfea2002.ntu.edu.sg/papers/2090.pdf.

Chong, Li Choy, Oliver Kabuth, and Klaus Kukovetz (editors), "The China Venture: Business Environment and Strategic Considerations," The Asia Research Center, The Research Institute for International Management, The University of St. Gallen, www.lim.ethz.ch/lehre/InternationalMgmtAsia.

Dodd, Randall, 2000, *The Role of Derivatives in the East Asian Financial Crisis*, Derivatives Study Center, CEPA Working Paper Series III (November), *International Capital Markets and the Future of Economic Policy.* A Project Funded by the Ford Foundation, Working Paper No. 20.

Eichengreen, Barry and Donald Mathieson, 1998, *Hedge Funds and Financial Market Dynamics*, Occasional Paper No. 166, Washington D.C.: International Monetary Fund.

Everbank:http://currency-investing.everbank.com/world-currency/world-currency-deposit-accounts/pro_wc_fx_renminbi.

Feng, Charles, 2003, CNY offshore NDF and onshore bond markets, Asia Fixed Income Research, Deutsche Bank.

Frankel, Jeffrey and Shang Jin Wei, 2003, *Managing Macroeconomic Crises: Policy Lessons*, Kennedy School of Government, Harvard University and Brookings Institution and International Monetary Fund (November).

Garber, Peter M., 1998, *Derivatives in International Capital Flow*, NBER Working Paper Series, Working Paper 6623: http://www.nber.org/papers/w6623.

Hanke, Steve H., March 15, 2003, John Snow is wrong about China exporting deflation, http://www.cato.org/dailys/03-15-03.html.

Hiscock, Geoff, 2003, "Currency pressure builds on China," CNN's Asia Business Editor, Wednesday, October 29, http://www.cnn.com/2003/BUSINESS/10/29/apec.special.yuan/eu/.

Hu, Fred, 2003a, "China needs a 'regime Change' — for its currency!," Goldman Sachs, China Insight, June 11.

Hu, Fred, 2003b, Revaluating or floating, Caijing Magazine, Fourth issue.

Hu, Fred, 2003c, Hong Kong Economic Daily, August 30.

IMF, 1999, *Involving the Private Sector in Forestalling and Resolving Financial Crises.* Washington, D.C.: Policy Development and Review Department.

IMF Office Memorandum on private market financing for emerging markets: Developments for the second quarter of 1997, July 17, 1997.

International CNN.com, July 18, 2003, Time not right for yuan to flout.

International Monetary Fund (IMF), July 23, 2003, International Herald Tribune online.

Ishii, Shogo, Inci Otker-Robe, and Li Cui, 2001,"Measures to Limit Offshore Use of Currencies: Pros and Cons", IMF Working Paper WP/01/43.

Japan Times, July 31, 2003, China under more pressure to revalue the yuan, http://www.japantimes.com/cgi-bin/getarticle.pl5?nb20030731a1.htm.

Kregel, J. A., 1998, "Derivatives and global capital flows: applications to Asia." *Cambridge Journal of Economics*, 22, 677–692.

Kuramitsu, Yumi, October 7, 2003, China yuan forward rate passes H.K. peg for 1st time, Bloomberg, 07:04 (New York).

Lall, Subir, 1997, *Speculative Attacks, Forward Market Intervention and the Classic Bear Squeeze*, International Monetary Fund, Research Department, authorized for distribution by Donald J. Mathieson, December, WP/97/164.

Lavin, D, 1998, "Profit at Société Générale up 34 percent; bank sees robust growth trend". *Wall Street Journal Interactive Edition*, 12 March.

Letter to President George Bush on July 31, 2003, www.nam.org/Docs/IEA/26896_LtrtoBushfromMembersofCongress-Yuan7-31-03.pdf.

Letter to Secretary John Snow on July 17, 2003, http://www.access.gpo.gov/-congress/ senate/senate05sh107.html.
http://schumer.senate.gov/SchumerWebsite/pressroom/special_reports/Ltr%20to%20Treasury%20on%20Yuan.pdf.

Li, Yuanhai and Ye, Yonggang, 2001, Forward Settlement — RMB Forward Market Research, Wuhan University Press.

Lo, Chi, August 19, 2003, Risks and opportunities of revaluing the renminbi.

Lu, Ning, 2004, "Difficulty to Float Governmental Shares," Oriental Morning Post, February 1, p. 11.

Martinsen, John, 2003, *Risk Takers: Uses and Abuses of Financial Derivatives*. Pearson Addison-Wesley.

Mecklai Financial and Commercial Services Ltd, 2004, Chinese Chequers, http://www.mecklai.com/mecklai/NTGEeness74.asp.

Murase, Tetsuji, October 2002, Japan and China: driving forces of a regional monetary arrangement in East Asia? Kyoto University.

Murray, Bruce, 2004, "China's economic performance and its impact on asia. Sponsored by the Asia Pacific Foundation of Canada, Canada China Business Council, and the Center for Chinese Research of the Institute of Asian Research at the University of British Columbia, ABD China Resident Representatives, June 21, Vancouver; available at: http://www.adb.org/PRCM/china-eco-performance.pdf.

Neftci, Salih N., 1998, *FX Short Positions, Balance Sheets and Financial Turbulence: An Interpretation of the Asian Financial Crisis*, CEPA Working Paper No. 11 (October).

Park, D. and C. Rhee, 1998, Currency crisis in Korea: how was it aggravated? *Asian Development Review*, 16, Asian Development Bank, 149–181.

Park, Daekeun, and Changyong Rhee, 2000, Measuring the degree of currency misalignment using offshore forward exchange rates: the case of the Korean financial crisis (Revised: February).

Park, Jinwoo, 2001, Information flows between non-deliverable forward (NDF) and spot markets: evidence from Korean currency. *Pacific-Basin Finance Journal*, 9(4), 363–377, August.

Park, K., 1998, Foreign Banks in S. Korea combined 97 net profit KRW 930.48B, *AP-DJ News Service*, March 13.

People's Daily, March 17, 2002, http://english.peopledaily.com.cn/200203/17/eng20020317_92259.shtml.

People's Daily, July 7, 2003, http://english.peopledaily.com.cn/200307/07/eng20030707_119666.shtml.

Prebon Yamane, Global Review 2003.

Report of The President's Working Group on Financial Markets Department of the Treasury, Board of Governors of the Federal Reserve System, Securities and Exchange Commission, Commodity Futures Trading Commission, 1999, *Hedge Funds, Leverage, and the Lessons of Long-Term Capital Management*, April 28.

Sesai, Sonali, 1998, Asian currencies look up as ringgit regains footing, *Indian Express Newspapers* (Bombay) Ltd.

Shuangning, Tang, 2003, "Facing WTO Challenges and Accelerating Banking Reform in China," www.cbrc.gov.cn/lingdaojianghua.

Smithson, Charles and Gregory Hayt, 2000, "Credit derivatives: the basics. *The Journal of Lending & Credit Risk Management*, (February), 58–60.

Special Report, August 18, 2003, Politics of yuan: debate over China's foreign exchange rate, http://www.asiasource.org/news/at_mp_02.cfm?newsid=100220.

Taylor, John B., October 30, 2003, Economic relations between the United States and China and China's role in the global economy, Under Secretary of Treasury for International Affairs, Committee on Ways and Means, http://www.ustreas.gov/press/releases/js956.htm.

The Independent, September 24, 2003, Pressure mounts on Chinese to float renminbi, http://news.independent.co.uk.

The Japan Times, 2003, China under more pressure to revalue the yuan, Japan, U.S. argue that unfairly low exchange rates are spreading deflation, trade deficits, http://www.japantimes.com/cgi-bin/getarticle.pl5?nb20030731a1.htm.

The Washington Post, June 18, 2003, China may float currency, Snow says.

Thompson, Peter, 1998, "Contract questions Cloud NDS Market", Asia Risk (December).

Thompson, Peter, 2001, "Non-deliverable Forwards," Derivatives Week

Tian, Xiaojun, 2004, "Impacts of Generalized China Stock Index Futures", Futures Daily, January 7, p. 3.

Tokyo-Mitsubishi View, August 2003, Rekindling debates over yuan revaluation and its prospect, Vol. 8(8), http://www.btm.co.jp/report/ecorev2001e.

Tsang, Donald, 1998, Speech at the Hong Kong Trade Development Council, Frankfurt, September 29.

US Consulate, Hong Kong, 2003, Greenspan sees China's currency peg unrelated to US job losses, Federal Reserve chairman repeats warnings against trade barriers, available via the World Wide Web at http://hongkong.usconsualte.gov/uscn/others/2003/121101.htm.

US–China ties: reassessing the economic relationship hearing before the Committee on International Relations, House of Representatives, one hundred eighth Congress, first session, October 21, 2003; Serial No. 108–70. Available via the World Wide Web at http://www.house.gov/international-relations.

US Department of the Treasury's Report to Congress on International Economic and Exchange Rate Policy Hearing before the Committee on Banking, Housing, and Urban Affairs, US Senate, one hundred seventh Congress, second session on the US Department of the Treasury's Report to Congress on International Economic and Exchange Rate Policy, May 1, 2002.

Wang, An, 2003, "Twenty Five Years," World Knowledge Publisher.

Wang, Lisa, August 7, 2003, Taiwan News.

Washington Monitor, October 3, 2003, A weekly review of U.S. trade policy developments affecting Japan, Vol. 7(39).

Watanabe, Kenichiro, Hiroshi Akama, and Jun Mifune, 2002, *The Effectiveness of Capital Controls and Monitoring: The Case of Non-internationalization of Emerging Market Currencies*, EMEAP Discussion Paper (January), International Department, Bank of Japan.

Wellons, Scott H.S., P.A., 2001, *International Finance: Transactions, Policy and Regulation*, eighth edition. New York: New York Foundation Press, p.1049.

Weston, Rae and Guy Ford, 2002, *Performance of Bank Stocks During and After Financial Crisis: An Analysis of Singapore and Hong Kong*. Macquarie Graduate School of Management, NSW, 2109, Australia.

Xie, Andy, November 4, 2002, China: say No to RMB revaluation, Morgan Stanley (Hong Kong), http://www.morganstanley.com/GEFdata/digests/20021104-mon.html#anchor5.

Yam, Joseph, 1999, *Causes of and Solutions to the Recent Financial Turmoil in the Asian Region*, A Symposium in Commemoration of 50 Years of Central Banking in the Philippines organized by the Bangko Sentral ng Pilipinas, Manila.

Yang, Yongzheng, 2003, "China's Integration into the World Economy: Implications for Developing Countries," IMF Working Paper 03/245.

Yu, Jialin, December 26, 2003, Closed-form likelihood estimation of jump-Di.usions with an application to the realignment risk of the Chinese yuan, Department of Economics, Princeton University, first draft January 30, 2003.

Zhang, Peter G., 1995, Barrings Bankruptcy and Financial Derivatives, World Scientific.

Zhang, Peter G., 1998a, Exotic Options — A Guide to Second Generation Options, World Scientific.

Zhang, Peter G., 1998b, IMF and Asian Financial Crisis, World Scientific.

Zhang, Peter G., 2000, "Asset Management Corporations in China," ICEA Research Paper.

Zhang, Peter G., 2003a, "Moving from Expansionary Fiscal Policy to Consumption Stimulation Policy," Working Paper.

Zhang, Peter G., 2003b, "Correlation Analysis between Copper Futures Trading at SHFE and LME," China Futures Daily, December 24, p. 4.

Zhang, Peter G., 2003c, Stock Index Futures & Options (forthcoming).

Zhang, Peter G., 2004, "Welcome the spring of derivatives industry in China." *Futures and Financial Derivatives Journal*, 13, 9–13.

Zhang, Peter G., 2004, Prepare for the spring of derivatives industry in China. *Futures and Derivatives Journal*, 12, 12–17 (in Chinese).

Zhang, Zhiwei, 2001, *Speculative Attacks in the Asian Crisis*, November, International Monetary Market, Working Paper authorized for distribution by Peter Isard, WP/01/189.

Index

Agricultural Bank of China 45, 224
American Currency Range Deposits 324
Asian financial crisis 4, 10, 25, 27, 30, 34, 36, 49, 53, 62, 88, 106, 118, 131, 134, 157, 158, 159, 160, 162, 163, 166, 170, 171, 172, 173, 175, 177, 183, 184, 187, 189, 192, 195, 196, 197, 201, 204, 205, 206, 209, 211, 215, 218, 220, 221, 223, 236, 237, 238, 243, 265, 294, 308, 309, 312, 313, 317, 331, 339, 342, 343, 349, 356, 358, 372, 373
at-the-money 302
Bank for International Settlement 104, 113, 114, 137, 141, 147, 183, 184, 214, 348
Bank of China 45, 223, 224, 355
Bear Spread 276
Bull Spread 272
call spread 305, 306
China Banking Regulatory Commission 41, 42, 367, 380
China Construction Bank 224, 229
China Insurance Regulatory Commission 41, 42, 71
China Securities Regulatory Commission 41, 369
Chinese yuan 3, 7, 124, 125, 130, 158, 191, 196
CNY forward 221, 223, 224, 225, 235, 264, 367, 372, 373, 380
CNY revaluation 3, 4, 5, 7, 11, 221, 237, 239, 240, 242, 251, 265, 269, 279, 280, 292, 297, 298, 300, 302, 308, 309, 311, 313, 317, 320, 332, 334, 337, 339, 341, 342, 348, 349, 350, 351, 352, 354, 355, 358, 361, 364
currency deposits with knock-out features 318
currency range deposits 318, 323, 324
Dual Currency Deposits 324
exotic options 146, 151, 152, 153, 317, 325, 327, 339
foreign direct investment 5, 21, 25, 26, 163, 236, 256, 265, 281, 308, 344, 367, 368, 376, 380

Foreign Exchange Forward Swaps 289
foreign invested enterprises 48, 353
forward 10, 11, 99, 101, 104, 105, 106, 107, 108, 109, 110, 111, 112, 118, 119, 120, 121, 122, 125, 126, 127, 129, 139, 140, 142, 155, 158, 169, 170, 175, 176, 177, 178, 179, 181, 182, 183, 184, 185, 186, 187, 190, 192, 193, 194, 195, 196, 197, 199, 209, 219, 221, 227, 231, 233, 254, 260, 262, 263, 264, 276, 279, 283, 284, 285, 289, 290, 291, 292, 297, 311, 313, 316, 329, 332, 339, 356, 357, 359, 367, 372, 373, 375, 376, 377, 378, 380
Hong Kong Monetary Authority 184, 185, 209, 215, 261, 356
hot money 341, 342, 343, 344, 345, 346, 347, 348, 349
implied volatilities 293, 295, 296, 297, 298, 299, 300, 311, 312, 316
Industrial and Commercial Bank of China 229
linked deposits 317, 318, 320, 326
non-deliverable forwards 158, 189, 201, 371
non-performing loans 45, 47, 53, 169
over-the-counter 151, 155, 157
People's Bank of China 39, 41, 223
qualified foreign institutional investors 57, 72, 73, 352, 368, 380
structured notes 158, 211, 216, 217, 218, 221, 331, 332, 338, 339,
the State Administration of Foreign Exchange 31, 32, 224
time spread 271, 310, 311
Volatility Smile 298
World Trade Organization 14, 19